150-175

Confrontation with the Warmakers, Washington D.C., October 27, 1967. Minoru Aoki.

ACTIVE NONVIOLENCE IN THE UNITED STATES

THE POWER OF THE PEOPLE

15616

Edited and Produced by Robert Cooney and Helen Michalowski

LAKE TAHOE COMMUNITY COLLEGE
LEARNING RESOURCES CENTER

COOPERATIVELY PUBLISHED

PUBLISHING INFORMATION

THIS BOOK was conceived of and undertaken more as a political project than an academic one. Besides recording the American tradition of nonviolence, *The Power of the People* served to draw nonviolent groups together in voluntary, unified action to produce the book independently. Subsequently, there is not a single publisher, but over 35 co-publishers who participated in this cooperative publishing effort by committing money or purchasing copies before publication.

AGAPE FOUNDATION
AMERICAN FRIENDS SERVICE COMMITTEE, AUSTIN
AMERICAN FRIENDS SERVICE COMMITTEE, CAMBRIDGE
AMERICAN FRIENDS SERVICE COMMITTEE, DAYTON
AMERICAN FRIENDS SERVICE COMMITTEE, PACIFIC NORTHWEST
AMERICAN FRIENDS SERVICE COMMITTEE, PHILADELPHIA
AMERICAN FRIENDS SERVICE COMMITTEE, SAN FRANCISCO
AMERICAN FRIENDS SERVICE COMMITTEE, SOUTHEAST
BRETHREN PRESS
CARBONDALE PEACE CENTER
CLERGY AND LAITY CONCERNED
COMMITTEE FOR NONVIOLENT ACTION
EAST LANSING PEACE EDUCATION CENTER
FELLOWSHIP OF RECONCILIATION
FRIENDS PEACE COMMITTEE
INSTITUTE FOR EDUCATION IN PEACE AND JUSTICE
INSTITUTE FOR NONVIOLENT SOCIAL CHANGE
INSTITUTE FOR THE STUDY OF NONVIOLENCE
INSTITUTE FOR WORLD ORDER
KOINONIA PARTNERS
THOMAS MERTON COMMUNITY
MODESTO PEACE/LIFE CENTER
MOVEMENT FOR A NEW SOCIETY
A.J. MUSTE INSTITUTE
NONVIOLENT STUDIES INSTITUTE
PAX CENTER
PEACE PRESS
PEACE STUDIES INSTITUTE
SAN JOSE CATHOLIC WORKER
SAN JOSE PEACE CENTER
WAR RESISTERS LEAGUE, DETROIT
WAR RESISTERS LEAGUE, KANSAS
WAR RESISTERS LEAGUE, SOUTHEAST
WAR TAX RESISTANCE FUND OF SYRACUSE PEACE COUNCIL
WOMEN'S INTERNATIONAL LEAGUE FOR PEACE AND FREEDOM, LOS ANGELES

Besides the contributions of these organizations, many other people lent their time, skill, and money to help produce this book in a manner consistent with the principles it records. Editors, printers, photographers, writers, typesetters, office workers and many others reduced their rates or donated their labor to make the independent publishing of *The Power of the People* a realistic endeavor. A financial summary of the publishing project can be found on the final page.

FIRST EDITION

Copyright © by Robert Cooney 1977
All rights reserved
Library of Congress catalog card number: 76-19519
International Standard Book Number: 0-915238-06-3 Hardbound
0-915238-07-1 Softbound

Printed and distributed by Peace Press, Inc.
3828 Willat Avenue, Culver City, California 90230
Discounts on bulk orders available.

Designed by Robert Cooney
Cover design by William I. Teitelbaum

ERRATA
The photographs of Susan Anthony and Lucretia Mott on page 32 are reversed.

Table of Contents

CHIEF SEATTLE'S MESSAGE

Nonviolence did not appear in this land with the arrival of European immigrants. Native Americans had a reverence for life, respected human dignity, and understood the interconnection of all things to an extent that has yet to be surpassed. The genocide perpetrated by the United States on the Indian tribes and cultures – a pattern which still continues today – remains one of the most thorough indictments of white civilization. In 1854, Chief Seattle, leader of the Suquamish tribe in the Washington territory, delivered this prophetic speech to mark the transferral of ancestral Indian lands to the federal government.

The Great Chief in Washington sends word that he wishes to buy our land.

The Great Chief also sends us words of friendship and good will. This is kind of him, since we know he has little need of our friendship in return. But we will consider your offer. For we know that if we do not sell, the white man may come with guns and take our land.

How can you buy or sell the sky, the warmth of the land? The idea is strange to us.

If we do not own the freshness of the air and the sparkle of the water, how can you buy them?

Every part of this earth is sacred to my people. Every shining pine needle, every sandy shore, every mist in the dark woods, every clearing and humming insect is holy in the memory and experience of my people. The sap which courses through the trees carries the memories of the red man.

The white man's dead forget the country of their birth when they go to walk among the stars. Our dead never forget this beautiful earth, for it is the mother of the red man. We are part of the earth and it is part of us. The perfumed flowers are our sisters; the deer, the horse, the great eagle, these are our brothers. The rocky crests, the juices in the meadows, the body heat of the pony, and man — all belong to the same family.

So, when the Great Chief in Washington sends word that he wishes to buy our land, he asks much of us.

So, the Great Chief sends word he will reserve us a place so that we can live comfortably to ourselves. He will be our father and we will be his children.

So we will consider your offer to buy our land. But it will not be easy. For this land is sacred to us.

This shining water that moves in the streams and rivers is not just water but the blood of our ancestors. If we sell you land, you must remember that it is sacred, and you must teach your children that it is sacred, and that each ghostly reflection in the clear water of the lake tells of events and memories in the life of my people. The water's murmur is the voice of my father's father.

The rivers are our brothers, they quench our thirst. The rivers carry our canoes, and feed our children. If we sell you our land, you must remember, and teach your children, that the rivers are our brothers, and yours, and you must henceforth give the rivers the kindness you would give any brother.

The red man has always retreated before the advancing white man, as the mist of the mountain runs before the morning sun. But the ashes of our fathers are sacred. Their graves are holy ground, and so these hills, these trees, this portion of earth is consecrated to us. We know that the white man does not understand our ways. One portion of land is the same to him as the next, for he is a stranger who comes in the night and takes from the land whatever he needs. The earth is not his brother, but his enemy, and when he has conquered it, he moves on. He leaves his fathers' graves behind, and he does not care. He kidnaps the earth from his children. He does not care. His fathers' graves and his children's birthright are forgotten. He treats his mother, the earth, and his brother, the sky, as things to be bought, plundered, sold like sheep or bright beads. His appetite will devour the earth and leave behind only a desert.

I do not know. Our ways are different from your ways. The sight of your cities pains the eyes of the red man. But perhaps it is because the red man is a savage and does not understand.

There is no quiet place in the white man's cities. No place to hear the unfurling of leaves in spring or the rustle of insects' wings. But perhaps it is because I am a savage and do not understand. The clatter only seems to insult the ears. And what is there to life if a man cannot hear the lonely cry of the whippoorwill or the arguments of the frogs around a pond at night? I am a red man and do not understand. The Indian prefers the soft sound of the wind darting over the face of a pond, and the smell of the wind itself, cleansed by a midday rain, or scented with the pinon pine.

The air is precious to the red man, for all things share the same breath — the beast, the tree, the man, they all share the same breath. The white man does not seem to notice the air he breathes. Like a man dying for many days, he is numb to the stench. But if we sell you our land, you must remember that the air is precious to us, that the air shares its spirit with all the life it supports. The wind that gave our grandfather his first breath also receives his last sigh. And the wind must also give our children the spirit of life. And if we sell you our land, you must keep it apart and sacred, as a place where even the white man can go to taste the wind that is sweetened by the meadow's flowers.

So we will consider your offer to buy our land. If we decide to accept, I will make one condition: The white man must treat the beasts of this land as his brothers.

I am a savage and do not understand any other way. I have seen a thousand rotting buffaloes on the prairie, left by the white man who shot them from a passing train. I am a savage and I do not understand how the smoking iron horse can be more important than the buffalo that we kill only to stay alive.

What is man without the beasts? If all the beasts were gone, men would die from a great loneliness of spirit. For whatever happens to the beasts, soon happens to man. All things are connected.

You must teach your children that the ground beneath their feet is the ashes of our grandfathers. So that they will respect the land, tell your children that the earth is rich with the lives of our kin. Teach your children what we have taught our children, that the earth is our mother. Whatever befalls the earth, befalls the sons of the earth. If men spit upon the ground they spit upon themselves.

This we know. The earth does not belong to man; man belongs to the earth. This we know. All things are connected like the blood which unites one family. All things are connected.

Whatever befalls the earth befalls the sons of the earth. Man did not weave the web of life; he is merely a strand in it. Whatever he does to the web, he does to himself.

But we will consider your offer to go to the reservation you have for my people. We will live apart, and in peace. It matters little where we spend the rest of our days. Our children have seen their fathers humbled in defeat. Our warriors have felt shame, and after defeat they turn their days in idleness and contaminate their bodies with sweet foods and strong drink. It

matters little where we pass the rest of our days. They are not many. A few more hours, a few more winters, and none of the children of the great tribes that once lived on this earth or that roam now in small bands in the woods will be left to mourn the graves of a people once as powerful and hopeful as yours. But why should I mourn the passing of my people? Tribes are made of men, nothing more. Men come and go like the waves of the sea.

Even the white man, whose God walks and talks with him as friend to friend, cannot be exempt from the common destiny. We may be brothers after all; we shall see. One thing we know, which the white man may one day discover — our God is the same God. You may think now that you own him as you wish to own our land; but you cannot. He is the God of man, and his compassion is equal for the red man and the white. This earth is precious to him, and to harm the earth is to heap contempt on its Creator. The white too shall pass; perhaps sooner than all other tribes. Continue to contaminate your bed, and you will one night suffocate in your own waste.

But in your perishing you will shine brightly, fired by the strength of the God who brought you to this land and for some special purpose gave you dominion over this land and over the red man. That destiny is a mystery to us, for we do not understand when the buffalo are all slaughtered, the wild horses are tamed, the secret corners of the forest heavy with the scent of many men, and the view of the ripe hills blotted by talking wires. Where is the thicket? Gone. Where is the eagle? Gone. And what is it to say goodbye to the swift pony and the hunt? The end of living and the beginning of survival.

So we will consider your offer to buy our land. If we agree, it will be to secure the reservation you have promised. There, perhaps, we may live out our brief days as we wish. When the last red man has vanished from this earth, and his memory is only the shadow of a cloud moving across the prairie, these shores and forests will still hold the spirits of my people. For they love this earth as the newborn loves its mother's heartbeat. So if we sell you our land, love it as we've loved it. Care for it as we've cared for it. Hold in your mind the memory of the land as it is when you take it. And with all your strength, with all your mind, with all your heart, preserve it for your children, and love it . . . as God loves us all.

One thing we know. Our God is the same God. This earth is precious to him. Even the white man cannot be exempt from the common destiny. We may be brothers after all. We shall see.

ACKNOWLEDGMENTS

Preparing this book has been an enlightening and fulfilling experience and we would like to thank the many people who shared the vision of this project and readily offered their help. Their support and cooperation encouraged our work and lifted our spirits during the long months of research, editing, fund raising, production and printing. Not only did these people provide material and resources to produce this book but their involvement also gave meaning to the idea of a cooperative publishing project.

We would particularly like to thank Marty Jezer, who wrote the basic text and allowed us free rein in its use, Henry Bass, Jan Addams, Jim Peck and Eileen Egan who generously contributed additional pieces. Larry Gara and Ann Davidon kindly reviewed the manuscript and made knowledgeable suggestions. Barbara Isaacs and others at Intermedia were exceptionally helpful with the ever-expanding typesetting work. Bob Zaugh and the good people at Peace Press lent invaluable help and encouragement from early conception to final publication.

For their help with the many different editorial, administrative and technical details of the project, we are very grateful to Regina Capella, Marianne Ferrarin, Donna Fletcher, Doug Gary, Paul Hammond, Susan Hester, Nick Hoy, Allison and Blaine Metcalf, Kathleen Mewshaw, Steve Perloff, Sharon Raichelson, and Eileen Savarese. We would also like to thank Marj and Bob Swann, Jim Forest, Nicola Geiger, Staughton Lynd, Roy Kepler, Henry Geiger, Bob and Janice Jackall, Steve Ladd, Barbara Deming, Bob Eaton, Igal Roodenko, and Sam Tyson for their encouragement and guidance in the course of this project; and Iris Moore, Joe Maizlish, Denny Pratt, W.H. and Carol Bernstein Ferry, Edward Ryerson, Susan Pines, Robert and Hildegarde Cooney, and our friends at Struggle Mountain and the Land for their many varied contributions.

The skill and generosity of a number of contemporary photographers helped make this book a unique and powerful documentary history. The enthusiasm and cooperation of Diana Davies, Bob Fitch, and John Goodwin in particular were contagious and deeply appreciated. George Ballis, Matt Herron, Danny Lyon, Minoru Aoki, Dorothy Marder, Theodore Hetzel, Janice Stockwell, George Cushing, Neil Haworth, Harvey Richards, Sid Sattler, Karl Bissinger, Tom Langston, Maury Englander, Terry Armor, Paul Kagan, and Mottke Weissman made their work available to us at minimum or no cost and with a great deal of trust and support for the effort. The late Ken Thompson's photographs are held by the Board of Global Ministries of the United Methodist Church, whose cooperation we greatly appreciate.

Many people and organizations were exceptionally generous in putting their material at our disposal for an extended period of time. Numerous libraries, archival collections, and nonviolent groups provided information, illustrations, and general assistance at various stages in the project. We would particularly like to thank the Fellowship of Reconciliation, War Resisters League, Institute for the Study of Nonviolence, Brethren Service Committee, Syracuse Peace Council, and various offices of the American Friends Service Committee. A special debt of gratitude is owed to Bernice Nichols at the Swarthmore College Peace Collection for her patience, support, and valuable aid in locating many of the illustrations which appear in this book. Each of the research centers and photographic agencies credited were also extremely helpful in providing material, often at reduced rates. In addition, dozens of groups publicized and promoted the book before publication by distributing brochures and running advertisements for us.

For contributing material, ideas, and inspiration, we are deeply indebted to Rick Boardman, Betty Brantner, Ernest and Marion Bromley, Art Danforth, Dorothy Day, Dave Dellinger, Ralph DiGia, Julius Eichel, Howard Everngam, Roy Finch and Margaret Rockwell Finch, Christopher Jones, Abe and Ida Kaufman, Randy Kehler, Ken Kolsbun, Ed Lazar, E. John Lewis, Dave McReynolds, Fred Moore, Lowell and Virginia Naeve, Wally and Juanita Nelson, Martin Ponch, Craig Simpson, and Stanley Vishnewski. The project also benefited greatly from the help of Maris Cakars, Chuck Matthei, Tom Gage, Bruce Martin, Marta Daniels, Dik Cool, Betty Roszak, Julius Lester, Franklin Zahn, Mark Morris, Jack Malinowski, Sherna Gluck, Tony Coluzzi, Ann Allen, Cesar Chavez, Bob Aldridge, Jock Brown, Alice Cox, Lucy Carner, Richard Deats, William Eshelman, Larry Erickson, Walter J. Fox, John Howard Griffin, Sandy Gottlieb, Donna Glickman, Ashton Jones, Brad Lyttle, Carole Nelson, Earl Reynolds, Vernon Schmid, John-i-thin Stephens, Roger Smith, Peter Klotz, Charles Chatfield, Peter Carroll, Joy Locke, Kay Boyle, Myles Horton, Adrian Wilson, Ed Guinan, Roger Dodds, Carol Bragg, Kit Bricca, Joel Shumer, Rob Leppzer, and many others.

Finally we would particularly like to thank Bob Overy for his warm friendship and knowledgeable guidance, Lee Swenson for his initial help and tenacious spirit, Bob Fitch for his clear photos and sound advice, and Jim Peck for his inspiration and support. We, of course, are solely responsible for any errors. We would appreciate being informed of any changes to be made in the information which appears in this book and receiving leads to other material relevant to this history. We are deeply grateful for all the help we received from people throughout the country similarly concerned about building a nonviolent society.

ROBERT COONEY
HELEN MICHALOWSKI

Palo Alto, California
August, 1976

Ken Thompson

PREFACE

There are quite a few books on the theory of nonviolence, but until now there has been no popular visual history on the practice of nonviolence in the United States. Here we have tried to document in one place the role nonviolence played in interconnecting the social movements of the 20th Century — for peace, unionization, suffrage, disarmament, civil rights and civil liberties — and to emphasize that a strong tradition of active nonviolence exists in this country. We have concentrated more on actions than on the theories behind the actions to better show what it is that nonviolent people *do*, and how their actions encouraged other actions and helped to bring us where we stand today.

While the organized struggle against war has been somewhat recognized and recorded, the people who resisted the first and second World Wars have been generally forgotten, and the effect of organized nonviolence has been virtually ignored by historians. The stories of Evan Thomas, Alice Paul, Jane Addams, Dave Dellinger, Jessie Wallace Hughan, Bayard Rustin, A.J. Muste and others have generally remained untold or been confined to individual treatments which fail to establish how much their efforts and the movements they were part of formed a whole.

Because of the way history is taught in schools and distorted by mass media, many people forget that history is actually made by people very much like themselves. Usual treatments of history, dominated as they are by wars and victorious leaders, tend to obscure the real processes involved in human development and social change. "Histories are *written* by intellectuals," Dave Dellinger once observed, "who generally give undue credit to other intellectuals for making history. But history is *made* by people who commit themselves, their lives, and their energies to the struggle. The best history," he continued, "is made by people who struggle against war, oppression, and hypocrisy and who also struggle to incorporate into their own lives and organizations the values that led them to oppose these evils in the first place."

Nonviolence is a relatively new idea which differs considerably from religious pacifism. While pacifism refers to the traditional belief that all killing, particularly in war, is wrong, contemporary nonviolence concerns itself with the implications of this belief in the whole social fabric. Nonviolence has a broader definition of what causes and constitutes violence, takes the initiative against the existing system of dominance and privilege, and gives more conscious attention to the building of an alternative social structure. In this book, we have concentrated on radical pacifists as the clearest exponents of nonviolence because they took the lead in developing nonviolent techniques and strategies, in addition to consistently opposing war and militarism and trying to lead nonviolent lives.

The word "nonviolence" first appeared in the U.S. in the 20th Century and the evolution of the concept can be traced through earlier changes in terminology. The word "nonresistance" was used from the 17th through the mid-19th Century; "passive resistance" and "moral force" were used by 19th Century abolitionists and labor organizers; and "non-violent resistance" appeared in the 1920's. Only after the second World War did the terms "revolutionary nonviolence" and "active nonviolence" begin to be used.

Little is known to date about the exact route by which radical pacifists, labor organizers, feminists, and socialists came to join ranks over the last quarter of the 19th Century, but certainly such a linkage between pacifists and mass movements for social change had taken place by the time of World War I. By 1930, Devere Allen, a Socialist Party leader, was calling for mass action and "non-violent attack to hasten the transformation of evil and unjust social situations." With such obvious connections between mass organizations and pacifists, and such clear acknowledgment of the need for nonviolent action to change unjust social situations, it came as a surprise to us to realize that it was not until the 1940's that pacifists in the U.S. began directly to challenge the prevailing social system by means of organized nonviolent action. The Congress of Racial Equality was founded in 1942; World War II conscientious objectors committed to aggressive nonviolence assumed control of the War Resisters League in 1948; and the same year Peacemakers was founded after radical war resisters

issued a call for a "more disciplined and revolutionary pacifism."

Radical pacifists not only began organizations expressly committed to using nonviolence to bring about social change, they also called what they were doing revolutionary. They realized that to implement their vision of freedom and equality required a far-reaching social program which would touch every aspect of American society. Moreover, they began to practice and develop nonviolent tactics and strategies as the means to make this revolution. Immediately after World War II, A.J. Muste wrote that humanity faced a major crisis in which "only a drastic change, such as is suggested by the terms rebirth, conversion, revolution, can bring deliverance. . . . War and the war system, as well as social violence, are inherent in our present politico-economic order and the prevailing materialistic culture." He called for "a nonviolent revolutionary movement" which would include both changes in external relationships and an inner transformation of the individual. These same insights were echoed by Vinoba Bhave of India in the first issue of *Liberation* magazine:

> If in spite of knowing the power of love, I were to go on crying for legislation instead of relying on and developing this power in society then I shall not have done my work. Therefore, I want to build up and we must build up that Power of the People which will be different from the Power of the State.
>
> We want to overhaul the entire social structure without recourse to violence. That is, we want both peace and revolution. Revolution is indispensible. Now if we want peace also, then we have to prove that peace too has the power to revolutionize society – not gradually but with the speed of revolution. If this is proved, violence will cease to be the indispensible adjunct of revolution and society will be saved.

Today the institutionalized violence of the American status quo and the need for fundamental changes in individual, social and political life are more widely acknowledged. Nonviolent revolution,

Suffrage Tableau on the steps of the U.S. Treasury Building, March 3, 1913. Library of Congress.

however, still remains more a direction of developing thought and action than a fully formed plan or ideology. Although significant progress has been made over the past 30 years in developing nonviolent strategies and tactics, many activists hesitate to call nonviolence revolutionary because a thorough social and economic program has not yet been formulated. Some have also expressed the concern that setting up revolution as the end, and fitting nonviolence into the means, might narrow down, distort, or even subvert the real meaning of nonviolence.

Nonviolence is a natural element which relies on the power of truth rather than force of arms and flows from a sense of the underlying unity of all human beings. There can be no sustained nonviolent struggle on a massive scale until social institutions based on nonviolent principles are built up. While nonviolent resistance and direct action are extremely important, at the core of nonviolence is unity based on love and the desire for justice and voluntary constructive work which will build up the structure of a new society. These beliefs and values will provide the foundation for our common future, fulfilling a tradition where conscience is stronger than custom, where personal risks are taken to better the common lot, and where the contradictions of the times are so grasped and reformulated as to suggest new and effective means to achieve a free and equal life for all.

RESEARCH NOTES

Our research into this history began in 1973, following publication of the War Resisters League's annual peace calendar, *50 Years of Nonviolent Resistance,* written by Marty Jezer. Although the calendar focused primarily on WRL's work, it suggested a broader history of nonviolence and served as the core of this book. We made some revisions and additions to the text and solicited chapters and profiles on topics left uncovered. Henry Bass wrote the Civil Rights chapter and Jan Addams wrote the chapter on the United Farm Workers Union. We also added the Introduction and appendices, and gathered all the pertinent photographs and illustrations we could find. While the editing and research proceeded, we also raised the funds to produce the book cooperatively and independently.

We worked backwards, in a sense, using people and ideas connected to nonviolence today to lead us to individuals and related events in the past. Again and again we realized how little work has been done in this field and how great the need is for more research and study, greater care in preserving material, and wider availability of basic information and writings. Subject headings for "Nonviolence" were virtually nonexistent, so material was drawn from a wide variety of areas to illustrate the people and events gathered here. Our research was done rather rapidly and on limited funds and so does not represent a comprehensive effort to locate material in this field.

We tried in the text to avoid using the masculine to refer to all humanity, but for want of a simple, consistent alternative, we let quotations stand as they are in the original.

We had to be very selective in our choice of what to include, which should not be seen as a dismissal of other areas or types of struggle. There is a tremendous amount more to nonviolence than we could present in these pages. While resistance and direct actions have been emphasized (and can best be pictured), there are many other ways of approaching and understanding nonviolence, and we encourage others to explore and popularize them.

The following books provided most of the information in this book: *Pacifism in the United States: From the Colonial Era to the First World War* and *Twentieth Century Pacifism* by Peter Brock; *For Peace and Justice: Pacifism in America 1914-1941* and *Peace Movements in America* by Charles Chatfield; *The Radical "No": The Correspondence and Writing of Evan Thomas on War* edited by Charles Chatfield; *Peace or War: The American Struggle, 1636-1936* and *The American Peace Crusade: 1815-1860* by Merle Curti; *Revolutionary Nonviolence* by Dave Dellinger; *The Resistance* by Michael Ferber and Staughton Lynd; *Century of Struggle: The Woman's Rights Movement in the United States* by Eleanor Flexner; *The Bending Cross: A Biography of Eugene Victor Debs* by Ray Ginger; *Living My Life* by Emma Goldman; *Peace Agitator: The Story of A.J. Muste* by Nat Hentoff; *The Essays of A.J. Muste* edited by Nat Hentoff; *Uphill with Banners Flying: The Story of the Woman's Party* by Inez Irwin; *The Quakers in the American Colonies* by Rufus Jones; *Radicalism in America* by Sidney Lens; *Nonviolence in America: A Documentary History* by Staughton Lund; *The American Peace Movement and Social Reform, 1898-1918* by Roland Marchand; *Men Against the State* by James Martin; *Black Freedom: The Nonviolent Abolitionists from 1830 through the Civil War* by Carlton Mabee; *Nonviolent Reform in the United States, 1860-1886* by Marjorie Mae Norris; *We Who Would Not Kill* by Jim Peck; and *Rebels Against War: The American Peace Movement, 1941-1960* by Lawrence Wittner.

The following publications are the primary (often only) sources for information on a particular group or movement: *Alternative, American Report, Catholic Worker, CNVA Direct Action, Compass, The Conscientious Objector, CORElator, Dissent, El Malcriado, Fellowship, The Industrial Worker, Liberation, Manas, Pacifica Views, Peacemaker, Politics, WIN, World Tomorrow* and *WRL News.* Many of these periodicals are out of print and so may be difficult to find except in large libraries, archival collections, or the files of the organizations themselves. Additional information came from personal interviews, pamphlets published by the Pacifist Research Bureau, the annual calendars of the War Resisters League, and from standard reference works.

Files relating to this history are scattered in library, university, and archival collections, personal and organizational files, historical societies and commercial photographic agencies all over the country. The Swarthmore College Peace Collection, Swarthmore, PA 19081, is the richest source of information pertaining to the contents of this book. The Sophia Smith Collection, at Smith College, Northampton, MA 01060, includes extensive photographic files covering women's rights, the abolition movement, William Lloyd Garrison and his family, as well as numerous other areas, and has a Picture Catalog available for $6.

The Garland Library of War and Peace includes 328 volumes of mostly out-of-print literature. In addition to many international peace histories, critiques of war, and theoretical works, the Garland Publishing Company has also reprinted writings by Gandhi, Tolstoy, William Lloyd Garrison, Adin Ballou, Jane Addams, Norman and Evan Thomas, Jessie Wallace Hughan,

A.J. Muste, and many others. The war-time editions of *Pacifica Views* have been reprinted in 19 volumes. Many editions also have insightful introductions written by contemporary peace historians. A complete catalog of the useful library is available from the Garland Publishing Company, 24 West 45th St., New York, NY 10036.

Navajivan Publishing House, Ahmedabad 14, India, is the principal source for publications by and about Gandhi, *satyagraha*, and nonviolent theory, including the works of Richard Gregg and numerous others.

Brief summaries of relevant Ph.D. dissertations, such as those mentioned in the *Reading List*, may be found in Xerox University Microfilms' *Dissertation Abstracts International (Section A Humanities and Social Sciences)*. Most university and large public libraries carry this reference work in which abstracts are arranged by subject and the year in which the Ph.D. was awarded. Complete dissertations are available on microfilm or in bound xerographic reproductions from Xerox University Microfilms, Ann Arbor, MI 48106.

KEY TO ABBREVIATIONS

ACLU	American Civil Liberties Union		MNS	Movement for a New Society
AFof L	American Federation of Labor		NAACP	National Association for the Advancement of Colored People
AFSC	American Friends Service Committee			
AQAG	A Quaker Action Group		NCPW	National Council for the Prevention of War
AUAM	American Union Against Militarism		NFWA	National Farm Workers Association
AWOC	Agricultural Workers Organizing Committee		NSBRO	National Service Board for Religious Objectors
CALC	Clergy and Laity Concerned		SCLC	Southern Christian Leadership Conference
CCCO	Central Committee for Conscientious Objectors		SDS	Students for a Democratic Society
CIO	Congress of Industrial Organizations		SNCC	Student Nonviolent Coordinating Committee
CNVA	Committee for Nonviolent Action		SPU	Student Peace Union
CNVR	Committee for Nonviolent Revolution		SSRS	Society for Social Responsibility in Science
CO	Conscientious Objector		UFW	United Farm Workers
COFO	Council of Federated Organizations		UN	United Nations
CORE	Congress of Racial Equality		VDC	Vietnam Day Committee
CPLA	Conference for Progressive Labor Action		WILPF	Women's International League for Peace and Freedom
CPS	Civilian Public Service			
CW	Catholic Worker		WRL	War Resisters League
FCNL	Friends Committee on National Legislation		WSP	Women Strike for Peace
FOR	Fellowship of Reconciliation		WTR	War Tax Resistance
IWW	Industrial Workers of the World (Wobblies)		WWWC	World Without War Council

THE ROOTS OF AMERICAN NONVIOLENCE 1650-1915

BY HELEN MICHALOWSKI

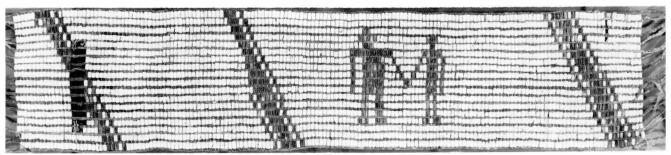

WAMPUM BELT PRESENTED TO WILLIAM PENN, 1681
Pennsylvania Historical Society

THE PACIFIST TRADITION

Nonviolence is a word which dates from the early 20th Century, but there is a strong pacifist tradition in the United States with roots reaching back to the colonial period. The most obvious and consistent element is the principled refusal to bear arms, for which religious pacifists won legal recognition during the 17th Century. Other components of contemporary nonviolence, such as the insistence upon freedom of conscience, the struggle to find a correct relationship with established authority, and the quest for community and a just social order can also be traced to the colonial period.

Traditional pacifism broadened in forms of organization from peace churches in the mid-17th Century to secular peace organizations in the early 19th Century. The number of people who promoted pacifism and their reasons for doing so increased, with humanitarian, philosophical, and political arguments joining the traditional religious ones. The most radical of the secular pacifist organizations was at the forefront of the abolition movement. By the time of the Civil War, pacifists practiced civil disobedience, tax refusal, public disturbances, boycotts, and direct actions such as sit-ins.

Although there were pacifist organizations prior to the Civil War, pacifism was still conceived as a personal creed and direct action was carried out on a more or less individual basis. Not until the 20th Century did people begin to think that pacifism was relevant to an organized mass movement for social change. This 20th Century development reflects an inheritance from the 19th Century women's and labor movements — more people grasped analyses of the existing social system as unjust and violent and had experience in methods of mass organization, new varieties of direct action, and alternative institutions.

Before the pacifist tradition in the U.S. is further detailed, it would be useful to point out some of the various principled positions historically held by pacifists. The word "principled" is stressed in order to omit from discussion those people who would use violence if they could (but for some reason cannot) and those who take no firm position with regard to human life and physical force, although they do not generally use violence.

There are at least five kinds of people who practice pacifism on principle: 1) Those who oppose certain violent conflicts, but not all violence, e.g., Dr. Francis Wayland of the American Peace Society who opposed the Mexican War on the grounds that it was a war of aggression; 2) Those who will not

PERSECUTION OF QUAKERS, 1656
American Friends Service Committee

personally use violence (although they will not interfere with the government's using violence) and who offer their services to alleviate suffering, e.g., Mennonites; 3) Those who will not personally use or cooperate with violence and who seek to alter undesirable situations by acts of good will and reconciliation, e.g., John Archdale, Quaker Governor of the Carolinas (1694-1697); 4) Those who will not personally use violence and who actively oppose injustice by means of writing, direct action, etc., e.g., William Lloyd Garrison of the New England Non-Resistance Society and editor of the abolitionist paper *The Liberator*; 5) Those who seek to rid their personal behavior of violence and exploitation, emphasize building the structure of a just society and who use organized nonviolent resistance and direct action to remove parts of the old structure which are obstacles to the new, e.g., A.J. Muste, 20th Century labor and anti-war activist. All of these types of principled pacifists exist in the United States today, although the last did not appear until the 20th Century.

In the following historical sketch it will be easier to talk about the period 1650-1915 if we let the term "nonviolence" refer to the 20th Century development and refer to the other, earlier forms by the more traditional term "pacifism." Although the development of modern nonviolence did not solely rely on — and was not limited to — absolute pacifists, the work of these people best exemplifies some of the most important elements of nonviolent philosophy and politics.

THE STRUGGLE FOR FREEDOM OF CONSCIENCE

Contemporary nonviolence, like traditional pacifism, assumes freedom of conscience which implies the right to act in accordance with what one believes to be true. Early American colonialists, some pacifist and some not, are responsible for winning legal recognition for this freedom. During the formative years of the colonies, Roger Williams, a laborer and minister, denounced the Puritan clergy's "bloody doctrine of persecution for the cause of conscience." For this and other assertions, such as insisting that the land belonged to the Indians, the General Court of Massachusetts tried and banished him in 1635. A year later, he purchased land from the Narraganset Indians who had given him refuge and he established the town of Providence. In 1638, the Puritans also banished Ann Hutchinson from Massachusetts because she publicly insisted that conscience has higher authority than the law. The pacifist Society of Friends was banned from Massachusetts from 1654 until 1661 because, in the words

STATUE OF MARY DYER
OUTSIDE THE BOSTON STATE HOUSE
Archives of the Commonwealth
of Massachusetts

of the General Court, Quakers were "a cursed sect of heretics who take upon themselves to be . . . infallibly assisted by the Spirit."

Ann Hutchinson's insistence upon the priority of personal conscience brought her into trouble with the Massachusetts authorities because a theological debate known as the "Antinomian Controversy" had political implications. "Antinomian" means opposed to the law and referred pejoratively to people who, in theological terms, believed grace rather than works to be the source of salvation. The leaders of the church in Puritan Massachusetts viewed this teaching as a threat because in practical terms it implied that something supercedes observance of the law.

While still in England, Ann Hutchinson became a follower of John Cotton, an Antinomian. When he moved to Boston, she and her husband came after him in 1634. Two months later, the local Puritan church accepted her and she soon came to be held in high esteem. She began to hold discussions for women about the weekly sermon and these became so popular that she organized another meeting for the men. About sixty people a week came to listen to her comments about the sermons of Cotton as

contrasted with the sermons of the other ministers whom she termed "legalists."

Ann Hutchinson was brought to trial after the Antinomians attempted to have one of their own persuasion assigned as minister in Boston. Among other things, she was accused of "having troubled the peace of the commonwealth and churches," "having divulged and promoted opinions that cause trouble," "having spoken divers [sic] things prejudicial to the honor of the churches and the ministers" and "having maintained a meeting in your home, not comely in the sight of God, nor fitting your sex."

Possessing an imposing familiarity with the Scriptures, Hutchinson brilliantly answered the charges brought against her. On the second day of the trial, she tried to explain how her own conscience led her to know what was right. In so doing, she spoke of hearing a voice in her soul and of immediate revelations. These words provided the judges with the grounds to find her "under a devilish delusion" and she was ordered banished.

Ann Hutchinson left Massachusetts and founded the town of Portsmouth, which, together with Roger Williams' Providence and the town of Newport (1639), grew into the colony of Rhode Island, the most democratic society of its time. In 1641, the assembled citizens of Rhode Island decreed: "It is ordered that none be accounted a delinquent for doctrine."

Ann Hutchinson's banishment preceded by less than a decade the founding of the Society of Friends (Quakers) by Margaret Fell and George Fox. When the Quakers left Europe to escape persecution, they were welcomed in Rhode Island. By contrast, the Puritans of Massachusetts in 1657 passed a law against the Society which called for a fine of one hundred pounds on anyone who brought a Quaker into the Colony and forty shillings for every hour that one concealed a Quaker. Any Friend who returned to Massachusetts after having been driven out should, if a man, have an ear cropped; for a second offense, the other ear; and for a third, have his tongue bored with a hot iron. If the offender was a woman, she was to be severely whipped and for the third offense have her tongue bored. Although safe in Rhode Island, the Friends purposefully went again and again to Massachusetts to spread their teachings, including the "heresy" of "Inner Light," i.e., personal knowledge of the truth, and they were punished again and again according to the law.

This early civil disobedience campaign of the Friends and their subsequent persecution came to the attention of King Charles II, in 1661, when the Society presented a list of sufferings to him. The list

CHURCH	ALTERNATE NAME	FOUNDER & DATE	PROSELYTIZE	USE PERSONAL VIOLENCE	ALLOW STATE VIOLENCE	VOTE	HOLD PUBLIC OFFICE	PAY WAR TAXES & FINES
Amish			NO	NO	YES	NO	NO	YES
Brethren, Church of the	Dunkers Tunkers German Baptist	Alexander Mack, Sr., 1708	NO	NO	YES	NO	NO	YES
Mennonites		Menno Simons, c. 1537	NO	NO	YES	NO	NO	YES
Nicholites	Joined Quakers c. 1800	Joseph Nichols, 1774	NO	NO	NO	YES		NO
Moravians		Count Nicholas Lewis of Zinzendorf, c. 1772 (Descendants of Unitas Fratum, c. 1457)	YES	NO		YES		YES
Rogerenes		John Rogers, Sr. (d. 1721)	YES	NO	NO	YES		NO
Schwenckfelders		Caspar Schwenckfelder c. 1560		NO	YES	YES	YES	YES
Society of Friends	Quakers	George Fox & Margaret Fell c. 1652	YES	NO	NO	YES	YES	NO
United Society of Believers in Christ's Second Coming	Millennial Church Shaker Church	Ann Lee, c. 1774	YES	NO	NO	YES	YES	NO

This chart of colonial peace churches illustrates varying positions pacifists have historically assumed with regard to civil authority. Many generalizations have been made and each generalization has exceptions. Within each church, people held shades of opinion and, through time, the churches changed. The Shakers, for example, did not come to the absolutist position until the War of 1812 and the Moravians gave up their pacifism by the beginning of the Civil War. After Friends resigned from the government of Pennsylvania in 1756, they did not generally hold public office until the turn of the 20th Century.

detailed searches, whippings, imprisonments, banishments, brandings, fines, ear croppings, sales into slavery, three executions (William Robinson, Marmaduke Stephenson and Mary Dyer) and five unsuccessful appeals to England. The authorities of Massachusetts countered by portraying the Quakers as persons not fit to inhabit the earth and as "malignant promoters of doctrines tending to subvert both our church and state."

Upon receiving further petitions and conducting an interview with English Quakers, King Charles issued a mandate for the government of Massachusetts to stop its persecution of the Society of Friends. Confronted with the King's decree, the Governor of Massachusetts ordered all imprisoned Quakers released. Although Friends continued to be abused for the next two years, the King's mandate marked a turning point in their treatment. In 1665, the royal commissioners commanded the General Court of Massachusetts to allow Quakers to go about their business unmolested.

William Penn's "Great Law" of 1682 guaranteed freedom of conscience for the people of Pennsylvania. Following the example set by the citizens of Rhode Island and the Society of Friends, freedom of conscience is written into the American Constitution as the first article of the Bill of Rights.

COLONIAL PEACE CHURCHES

As a result of religious convictions which rejected war, colonial peace churches asserted that the state has no authority over matters of conscience. This assertion brought them persecution by both European and colonial governments.

Many of the peace churches, e.g., Mennonites, Brethren and Amish, took literally the New Testament injunction, "Resist not evil." Members came to be called *nonresistants* and, for the most part, followed a program of withdrawal from the world. These churches identified civil authority with the violence state governments employ to maintain their power. Therefore, they forbade *willful* participation in government, e.g., holding office or voting, since such action would bring members to occasions when they had to inflict injury or elect others who would inflict injury.

In practice, the nonresistance of these churches meant obeying the existing civil authority up to the point of actually, personally using violence. Since taxes were "Caesar's due," members paid taxes even when the money clearly went to support war. When drafted, members paid to be exempted or accepted alternative service. They did this in the name of not resisting evil. Thinking a violent state appropriate for an unjust society, they expected the governments would protect citizens, and by arms if necessary; but they did not personally want any part of it.

Other colonial churches, e.g., the Society of Friends and Shakers, held a different world view. Instead of thinking of their churches as islands to be preserved from inundation by the world's sinfulness, they thought that their vision would overcome the world and they energetically promoted their ideas.

Churches typified by the Quakers did not identify civil authority with state violence and so they did not object to active participation in politics. When the Society of Friends established the government of Pennsylvania, they intended that civil authority should flow from the power of the people's experience of "Inner Light," i.e., direct personal knowledge of the good.

In practice, the pacifism of these churches did not permit anything that could be construed as support of state violence. Church members refused war taxes, would not pay to be exempted from the militia, and would not perform alternative service. In short, they were absolutists. While they endorsed government per se, they would not cooperate with civil authority in causing injury. If this meant breaking the law, then they were ready to practice civil disobedience and to accept the consequences of their beliefs.

EARLY CONSCIENTIOUS OBJECTORS

Just as colonial Friends risked life, limb and property to establish freedom of conscience, early pacifists risked all to follow the dictates of conscience and resist war. At least through the Civil War, these people were called "nonresistants," "noncombatants," "those scrupulous against bearing arms," etc., because the term "conscientious objector" had not yet been coined. The first settlers in the New World to refuse to bear arms were probably Dutch Mennonites who were living on Manhattan in the early 1640's. The earliest recorded case of persecution for a pacifist stance dates from 1658 when Richard Keene, a Maryland Quaker, refused

to be trained as a soldier. The sum of £61.15s was taken from him, and the sheriff, saying, "You dog, I could find in my heart to split your brains," drew his cutlass and struck him on the shoulder. During the Colonial period, all of the peace churches resisted militia duty in one way or another. Sometimes they moved en masse as, for example, the Moravians who migrated from Oglethorpe's Georgia in 1739 rather than fight the Spaniards in Florida during the War of Jenkin's Ear.

Due to their prolonged refusal to muster for the militia, many of the colonial peace churches had gained partial recognition for their pacifist positions by the time of the Revolutionary War. Pacifists had been harassed and their property had been seized so many times, that their neighbors were familiar with their arguments and acknowledged that they derived from conscience and not from cowardice. Virginia and North Carolina exempted those who could produce a certificate of membership in a recognized peace church. In 1775, Pennsylvania passed a law which exempted members of peace churches who were willing to pay a commutation fee of £2.10s in order to be excused. A penalty of seizure of goods or four months imprisonment was levied for refusal of the commutation fee. New Jersey, New York, Maryland and Delaware had similar laws. Massachusetts had given Quakers a complete exemption in 1775, but later the law was changed to an exemption with the payment of a commutation fee of £10 and a penalty of two months imprisonment for refusal.

Many noncombatants were satisfied with the exemption laws, for they were willing to pay the fees or to perform alternative service as wagon drivers or nurses. However, some churches, such as the Friends and Rogerenes, refused any cooperation. The seizures of property, imprisonments and persecutions recorded during the war pertain mainly to these absolutists or to members of exempted peace churches who were old enough to be conscripted but not old enough to be baptized and therefore could not produce a certificate of membership.

Pacifists unwilling or unable to be exempted under the laws of the time were either imprisoned, fined and fined again, or they moved west or to Canada. Occasionally, some were individually excused. Seven Quakers, for example, were seized for the army and forced to march with rifles strapped to their backs. Often they went hungry because they would not eat army rations. When these men were brought to General Washington's encampment, he ordered them discharged and sent home.

Although most of the noncombatants during the

MILITARY GLORY
BY THOMAS NAST, 1870
New York Public Library

Revolutionary War came from the peace churches, the names of some principled war resisters unaligned with these churches are known to us, e.g., Joseph Healy, a Connecticut shoemaker; John Baker, a Connecticut farmer; E. Estabrook, a Baptist minister from New Hampshire; Jesse Lee, a Methodist preacher from North Carolina; and Thomas Watson, a British army deserter.

During the Civil War, the peace churches, with some exceptions, repeated the same pattern of graduated opposition they practiced in the Revolutionary War. The strong abolitionist attitudes of these churches made the decision against war more difficult and many individual members participated in the conflict. This participation was also due in part to the churches' neglect of instructing their young in the traditional pacifist principles. The Moravians, as a church, had abandoned their pacifism by the outbreak of the Civil War.

The great majority of members of the Amish, Church of the Brethren, Mennonites, Society of Friends, Rogerenes and Shakers held to their antimilitarism. Most of the noncombatants during the

war were from these churches or from the peace churches which had developed since the Revolutionary War such as the Seventh Day Adventists, Second Adventists, Christadelphians and Brethren in Christ (River Brethren). Other noncombatants came from the secular New England Non-Resistance Society and the Hopedale and Oneida communities.

The general public accepted pacifism, still not completely, but more easily during the Civil War than during the Revolutionary War because people had even more familiarity with the idea. Most states had passed laws exempting from the militia those who could prove membership in a recognized peace church. When the war started, federal conscription laws superceded the state laws and pacifists had to wage another set of battles to gain legal recognition. This was easier in the North than in the South. The conscription law of the North provided for alternative service or a commutation fee. No provision was made, however, for refusal to cooperate in any way. Thus, Quakers, Shakers, Rogerenes, Brethren in Christ and other absolutists, as well as those too young for formal membership in the churches practicing adult baptism, underwent a long list of hardships ranging from minor seizures of goods to death in army prisons.

President Abraham Lincoln and Secretary of War Edwin Stanton understood the arguments of absolute pacifists and released from the army prisons those individuals who were brought to their attention. Stanton offered to set up a special fund designated solely for the education of freed slaves if these absolutists would pay the commutation fee. Quakers refused the concession, for as the 1865 Yearly Meeting stated:

> *Believing that liberty of conscience is the gift of the Creator to man, Friends have ever refused to purchase the free exercise of it, by the payment of any pecuniary or other commutation, to any human authority.*

Lincoln tolerated the circulation of anti-war tracts among the military, held personal interviews with individuals professing the absolutist position, and did what he could to prevent anything resembling persecution for matters of conscience.

Noncombatants in the Confederate states suffered more than their pacifist comrades in the North. Because the South was harder pressed for men and matériel and less familiar with the pacifist position, the Confederate conscription law of 1862 did not provide for an exemption based on conscience. Southern Mennonites, Brethren (Dunkers) and Quakers joined forces to lobby for

**WILLIAM PENN'S MESSAGE TO THE
INDIANS OF NORTH AMERICA, 1681**
George M. Cushing/Massachusetts
Historical Society

bread and water diets, and threats of death. The men were not the only ones to suffer; there are recorded cases of civilians having their hands squeezed between fence gates while being questioned as to the whereabouts of draft-age men and one case of a woman being hanged until dead for refusing to tell where a man in her family had gone.

Some of the names of those resisting the Civil War have been passed down to us, e.g., the brothers Mahlon and Joshua Kemp; Addison Harper, who resigned his commission with the Confederate army; Jesse Buchner, who resigned his commission; Rufus P. King, who at first accepted alternative service and then deserted; a man named Blackmore, who died in camp; John Wesley Pratt, a New England Non-Resistance Society absolutist; Jesse Macy, a Quaker who accepted alternative service; Ben P. Moore, an absolutist; Cyrus Pringle, an absolutist who was tortured; Jesse Gordon and M. G. Bradshaw, who were exempted by Stanton; the brothers William, Himelius and Jesse Hockett, all absolutists, the latter two suffering hanging by the thumbs and repeated bayonet prickings. Gideon Macon was about to be hanged when the regiment he was with was forced to retreat and Seth Loflin would have been shot, but the twelve men on the firing squad refused to carry out the court martial sentence.

THE QUEST FOR A
JUST SOCIAL ORDER:
THE SOCIETY OF FRIENDS

Early pacifists challenged the supposition that society must be based on violence not only by resisting war, but also by building communities where they worked to eliminate injustice. In the attempt to create and maintain a just social order most of the peace churches secluded themselves. The Society of Friends, however, took a large and active part in public affairs and worked for a just order which confronted rather than avoided the problems of the world. On a personal level, Friends tried to eliminate violence from their daily lives and they transacted their business fairly and honestly. When Quakers gave their word, they bound themselves completely. Members of the Society who fell short of these standards received friendly counsel from other members of the Society.

On a public level, Friends tried to prevent violence by removing its causes. As results of this approach, they made highly effective diplomats; they enjoyed amicable relations with the Native Americans; in Pennsylvania they created the most progressive penal code in the world up to that time;

legal recognition of their positions. The Brethren and Mennonites met with success when later that year the law was changed to allow a commutation fee. One of the foremost lobbyists, the Brethren leader John Kline, was assassinated in 1864 while still active on behalf of imprisoned pacifists.

Leaders of the Confederacy, such as Assistant Secretary of War John A. Campbell, cooperated with pacifists more than regimental officers did. General T. J. "Stonewall" Jackson, considering the problems created by conscience in the ranks, said that it was better to send the pacifists home and let them work on their farms.

In both the North and the South, it was the regimental officers who handed out the harshest treatment to noncombatants, while in many cases the lower ranks were friendly to pacifists. Although no noncombatants were executed, many died from illnesses resulting from their treatment by the army. Cruelties inflicted included: repeated piercings with a bayonet, hanging by the thumbs, beatings, deprivation of sleep and of means of washing, and, in the period prior to and following the Revolutionary War, Friends carried out an extensive campaign for the abolition of slavery.

The public involvement of the Quakers made them highly visible and influential throughout the colonies. Although best known for founding the state of Pennsylvania, Friends also participated at high levels in the administrations of Rhode Island, New Jersey, New York and the Carolinas.

John Archdale's governing of the Carolinas (1694-97) provides a good example of Quaker wisdom cutting through political controversy to arrive at the heart of an issue. The Proprietors of the Carolinas appointed Archdale, also a Proprietor, as governor because South Carolina was torn with dissension between high churchmen and low churchmen. Archdale resolved the conflict by bringing the disputing parties into balanced participation in the Council. Archdale also eased the discrimination against the French Huguenots in the colony at a time when there was much bad feeling between the English and the French. When Archdale arrived, the French could not vote or hold seats in the Assembly. Archdale succeeded in tempering the hostilities and by the time he returned to England, he had opened the way for passage of an act which provided: "All aliens of what nation soever, which now are inhabitants of South Carolina shall have all rights, privileges and immunities which any person born of English parents within this province has."

The Society of Friends pursued an Indian policy based, first, on their regard for the Native Americans as people. Friend John Woolman expressed the common Quaker attitude:

> Love was the first motion, and thence arose a concern to spend some time with the Indians, that I might feel and understand their life and the spirit they live in, if haply I might receive some instruction from them, or they might be in any degree helped forward by my following the leadings of Truth among them.

Secondly, Quakers acted on their insight that conflict is best overcome by clearing away its causes. Besides compensating the Indians for their land, Friends also gave Indians the benefit of the doubt when trouble arose. In 1688, for example, rumors circulated in Pennsylvania that 500 Indian warriors were preparing to attack. Friend Caleb Pusey volunteered to investigate, if the Council would appoint five others to accompany him. When the unarmed Quakers arrived at the place where the warriors were supposed to be massing, they found just the chief lying on his bed with women and

A
CAUTION
T O
GREAT BRITAIN
A N D
Her COLONIES,
I N

A short REPRESENTATION of

The CALAMITOUS STATE of the

ENSLAVED NEGROES

In the BRITISH DOMINIONS.

By ANT. BENEZET.

PHILADELPHIA Printed :

LONDON Reprinted, 1767.

TITLE PAGE FROM
QUAKER TRACT, 1767
George M. Cushing/Massachusetts Historical Society

children around him.

The Friends' attitude and the measures they instituted enabled the people of Pennsylvania, Indian and white, to enjoy fraternal relations for 60 years. Only when Thomas Penn abandoned his father's policy of dealing fairly with the Indians, and when Friends no longer were able to restrain the colony's non-Quaker majority from provoking the Indians, did the people of Pennsylvania bring down upon themselves the hostilities of the French and Indian War.

The "Great Law" which William Penn introduced in 1682, made murder and treason the only capital offenses, while in England over one hundred crimes were punishable by death. The "Great Law" stipulated that when Indians came to trial, one half of the jury should be Indian and the testimony of Indians should be given the same weight as that of Englishmen. Under Penn's laws, Pennsylvania never experienced the witch hunts that crazed New England. Only one woman was charged with being a witch in Pennsylvania and Penn tried her himself. The woman was found to be guilty of having the reputation of a witch but innocent as indicted and she was released to the care of her neighbors.

Though not initially opposed to slavery, Friends were the first to recognize the injustice of the sys-

MEETING ANNOUNCEMENT FROM THE
MASSACHUSETTS PEACE SOCIETY, 1818
Swarthmore College Peace Collection

DAVID LOW DODGE
Swarthmore College Peace Collection

tem and to respond in an organized fashion. As early as 1688, a group of Mennonites who had become Quakers in Germantown, Pennsylvania, under the leadership of Francis Daniel Pastorius, addressed a protest against slavery to the London Yearly Meeting. Five years later, in New York, George Keith printed *An Exhortation and Caution to Friends Concerning Buying or Keeping of Negroes.* These first appeals from Quakers to Quakers objected to slavery on the grounds that slaves were wrongfully gained as spoils of war and that they could be kept in their servitude only by means of violence.

The initial response of Friends in government to the slavery issues being raised at the Meetings was marked with contradictions. In 1705, Quakers in Pennsylvania made an effort to hinder the slave trade by taxing the owners of imported slaves forty shillings per head. Yet, that same year, they made certain crimes capital offenses for blacks that were not punishable by death for whites.

In 1712, the Pennsylvania legislature levied a prohibitive duty of £20 on every slave imported to the colony. In 1730, the Philadelphia Yearly Meeting declared the purchase of a slave to be grounds for disownment and, by 1754, many Quakers, most notably John Woolman and Anthony Benezet, were teaching that, apart from the violence by which slaves were obtained, slavery was wrong in itself as an abrogation of human rights.

The tempo of the struggle against slavery picked up after 1756 when Friends turned to moral causes with increased zeal after their withdrawal from the government of Pennsylvania. The 1758 Philadel-

phia Yearly Meeting encouraged Quakers to start a campaign to turn others away from holding slaves. By 1780, practically no Friends in the United States held slaves and due to Quaker example and efforts, various states, starting with Pennsylvania, began to pass laws abolishing slavery within their borders.

Out of a general population of 2,500,000 in North America at the end of the colonial period, Friends numbered about 50,000. These people helped to found the country, not only as honest, hard working settlers, but also as administrators, law givers and agitators. Their unrelenting search for the best in human society brought them to start not only public schools but also abolition societies and the "Friendly Association for Gaining and Preserving Peace with the Indians by Pacific Measures."

Because Friends accepted everyone into their communities, they soon lost their majority standing. Even as a minority, Friends continued in power for a time due to their progressive leadership which extended civil liberties to the citizenry, kept the people out of wars, and promoted a high level of prosperity. Quaker administrators proved to be scrupulous in their care of the public interest. As Friends became increasingly a minority, however, it grew more difficult for them to implement their methods of maintaining social order and preserving the peace. In positions of public responsibility, some Quaker governors compromised the Quaker teaching about war. Others, such as members of the Pennsylvania Assembly in 1756, withdrew from public office rather than be responsible for mounting a militia for the French and Indian War.

The Society of Friends never really set out to experiment with government. They experimented with a religious concept and drew socially relevant conclusions from their Principle of Inner Light.

THE FIRST SECULAR PEACE ORGANIZATIONS

Beginning in 1815, churchmen professing religions not traditionally pacifist founded organizations to promote the cause of peace. These organizations, such as the New York Peace Society, Massachusetts Peace Society, and American Peace Society, are called secular, although most of their members were churchmen, because membership in the society did not depend on membership in a church.

Secular efforts to popularize the cause of peace took two different courses. The program more easily accepted by the general public called for outlawing wars of aggression. The other called for eradicating all violence, domestic and international. The two strains of thought found expression in the debate about offensive versus defensive wars: "Do we object to all wars or only to wars of aggression?" Because the organizations were trying to reach a broad audience, the debate concerned tactics as much as it did principles. Would greater effect be had by promoting advanced ideas or by gaining the allegiance of more people?

Eventually, this debate led to splits within the secular peace movement. The peace societies which emerged, the New England Non-Resistance Society and the League of Universal Brotherhood, were more truly secular. In addition to the problem of war, the new organizations took up the problems of slavery, minority rights, women's rights, and prisons. Unlike the older organizations, which sought to influence professionals and "important" people, the newer organizations gave their attention to the more common populace.

In 1815, when David Low Dodge, a New York merchant, started the New York Peace Society and Noah Worcester, a Congregational minister, founded the Massachusetts Peace Society, the different considerations about the purpose of a secular peace organization were not so well articulated. Both Dodge and Worcester personally denounced offensive and defensive wars, as well as the use of injurious force in self-defense. This complete pacifist position was emphasized by the New York Peace Society, while the Massachusetts Peace Society gave more emphasis to promoting a world court as an alternative to war.

These first secular peace organizations carried out their work by means of speaking engagements and publishing. They directed their efforts to ministers, so that they would instruct their congregations, and to high placed people, so that they would use their influence to turn the government away from war. At its peak in 1818, the Massachusetts Peace Society had 1,000 members, many of whom were actively enlisted military officers.

While Biblical arguments continued to be used, other reasons to forego war began to be developed. Noah Worcester wrote *A Solemn Review of the Custom of War* (1814) in which he maintained that wars should not be fought to right wrongs because the people killed are not the people most responsible for the wrongful national policy. Dodge wrote in his book *War Inconsistent with the Religion of Jesus Christ* (1815) that war is a waste of resources; that it is biologically unsound because it selects out the young and healthy; and that it is not effective because the peace and liberty it is purported to achieve are aborted by the hatred and desire for revenge which it generates. Samuel Whelpley of the New York Society wrote a series of open letters to the Governor of Massachusetts in which he connected war with the defense of property.

In 1828, the Massachusetts and New York Peace Societies, together with other secular peace groups which had developed in the meantime, joined to form the American Peace Society, for which Worcester wrote the constitution. Under the leadership of William Ladd, Worcester's successor as the foremost peace organizer, the American Peace Society continued to solicit the support of influential people in organizing meetings, publishing, speaking and petitioning state and federal governments. Members of the Society criticized U.S. expansionist policy and argued for disarmament, but the Society focused its greatest attention on establishing a world court.

The official position of the American Peace Society increasingly emphasized only wars of aggression. This growing conservatism resulted in two schisms; the first, in 1838, led to the formation of the New England Non-Resistance Society, and the second, in 1846, led to the formation of the League of Universal Brotherhood. During the Civil War, the American Peace Society issued a statement declaring the conflict to be an internal police action and, thus, not within its field of concern.

The lobbying and educational efforts of the American Peace Society in its later years led directly to the establishment of the Hague Court (1899), the first permanent tribunal for international arbitration, and paved the way for the League of Nations, predecessor of today's United Nations.

WILLIAM LLOYD GARRISON
Sophia Smith Collection/Smith College

ADIN BALLOU
George M. Cushing/Massachusetts Historical Society

THE NEW ENGLAND
NON-RESISTANCE SOCIETY

By 1838, some members of the American Peace Society felt that they could no longer work within the Society's official program of moderate reform. These members, discontented because the American Peace Society would not come out against all state and personal use of violence, withdrew to start the New England Non-Resistance Society, the boldest pacifist organization in the 19th Century. Members of the New England Non-Resistance Society were committed to radical social change without violence. They took the offensive against injustice and also made important theoretical contributions to the development of nonviolence.

Henry Clarke Wright, a Congregational minister and stormy abolitionist, led the discontented members in their attempts to radicalize the American Peace Society. Wright was ably assisted by Samuel J. May, a Unitarian minister who championed temperance, penal reform, women's rights and the causes of oppressed people — from Native Americans to immigrant Irish. William Lloyd Garrison, a pacifist and leading abolitionist, supported their efforts, although he was not a member of the American Peace Society. In his abolitionist paper *Liberator*, Garrison criticized the American Peace Society, saying that such mild organizations:

> . . . are mischievous, instead of being beneficial, because they occupy the ground without being able to effect the object. What a farce it is to see a Peace Society enrolling upon its list of members, not converted but belligerent commanders-in-chief, generals, colonels, majors, corporals and all! What a wonderful reform may be expected where there are none to be reformed!

Garrison once told William Ladd, the President of the American Peace Society, "Be assured that . . . until your cause is honored with lynch law, a coat of tar and feathers, brickbats and rotten eggs — no radical reform can take place."

Under Wright's leadership, the radicals called a convention to which they invited all whom they hoped would share their views. Garrison and his followers came; George C. Beckwith, Secretary of the American Peace Society and editor of its paper *Advocate of Peace*, arrived with his contingent. After a few hours, Beckwith and his sympathizers left, saying that they objected to women being admitted to full membership in the convention and its committees. Most of the debate centered around the successful resolution that "human life is inviolable and can never be taken by individuals or nations . . ." The convention set up the New England Non-Resistance Society and Garrison headed the committee to draft the Constitution and Declaration of Sentiments.

The Declaration which Garrison wrote says in part:

> *We cannot acknowledge allegiance to any human government. . . . Our country is the world, our countrymen are all mankind. . . . We register our testimony, not only against all war – whether offensive or defensive, but all preparations for war, against every naval ship, every arsenal, every fortification; against the militia system and a standing army; against all military chieftains and soldiers; against all monuments commemorative of victory over a foreign foe, all trophies won in battle, all celebrations in honor of military or naval exploits; against all appropriations for the defense of a nation by force and arms on the part of any legislative body; against every edict of government requiring of its subjects military service. Hence, we deem it unlawful to bear arms or to hold a military office. . . . We cannot sue any man at law to compel him by force to restore anything which he may have wrongfully taken from us or others; but if he had seized our coat, we shall surrender up our cloak rather than subject him to punishment.*

Like the nonresistant peace churches, the New England Non-Resistance Society would not use violence or participate in government; unlike those churches which withdrew from the world, the New England Non-Resistance Society directly challenged the injustice of the contemporary society and actively campaigned for change.

While most of the work centered in New England, active branches also operated in Ohio, Michigan and Indiana. The Society's views found expression in the *Liberator*, and from 1839 until mid-1842, the Society published its own paper, *Non-Resistant*, which in 1840 had 1,000 subscribers. Rank and file members of the Society disturbed church meetings to call attention to the churches' inaction concerning slavery. For their efforts, the

MARIA CHAPMAN
George M. Cushing/Massachusetts Historical Society

members as well as their leaders often faced the violence of angry mobs, but always they refused to return the injury. The Society attributed to this nonresistance the fact that none of its members were ever killed.

Several capable and energetic women furthered the organization and the principles of the New England Non-Resistance Society. Among them were: Lucretia Mott, abolitionist and women's rights advocate; Sarah and Angelina Grimké, early feminists and abolitionists; Lydia Maria Child, novelist; Maria Chapman, abolitionist; Abby Kelly, Quaker and women's rights advocate; and Ann Weston, nonresistance activist.

William Lloyd Garrison led the abolitionist work. Henry C. Wright, an apt organizer, traveled throughout this country and to England, where he made considerable impact on the anti-militarist movement just beginning there. Of the group, Adin Ballou did the most to further pacifist theory. Later, Russian novelist and pacifist Leo Tolstoy corresponded with Ballou, translated some of his work and propagated his writings in Russia. Mohandas Gandhi was also influenced by the work and thought of Adin Ballou and William Lloyd Garrison.

HENRY DAVID THOREAU
Library of Congress

The ideology developed by the New England Non-Resistants was not a well rounded creed but a constant examination of philosophy and technique. The members agreed that the existing system could not be reformed and they sought a clear break with it. They maintained a determined "no government" position and, as a result, they avoided electoral politics as a means to their ends. Instead, they appealed directly to individuals and encouraged a revolution of the inner person.

Henry David Thoreau's celebrated essay "Civil Disobedience" owes much to the Christian anarchism articulated by Garrison and Ballou. The essay was written in 1846, after Thoreau spent a night in jail for refusing to pay the Massachusetts poll tax. Thoreau's action stemmed from his opposition to the war with Mexico, which he believed was intended to spread slavery. Though neither a pacifist nor a member of the New England Non-Resistance Society, Thoreau was still familiar with their position. He distinguished himself from the New England Non-Resistants by stating in his essay, ". . . unlike those who call themselves no-government men, I ask for, not at once no government, but *at once* a better government." The essay goes on to argue the necessity for individuals to act according to the dictates of conscience even though this entails resistance to the state.

In developing its theory and practice of non-resistance, the Society gave more consideration to domestic defense from anti-social forces than it did to a nation's protecting itself from external attack. Considering criminals, Adin Ballou introduced the concept of "noninjurious force" which limited the use of force to restraining dangerous persons in such a way that would not harm them. The reformation of criminals, Ballou suggested, was dependent upon the power of the community's concern for them. Charles K. Whipple urged that policemen be recruited from tried nonresistants who would act without weapons but with the full support of the community. The Non-Resistants insisted upon the need to eliminate the social and economic causes of crime.

Adin Ballou distinguished three kinds of principled pacifism: Philosophical, pacifism based on the principle that violence is irrational; Sentimental, pacifism based on humanitarian principles and the belief in human perfectibility; and Christian, pacifism based on a desire to follow the example of Jesus Christ. Ballou was the first to suggest that there could be principled pacifism not based on religious considerations.

Ballou also enunciated the Law of Reciprocation. This "law" means that absorbing injury and responding with a benevolent insistence upon justice perfects human society, while to return injury with injury results in further injury. The Non-Resistants repeatedly made the point that humans have followed the latter course throughout history with the only result being a world filled with violence and insecurity.

Concerned as they were with the abolition of slavery, and living in a world which had witnessed several revolutions and attempted revolutions, the New England Non-Resistants particularly examined the relationship of pacifism to struggles for freedom from oppression. Charles K. Whipple foreshadowed Gandhi's thinking as to technique when he wrote *Evils of the Revolutionary War* (1839). Whipple accepted the aims of the Revolutionary leaders but maintained, "We should have attained independence as effectually, as speedily, as honorably, and under very much more favorable circumstances, if we had not resorted to arms." In order to accomplish their goals, the colonists would have had to 1) refuse all unjust demands; 2) efficiently make their cause known; and 3) endure the reprisals that undoubtedly would follow.

Whipple suggested that the colonists surely would have suffered, but nothing approaching the calamities of war. Moreover, if they had had the mindfulness to conduct their revolution without violence, the nation which they founded would have enjoyed many benefits. There would not have followed a half century of hostilities with England; slavery would not have been written into the Constitution; Indians would have been treated differently; and the spirit of revenge would not have pervaded the foreign relations of the country and its penal system.

The New England Non-Resistance Society held its last regular meeting in 1849. With the rising tide of militancy among the nation's abolitionists, the Non-Resistants were torn between their commitment to pacifism and their commitment to abolition. While maintaining their personal allegiance to nonresistance, Garrison and Wright advocated that people should be true to their sense of right and employ violence to help the slave if they would use violence in self-defense. The Non-Resistants had not managed to mature their theory into broad and effective practice and, as a result, ended their dual public campaign for both pacifism and social justice.

THE LEAGUE OF UNIVERSAL BROTHERHOOD

The League of Universal Brotherhood, founded in 1847 by Elihu Burritt, was the first secular pacifist organization to directly seek the support of common working people. Moreover, Burritt's League became the first secular pacifist organization to gain international status. It had branches in the United States and in Britain and carried its educational work to Holland, Germany, France and Italy.

A blacksmith by trade, Burritt educated himself to a working knowledge of some forty languages. One day, while studying geography, he was struck by the interrelation of the earth's climates. This, reinforced by the relationships he found between languages, gave him insight into the unity and interconnection of all things. As a practical result, he advocated socialism and devoted himself to bringing an end to the mutual slaughter of workers when governments declare war.

Burritt began his organizational work by joining the American Peace Society in 1843, and soon he became one of the leading activists. He served on the Executive Board and edited the newspaper *Advocate of Peace* (adding *and Universal Brotherhood* to the name). In 1846, Rev. George C. Beckwith, who had led the opposition to the radicals in 1838, succeeded in modifying the American Peace Society's constitution and, in effect, weakened the statement of principles. Beckwith had mobilized the conservative majority to make the changes so that membership would be more appealing to people who opposed international wars of aggression but who did not necessarily oppose defensive wars or capital punishment. Burritt and several others, including Samuel Coues, then President of the Society, resigned their positions on the

ELIHU BURRITT
J.C. Buttre/Library of Congress

Executive Board, although they did not resign from the Society. In their letter of resignation, they stated their conviction that no increase in membership could compensate for abandoning the fundamental principle that human life is sacred and inviolable.

The League of Universal Brotherhood provided an organization for those who held the full pacifist position which the American Peace Society had relinquished. In addition to propagating ideas about the necessity of forgoing war, the League promoted increased international understanding. Members lobbied and carried out extensive press campaigns for ocean penny postage and for more lenient immigration laws. They encouraged communities to set up "sister city" relationships with foreign communities and to institute exchange programs whereby people could live in another country for a time. Members of the League also organized international peace conferences.

Burritt instituted the first peace pledge. Through the efforts of the League in the United States and in England, over 50,000 people signed this statement:

> *Believing all war to be inconsistent with the spirit of Christianity, and destructive to the best interests of mankind, I do hereby pledge myself never to enlist or enter into any army or navy, or to yield any voluntary support or sanction to the preparation for or prosecution of any*

CAUTION!!
COLORED PEOPLE
OF BOSTON, ONE & ALL,

You are hereby respectfully CAUTIONED and
advised, to avoid conversing with the
Watchmen and Police Officers
of Boston,

For since the recent ORDER OF THE MAYOR &
ALDERMEN, they are empowered to act as
KIDNAPPERS
AND
Slave Catchers,

And they have already been actually employed in
KIDNAPPING, CATCHING, AND KEEPING
SLAVES. Therefore, if you value your LIBERTY,
and the *Welfare of the Fugitives* among you, Shun
them in every possible manner, as so many *HOUNDS*
on the track of the most unfortunate of your race.

Keep a Sharp Look Out for
KIDNAPPERS, and have
TOP EYE open.
APRIL 24, 1851.

POSTER PRODUCED BY
UNITARIAN MINISTER
THEODORE PARKER, 1851
Unitarian Universalist Association

*war, by whomsoever, for whatsoever
proposed, declared, or waged. And I do
hereby associate myself with all persons,
of whatever country, condition, or
color, who have signed, or shall hereafter sign this pledge, in a "League of
Universal Brotherhood"; whose object
shall be to employ all legitimate and
moral means for the abolition of all war,
and all spirit, and all the manifestation
of war, throughout the world; for the
abolition of all restrictions upon international correspondence and friendly
intercourse, and of whatever else tends
to make enemies of nations, or prevents
their fusion into one peaceful brotherhood; for the abolition of all institutions
and customs which do not recognize the
image of God and a human brother in
every man of whatever clime, color, or
condition of humanity.*

The ambitions of the League went beyond the
abolition of all war. Burritt described the League's
objectives in 1846:

*Its operations and influence will not be
confined to the work of mere abolition
[i.e., of war]; as if nothing more were
requisite for the symmetrical development of society, or the universal growth
of human happiness, than the axe be
laid to the root of existing evils. It will
seek to build up, as well as to pull down
. . . Long after nations shall have been
taught to war no more, long after the
mere iron fetters shall have been
stricken from the limbs of every last
slave, and every visible yoke shall have
been broken, and every formal bastille
of oppression levelled with the ground,
there will be a work for the League.*

By 1857, the League of Universal Brotherhood
had exhausted itself as a separate organization. The
British branch joined the London Peace Society
and the U.S. branch melted into the American
Peace Society. The League declined primarily
because people found it easier to sign the pledge
than to keep it, particularly in face of the Crimean
War in Europe and the fast approaching Civil War
in the United States. After the demise of the
League, Burritt continued to be recognized as a
leader among active pacifists, especially because he
was one of the few to maintain an absolute renunciation of armed force throughout the Civil War.

The League is important as the first secular
peace organization to bring peace propaganda
directly to common people. The laborers and farmers who constituted the vast majority of its membership circulated the pledge among their peers and
collected signatures for it. Burritt's "Olive Leaves,"
short statements on peace issues, were printed in
the popular press on both sides of the Atlantic and
were read by tens of thousands of people in all walks
of life. In the middle of the 19th Century, Burritt's
name was a household word and the work of the
League was often far more visible than the work of
the American Peace Society. The League is also
important because it did more than present the
negative case against war; it emphasized a positive
philosophy of peace action.

THE ABOLITION MOVEMENT

Committed pacifists led the organized abolition
movement from its very beginning. The Society of
Friends started the first anti-slavery society in 1780
and, in time, their efforts resulted in northern
states passing emancipation laws. William Lloyd
Garrison, a pacifist and one of the most radical of the
early abolitionists, founded the New England Anti-

Executive Committee of the Pennsylvania Abolition Society, 1850. Standing: unidentified, Edward M. Davis, Haworth Wetherald, Abby Kimber, unidentified, Sarah Pugh; seated: unidentified, Margaret Jones Burleigh, unidentified, Robert Purvis, Lucretia Mott, and James Mott. Eight of the group were members of the Society of Friends. Sophia Smith Collection/Smith College.

slavery Society in 1832 and, a year later, was one of the founders of the American Anti-slavery Society. Members of both these organizations declared their determination to end the violence of slavery without themselves having recourse to violence. In fact, early Garrisonian abolitionists, black and white, male and female, again and again proved their capacity to absorb injury without retaliating.

Black slaves bore great suffering, and while they sought relief, very few called for revenge. Besides a limited number of armed insurrections, black resistance to slavery ranged from work slowdowns to running away. Because the most severe penalties were inflicted on recaptured slaves, those who tried to escape did so at great personal risk. Nonetheless, thousands of blacks made their way to freedom, usually without help from anyone else. Some received assistance from the Underground Railroad, a network of people, many of them members of the Society of Friends, who hid escaped slaves and helped them reach the next stopping point on the way north.

Both abolitionists and blacks fighting racism used the technique of the boycott. Boycotts of slave produce became so popular in the North that several stores opened which carried only free labor goods. Abolitionists also boycotted churches that did not firmly oppose slavery. Individual ministers relinquished their pulpits or refused assignment to pro-slavery congregations, and church members refused to acknowledge fellowship with slave holders. Because of this, some national denominations split. The Methodists, for example, divided in 1846 when the anti-slavery members formed themselves as the Wesleyan Methodist Church. In a boycott which lasted eleven years, black parents withdrew their children from segregated schools in Boston. The parents reasoned that "separation from the rest of the community . . . postpones that great day of reconciliation which is sure to come." As a result of their action and perseverance, Boston, in 1855, became the first major city in the United States to initiate integration of its public education system.

To challenge the racist status quo, blacks and some white abolitionists pioneered in a number of bold and consciously nonviolent actions such as sit-ins, eat-ins and walk-alongs. Blacks sat in the white sections of railroad cars, waited to be served

FREDERICK DOUGLASS
Sophia Smith Collection/Smith College

SOJOURNER TRUTH
Sophia Smith Collection/Smith College

at white tables, and tried to integrate steamboats. Blacks and whites walked down the street, arm in arm, male and female, or they sat down to eat together. Often these actions brought the practitioners violent reprisals and they usually maintained their nonresistance. Frederick Douglass, a runaway slave and, in time, a towering figure among blacks by virtue of his staunch abolition work, participated in a great many of these direct actions. Having aligned himself with Garrison in 1841, Douglass practiced nonresistance for years and more than once, in the course of trying to end prejudice and slavery, took beatings without retaliating.

Black leaders understood that violence would not solve the problem of white hatred. In 1846, Douglass opposed war as a means of emancipation and he added, "Were I asked the question whether I would have my emancipation by the shedding of one single drop of blood, my answer would be in the negative." In 1849, while affirming the right of slaves to revolt, he continued to assert that the "only well grounded hope of the slave for emancipation is the operation of moral force." Sojourner Truth, a former slave and widely respected abolitionist, voiced her opposition to the use of force to effect emancipation and she insisted that only a change of heart on the part of whites would ensure lasting liberty.

Several events in the middle of the 19th Century made it increasingly difficult for abolitionists to

maintain their nonresistance stance. The most notable of these events were the murder of Rev. Elijah Lovejoy, passage of the Fugitive Slave Act, and John Brown's raid. The Rev. Elijah Lovejoy, a leading white abolitionist, was killed in 1837 while defending his printing press with guns. The abolition movement as a whole split in the ensuing debate as to whether abolitionists should defend themselves by arms. The Garrisonian wing held to the position that abolitionists had pledged themselves to forego violence, even in self-defense. The Fugitive Slave Act of 1850 was so weighted in favor of the slaveholders and so increased the danger to even free northern blacks, that blacks began to arm themselves. Frederick Douglass abandoned his nonresistance and supported them, but the Garrisonians declared the law null and void and organized people to follow slave hunters around while announcing the purpose of their business and otherwise getting in their way. In 1859, John Brown led an armed attempt to encourage a slave insurrection, an action which severely challenged the nonresistants because they possessed great respect for courage and principled determination. At a meeting commemorating Brown's execution, Garrison affirmed his personal commitment to nonresistance, but rejoiced that those who believed in armed force would use their weapons to end the oppression of slavery.

Still, a number of nonresistants remained constant in their absolute condemnation of violence as a viable means. In response to John Brown's raid, Charles K. Whipple wrote *The Non-Resistance Principle: With Particular Application to the Help of Slaves by Abolitionists* (1860). In this work Whipple maintained that the slave's "first duty of good will to the slaveholder is utterly to refuse any longer to be a slave. . . Quiet, continuous submission to enslavement is complicity with the slaveholder." Whipple went on to write of the corresponding duty of abolitionists:

> If also it be necessary. . . to seize and put under restraint, by uninjurious means, the persons of any slaveholders, until the departure of the slaves is safely effected, this would be perfectly right, for it is only what the government ought long since to have done. A slaveholder is a public nuisance; a person eminently dangerous to the community; and if the government does not do its duty in restraining him, any person who has the power may properly use all uninjurious means to do it.

A year before the publication of Whipple's work, Adin Ballou argued against those who wanted to encourage slave rebellions by saying, "[If the slaves are freed by rebellion,] what is to be done with them for the next hundred years?. . . How are they to be employed, trained for liberty and organized into well ordered communities? And above all, how is this work to be accomplished with the great mass of the whites in the country full of horror, loathing and revenge toward them?"

After the Civil War, most blacks still lived in the South and they still had to bear the animosity of whites who instituted the Ku Klux Klan, castration, lynching, the poll tax, literacy tests and sharecropping in order to keep blacks out of equal participation in society. After ratification of the 14th and 15th Amendments, blacks found that rights guaranteed by law were precarious as long as their fellow white townspeople remained unchanged or, worse, hardened in their inability to see blacks as people.

THE WOMEN'S RIGHTS MOVEMENT

Without using violence, women effected pervasive changes in the social fabric of the United States over the course of the 19th and early 20th Centuries. Many of the most important leaders of the women's movement were members of the New England Non-Resistance Society and/or Quakers and the more radical groups and actions were organized by

SARAH M. GRIMKÉ
Library of Congress

ANGELINA E. GRIMKÉ
Library of Congress

SUSAN B. ANTHONY
Sophia Smith Collection/Smith College

LUCRETIA MOTT
Sophia Smith Collection/Smith College

pacifists. To the movement's political and legal efforts, pacifists added direct action, civil disobedience, public disruptions and passive resistance in order to highlight the women's cause and determination.

Apart from early efforts toward equal education, women first challenged their institutionalized subservience by insisting on their right to speak and to act publicly. Angelina and Sarah Grimké of the New England Non-Resistance Society became early champions of women's rights after being virulently criticized by clergymen for daring to address public meetings about abolition. Lucretia Mott, a Quaker and New England Non-Resistant, and Elizabeth Cady Stanton were refused as delegates to the 1840 World Anti-Slavery Convention in London, although they were both staunch abolitionists. As a result of this and other sexist experiences, the two women in 1848 called the Seneca Falls convention to discuss women's rights. During the convention, Stanton issued the first call for woman's suffrage.

Quakers held leadership positions in the women's movement far out of proportion to their relative number in the general population. Of all the major denominations, only the Friends commonly accepted women as speakers at meetings and as religious leaders. Thus, in addition to firm convictions, Quaker women possessed confidence and public speaking skills which were denied to most women.

Women developed not just speaking skills but also valuable organizational skills while doing abolition work and when they took up their own struggle, they received the support of black abolitionists. Frederick Douglass encouraged Elizabeth Cady Stanton's call for women's suffrage in 1848 and black abolitionists Francis E. W. Harper and Sarah Remond drew the connections between the women's and the blacks' struggles for freedom. It was in order to quiet a heckler at a 1851 women's rights convention in Akron, Ohio, that the eminent abolitionist Sojourner Truth delivered her famous "Ain't I a Woman" speech.

The man over there says women need to be helped into carriages and lifted over ditches, and to have the best places everywhere. Nobody ever helps me into carriages or over puddles, or gives me the best place – and ain't I a woman? . . . I could work as much and eat as much as a man – when I could get it – and bear the lash as well. And ain't I a woman? I have born thirteen children, and seen most of 'em sold into slavery, and when I cried out with my mother's grief, none but Jesus heard me – and ain't I a woman?

Shortly after the Civil War, the Equal Rights Association was organized to promote voting rights for both blacks and women. In 1868, the Association began to pull back from the women's cause and women were asked to quiet their demands for suffrage so as to facilitate passage of the 15th Amendment which enfranchised black males.

Susan B. Anthony, a Quaker and the leading organizer of the women's movement for 50 years, and Elizabeth Cady Stanton, the movement's leading theoretician, firmly believed that blacks and women both could win the vote. So the two women withdrew from the Equal Rights Association in order to organize the National Woman's Suffrage Association in 1869.

The National Woman's Suffrage Association emphasized work for a federal amendment to guarantee women the right to vote, but also concerned itself with many other problems which women faced: women driven to prostitution as their only means of livelihood; long hours and short pay for working women; grossly unfair divorce and inheritance laws. Under Susan Anthony's leadership, the National Association encouraged civil disobedience, tax refusal and public demonstrations such as interrupting the 1876 national Centennial celebration in order to present the Declaration of Women's Rights.

By contrast, the American Woman's Suffrage Association, founded shortly after the National and under the leadership of Lucy Stone and Julia Ward Howe, emphasized state referenda as the way to woman's suffrage and devoted its whole attention to winning the vote. For reasons of "respectability," the American Association avoided close relationships with working class women, social outcasts and divorcees and it did not support the more militant actions of the National.

In 1890, the two organizations combined forces as the National American Woman's Suffrage Association with Elizabeth Stanton as the first president. Anthony succeeded her in 1892 and served until 1900 when, due to advanced years, she chose Carrie Chapman Catt as her successor and stepped down. The two organizations had merged in order to carry on work both for a federal amendment and for state enfranchisement, but very shortly all the attention came to be focused on state referenda. The women's movement became increasingly conservative and nearly moribund until Alice Paul revived it by demanding a federal amendment in 1913.

Ratification of the 19th Amendment, the "Anthony Amendment," in 1920 represents only one accomplishment of the women's movement to that date. Over the 19th Century, women won access to education and some very strong women began to enter the professions. Slowly and unevenly, states passed legislation recognizing the rights of married women to hold property, to keep their own earnings, to make a will, to have custody of their own children and to inherit a deceased husband's estate. Slowly and painfully, married women began to rise from what was called in the law their "civil death;" they began to have some legal existence.

THE LABOR MOVEMENT

Like the 19th Century women's movement, the early labor movement was not self-consciously pacifist on principle. Yet, workers endured violence ranging from starvation wages to being shot down and, for the most part, still struggled to improve their situation without resorting to violence. While many labor leaders avoided violence because they thought it impractical, there were many others, who with George E. McNeill, an abolitionist turned labor organizer, believed "in the passive force of nonresistance."

Labor entered the most stormy period of its history in the years after the Civil War. While capital rapidly concentrated in fewer and fewer hands, workers still did not have the legal right to organize. The industrial revolution obliterated the self-esteem and the earnings of skilled craftsmen by putting them on a par with unskilled laborers tending machines. Workers lived in tenement slums; they received no compensation when they suffered injuries on the job; and they were at the mercy of employers who proclaimed it their right to fire or cut wages at will. When workers banded together to improve their lot, they were branded as criminals by the press, the churches, and the courts.

To better their condition, laborers educated themselves about collective activity and began to organize themselves into unions. This was not easy since employers summarily dismissed and blacklisted organizers and then instituted "yellow dog" contracts which made employment contingent upon never joining a union. Since workers had no legally recognized rights, they began to popularize the idea of arbitration so that employers would feel some compunction to deal with labor's grievances. Almost as a whole, employers violently opposed arbitration because they claimed the absolute right to do whatever they pleased with their own businesses. Workers, sorely pressed under the weight of the capitalist system, endeavored to understand the nature of their oppression as wage earners and they elaborated various economic alternatives, one of the most common being worker and consumer cooperatives. They also came to realize that only a small part of the time they labored went to pay their wages; the rest of the time paid for the factory, the materials and tools, and the income and profits of

EZRA H. HEYWOOD
Brown University

the owners. To mitigate this exploitation, labor agitated, educated, lobbied and struck for the eight-hour work day.

While labor did not receive much organized support from the peace societies in the period after the Civil War, it did receive strong support from individual pacifists, one of whom was Ezra Heywood, formerly a member of the New England Non-Resistance Society. An ardent abolitionist, Heywood withdrew from the abolition movement at the outbreak of the Civil War. While he continued to denounce slavery, he publicly condemned the war the entire time it lasted and supported the absolute position taken by the Society of Friends and the Shakers. After the Civil War, he was one of the founders of the Universal Peace Union, which was basically a regrouping of the old New England Non-Resistance Society.

Heywood was a native anarchist, a convert of Josiah Warren and a teacher of Benjamin Tucker, both significant early American anarchists. Considering individuals in free association to be the source of social energy and balance, anarchists taught that piecemeal political reforms could never correct the continual economic disorder. Anarchists urged people to withdraw their support from the existing order and, instead, to build non-coercive alternatives such as cooperatives and land reform.

Under Heywood's guidance, the Worcester Labor Reform League came into being in 1867 to educate the public about the rights of labor. By 1871, the organization had grown into the American Labor Reform League which continued to vigorously support the women's struggle for equal pay and the movement for the eight-hour day. Working closely with the Knights of St. Crispin and the Sovereigns of Industry, the League called conferences which were addressed by such labor activists as Isaac Myers, President of the Colored National Labor Union and William Sylvis, President of the National Labor Union. The League endeavored to encourage working class self-consciousness but did not subscribe to the inevitability of class war.

Pamphlets which Heywood wrote over a 25 year period utterly rejected the taking of profits and the inheritance of land or the rights to raw materials. He called for a monetary system based upon the value of labor rather than upon gold and he condemned the economic subjugation of women. Unlike other anarchists of the period, Heywood did not write in isolation; from 1872 until 1882 he published a four-page monthly called *The Word* which carried articles by writers from a broad spectrum of radical perspectives, and he published booklets which disseminated the ideas of men and women who wanted to restructure the country's economic, social, and political system.

Heywood was imprisoned twice on charges of sending obscene material through the mails, charges which ostensibly resulted from his printing articles by radical feminists, including his wife. Heywood thought that his statements about labor and government had more to do with the reasons for his arrests. After six months of the first two-year sentence, President Hayes pardoned him in December 1878 due to public pressure. Heywood served the second two-year sentence in full and died in 1893, within a year of his release.

Three of the most important labor organizations of the 19th Century, the National Labor Union, the Knights of St. Crispin, and the Knights of Labor, all condemned labor violence and tried to institute alternatives that would not only check the injustice suffered by workers, but also advance human progress on the whole.

The National Labor Union (1866-70), the first national labor federation of any duration, promoted cooperatives, urged voluntary arbitration, and dispatched organizers to encourage the formation of unions around the country. The union held high aspirations that the struggle of workers would transform the whole society. William Sylvis, an iron-molder and President of the NLU, urged his membership to prove themselves morally superior to their employers and to ". . . make the union a power it will never be so long as we rely upon mere brute

force to carry our point." Sylvis spent his energies
to bring about the day when

> . . . all mankind shall be free, when the
> whole human family shall become
> united in one common brotherhood;
> when the broad banner of political,
> social and religious freedom shall wave
> over every land, under whose ample
> folds all the nations of the earth can find
> protection, and when reason, directed
> by moral principle, shall rule all the
> nations of the earth.

As a prototype, the National Labor Union contained many diverse elements. Some members
wanted to use electoral politics while others
insisted that all energy should be concentrated on
building unions. Some favored the admission of
women and blacks while others regarded these
workers as a threat. The resulting disputes and the
depression of the 1870's led to the dissolution of the
NLU. Before its demise, however, the federation
served to isolate and define the major problems
facing labor, it initiated the eight-hour work day
movement, built unions, and educated for
cooperation.

The Knights of St. Crispin (1867-73), the shoe-
makers' union, was the most powerful union in its
day. At its height in 1872, it had a combined membership of 50,000 in approximately 300 lodges.
Crispins fought for the eight-hour work day, succeeded in their drive for a Bureau of Labor in
Massachusetts, and founded their own Labor Party.
In their attempt to reconcile the interests of capital
and labor, Crispins started several cooperatives
and, in struggles to limit the work force and to
stabilize wages, they relied on voluntary arbitration. When, as the last recourse, they did strike,
they insisted that there be no worker violence.
Although they were in desperate straits, Crispins
more than once called off their strikes when violence seemed imminent.

The factory owners systematically set out to
destroy the union. They succeeded by locking out
union members while refusing to negotiate with
them and by offering higher wages to scab laborers.
Both the union and its cooperatives went under in
the depression of 1873.

The Knights of Labor (1869-86+) received direction from Uriah Stephens, founder and president;
George E. McNeill, Bay States organizer; and
Terence V. Powderly, president. They were men
firmly convinced about the power inherent in a just
cause and they relied on this rather than on class
war to accomplish their end. As a result, the
Knights of Labor advanced cooperatives and volun-

The Worker's May Pole
by Walter Crane

tary arbitration. By 1886, the Order operated 140
cooperatives and it had conciliated over 300 labor
conflicts in New York alone. The Knights avoided
strikes except as an absolute last resort and then
members were called on to be disciplined and to
use no violence.

After the Knights regained wages cut from railway workers in 1885, the union emerged as undis-
puted leader of the labor movement and the
national membership jumped from 104,000 in that
year to 700,000 in 1886. Blacks, women, skilled and
unskilled workers were all invited to join in one
great union which aimed eventually to abolish the
wage system.

Accomplishments of the Order go beyond the
short-lived gains won for some workers. The
Knights of Labor raised the hopes of skilled and
unskilled workers alike and gave them a sense of
power and unity they had never had before. Also, as
an indirect result of the Knights' agitation, states
began to pass labor reform legislation. These laws
established boards of arbitration, regulated child
labor, protected women in industry, called for

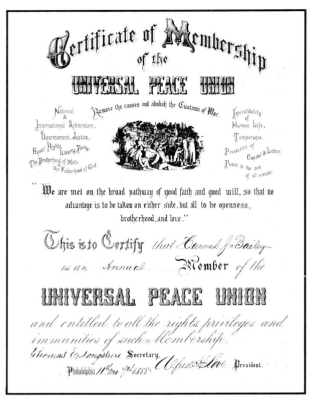

MEMBERSHIP CERTIFICATE FROM THE
UNIVERSAL PEACE UNION, 1888
Swarthmore College Peace Collection

safety inspection of work places and made some changes in the legal length of the working day. Because of loopholes, much of this early legislation proved ineffective, but nonetheless, it laid the basis for later, more effective labor laws.

Though the Knights of Labor continued well into the 20th Century, the Order declined rapidly after 1886. The disintegration resulted from Powderly's gradualism, from the national reaction to the Haymarket bombing, and from Samuel Gomper's determination to destroy the Knights in his efforts to build the American Federation of Labor.

Powderly withdrew the Knights' support from a general strike for the eight-hour work day which was called for May 1, 1886. With his union's membership having quadrupled in one year and with mounting animosity toward labor, Powderly wanted first to educate the new members and the general public about the eight-hour movement. So, although the Knights had earnestly supported the movement in the past, Powderly held back from the general strike. At the same time, Powderly's desire to win public opinion to the side of labor also kept him from lending his union's support to the anarchists framed and subsequently executed for the Haymarket bombing which took place at a rally called to build the May 1st general strike.

Workers, impatient with their intolerable condition and Powderly's insistence on gradual change, left the Knights of Labor by the thousands.

Within weeks of Haymarket, a conference of trade union leaders launched the American Federation of Labor. They offered a treaty to the rival Knights but the Knights found the terms unacceptable. In the ensuing battle for the allegiance of workers, the Knights of Labor lost out. With single-minded determination to build unions, the American Federation of Labor left behind blacks and the unskilled as too much of a burden. Instead of looking for "the entire redemption of the world's toilers," as Uriah Stephens had phrased the mission of the Knights of Labor, the AF of L wanted only to have a bigger piece of the economic pie.

From the beginning, the labor movement gathered strength from a combination of strong currents — utopian reformers who addressed themselves to all the problems of society; socialists, anarchists and communists who wanted to abolish the capitalist state; and "pure and simple" unionists who avoided politics and put all their energy into building unions. Often these different currents regarded each other as opponents second only to the owners and their police. In time, the movement came to be dominated by those who accepted competition and the profit motive and, as a result, many of the basic social and economic problems facing the country remained to be solved.

CONCLUSION

Not until the passage of the Wagner Act in 1935 were some workers guaranteed the right to organize. It took women three quarters of a century to gain the vote. Blacks by 1870 learned that the "right to vote" did little if anything to ensure them justice and equality of opportunity and once again they turned to direct action, such as the 1870 campaign in Louisville, Kentucky to win such simple things as the right to ride public street cars. In these struggles for liberation on the part of working people, women, and blacks, eventual gains followed long, hard years of abuse suffered by people who rarely saw the fruit of their own labor. Each of these movements changed more of the mass consciousness than became codified into law and in each, people committed to pacifism sought tactics which offered an option besides violence or submission — tactics such as boycotts, cooperatives, withdrawal of labor and/or financial support, direct action and civil disobedience.

Secular peace societies never recovered the vitality they had before the Civil War. By refusing to call the Civil War a war, the American Peace Society had compromised itself, and continuing to rely heavily on the influential and well to do, it grew ever more conservative in limiting its definition of violence to international war. The Universal Peace Union, founded in 1865, was in its origins a direct continuation of the New England Non-Resistance Society. Smaller than the American Peace Society and initially not so well-connected, the Universal Peace Union based itself on the absolutist position that human life is inviolable and cannot be taken by either governments or individuals. Unlike the American Peace Society, the Universal Peace Union encouraged unilateral disarmament, undertook several campaigns on behalf of oppressed ethnic groups and talked about, although it did not do much toward, the "emancipation of labor." The Universal Peace Union, active until 1913, never matched the vigor of the New England Non-Resistance Society in its action or analysis and as time went on the Union's list of vice-presidents came to include people who could hardly be called radical pacifists, e.g., William H. Taft, Andrew Carnegie, and the Mexican dictator Porfirio Díaz.

In the second half of the 1880's, Tolstoy's writings on nonresistance began to circulate in the U.S. and several Tolstoy clubs sprang up to promote his ideas. Jane Addams, social reformer and world famous peace worker, was influenced by Tolstoy in her approach to peace and social problems. Tolstoy's teachings were also promoted by the politician William Jennings Bryan and the lawyer Clarence Darrow, but their nonresistance was ambivalent. Bryan resigned as Secretary of State in 1915 due to his opposition to growing U.S. involvement in World War I, although the year before he had used war ships to carry out U.S. policy in the Caribbean. Darrow valued Tolstoy's explication of nonresistance primarily for its relevance to problems of law enforcement and criminal reform, but he did not completely think through its application to international affairs. With the German invasion of Belgium in 1914, Darrow abandoned the Tolstoyan nonresistance he had advocated for more than ten years.

By the first decade of the 20th Century, the "peace movement" had gained considerable strength as one of many reforms to be attained in a reform-minded age. The peace cause was respectable and enjoyed the allegiance of a number of the nation's political, business, religious, and academic organizations. Still, only a minute portion of the movement held the absolutist position or anything resembling "radical pacifism" with its call to eradicate all violence from the social structure. For the great majority, peace referred only to international relations and even then very few understood what the socialists and labor organizations were saying about rival imperialisms as a cause of war.

With the advent of the first World War, serious peace activists developed new organizations to replace those dominated by the wealthy and highly-placed. The most important of these were the Women's Peace Party, founded in 1914 and comprised of radical pacifists and feminists active in the women's rights movement; the American Union Against Militarism, founded in 1916 by radical pacifists and socialists; and the People's Council of America, founded in 1917 and comprised of radical pacifists, socialists, and organized labor.

The traditional peace churches were relatively quiet in their pacifist teaching in the late 1800's, but began to renew their outreach around the turn of the 20th Century. Friends, such as Rufus Jones and Henry Cadbury, began a more sophisticated analysis of the causes of war and began to bring pacifist ideas to an audience broader than their own Society. In 1906, Mennonites took the initiative in organizing the nondenominational Intercollegiate Peace Association which endeavored to bring peace issues to the college population. These churches also began to broaden their conception of violence so that it no longer was looked upon simply as sin but came to be seen as having social and economic causes. The practical line of thought articulated by William James in his 1910 essay "The Moral Equivalent of War," that pacifists had to organize along the virtues of discipline, service, self-sacrifice and comraderie — virtues long misappropriated by the military — influenced the Friends to begin the American Friends Service Committee in 1917.

In two hundred and fifty years the traditional pacifist position — molded and influenced by the social movements of the 19th Century — changed substantially from the religious creed of the colonial peace sects. It grew from emphasizing the negative case against war to a broader position, justified by secular as well as religious beliefs, which sought to establish a positive philosophy of constructive action for domestic and international peace.

The growing secularization of pacifist ideas and organizations spread nonviolent principles wider than ever before and helped draw many more people into the struggle for fundamental social change. When, during the 20th Century, radical activists referred back to the achievements and lessons of earlier pacifists, they found that their contemporary efforts were both the result and a further extension of the tradition of active nonviolence in the United States.□

CHAPTER 1

WORLD WAR I
AND AMERICAN OPPOSITION

THE ANTI-ENLISTMENT LEAGUE
The nonviolent movement as a radical political force in America began to coalesce during the first World War. Pacifism still had a religious orientation and of the three traditional peace churches — Brethren, Mennonite and Quaker — it was primarily the Quakers whose social vision was translated into political form. When the war broke out in Europe in 1914 there was no pacifist movement around which a cohesive nonviolent resistance could be formed. Most Americans, including President Woodrow Wilson, were publicly opposed to

United States participation in the war in Europe. However, when Wilson, in violation of his promises in the 1916 Presidential campaign, asked Congress for a Declaration of War, popular opinion swelled behind him, and even liberal peace organizations like the American Peace Society declared their support, claiming that peace could not be attained unless Germany and its allies were defeated.

The first organized opposition to the war came in the spring of 1915 when Jessie Wallace Hughan, Tracy D. Mygatt, Evelyn West Hughan and Frances Witherspoon formed the Anti-Enlistment

Eugene Debs immediately after his release from the Atlanta Penitentiary, 1921. Tamiment Library/NYU.

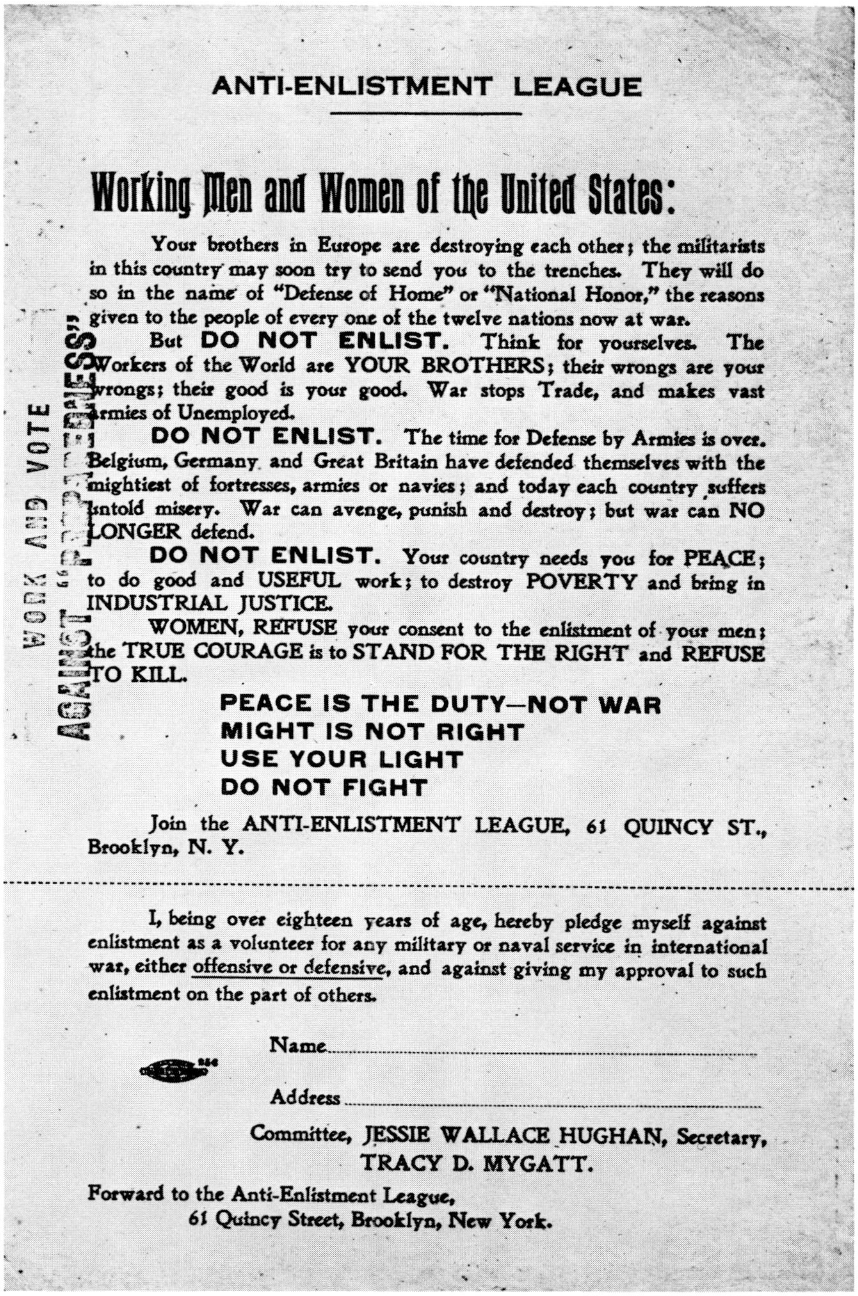

ANTI-ENLISTMENT LEAGUE

Working Men and Women of the United States:

Your brothers in Europe are destroying each other; the militarists in this country may soon try to send you to the trenches. They will do so in the name of "Defense of Home" or "National Honor," the reasons given to the people of every one of the twelve nations now at war.

But **DO NOT ENLIST.** Think for yourselves. The Workers of the World are YOUR BROTHERS; their wrongs are your wrongs; their good is your good. War stops Trade, and makes vast Armies of Unemployed.

DO NOT ENLIST. The time for Defense by Armies is over. Belgium, Germany and Great Britain have defended themselves with the mightiest of fortresses, armies or navies; and today each country suffers untold misery. War can avenge, punish and destroy; but war can NO LONGER defend.

DO NOT ENLIST. Your country needs you for PEACE; to do good and USEFUL work; to destroy POVERTY and bring in INDUSTRIAL JUSTICE.

WOMEN, REFUSE your consent to the enlistment of your men; the TRUE COURAGE is to STAND FOR THE RIGHT and REFUSE TO KILL.

PEACE IS THE DUTY—NOT WAR
MIGHT IS NOT RIGHT
USE YOUR LIGHT
DO NOT FIGHT

Join the ANTI-ENLISTMENT LEAGUE, 61 QUINCY ST., Brooklyn, N. Y.

I, being over eighteen years of age, hereby pledge myself against enlistment as a volunteer for any military or naval service in international war, either offensive or defensive, and against giving my approval to such enlistment on the part of others.

Name...

Address...

Committee, JESSIE WALLACE HUGHAN, Secretary,
TRACY D. MYGATT.

Forward to the Anti-Enlistment League,
61 Quincy Street, Brooklyn, New York.

Leaflet from the Anti-Enlistment League, 1915. Swarthmore College Peace Collection.

League. In two years, the League enrolled 3,500 young men who pledged:

> *I, being over eighteen years of age, hereby pledge myself against enlistment as a volunteer for any military or naval service in international war, either offensive or defensive, and against giving my approval to such enlistment on the part of others.*

Under the chairpersonship of Frances Witherspoon, the League made a special effort to get support in the colleges. "Each day this country approaches one step nearer the 'armed camp' once denounced, now urged, by President Wilson," went a form letter sent out to the students. "In addition to exorbitant demands on Congress, the militarists plan . . . to turn our little school-boys into strutting soldiers; already they make inroads into the life of our colleges; in several instances, military tactics ranks for a degree with academic training. . . ."

The League was aimed only at voluntary enlistments, however. With the beginning of conscription in 1917 following America's entry into the

Swarthmore College Peace Collection

JANE ADDAMS
(1860 - 1935)

Jane Addams' outstanding contributions to international peace and social reform place her in the forefront of early nonviolent activists. Born in Rockford, Illinois, she seized early on the idea that the nurturing and protective function of women creates a greater sense of moral obligation in them than in men and that this obligation has a direct bearing on urban-industrial society. While initially motivated by ideas of Christian benevolence, she later became more pragmatic in her ethical reasoning and spoke specifically of the values of freedom and justice, democracy and culture. She asserted consistently that war destroys social reform and that reform and peace are inseparable parts of a single hope for the human race.

In 1889 she founded Hull House, one of the first settlement houses in America, which tried to answer the immediate needs of a poor immigrant neighborhood in Chicago. At a time when many viewed the immigrants with fear, Addams welcomed the cultural diversity they brought to American life. She realized, however, that social clubs and neighborhood services alone were insufficient to meet the deep-seated problems of the poor community. She made Hull House a center of social reform and attracted other capable people, such as Alice Hamilton, Julia Lathrop, and Florence Kelley to join in the work. Due to their efforts, Hull House exerted increasing influence in the state's political battles for child labor laws, protection of immigrants, industrial safety, recognition of labor unions, and limitation of working hours. Jane Addams served as the common bond uniting the various projects and she helped her co-workers understand the broader significance of their activities.

Addams wrote and spoke forcefully about the efforts of working people to organize and helped to negotiate numerous labor disputes. The exposé she wrote of the causes of the Pullman strike was publicly banned for twelve years. She also joined in the Chicago municipal suffrage campaign in 1907, and, as vice-president of the National American Woman Suffrage Association from 1911 to 1914, she spoke widely for the cause.

When the first World War broke out in Europe, Addams turned her whole attention to working for peace. She helped found the Woman's Peace Party in January 1915 and that April was chosen president of the International Congress of Women at The Hague. She joined the delegations which were sent by the Congress to the heads of warring and neutral nations to urge constant peace negotiations. She also tried unsuccessfully to persuade President Wilson to initiate a conference of mediation. She helped found the Anti-Preparedness Committee in 1915, which grew into the American Union Against Militarism, and was also involved in organizing the National Association for the Advancement of Colored People and the American Civil Liberties Union. During the war, in opposition to the government and isolated from many of her former friends, she still lectured throughout the country on behalf of increased food production to aid victims of the war. In 1919 she was elected first president of the Women's International League for Peace and Freedom and she held this post until her death.

A modest and good natured woman, although somewhat aloof personally, Jane Addams was widely recognized and honored throughout the world during her life. Her birthdays were widely celebrated and she regularly ranked first on lists of "America's Greatest Women." In 1931, four years before her death, she was awarded the Nobel Peace Prize and donated the money, some $16,000, to the WILPF.

Immigrants, New York City, c. 1900. Library of Congress.

war, it ceased to function, though in terms of structure and the people involved, it may be considered
the forerunner of the War Resisters League.

Wilson did not have the unanimous support of
Congress for his declaration of war. In the House,
the first Congresswoman, Jeannette Rankin, joined
with over 50 others in voting against the war. In the
Senate, Robert M. LaFollette tried to filibuster
against the war and was joined by five other Senators in finally voting No. But most opposition to the
war came from the radical left, from the Wobblies of
the syndicalist Industrial Workers of the World,
from anarchists like Emma Goldman and Alexander
Berkman, and from the Socialist Party, which had
become an important force in American politics.

In January 1915 the Woman's Peace Party was
formed and in April members met with women
from other countries at a Peace Congress in The
Hague. The Women's International League for
Peace and Freedom (WILPF) was formed then,
with pacifist leaders Jane Addams and Emily
Greene Balch among its founders. The American
Friends Service Committee (AFSC) was organized
in April 1917 and within five months had trained
and sent 100 conscientious objectors to the war
zone to do medical and relief work.

American peace delegates aboard the *Noordam* on their way to the International Peace Congress in The Hague, April 1915. Mrs.
Emmeline Pethic-Lawrence is on the far left and Jane Addams is next to her in the foreground. Bain Collection/Library of Congress.

Leaflet from the Woman's Peace Party, 1915. Swarthmore College Peace Collection.

WOMEN'S INTERNATIONAL LEAGUE
FOR PEACE AND FREEDOM
(Founded 1915)

Leading American feminists and peace advocates founded the Woman's Peace Party in January 1915 and immediately joined with their European comrades in a call for an international convention of neutral nations in the interest of early peace. Jane Addams, prominent social reformer and chairperson of the Woman's Peace Party, was asked to preside at the gathering which met in The Hague in late April of that year with over 1000 women from a dozen countries. The Congress organized a Women's International Committee for Permanent Peace, with headquarters in Amsterdam, and sent delegations to the heads of warring and neutral nations to urge neutral mediation of the war. Many of President Wilson's "Fourteen Points" were based on the resolutions presented to him from The Hague meeting.

The second Women's Peace Congress in 1919 voted to continue the organization permanently as the Women's International League for Peace and Freedom. Its goal has remained to unite women in all countries who are opposed to every kind of war, exploitation, and oppression. League members work for universal disarmament and for the solution of conflicts by the recognition of human solidarity, by conciliation and arbitration, by world cooperation, and by the establishment of

American delegates from the Woman's Peace Party at The Hague International Peace Congress where the Women's International League for Peace and Freedom was formed, April 1915. Front row, left to right: Mrs. Louis Post, Jane Addams, Fanny Fern Andrews, Rose Morgan French; Second row: Mrs. Evans, unidentified, A. Evelyn Newman, Alice Hamilton, unidentified, Florence Holbrook, unidentified, Angela Morgan, unidentified, Mrs. Robert W. Kohlhamer, unidentified; Third row: Emily Greene Balch, Alice Carpenter, Mrs. Mabel M. Irwin, Lucy Biddle Lewis, Julia Grace Wales, Mrs. William I. Thomas, Mrs. William Bross Lloyd, unidentified, Constance Drexel, unidentified, unidentified; Fourth row: Mabel Kittridge, Sophonisba P. Breckinridge, Anna M. Klingenhagen, Mrs. Mary Cruttenden, Leonora O'Reilly, Rebecca Shelley, unidentified, unidentified; Back row: Mary Heaton Vorse O'Brien, Mrs. Juliet Barrett/Rublee, Grace Abbott, Grace DeGraff, A. Emily Napieralski, Madeline Doty, unidentified, Mary Chamberlain, Mrs. Frank H. Cothren, Louis Lochner, Mrs. Anna M. Schaedler. Swarthmore College Peace Collection.

social, political, and economic justice for all, without distinction of sex, race, class, or creed. The U.S. section of the WILPF now includes over 140 branches in cities across the country and is one of the most powerful and vigorous of the 30 sections of the International, headquartered in Geneva.

Since the first Congress, WILPF has sent peace missions to diplomatic centers and areas of tension throughout the world. It has arranged International Summer Schools where young people study international problems and has widely distributed peace education materials. In the 1930s, the League lobbied for disarmament legislation and sparked the famous Congressional investigation of the munitions industry. In 1932, to support the World Disarmament Conference, WILPF organized a Peace Caravan which travelled from Hollywood, California to Washington D.C., making front-page news in each of the 125 cities along the way. In an effort to halt H-bomb tests in the Fifties, the WILPF gathered thousands of signatures in one of its many petition campaigns. The League again asked women to use their power to end the war in Vietnam in 1965 and launched a world drive for signatures.

In 1971, the WILPF International Congress declared:

> The WILPF has a duty to study and work towards developing methods for the effective use of non-violent means; to make the public aware of the problems of the oppressed and the exploited; to analyze the structure of power in society and the use made of it; to engage ourselves actively in non-violent movements for change.
>
> A society that is military and exploitative generates movements for rapid change towards social justice. It is a human right to resist injustice and to be neither silent witness nor passive victim of repression. Although we reaffirm our belief that violence creates more problems than it solves, we recognize the inevitability of violent resistance by the oppressed when other alternatives have failed.

The League includes women from all backgrounds and walks of life whose efforts throughout the century have encouraged and sustained organized work for peace and social justice. Leaders in WILPF have included Jane Addams, Jeannette Rankin, Emily Greene Balch, Hannah Clothier Hull, Dorothy Detzer, Dorothy Medder-Robinson, Dorothy Hutchinson and Katherine Camp.

WOMEN OF AMERICA
What Will Your ANSWER BE?
When Your Children Ask
WHAT DID YOU DO
IN 1916
To Help the Protest Against Militarism?
Join the WOMAN'S PEACE PARTY
70 Fifth Avenue, New York City
JOIN TODAY!

Leaflet from the Woman's Peace Party, 1916. Tamiment Library/NYU.

Jane Addams and Mary McDowell at the Democratic National Convention, 1932. Swarthmore College Peace Collection.

THE CONSCIENTIOUS OBJECTORS

There were 4,000 conscientious objectors during World War I. The government allowed for noncombatant service in the military, and after 1918 offered those objectors who would not accept this status the alternative of working in agriculture, but still under military authority. The men granted noncombatant classification by their local boards numbered 20,873 and an indeterminable number claimed exemption as conscientious objectors which their boards refused. Absolutists who would not accept any service under military authority served harsh sentences in military prisons. There they were joined by the many political objectors who did not possess the religious qualifications to gain government approval as legitimate COs.

Conscientious objectors facing prison in World War I had virtually no organizational support. A section of the Fellowship of Reconciliation (FOR), founded in Great Britain in 1914, was begun in the United States the following year. It brought together religious pacifists from the different peace churches, but did not advocate conscientious objection in itself or service the political objectors who were given the harshest sentences. In November 1915, the Anti-Militarist Committee was formed in New York to counter President Wilson's preparedness program. The next year it became a national organization under the name of the American Union Against Militarism (AUAM) with a full-time lobbyist in Washington. Among its leaders were the Rev. John Haynes Holmes of N.Y. Community Church, social workers Lillian Wald and Jane Addams, editor Max Eastman, conservationist Amos Pinchot, Rabbi Steven S. Wise and Norman Thomas, who was then active in the Fellowship of Reconciliation. When the nation entered the war, the aims of the AUAM changed from opposition to militarism as "repugnant to American traditions and institutions" to the "preservation of democratic institutions and liberties in time of war. . . ." Roger Baldwin, who in 1918-1919 served a year in prison for refusing to take his army physical, headed the AUAM's Bureau of Conscientious Objectors and guided its evolution into the American Civil Liberties Union.

The usual prison sentence meted out to absolutist COs was from 20 to 25 years. Life sentences

World War I conscientious objectors in prison at Fort Douglas, Utah, 1919. Front row, left to right: Knude Lassen, Jacob Schneider, Harry Clave, Francis Steiner, Julius Eichel, Frank Minnick, Frank Moser, Julius Katz; Second row: Fred Briehl, Robert Cage, William Sandberg, Ben Salmon, David Eichel, Meyer Bernstein, Sam Sterenstein, Fred Jerger, Thomas Shotkin; Back row: Emanuel Silver, Jacob Haugen, William Doty, Sam Cutler, Nicolo Locosale. Julius Eichel Collection.

were given to 142. Seventeen were given death sentences, later commuted, though one CO escaped execution only by going overseas and accepting duty to fetch wounded from No Man's Land. In actuality, however, no objector served more than three years in prison as all were released by November 1920.

Prison life was brutal for World War I COs, as they were portrayed by the government as cowards and shirkers, as men who would not do their patriotic duty. Torture and brutality were commonplace. In October 1918, a group of Molokans, Christian nonresisters and emigrants from Russia, were brought to Fort Leavenworth, Kansas, to serve their time. Because they would not work under military orders, they were thrown into the hole, manacled to the cell bars in a standing position for nine hours each day, and prohibited from receiving or sending out mail. Other COs tried to protest their mistreatment, but prison officials intercepted their protests in the mail. On November 2, 1918, Evan Thomas, serving a lifetime sentence as a CO, went on a work strike in protest. He, too, was thrown in the hole and manacled to the bars. Other COs joined the strike and followed Thomas to the hole, where they were not allowed to speak to one another. Guards, revolting at this brutality, refused to enforce the no-talking rule, and soon news of the strike and the treatment of the Molokans got out. After seven weeks in solitary, Thomas and the other COs were released and the War Department made manacling illegal. This was just one of many reforms the COs forced the government to make during this period.

Prison reform came too late to save from death the two Hofer brothers who, with two other Christian nonresisters, spent five days in strait jackets, locked to a ball and chain in a wet, pitch black dungeon cell at Alcatraz in California. Much of this time they were made to stand, their hands manacled to the bars. Transferred to Leavenworth, they were again placed in the hole, where the two brothers contracted pneumonia and later died.

Some objectors refused even to register for the draft and served short sentences in civilian prisons. Often, upon their release, they were arbitrarily drafted and forced either to accept military service or risk long sentences in military jails.

It was not until after the war that political objectors had an organization to support and advance their views. The War Resisters League (WRL) was

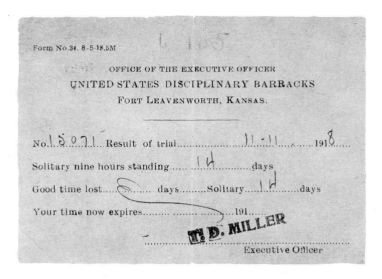

founded in 1923 on the initiative of Jessie Wallace Hughan, Tracy D. Mygatt and Frances Witherspoon when it became evident the FOR could not relate to nonreligious COs. Anyone could become a member of the League if he or she signed a pledge renouncing participation in war. Much of the organization's support came from pacifist members of the Socialist Party and for many years the WRL did most of its work in the educational field, advocating conscientious objection and giving legal advice and support to those who needed it.

Prison order sentencing conscientious objector David Eichel to 14 days solitary confinement, standing nine hours a day, on a bread and water diet for his refusal to work in Leavenworth Federal Prison, November 1918. Julius Eichel Collection.

Barbed-wire fence surrounding Fort Douglas, Utah, internment camp where war resisters were held, 1919. Julius Eichel Collection.

TRACY MYGATT
(1885 - 1974)

FRANCES WITHERSPOON
(1887 - 1974)

Tracy Mygatt and Frances Witherspoon were life-long friends and vigorous co-workers for peace and human rights. They graduated from Bryn Mawr in 1908 and worked together until their deaths within three weeks of each other in 1974. Their work against war and militarism spanned from the Anti-Enlistment League, which they helped found in 1915, to anti-Vietnam war protests in the 1960s. They were the first organizers of the

War Against War Exhibit

"Seeing is believing."

5,000 to 10,000 people a day came to see the War Against War Exhibit in New York last May. This Exhibit set forth graphically and pictorially the stupidity and futility of the whole war system. Those who saw it never forgot it. It was so simple a child could understand it, so comprehensive it made the idea of world organization seem a practicable reality.

The original War Against War Exhibit which cost several thousand dollars to produce has now been reproduced in poster form and can be secured complete for $8.00 (transportation included).

SPECIMEN PANELS.

The Exhibit consists of 23 panels (3 by 5 ft.) and seven cartoons (2 by 3 ft.) printed in one, two and three colors on bill poster paper, suitable for indoor or outdoor use. The posters can be pasted on muslin or cardboard or simply tacked up for temporary use. (The large panels are each printed in two sections.) They are effective when displayed singly but are especially designed to be hung as an exhibit and thus form a complete graphic indictment of war.

The Exhibit is shipped in a large paste-board tube, is light, compact, and easily transported.

We especially recommend it for the immediate use of

Peace Organizations	Social Settlements
Anti-Militarist Societies	Civic Centers
Labor Unions	Village Improvement Associations
Granges	Clubs and Churches
Schools and Colleges	Chautauquas

and

All Individuals who want to do their part toward winning the battle of democracy against militarism.

A special letter will be furnished on request, giving suggestions and directions for additional features, publicity schemes, literature, speakers and all the points which make an exhibit draw a big crowd.

WAR AGAINST WAR EXHIBIT, $8.00

produced by

THE AMERICAN UNION AGAINST MILITARISM
Munsey Building, Washington, D. C.

woman's suffrage movement in Pennsylvania and, before World War I, they organized "church raids" in New York to open up churches for aid and shelter to the large number of unemployed.

During the war, they set up the Bureau of Legal Advice in New York City which provided the first organized help for conscientious objectors and, after the armistice, they organized the first parade for amnesty for war resisters. With Jessie Wallace Hughan and John Haynes Holmes, they founded the War Resisters League in 1923. Their writings included hundreds of letters over the years to members of Congress, world leaders, and newspaper editors, as well as articles, petitions, plays and short stories. Tracy Mygatt was a founder of the Campaign for World Government and both women were socialists, feminists, and active members of the FOR, ACLU, SANE, WILPF, World Federalists, and the U.N. Association.

Leaflet from the American Union Against Militarism, c. 1916. Swarthmore College Peace Collection.

Sophia Smith Collection/Smith College

ROGER BALDWIN
(Born 1884)

A political reformer and early pacifist leader, Roger Baldwin was born in Wellesley, Massachusetts, graduated from Harvard, and moved to St. Louis, Missouri, to engage in social work. At the outbreak of World War I, he declared himself a conscientious objector and volunteered his services to the American Union Against Militarism. Baldwin was largely responsible for the evolution of the American Civil Liberties Union from the AUAM's Bureau for Conscientious Objectors and he guided the ACLU as director from 1917 until 1950.

In 1918, he was arrested for refusing to fight in the military and was imprisoned for a year. Before sentence was passed, Baldwin declared to the court:

> The compelling motive for refusing to comply with the draft act is my uncompromising opposition to the principles of conscription of life by the state for any purpose whatever in time of war or peace . . . I am opposed to this and all other wars. I do not believe in the use of physical force as a method of achieving any end, however good. I am not complaining for myself or others. I am merely advising the court that I understand full well the penalty of my heresy and am prepared to pay it. The conflict with conscription is irreconcilable. Even

TO MEN OF MILITARY AGE OPPOSED TO WAR!

Register June 5th — and when you register, state your protest against participation in war

You can only make your protest effective by registering. See that the clerk puts down your claim to exemption from service as a "conscientious objector to war"

Read the following statement signed by men and women active in the anti-militarist movement:

The presence in this country of a considerable number of so-called conscientious objectors is generally known. In recent weeks these objectors, confronted by the Conscription Act, have been undecided as to whether they should make known their conscientious scruples against war by refusing to register, or refusing military service (as distinct from alternative civil service which may conceivably be secured hereafter) when actually drafted by the process of selection.

In realization of the necessity of concerted action in this crisis and in answer to appeals for counsel in the matter, the undersigned, after consideration which has in some cases reversed original opinion, unite in stating their belief that **all conscientious objectors should register and indicate in the way provided by the law their personal opposition to participation in war.**

Obedience to law, to the utmost limit of conscience, is the basis of good citizenship. Public understanding and sympathy, in this case, should not be alienated by misdirected action. The moral issue involved should not be confused. The opportunity provided by the act to specify one's claims to exemption from military service should not be missed by those who desire to state their objection to that service on religious or other conscientious grounds.

We therefore urge all conscientious objectors to register, stating their protest in such form as they may think best, at that time. We request that the widest possible publicity be given to this statement.

LILLIAN D. WALD, New York City.
JOSEPH D. CANNON, New York City.
OSWALD GARRISON VILLARD, New York City.
JOHN HAYNES HOLMES, New York City.
MRS. FLORENCE KELLEY, New York City.
MRS. GLENDOWER EVANS, Boston, Mass.
BENJAMIN C. MARSH, New York City.
NORMAN M. THOMAS, New York City.
ZONA GALE, Portage, Wisconsin.
HAROLD A. HATCH, New York City.
OWEN R. LOVEJOY, New York City.

JESSIE M. HUGHAN, Brooklyn, N. Y.
JONATHAN C. DAY, New York City.
ROGER N. BALDWIN, St. Louis, Mo.
WM. F. COCHRAN, Baltimore, Md.
WINTER RUSSELL, New York City.
FREDERICK P. LYNCH, New York City.
HENRY R. LINVILLE, New York City.
ALICE LEWISOHN, New York City.
AGNES B. LEACH, New York City.
JOHN LOVEJOY ELLIOTT, New York City.
HENRY R. MUSSEY, New York City.

ENDORSED BY
THE AMERICAN UNION AGAINST MILITARISM
Munsey Building, Washington, D. C.   New York Office: 70 Fifth Avenue.

A bureau of aid and advice for conscientious objectors has been established by the American Union, working in co-operation with representatives of other interested agencies. Those wishing to register with the bureau sign here and mail in. Contributions for the support of the bureau will be warmly appreciated.

| American Union Against Militarism, |
| 70 Fifth Avenue, New York City. |
| Please register me as a conscientious objector of military age. |
| Signed .... |
| Street address .... |
| City and State .... |

the liberalism of the President and the Secretary of War in dealing with the objector leads those who are "absolutists" to a punishment longer and severer than that of desperate criminals.

But I believe most of us are prepared even to die for our faith, just as our brothers in France are dying for theirs. To them we are comrades in spirit — we understand one another's motives, though our methods are wide apart. We both share deeply the common experience of living up to the truth as we see it, whatever the price. Though at the moment I am of a tiny minority, I feel myself just one protest in a great revolt surging up from among the people — the struggle of the masses against the rule of the world by a few, profoundly intensified by the war. It is a struggle against the political state itself, against exploitation, militarism, imperialism, authority in all forms.

Leaflet from the American Union Against Militarism, c. 1916. Swarthmore College Peace Collection.

Leaflet from the People's Council for Democracy and Peace, a radical anti-war coalition of peace, labor and farm groups, 1917. Swarthmore College Peace Collection.

Anti-conscription parade organized by the Woman's Peace Party, New York City, 1916. Brown Brothers.

Boston Globe

EMMA GOLDMAN
(1869 -1940)

A Russian-born anarchist, Emma Goldman came to the U.S. in 1886 at the age of 17. She was a short, thick-set, modest woman who spoke clearly and forcefully about the poverty, injustice, and lack of opportunity which she saw all around in her new country. At first, Goldman advocated violence as a means of obtaining social and economic justice, but later she abandoned that position as impractical. She came to teach that violence can never constitute the means of liberation, although she understood how people could be driven to it out of desperation.

Because violence is a fundamental characteristic of the state, Goldman chose not to advocate violence to overthrow the state, but urged collective withdrawal of labor from the exploitative social system and from production for war. Without workers or soldiers, the system itself must inevitably collapse and the way would be cleared for a decentralized order in which people would work cooperatively without coercion. In 1917, she and Alexander Berkman organized the No-Conscription League to encourage resistance to World War I. For "conspiring against the draft," she was fined $10,000 and imprisoned for two years. Immediately after her release, she was deported back to Russia. Although an enthusiastic supporter of the Russian revolution at the beginning, she (and Berkman) later left the Soviet Union disillusioned with the repressive measures of an increasingly centralized Bolshevik state.

In 1909, Emma Goldman had spoken in St. Louis and in the audience was Roger Baldwin, then a young social worker. The meeting left Baldwin strongly moved and he began to turn from juvenile court work to examining the root causes of the poverty which brought the children before the court in the first place. He attributed this radicalization to the influence of Goldman and wrote:

> Emma Goldman impressed me deeply, a selfless woman whose whole being was absorbed in the social problem. She was self-educated, always studying, always reading, and deeply cultivated in the fields of literature and art. But, above all, she was the militant woman of the left, a far-visioned idealist who could see a society so good that you didn't need governments to hold it together.

Leaflet from the No-Conscription League, 1917. Tamiment Library/NYU.

Tamiment Library/NYU

EUGENE V. DEBS
(1855 - 1926)

Eugene Victor Debs, a founder of the Socialist Party and an outstanding political leader, was a pioneer of industrial unionism in the United States. When the working class in this country was still atomized and disorganized, Debs pulled together the first enduring class-based political organization and gave socialist principles their first real hearing in America.

Debs achieved prominence as a labor organizer and strike leader well before he came to socialism. Born in Terre Haute, Indiana, Debs worked as a locomotive fireman and served in the Indiana legislature in 1884. In 1893, he organized the American Railway Union and a year later led a strike against the powerful Pullman Company, which had just cut wages by as much as 50%. Pullman crushed the strike with unprecedented support from the federal government and Debs was sentenced to six months in prison for violating a court injunction against the strike. While in prison, Debs was introduced to Marx's *Capital* and within two years, by the time he was 41, he was totally committed to socialism.

As a popular socialist leader and orator, Debs was widely admired as a man of great personal gentleness and compassion who eloquently voiced the sentiments of the rank and file. "I am not a labor leader," he once said. "I don't want you to follow me or anyone else. If you are looking for a Moses to lead you out of the capitalist wilderness you will stay right where you are. I would not lead you into this promised land if I could, because if I could lead you in, someone else would lead you out." Though not a pacifist, he recognized the dangers inherent in violent revolution. "To the extent that the working class has power

based on class consciousness," he wrote, "force is unnecessary; to the extent that power is lacking, force can only result in harm."

Before and after the United States entered World War I, Debs travelled throughout the country denouncing the war as an international capitalist battle for markets and profits. He was charged with violation of the Espionage Act in 1918 and sentenced to ten years in a federal prison.

> *They are trying to send us to prison for speaking our minds. Very well, let them. I tell you that if it had not been for men and women who in the past have had the moral courage to go to prison, we would still be in the jungles.*

Sixty-three years old and in poor health, Debs was still able to begin his sentence with the statement, "I enter the prison doors a flaming revolutionist — my head erect, spirit untamed and my soul unconquerable." Debs was pardoned late in 1921 and returned to guide the crippled Socialist Party until his death in 1926.

SOCIALIST PARTY
FOR PRESIDENT

EUGENE VICTOR DEBS

Postcard from Eugene Debs' 1920 presidential campaign. Tamiment Library/NYU.

SOCIALIST OPPOSITION

The Socialist Party in America, organized by Eugene Debs in 1901, had thousands of members and drew hundreds of thousands of votes during the "Golden Age of American Socialism" in the early 1900s. By 1912, over a thousand party members held elected political offices in 337 towns and cities across the U.S. There were 323 Socialist papers and periodicals, including five dailies, 262 weeklies, 10 monthlies plus 46 publications in foreign languages, of which 8 were dailies. Debs was the chief contributor to the most important of the Socialist papers, the *Appeal To Reason,* which reached a circulation of 600,000 in 1912.

The American left, and the Socialist Party in particular, stood virtually alone in its political opposition to the first World War. In Europe the majority of the radical parties lined up behind their governments in support of the conflict. According to Jessie Wallace Hughan:

> *Though the international socialist movement was theoretically opposed to war, viewing it only as a battle between vested competing interests of the ruling, capitalist class, they had no concrete proposal about what to do in the event of*

the actuality of war, no program, no alternative; thus, when World War I broke out, individual socialists, most of the national sections of the Socialist International, and the many different socialist parties were swept up by national fervor.

The opposition of radicals to war was limited only to what they, like the liberal peace societies, subjectively considered to be an unjust war. In Hughan's words:

> *They fell an easy prey to the propagandists which in every country proved that particular government to be fighting the battles of freedom.*

In the United States the left held to its anti-war principles. With the outbreak of the war in Europe in 1914, the American Socialist Party declared its opposition to "this and all other wars." The Wobblies called for a general strike, in all industries, should the United States enter the fray. In 1916 Congressional elections, the Socialists proclaimed, "Every Socialist ballot is a protest against the war," and a Wobbly sticker read, "Don't be a soldier, be a man."

The day after the United States entered the war,

Socialist conscientious objectors at Fort Douglas, Utah prison camp, 1919. Julius Eichel Collection.

on April 7, 1917, the Socialist Party, meeting in an extraordinary session, passed what has since become known as the St. Louis Resolution, which began:

> *The Socialist Party of the United States in the present grave crisis reaffirms its allegiance to the principle of internationalism and working class solidarity the world over, and proclaims its unalterable opposition to the war just declared by the government of the United States. . . .*

In May 1917 Congress passed the first conscription act since the Civil War. In June the Espionage Act was approved giving the government the right to censor newspapers, ban publications from the mail and imprison anyone who "interfered" with conscription or the enlistment of soldiers. The penalties for these crimes were harsh, twenty years and a $10,000 fine, and they were used by the government to destroy the American radical movement.

Much of the leadership of the Socialist Party, which under Eugene V. Debs had garnered almost 900,000 votes in 1912, was sent to prison. Kate Richard O'Hare got five years for an anti-war speech in North Dakota and Rose Pastor Stokes received ten years for a letter to a newspaper in which she said:

> *No government that is for the profiteers can also be for the people; and I am for the people, while the government is for the profiteers.*

Victor Berger, the Socialist Congressman from Wisconsin, was sentenced to twenty years by Judge Kenesaw "Mountain" Landis, who went on to win fame as major league baseball's commissioner. The Supreme Court eventually overturned this decision, but Landis would have preferred to have "Berger lined up against the wall and shot."

EUGENE DEBS

The most important anti-war confrontation involved Eugene Debs, the popular leader of the Socialist Party. Debs, from the beginning, had stood adamantly against the war and was one of the forces behind the party's adoption of the St. Louis Resolution. A fervent internationalist who never sacrificed his humanism for radical rhetoric, Debs once said, "I have no country to fight for; my country is the earth and I am a citizen of the world."

With the United States' entry into the war and the passage of the Espionage Act, Debs went out on

Socialist anti-war meeting, Union Square, New York City, August 8, 1914. Bain Collection/Library of Congress.

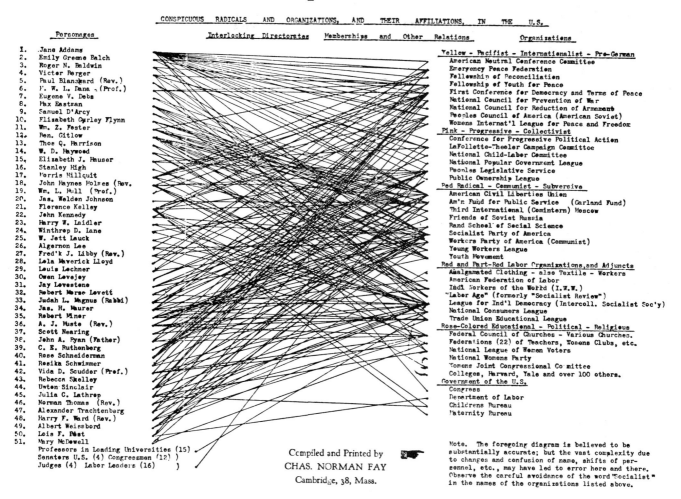

a speaking tour deliberately to court prosecution for his anti-war views. On June 16, 1917, before a cheering throng of workingmen and women in Canton, Ohio, Debs concluded a speech against the war by exclaiming:

> . . . The master class has always declared the wars; the subject class has always fought the battles. The master class has had all to gain and nothing to lose; the subject class has nothing to gain and all to lose – especially their lives.

Two weeks later Debs was arrested for this speech, found guilty and sentenced to ten years in prison.

On the day of sentencing, September 14, 1918, he addressed the court:

> Your honor, years ago I recognized my kinship with all living beings, and I made up my mind that I was not one bit better than the meanest on earth. I said then, I say now, that while there is a lower class, I am in it; while there is a criminal element, I am of it; while there is a soul in prison, I am not a free man.

While prisoner No. 9653 in the Atlanta Penitentiary, Debs ran for President in 1920 and received 915,490 votes. Despite public pressure and against the recommendations of Cabinet members, President Wilson refused to pardon Debs. The Socialist leader, by now old and in poor health, had to wait for Warren Harding to do so on Christmas Day 1921; but the pardon, while giving Debs his freedom, did not restore his civil rights.

Chart of "Conspicuous Radicals and Organizations" in the U.S., c. 1922. Swarthmore College Peace Collection.

INDUSTRIAL
WORKERS OF THE WORLD
(Founded 1905)

The Industrial Workers of the World (IWW) did not on principle reject violence, especially in self-defense. Contrary to popular opinion, however, the union did reject violence in its theory and practice. In 1907, the IWW's publication stated that violence which "is the basis of every political state in existence, has no place in the foundation or superstructure of this organization."

In theory, the IWW looked forward to a revolution without bloodshed. They reasoned that workers who waged violent struggles would not be properly trained to lead in the new society. Wobblies struck for immediate gains in order to prepare for the great general strike which would paralyze the economy until the owning class handed over the means of production to the working class.

In tactics, Wobblies understood the advantage of let-ting the public compare peaceful workers with violent employers. Wobblies calmed labor violence at the 1909 strike at the McKee Rocks Pressed Steel Car Works. They took beatings and imprisonment with patience and courage during their 1909-1911 campaign on the West Coast for the right to speak publicly and to organize. In 1913, the IWW Secretary-Treasurer, William D. "Big Bill" Haywood, shouted to massed strikers in Patterson, New Jersey that their power rested in their folded arms. While calls for violence from individual Wobblies were the exception, not the rule, advocacy of violence to any extent made it easier for the enemies of the IWW to further defame the union.

The union's militant activism and radical insistence upon the rights of unskilled laborers to organize made it a force to reckon with in the years prior to World War I. When the IWW called for a general strike in opposition to the war, the U.S. government moved quickly and ruthlessly to destroy the working-class organization.

Mayday rally, Union Square, New York City, 1912. Bain News Service/Library of Congress.

Bottom right: Cartoon from *Solidarity*, the newspaper of the Industrial Workers of the World.

THE RED SCARE

The repression that accompanied the war, the loss of more moderate members to the cause of militarism, and the ideological disputes that accompanied the successful Bolshevik Revolution in Russia, shattered the Socialist Party. The Wobblies fared no better. In Arizona during the summer of 1917, 1200 Wobblies and their sympathizers were herded into a ballpark by armed businessmen and shipped in cattle cars to the middle of the desert where they were abandoned. In Butte, Montana, Frank Little, an IWW organizer, was dragged from his bed by masked men and hanged from a railroad trestle. On September 5, every IWW meeting hall was raided and a few days later more than 160 leaders, including "Big Bill" Haywood and Elizabeth Gurley Flynn, were arrested and charged with treason. Most of their leaders were sent to prison, while Haywood, probably their most famous leader, jumped bail and fled to the Soviet Union to experience a "socialist" revolution first hand.

At the time the conscription law was passed, the anarchists Emma Goldman and Alexander Berkman attempted to organize a No-Conscription League to "resist conscription by every means in our power." They were given the maximum sentence of ten years and $10,000 and later deported. In September 1918, in what John Reed called "the blackest month for freedom our generation has known," federal agents raided radical organizations throughout the nation. Thousands were imprisoned and 500 deported. Harassment continued throughout the winter as Woodrow Wilson's Attorney General, A.

A BIRD THAT LAYS SUCH ROTTEN EGGS IS LONG OVERDUE FOR EXTINCTION

Mitchell Palmer, conjured up a "Red Scare" to justify his raids. William Leuchtenberg has described some of these raids:

> In one city prisoners were handcuffed, chained together and marched through the streets. In New England hundreds of people were arrested who had no connection with radicalism of any kind. In Detroit 300 people were arrested on false charges, held for a week in jail, forced to sleep on the bare floor of a vile corridor, and denied food for 24 hours, only to be found innocent of any involvement in a revolutionary movement.

With the war's end, the Left was shattered and the Nineteen Twenties became a time for regrouping. □

1200 members of the Industrial Workers of the World are marched between armed citizens from Bisbee to Warren, Arizona, during the Red Scare, 1917. Brown Brothers.

Literature scattered over the street after soldiers and sailors wrecked Socialist Party headquarters in Boston, c. 1917. Underwood and Underwood.

CHAPTER 2

WOMAN'S SUFFRAGE

RENEWING THE STRUGGLE

Despite World War I and President Wilson's repressive policy towards dissenters, militant feminists continued to agitate and take direct action for equal rights for women. The cutting edge of this movement was the Woman's Party, whose leader was Alice Paul, a Quaker who had been imprisoned in England as a participant in Sylvia Pankhurst's direct action suffrage campaign. Other members of this group were Lucy Burns, who with Paul helped form the Women's Peace Society, the absolutist offshoot of the Women's International League for Peace and Freedom, and Crystal Eastman, an active member of the American Union Against Militarism.

These women recognized the need for a Constitutional amendment guaranteeing women the right to vote and so, the day before Wilson's inauguration

in 1913, they organized a suffrage parade in Washington, D.C., with 5,000 women participating. A near riot broke out as swarms of spectators, many of them Wilson supporters in the city for the inaugural, tried to break up the demonstration. Military troops finally had to be called out, much to the embarrassment of the administration. An observer reported that:

> *Passing through two walls of antagonistic humanity, the marchers for the most part kept their temper. They suffered insults, and closed their ears to jibes and jeers. Few faltered, though some of the older women were forced to drop out from time to time.*

The parade received a good deal of publicity and marked the beginning of the revival of the movement for a federal suffrage amendment.

Woman Suffrage parade, Washington D.C., March 3, 1913. G.V. Buck/Library of Congress.

What Is The Paramount Issue Before Congress?

National Defense? NO!

WOMAN SUFFRAGE

Democracy Must Determine Its Own Defense

The women of the United States should be consulted on defense.

A government responsible to all women, as well as all men, will be less likely to go to war, without real necessity.

THE FEDERAL SUFFRAGE AMENDMENT

"The right of citizens of the United States to vote shall not be denied or abridged by the United States, or by any State, on account of sex."

READ THE ANSWER TO YOUR FAVORITE OBJECTION

OBJECTION 1

Some Congressmen say that they cannot vote for the amendment, because they do not believe in woman suffrage.

ANSWER 1.

This need not deter them.

By voting for the amendment, Congress merely passes the question on for the Legislatures of the States to decide.

ANSWER 2.

Many Congressmen did not believe in the Direct Election of Senators, yet voted for the amendment, because of party pressure. The welfare of political parties now demands the passage of the Suffrage Amendment. The Western Women Voters have decided to penalize the party which has the power and does not use it to secure its passage.

OBJECTION 2

Some Congressmen say that they cannot vote for it because they do not approve of the provision in the Constitution for ratifying amendments, by which a State with a large population counts for only one vote, and carries no more weight than a State with a scanty population.

ANSWER.

Women are not responsible for this law. It was put into the Constitution to please the State Rights men, who did not want large States to discriminate against small States.

It is not a sincere objection, as it was not raised against the Income Tax and Direct Election of Senators amendments.

OBJECTION 3

Some Congressmen say that the amendment violates the principle of local self-government.

ANSWER.

On the contrary, it establishes local self-government for women, nation-wide. It is of the same nature as the clause in the Constitution forbidding any State to deny a citizen the right of trial by jury—a just principle valid in every part of the United States.

OBJECTION 4

Some Congressmen say that there is not a sufficient demand for National woman suffrage, and that it is not wise to go ahead of public opinion.

ANSWER 1.

There is a far greater demand than there was for the Income Tax or Direct Election of Senators amendments. There is practically no demand for the enfranchisement of Philippine men; yet the Democratic Party proposes to grant it.

ANSWER 2.

Even the opponents of woman suffrage admit that it is bound to come; this proves the strength of the demand.

Write your Senators and Congressmen to urge the passage of the amendment.

CONGRESSIONAL UNION FOR WOMAN SUFFRAGE,
National Headquarters, 1420 F Street, Washington, D. C.
New York Headquarters, 13 East 41st Street
Telephone, 5444 Murray Hill

THE CONGRESSIONAL UNION FOR WOMAN SUFFRAGE

Congressional interest in woman's suffrage in 1913 was at an all time low: the Senate had not debated the question since 1887 and the issue had never reached the floor of the House. Between 1913 and 1915, Alice Paul, chairperson of the Congressional committee of the National American Woman Suffrage Association, organized a national campaign to defeat Democrats coming up for election. The Democratic party, then in power, was making no visible effort to enfranchise American women. The National Association, however, considered the drive for a federal amendment to be premature, so Paul and the women around her split off to form the Congressional Union for Woman Suffrage.

As a result of the Congressional Union's efforts, suffrage came to a vote in the Senate in 1914 where it was narrowly defeated by two votes. The House finally considered the question in the beginning of 1915, but although 174 representatives favored it, 204 were opposed. The strength of the Congressional Union was being felt, however, and many women began to hold greater hope in the Union than in the National Association's program. In 1915, after losing three important campaigns to gain the vote by state referenda, and losing the allegiance of many of its members, the National Association, under the direction of Carrie Chapman Catt, rejoined the campaign for a federal amendment. Congress remained recalcitrant, however, and for

Leaflet from the Congressional Union for Woman Suffrage. Sophia Smith Collection/Smith College.

the next two years it used all manner of procedural tactics to block the suffrage measure.

Beginning January 10, 1917, Paul and other Congressional Union members began a silent vigil at the White House, probably the first demonstration ever held at the President's mansion. The vigil, which demanded that Wilson keep his promise to fight for a constitutional amendment giving women the right to vote, lasted into the spring despite frequent attacks by observers, including soldiers on leave and police. More than once the war news was crowded off the front page by the activities of Alice Paul and Lucy Burns. The public actions included special "watchfire" burnings of quotes by President Wilson — his unfulfilled campaign promises.

On May 22 the police began to arrest the demonstrators for "obstructing sidewalk traffic." In all, 218 women from 26 states were arrested and 97 were imprisoned. Their reports on prison conditions at Occoquan prison in Virginia and the city jail in Washington caused a scandal. And always there were more women to take the places of those arrested on the vigil line. The National Association

completely disassociated itself from Alice Paul's nonresisting militants and also opposed the Woman's Party stand against the war. The demonstrations continued and brought great pressure upon the government to pass the nineteenth amendment.

HUNGER STRIKE

Most of the women served sixty days for their action, though a few, like Rose Winslow, got seven months for "obstructing traffic." In prison, the women continued their protest, demanding that they be treated as political prisoners, refusing to work and, finally, going on a hunger strike which earned their cause publicity and widespread support.

Doris Stevens, one of the prisoners, wrote a book *Jailed for Freedom* that described these actions. Writing of the hunger strike, she said:

> *When the Administration refused to grant the demand of the prisoners – and of that portion of the public which supported them – for the rights of political*

Suffrage vigil and watchfire, in which President Wilson's unfulfilled campaign promises were burned, in front of the White House, Washington D.C., 1917. Library of Congress.

SENATORS vs. WORKING-WOMEN

Sentimentality of New York Senators
in Equal Suffrage Debate Answered
by Common Sense of Working Women

JOINT MASS-MEETING

**Wage-Earners' League and Collegiate
Equal Suffrage League**

Cooper Union, April 22d, 8 p.m.

"Now there is nobody to whom I yield in respect and admiration and devotion to the sex." Answered by MOLLIE SCHEPPS, Shirt Waist Maker.

"Cornelia's Jewels. Where are they to-day?"
Answered by MELINDA SCOTT, Hat Trimmer.

"The anti-suffragists tell me: 'Be careful, be careful, how you destroy the incentive to motherhood. We speak for motherhood. Save that.'"
Answered by LEONORA O'REILLY, Shirt Maker.

"Women—they are peaceful; they are sympathetic; they minister to man in the home." Answered by MRS. HEFFERLY, Neckwear Maker.

"Now there is no question in the world to my mind but what the family and family relation are a more important thing than any law or any law-making or holding of office." Answered by MAGGIE HINCHEY, Laundry Worker.

"We want to relieve women of the burdens and responsibilities of life."
Answered by CLARA LEMLICH, Shirt Waist Maker.

"Get women into the arena of politics with its alliances and distressing contests—the delicacy is gone, the charm is gone, and you emasculize women."
Answered by ROSE SCHNEIDERMANN, Cap Maker.

Instructions for the Suffrage Parade, May 4th
Elizabeth Freeman of England

Free tickets can be obtained at the Women's Trade Union League, 43 East 22nd Street. Admission without ticket after 8 P.M.

Working Women! Don't fail to come and hear what Senators McClellan, Thomas, Sage and some of the Assemblymen have said about women

They forgot all about the four-hundred thousand working women in New York City. They forgot the eight hundred thousand working women in New York State. Come just to show the gentlemen we have arrived.

Members of the Votes for Women Club at Hamline College, St. Paul, Minnesota, 1913. Minnesota Historical Society.

Notice of a suffrage rally. Sophia Smith Collection/Smith College.

Suffrage workers before billboard, New York City, 1917. Sophia Smith Collection/Smith College.

Library of Congress

ALICE PAUL
(Born 1885)

Alice Paul, a Quaker born in Moorestown, New Jersey, devoted her whole life to securing equal rights for women in the United States and throughout the world. After graduating from Swarthmore College in 1905, she went to London to do social work and there became involved in Sylvia Pankhurst's direct action campaigns for woman's suffrage. While working with the English movement, she gained first-hand experience with direct action, imprisonment, hunger strikes and painful force-feedings. When she returned to the U.S. in 1910, she began speaking to

News from the Front

American suffrage groups on the lessons of the British movement and she led the militant nonviolent campaigns which finally forced Congress to grant American women the right to vote.

Alice Paul formed the Congressional Union for Woman Suffrage in 1913 and served as chairperson until 1917 when it merged with the Woman's Party to form the National Woman's Party. In 1915 she also helped found the Women's Peace Society, an offshoot of the WILPF and absolutist in its pacifism. By 1923, she had obtained three law degrees and had written the first women's equal rights amendment to be introduced to Congress. From 1927 to 1937, she served as chairperson of the Woman's Research Foundation and from 1930 to 1933 also chaired the nationality committee of the Inter-American Commission on Women. Representing this organization and other women's and equal rights groups, she lobbied in Geneva for the recognition of complete equality of women throughout the world. In 1938 she founded the World Women's Party for Equal Rights which successfully pressed the United Nations to include equal rights for women in its charter.

At the outset of the second World War, when she returned from her work in Geneva, Alice Paul observed that the present world crisis had come about without women having anything to do with it. "If the women of the world had not been excluded from world affairs," she said, "things today might have been different."

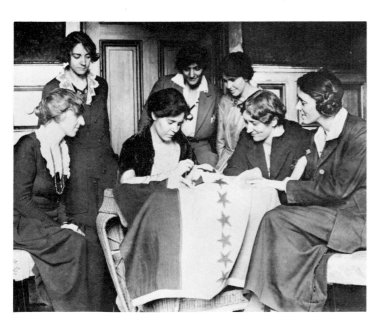

Cover of *The Suffragist*, the weekly publication of the National Woman's Party, June 23, 1917. Sophia Smith Collection/Smith College.

Celebrating ratification of the suffrage amendment, Alice Paul sews the 36th star, representing Tennessee, on the Woman's Party's suffrage banner, Washington D.C., August 19, 1920. Schlesinger Library/Radcliffe College.

prisoners, it was decided to resort to the ultimate protest weapon inside prison. A hunger strike was undertaken, not only to reinforce the verbal demand for the rights of political prisoners, but also as a final protest against unjust imprisonment and increasingly long sentences. This brought the Administration face to face with a more acute embarrassment. They had to choose between mere stubborn resistance and capitulation. . . .

The decision to go on an organized hunger strike was a deliberate and possibly an unprecedented attempt to win a political reform through nonviolent means. "All the officers here know we are making this hunger strike that women fighting for freedom may be considered political prisoners," Winslow wrote. "There have been sporadic and isolated cases of hunger strikes in this country but to my knowledge ours was the first to be organized and sustained over a long period of time. . . ."

Hunger strikes had been used successfully by political prisoners in Russia, by Sylvia Pankhurst and other members of the British suffrage move-ment, as Alice Paul knew, and by Irish nationalists imprisoned without trial by the English for agitating for Irish independence. "And so it was that when we came to the adoption of this accelerating tactic," wrote Stevens, "we had behind us more precedents for winning our point than we had for losing." The hunger strikers were painfully forcefed and many, including Paul, were placed in solitary confinement.

While being held incommunicado in jail, Alice Paul received a visit from David Lawrence, a newspaperman closely associated with Wilson's administration. President Wilson would see to it that Congress passed the suffrage bill, Lawrence told her. He added that if the administration granted the women's demand to be treated as political prisoners, it would have to treat groups which opposed the war as political prisoners also, and that would "throw a bomb in our war program." "It would never do," he said. "It would be easier to give you the Suffrage Amendment than to treat you as political prisoners." Congress passed the woman's suffrage amendment early in 1918 and it was ratified by the states on August 26, 1920.□

Suffragist being forcefed. Drawing from the Women's Social and Political Union, England.

CHAPTER 3

THE LABOR MOVEMENT

THE LAWRENCE STRIKE

During the war about 70 ministers, most of them Protestants, lost their pulpits on account of their pacifism. One of these, a Presbyterian named A. J. Muste who had served a white, middle class congregation in Newton, Mass., joined with other pacifist churchmen in a religious community in Boston called The Comradeship. The communards of this group, in Muste's words, sought "to organize our lives so that they would truly express the teachings and spirit of Jesus, or, in other terms, faith in the way of truth, nonviolence, and love."

In January 1919 it became apparent that a general strike of textile workers was soon to break out in nearby Lawrence, Mass. The Comradeship started to make frequent trips to Lawrence to see if they could offer service. None of them had any exper-

ience in labor disputes and they were uncertain about what exactly they could do. But as Muste later wrote:

We had also a feeling that nonviolence had to prove itself in actual struggle; otherwise it was a mere abstraction or illusion. I recall that some of us felt the sting of the charge that, during the war, while others risked their lives, we had stood on the sidelines and 'had it easy.' Here a struggle was developing in our own back yard. Did our nonviolence have any relevance to the impending conflict?

The 30,000 Lawrence mill workers, most of whom were immigrants, spoke a variety of languages. The A. F. of L., which represented only

Parade of Unemployed, New York City, May 30, 1909. Bain News Service/Library of Congress.

skilled craftsmen and opposed the idea of industrial unionism, refused to support the demands of the workers, which were not at all excessive. The average wage of textile workers was $11 for a 54 hour week. Management proposed to cut the work week to 48 hours with more than a ten percent reduction in take home pay. The workers wanted "54-48" — 54 hours' pay for 48 hours work.

With no experienced leaders in their own ranks and no support from the labor movement, the workers turned to The Comradeship and Muste became executive secretary of the strike committee. The strike was 100% effective from the beginning, despite brutal behavior by the police. Although strike leaders seldom walked picket lines in those days for the obvious reason that they were easy targets for the police, Muste joined the strikers at their head. He was cut off by police on horseback and severely beaten.

As the strike continued past the first months with no break in the solidarity of the workers, the police escalated their strike-breaking tactics. Placing

Striking textile workers confront National Guard troops, Lawrence, Massachusetts, 1912. Brown Brothers.

Protest against child labor, c. 1910. Bain News Service/Library of Congress.

machine guns at key points along the principal streets of Lawrence was a clear provocation to the strikers to use violence. Militants among the workers, later discovered to be spies for management, urged all-out war. "The police are only a couple of hundred. We are thirty thousand," one urged. "Let's seize the machine guns this afternoon and turn them on the police." But the strikers refused to jump at this bait. They voted to remain nonviolent.

Muste recalled that, before going out to confront the machine guns, he told the workers:

> . . . that to permit ourselves to be provoked into violence would mean defeating ourselves; that our real power was in our solidarity and our capacity to endure suffering rather than give up the right to organize; that no one could 'weave woolens with machine guns'; that cheerfulness was better for morale than bitterness and that therefore we would smile as we passed the machine guns and the police on the way from the hall to the picket lines around the mill.

In the fifteenth week of the strike, with the workers' resources running out, management capitulated.

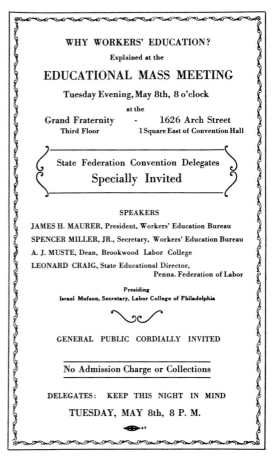

WHY WORKERS' EDUCATION?

Explained at the

EDUCATIONAL MASS MEETING

Tuesday Evening, May 8th, 8 o'clock

at the

Grand Fraternity - 1626 Arch Street
Third Floor   1 Square East of Convention Hall

State Federation Convention Delegates
Specially Invited

SPEAKERS

JAMES H. MAURER, President, Workers' Education Bureau

SPENCER MILLER, JR., Secretary, Workers' Education Bureau

A. J. MUSTE, Dean, Brookwood Labor College

LEONARD CRAIG, State Educational Director,
Penna. Federation of Labor

Presiding
Israel Mufson, Secretary, Labor College of Philadelphia

GENERAL PUBLIC CORDIALLY INVITED

No Admission Charge or Collections

DELEGATES: KEEP THIS NIGHT IN MIND

TUESDAY, MAY 8th, 8 P. M.

Parade of striking textile workers, Lawrence, Massachusetts, 1912. Brown Brothers.

Leaflet for workers' education meeting, c. 1928. Swarthmore College Peace Collection.

DEVERE ALLEN
(1891 - 1955)

Driven by the desire to make pacifism practical, Devere Allen was one of the first to articulate the need for and the characteristics of modern nonviolence. A writer and editor by vocation, he recorded, analyzed, and helped organize the pacifist movement in the interwar years. Active in the national councils of the Socialist Party, he also served as that party's chief advocate of war resistance during the Thirties and Forties.

Allen began to analyze pacifism in the Twenties. In 1929 he edited *Pacifism in the Modern World,* a collection of articles demonstrating the relevance of pacifism to social problems, and a year later wrote *The Fight for Peace.* This major historical work not only recorded the growth of the secular peace movement, but also criticized that movement for the fact that, like the stereotyped symbols of peace, "spokesmen for peace have so long either bleated like lambs, cooed like doves, or quivered vernally against the harsh and wintry gales of war." Allen insisted that pacifists have to be realists, for "the overthrow of oppression is a problem of sociology, psychology and economics, and is only incidentally a problem of physical power." He ended the historical work by calling for an active nonviolence:

> It is necessary for modern pacifism to have at least certain fairly definite hypotheses on which to base non-violent action. Three general types are required: non-violent resistance to a hostile aggressor; non-violent attack to hasten the transformation of evil and unjust social situations; and non-violent mass action for the prevention of war.

An active member of the Fellowship of Reconciliation, Allen wanted to de-emphasize the religious basis for pacifism and to stress instead its ethical side. His views and analyses found expression in *The World Tomorrow,* a journal closely associated with the FOR. Allen worked as an editor of the magazine from 1921 until 1931 and was instrumental in making it one of America's most vigorous little magazines of the period.

In 1933, Allen and his wife Marie launched their No-Frontier News Service to circulate reports on international developments. The news service, later known as Worldover Press, reported and analyzed events not covered in the regular press and by 1955 served 700 newspapers and magazines in 62 countries. It also served to remind the pacifist community of the need to deal with issues in international terms.

A Socialist leader, Allen joined his close associate Norman Thomas in opposing labor violence and, as a board member of the League for Industrial Democracy, tried to apply pacifism to labor relations. Allen realized that violence formed a poor strategy for workers because it not only compromised their democratic ideals but also mobilized the middle class against them and further concentrated state power. He believed that the only sure ground for international peace was organized mass action and not the agreements made by heads of state. When the Socialist Party held its national meeting in Detroit in 1934, Allen wrote the Declaration of Principles which called for acceptance of the general strike as the surest defense against fascism. "I profoundly believe," he wrote in 1931, "that human relations can never be put on a higher level until we learn to fight radically for social progress by non-violent methods."

Children and striking workers from the Passaic, New Jersey, textile mills picket the White House after President Coolidge refused to see them, Washington D.C., April 15, 1926. Devere Allen and other Fellowship of Reconciliation members were active in the Passaic strike. Library of Congress.

SACCO AND VANZETTI

The radical pacifist movement, like the Left in general, barely stayed alive during the Twenties. The effects of the Palmer Raids and the "red scare" were felt for the duration of the decade. The case that symbolizes the repressive atmosphere of those years was that of two Italian workingmen, Nicola Sacco and Bartolomeo Vanzetti.

Sacco was a shoe cutter, Vanzetti a fish peddler;

both were committed activists in the anarchist movement around Boston. Sacco was also a conscientious objector during World War I. On May 9, 1920, they were arrested for distributing circulars announcing a protest meeting for one of their friends, Andrea Salsedo, who died or was killed while held for eight weeks in secret custody by Justice Department officials. The day after their arrest, Sacco and Vanzetti were charged with murdering a paymaster and guard during a $15,000 payroll robbery at South Braintree, Mass., three weeks earlier.

The trial of Sacco and Vanzetti was an outrageous pretension at justice. They were tried more for their radical beliefs than for their alleged involvement in the crime. Of Vanzetti, Judge Webster Thayer told the jury, "This man, although he may not have actually committed the crime attributed to him, is nevertheless morally culpable, because he is the enemy of our existing institutions."

Despite shaky evidence by the prosecution and convincing evidence for the defense that the accused were elsewhere at the time of the crime (the head of the Justice Department in Boston eventually submitted sworn affidavits that the government knew Sacco and Vanzetti were innocent but prosecuted them exclusively for their political beliefs), the two were found guilty and sentenced to death. The case became a cause célèbre throughout the world for the next six years, but the two radicals lost all judicial appeals and were electrocuted August 23, 1927.

Their final words still echo throughout the radical tradition:

> *Only two of us will die – our ideal, you, our comrades will live by millions. We have won. We are not vanquished. Just treasure our sufferings, our sorrows, our mistakes, our defeat, our passion, for future battles for the great emancipation. We embrace you all and bid you our extreme good-bye. Now and ever, long life to you all. Long live liberty.*

Bartolomeo Vanzetti, in a last letter just prior to his execution, wrote,

> *If it had not been for these things, I might live out my life talking at street corners to scorning men. I might have died, unmourned, unknown, a failure. Now we are not a failure. This is our career and our triumph. Never in our full life could we have to do such work*

Bartolomeo Vanzetti and Nicola Sacco are led into court, Boston, Massachusetts, October 31, 1921. *Boston Globe.*

Support demonstration for Sacco and Vanzetti, Boston, Massachusetts, May 1, 1925. *Boston Globe.*

for tolerance, for justice, for man's understanding of man as now we do by accident. Our words – our lives – our pains O nothing! The taking of our lives – lives of a good shoemaker and a poor fish-peddler – all! That last moment belongs to us – that agony is our triumph.

CLASS STRUGGLE

Class war seemed to be breaking out in the United States after the first World War, as labor fought for the right to organize against a managerial elite that expected and usually got the support of the government in breaking any and all strikes.

Radical pacifists had always been involved with the working people's struggle to organize. In the

From the Depths, photogravure by William Balfour Kerr, 1906. Library of Congress.

20s, both Evan Thomas and A. J. Muste organized textile workers, and pacifists in many parts of the country were involved in organizing and workers' education. Muste went on to head the Brookwood Labor College in Katonah, New York, where many of the future leaders of the CIO were trained. Founded in 1919 by pacifists William and Helen Fincke, Brookwood was the first resident workers' college in the country. A number of Fellowship of Reconciliation members were involved in the college, including John Nevin Sayre, Sarah Cleghorn, Tucker P. Smith and Muste, who directed the college from 1921 until 1933 when it split over the issue of violence in the labor movement.

As pacifists still lacked the means of applying nonviolence to explosive social situations, many,

including Muste, abandoned their pacifism to take the position that labor must be supported even if that meant condoning or using violent methods. After Brookwood, Muste helped start the Conference for Progressive Labor Action (CPLA) which, with the decline of the Socialist Party, became the radical alternative to the Communist Party USA, then closely following the Stalinist line for the benefit of the Soviet Union. "The Muste-ites," as members of the CPLA were called, sought to reform the AF of L from within, and stood for industrial unionism, the end of discrimination within the labor movement, unemployment insurance and other social benefits, recognition of the Soviet Union, and an "anti-imperialist and anti-militarist internationalist labor movement." In 1933 the CPLA formed the Workers Party, a "democratically organized revolutionary party," which merged a year later with the Trotskyist Communist League of America.

Muste abandoned the orthodox left in 1936, after a tour of Europe and a visit with Trotsky, and once more became a pacifist. Now, however, he no longer advocated a traditional form of pacifism. Muste urged an active nonviolence oriented to the great social problems of the time, a nonviolence that was anti-capitalist in orientation, cognizant of the problems of "human behavior," and based on a principled morality which, he felt, was still the basic dynamic for durable change.

Police charge strikers outside Republic Steel Corporation in Chicago during the CIO organizing drive in 1937. Eleven strikers were killed and nearly one hundred were injured. UPI.

Edith Berkman, an organizer for the National Textile Workers' Union, is arrested by plainclothes police in Lawrence, Massachusetts, February 27, 1931. Wide World.

THE SIT-INS

As a labor organizer with the CPLA in 1936, Muste helped organize a strike of the Goodyear Tire workers in Akron, Ohio, and largely through his suggestions, the tactic of the sit-in was introduced to the organizing efforts of the American labor movement, especially the Congress of Industrial Organizations (CIO). In the mid-30s, the sit-down strike was a vital element of the unionists' strategy. Underpaid clerks in New York's Woolworth dime-stores staged a sit-down in which they locked themselves inside and slept behind the counters. The sit-in became the subject of good-humored jokes; it was sweeping the country.

The idea of the sit-in strike goes back to the early 1900s when women garment workers, forbidden by contract to strike, often stopped working when they had a grievance and remained at their sewing machines until the issue was settled. In 1933, 2,500 employees of the Hormel Packing Company in Austin, Minn. refused to work or budge from their machines for three days until their strike against the speed-up and for shorter hours at better pay was won. But it was in the Goodyear strike that the sit-in tactic was popularized throughout the country. The technique was first used at Akron by the union baseball team which sat down on the field until they were provided with an umpire who was also a union man. During the winter of 1936, when Goodyear refused to enter into collective bargaining with the union, the tactic was recalled. In one Goodyear plant, there were 58 separate sit-downs that year. The tactic greatly minimized the violence that management could use against the workers. If the men remained in the factory, near their machines, management could not risk a physical attack which might lead to the destruction of their machinery.

From Goodyear, the sit-down tactic spread to other plants and industries, but the most important sit-in occurred in December 1936 during the campaign by the United Auto Workers (UAW) to win recognition from General Motors. The campaign had been going on for some time, but GM was unyielding in its refusal to recognize the UAW as representative of the GM workers. The sit-in began at the Fisher Body Plant in Flint and led to a strike

Sit-down strikers at Fisher Body Plant #3, Flint, Michigan, February, 1937. Sheldon Dick/Library of Congress.

Top left: Workers honor fallen comrade, Minneapolis, Minnesota, 1934. UPI.

that, by February 1937, involved 200,000 workers and cut the production of GM cars from 53,000 per week to 1,500.

Yet, the company would not negotiate, insisting that the Fisher Body workers first relinquish control of the plant. A court order forbidding the workers to remain in the plant was ignored and later the judge was discovered to be a GM stockholder. The company next tried to starve out the workers by prohibiting food from reaching them. It also turned off the heat in an attempt to freeze them out. Neither tactic worked. When the company tried to co-opt the idea of unionism by creating a company union, the workers made a bluff attack on the personnel office in Flint and then rushed in and took control of an unprotected plant that was the key production factory for Chevrolet. The police then tried to charge the main gate and were repulsed by the Woman's Emergency Brigade: the wives, sisters and woman friends of the occupying workers locked arms and barred the police from invading the plant.

More injunctions followed, but the police lacked the power to enforce them. Finally, the National Guard was called out and surrounded the plant, but under the command of Governor Frank Murphy, who was sympathetic to labor's cause, they remained neutral.

On February 11, 1937, with the help of Governor Murphy, GM capitulated and recognized the United Auto Workers as bargaining agent for the workers. After 44 days of occupation, the workers emerged from the plant singing "Solidarity Forever." After Flint, the sit-in became commonplace throughout industry and, flushed with this major victory, the CIO was able to organize other basic industries on an industry-wide basis.

Woolworth's employees during their sit-down strike for union recognition, New York City, March 17, 1937. Wide World.

Sit-down strikers dance during their occupation of the Chevrolet Fisher Body plant in St. Louis, Missouri, March 11, 1937. Wide World.

Starving cow and horse are led into the State Capitol by farmers dramatizing their demand for relief, c. 1935. Minnesota Historical Society.

During the sit-in, the workers created their own government and enforced their own discipline. Recreation and education were provided. The machinery was kept up and rules of conduct imposed. Food was a major problem. During the Midland Steel strike, the Milk Drivers Union sent in 30 gallons of milk per day. The cooks union provided chefs to feed the GM men, as they did during four other sit-down strikes. "The food goes into the factories in twenty kettles of various sizes," the cook for the GM strikers has recalled. "The amount of food the strikers use is immense. Five hundred pounds of meat, 1,000 pounds of potatoes, 300 loaves of bread, 100 pounds of coffee, 200 pounds of sugar, 30 gallons of milk, four cases of evaporated milk" a day. Often, the food was delivered to the workers in baskets by rope. The sit-ins succeeded in winning union recognition where decades of conventional strike actions failed.□

Sit-down strikers celebrate the agreement between the United Auto Workers union and General Motors officials, Flint, Michigan, February 11, 1937. Brown Brothers.

Victorious auto workers end their sit-in at the Dodge factory, March 26, 1937. Brown Brothers.

FELLOWSHIP OF RECONCILIATION
(Founded 1915)

The Fellowship of Reconciliation (FOR) was the central pacifist organization in the United States during the first half of the Twentieth Century. It helped to bring a broadened and more progressive constituency into the peace movement and under its influence, pacifism became more of an aggressive, creative and radical force, with less of its educational and legalistic aura.

The FOR was founded in England in 1914, a result of a pledge by two Christian ministers, Henry Hodgkin of England and Sigmund Schultze of Germany, not to let the war destroy their friendship or interrupt their work for peace. A few months later, in 1915, the FOR was established in the U.S. with the help of Gilbert Beaver, Edward Evans, Charles Rhoades, and others, and FOR groups were subsequently organized in 27 other countries, with an International Secretariat in Brussels.

Throughout World War I, the Fellowship raised vehement protest against the evils of massive warfare and, after the Armistice, it emerged as one of the more outspoken and action-oriented of the peace societies formed during the war. Its members included ministers, students, teachers, YMCA and social workers, professional people and others of many faiths "who recognize the essential unity of all humanity and who have joined together to explore the power of love and truth for resolving human conflict."

After the war, the Fellowship encouraged its members to unite the Christian ideals of loving service and community with a commitment to nonviolent social action. FOR members supplied nonviolent leadership and support in labor struggles and strike relief efforts in the Twenties and Thirties, wrote for and edited the radical religious journal *The World Tomorrow* (published from 1918 until 1934), and were influential in the No More War movement. They also helped build coalitions of peace groups and serviced conscientious objectors in the years just prior to the second World War.

While involved in disarmament, peace education, and social reform efforts in the mid-30s, the Fellowship began to prepare for the war by developing a "crisis strategy" involving the creation of both community and denominational groups to identify, recruit and organize pacifists during wartime. By 1936, there were over sixty local Fellowships and FOR membership increased from about 5,000 in 1938 to just under 15,000 at the war's end.

During World War II, when the Japanese-Americans were forcefully relocated from the West Coast in 1942, the FOR protested to the government, agitated for release and resettlement, and provided friendship and relief to

New Yorkers stage sit-in at Home Relief Station demanding more food, New York City, c. 1937. UPI.

Japanese-Americans in internment camps. While many of FOR's members and staff were in prison or CPS camps for their opposition to the war, the FOR published a special supplement to its magazine *Fellowship* which exposed the Allied policy of saturation bombing and the terrible suffering it caused civilians in Europe. This passionate protest, written by British pacifist Vera Brittain, won the endorsement of 28 prominent American religious leaders and was widely publicized and debated by the American press and radio.

After years of planning and work for racial equality, the FOR made a substantial contribution to the civil rights movement after World War II. The Fellowship helped found the Congress of Racial Equality in 1942 and co-sponsored the first Freedom Ride in 1947. FOR organizers, such as Glenn Smiley and James Lawson, trained Southern civil rights groups in nonviolent direct action, worked in Montgomery during the bus boycott, and were involved in many of the subsequent civil rights campaigns in the North and South.

A.J. Muste served as Executive Secretary of the FOR from 1940 until 1953, sharing this position for part of that time with John Nevin Sayre, who was also International Secretary. During this period, Bayard Rustin, George Houser, and John Swomley were active in FOR youth, inter-racial, and anti-conscription campaigns.

The Fellowship stood up for free speech and civil liberties during the McCarthy era, campaigned for commutation of the death sentence imposed on Ethel and Julius Rosenberg, and organized a Carnegie Hall meeting in 1956 to give Communists (and pacifists) an opportunity to speak publicly.

The Fellowship co-sponsored the first important demonstration against the war in Vietnam in 1964 and was active in many protests throughout the following years. FOR members joined in coalition actions and organized projects aimed at educating the public about the war and relieving some of the misery of those directly affected by the fighting. They ran full page ads in newspapers calling for an end to the war, sent an early inter-denominational investigating group to Vietnam, and raised sums for relief. In 1965 the Fellowship established the main American link with the pacifist Buddhist resistance movement in Vietnam. The FOR continued to speak out against American militarism after the war and campaigned for disarmament and a reappraisal of American priorities for "the endangered human species."

Out of the FOR grew such organizations as the National Conference of Christians and Jews, American Civil Liberties Union, National Religion and Labor Foundation, War Resisters League, Workers Defense League, Committee on Militarism in Education, American Committee on Africa, National Council Against Conscription, Peacemakers, Society for Social Responsibility in Science, Church Peace Mission, and Dai Dong. After over 60 years, the Fellowship of Reconciliation continues to be an important force in the development and practice of active nonviolence in the United States.

John, Anna, and A.J. Muste at Brookwood Labor College, Katonah, New York, c. 1930. Fellowship of Reconciliation.

Quaker Robert Jones and John Nevin Sayre of the Fellowship of Reconciliation on a peace mission in Nicaragua in 1927. Fellowship of Reconciliation.

CHAPTER 4

THE ANTI-WAR MOVEMENT

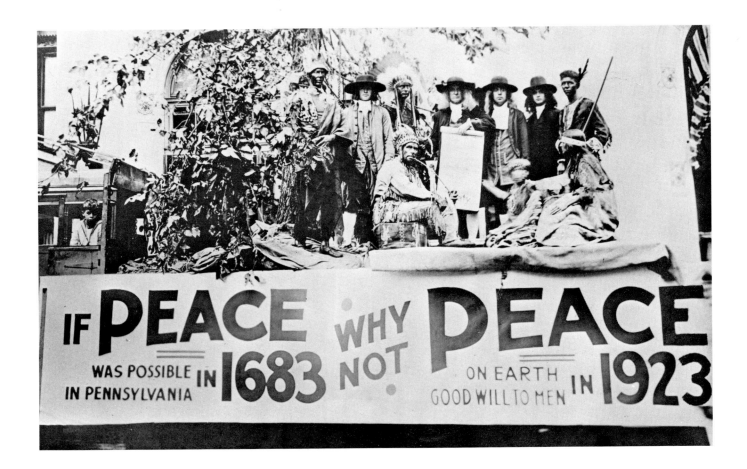

NO MORE WAR

Throughout the Twenties, the Women's Peace Society, the Fellowship of Reconciliation, the War Resisters League and a number of smaller ad hoc groups continued to agitate against and to argue the folly of the first World War. There were many street demonstrations, usually to commemorate specific holidays, such as Armistice (now Veterans) Day. These demonstrations were highly theatrical events, complete with songs, candlelight ceremonies and prayer services. The Women's Peace Society leafleted department stores to "protest against the display and sale of war-like toys," and took the message to Wall Street with a No More War Day rally, featuring speakers, leaflets and a float, in front of the Sub-treasury Building.

Superficially, at least, the movement was successful. The Conference for Progressive Political Action — a coalition of farmer, labor and socialist groups — led by the anti-war Senator from Wisconsin, Robert M. LaFollette, won more than 16% of the Presidential vote in 1924. Congressional investigations into the causes of World War I placed the onus on the armament industry and big business. Internationally there were a series of steps taken towards disarmament that culminated in the 1929 Paris Peace Pact which outlawed war as a solution to international problems. Sixty-two nations eventually signed the pact, including the United States and every other major belligerent in the next World War.

The most striking example of this strong anti-war

Peace Parade, 1923. Swarthmore College Peace Collection.

feeling was the British Oxford Pledge — "in no circumstances [to] fight for . . . King and Country" — which aroused the support of thousands of young men, including the cream of the student population. But the pledge demanded no commitment other than a signature on a dotted line. It ignored the serious tensions brought about by the worldwide depression, a growing class struggle, and the rise of totalitarianism in Nazi Germany and the Soviet Union.

The American parallels to these sincere but often naive yearnings for peace included public declarations by young men renouncing war at the annual Armistice Day eve dedication services, held by the WRL under the direction of Tracy Mygatt and Frances Witherspoon. From 1931 to 1934, scores of liberal, radical and pacifist groups sponsored a series of No More War parades which grew from 300 participants to more than 20,000. The Oxford Pledge Movement also spread to college campuses in America. At a Conference on Militant Pacifism, organized by the WRL in May 1931, Jessie Wallace Hughan urged radical pacifists to continue their efforts: "This is the time for us to work fast, not when the war comes."

Radical pacifists were encouraged by the support of the German physicist, Albert Einstein, who, in a visit to the United States in 1931, endorsed the objectives of the League and said that "even if only 2% of those assigned to perform military service should announce their refusal to fight . . . governments would be powerless. . . ." Beginning in 1934, students began publicly renouncing war, often in large public demonstrations. In April 1934, 500 Vassar women in caps and gowns marched through the streets of Poughkeepsie, N.Y., behind the president of the college, chanting "No more battleships. We want schools."

On April 12, 1935, 60,000 college students around the nation went on strike against war. The next November, 20,000 students in New York marched in the streets and at the City College, 3,500 students booed the president of the college when he objected to the reading of the Oxford Oath.

Far more impressive in buoying up the spirits of the pacifist movement during the early 30s were reports coming from India of Gandhi's use of nonviolent tactics and civil disobedience on a mass scale to win independence for his nation from Great Britain. The FOR organized the American League for India's Freedom to give financial support to Gandhi's 1930 march to the sea, a mass civil disobedience action challenging the British monopoly

Roger Baldwin leads students in reciting the Oxford Pledge at an anti-war rally at Columbia University during the nation-wide student strike against war, New York City, April 12, 1935. UPI.

The Appropriation Pie

(From Labor, December 11, 1920)

United States Appropriations, 1920

I.	Past Wars	$3,855,482,586	68%
II.	Future Wars	1,424,138,677	25%
III.	Civil Departments	181,087,225	3%
IV.	Public Works	168,203,557	3%
V.	Education and Science	57,093,661	1%
	Total	$5,686,005,706	100%

(Analysis by Dr. Edward B. Rosa, of the United States Bureau of Standards)

NO MORE WAR!

This cry is being raised throughout the world.

In England, France, Germany, Austria, Holland, Switzerland, Czecho-Slovakia, Hungary, Portugal and Sweden men and women are uniting, on the anniversary of the Great War, to voice their demand that there shall never again be such a cataclysm of murder and destruction.

Statesmen and diplomats, financiers and conferences, will not end war. War will never be abolished until you men and women, you fathers and mothers, you workers, you who pay the price of war in sorrow and suffering, in disease and death, in unemployment and poverty, raise your voices to say that there shall be

NO MORE WAR

Men and women of New York City will express their opposition to war on

Saturday Evening, July 29th, 1922

BY A

TORCH-LIGHT PARADE and MASS-MEETING

ARRANGED BY

THE WOMEN'S PEACE SOCIETY
THE WOMEN'S PEACE UNION of the WESTERN HEMISPHERE
THE FELLOWSHIP OF RECONCILIATION

and other organizations. The parade will form at Union Square at 7:30.
Come and join us in an imposing protest against war!

MARCH WITH US FOR PEACE!

Declare your willingness to march in the No-More-War Parade by signing the attached slip. Do it now!

I expect to march in the No-More-War Parade on July 29th.

Name

Address

Telephone Number

Return to Miss HENRIETTE HEINZEN, *Parade Secretary,*

Vanderbilt 3522

WOMEN'S PEACE SOCIETY
Room 1101, 505 Fifth Avenue, New York.

There will be a special Men's Section.
Women are asked to wear white, if possible.

We need volunteer workers.
Can you help?

Pass this word on

---

on salt. An American disciple of Gandhi, Richard Gregg, published a book in 1934 called *The Power of Nonviolence*, which argued that nonviolence was a more practical means of creating social change and defending one's homeland against armed invasion than was violence or armed might. Gregg was among the first to understand, explain and popularize nonviolence as an effective tactic in the United States.

THREAT OF FASCISM

Pacifists were among the first to recognize that the rise of fascism in Europe posed a serious threat to the people of the world. The first demonstration against the German treatment of the Jews and other minorities occurred in 1933 under the pacifist leadership of Rabbi Stephen S. Wise and Rev. John

---

Leaflet from the Women's Peace Society, 1922. Swarthmore College Peace Collection.

Leaflet from the American Union Against Militarism, 1920. Swarthmore College Peace Collection.

Ernest Shirely and Everett Walsh on one of the American Friends Service Committee's peace caravans, 1931. AFSC.

Wanted! 25,000 to March in the
NO MORE WAR PARADE

May 18th, 1935

> OFFICE:
> Room 306, 2 Stone Street
> New York City
> Tel. BOwling Green 9-9735

Fellow Citizens:—

Another great No-More-War-Parade is planned for Saturday afternoon, May 18th, 1935. The citizens of this country do not want war but America is again insanely rushing toward international conflict. Nationalism, greedy imperialism, economic insecurity, competitive armaments, and ancient fears are pushing the nations blindly, unwillingly into war.

These forces must be opposed by an aroused populace and an organized workers' movement which knows the cost and futility of war and is prepared by virtue of numbers and organization to demand peace.

The Munitions Inquiry showed the extent to which private industry can debauch governments; the navy proposes to maneuver in threatening proximity to Japanese waters; civil liberties are already endangered by those who see nothing but traditional flag-waving patriotism; government war expenditures are greater than ever in our history.

Let us give fair warning! We will not support our government in any war to which such activities may lead.

Let us now in this great Peace Demonstration, join with many thousands in a crusade for a warless world. Another year may be too late. This is the hour!

March in the NO MORE WAR PARADE! Enlist others! Mobilize the army of Peace!

Do not hold back the blank below more than a week; return as soon as possible with as many enlistments as you can get.

- -

ROSTER

I WILL MARCH! Send me a card later with final instructions. Send me copies of this call.

NAME	ADDRESS	ORGANIZATION (if any)

Attach a sheet for additional names and mail to:

NO MORE WAR PARADE COMMITTEE
ROOM 306   2 STONE STREET, N. Y. C.

Haynes Holmes. When President Franklin D. Roosevelt refused to lower immigration barriers to allow Jews entry into America to escape German persecution, pacifists protested vigorously, in marches and in words. In 1934 the War Resisters League urged the government "to display its traditional tolerance toward victims of racial and political persecution and suspend its quota regulations until all those oppressed shall have been afforded the refuge they need." The WRL also asked "pacifists and humanitarians who are in a position to do so to sponsor the entrance of one or more such refugees and give the necessary assurances and undertakings as required by the Immigration authority."

Peter Maurin, who with Dorothy Day founded the Catholic Worker movement in 1933, also spoke out against Roosevelt's refusal to admit Jewish

Leaflet from the No More War Parade Committee, 1935. Swarthmore College Peace Collection.

Students Zoe Wise and Mary Stevens, on one of the American Friends Service Committee's peace caravans, talk about international issues and the need for world peace over a St. Joseph, Missouri, radio station. AFSC.

Peace demonstration at Phyllis Wheatley House, Minnesota. Minnesota Historical Society.

Schlesinger Library/Radcliffe College

JEANNETTE RANKIN
(1880 - 1973)

A pacifist and the first Congresswoman in America, Jeannette Rankin voted against U.S. entry into the first World War and, a quarter century later, cast the only vote in Congress against the second. Born on a ranch near Missoula, Montana, she began her political career with the suffrage movement in 1910. She became field secretary for the National American Woman's Suffrage Association in 1912, and she spoke in Montana, Washington, and California and lobbied in Washington D.C. for the right of women to vote.

SECURITY
THROUGH
FEDERATION

DEMAND DRASTIC REDUCTIONS IN ARMAMENT BUDGETS

WORLD PEACE POSTERS — 31 UNION SQUARE, NEW YORK

She was elected to Congress in 1916 and was one of the few to vote against the declaration of war the next year. Her vote was the first ever cast on the issue of war by any female parliamentarian in the history of the Western world and, as a consequence, she lost her seat in Congress in the subsequent campaign.

During the Depression, Rankin lobbied for the National Consumers League and the National Council for the Prevention of War. A member of the Women's International League for Peace and Freedom, she lectured throughout the country on behalf of peace measures and neutrality legislation, proposed legislation against war profiteering, and testified before the Senate committee investigating the munitions industry.

She was elected to the House of Representatives for a second term at the onset of the second World War. On December 8, 1941, she stood alone as the only member of Congress to vote against the declaration of war. "I want to stand by my country," she said, "but I cannot vote for war." Nearly 27 years later, at age 88, she led 5,000 women in the Jeannette Rankin Brigade as they marched on Washington to protest the U.S. war in Vietnam.

Anti-war post card from World Peace Posters. Swarthmore College Peace Collection.

Jeannette Rankin before leaving Washington D.C. on a speaking tour in behalf of a peace plank in the Republican and Democratic party platforms, June 3, 1932. Wide World.

Swarthmore College Peace Collection

FREDERICK J. LIBBY
(1874 -1970)

As head of the National Council for the Prevention of War for over 20 years, Frederick Libby was at the center of the peace movement's disarmament crusade. A complete pacifist, he devoted himself to encouraging anti-war sentiment in the U.S. during the Twenties and Thirties and, in an effort to elicit a broad base of support, he took particular care to address farmers and housewives.

Libby grew up in Maine where his father was a country doctor and his mother was a school teacher. He worked as a high school principal and Congregational minister before becoming a member of the Society of Friends and turning to full-time work as a peace advocate in 1921. Under Libby's guidance, the NCPW became the most active and effective pressure group in Washington for disarmament and neutrality legislation.

As the peace movement's Congressional lobby, the National Council did not itself have members but consisted of affiliated groups, both pacifist (such as the Fellowship of Reconciliation and the Brethren Service Committee) and non-pacifist (such as the American Federation of Teachers and the YWCA). At its peak in 1935, the NCPW included 21 participating organizations and 10 additional cooperating agencies, had a staff of 18 people, and operated on a budget of over $100,000. *Peace Action,* the monthly newsletter, achieved a circulation of over 20,000 and the national headquarters distributed between one million and two million pieces of peace literature yearly throughout the Thirties. When the second World War was declared, the NCPW, by then in decline, pledged not to obstruct the war effort but rather to work for an early and just peace by negotiation.

Swarthmore College Peace Collection

DOROTHY DETZER
(Born 1900)

Dorothy Detzer, a leading peace lobbyist during the 1930s, sparked Senator Gerald Nye's 1934 Senate committee investigation of the munitions industry. Working closely with Frederick Libby of the National Council for the Prevention of War, she and her staff developed material for the committee and helped to line up Congressional support. Dorothy Detzer personally selected the committee's chief investigator.

The disclosures that were made by the Nye committee demonstrated to millions of people that traffic in armaments leads to war. The Committee charged that private armament interests circumvented national policies as defined in arms embargoes and treaties, sold weapons to both sides in time of war, bribed government officials, lobbied for military appropriations and against embargoes, stimulated arms races between friendly nations, and thrived on excess profits and favoritism from the government.

Dorothy Detzer was national secretary of the Women's International League for Peace and Freedom from 1924 to 1947. Throughout this period, she led the WILPF's campaign for total disarmament and devoted particular attention to the abolition of chemical warfare. She held leadership positions in several of the coalitions developed during the Thirties in attempts to forestall World War II. When the war came, she continued to maintain her absolute pacifism and stated that "as pacifists, we can never yield our inalienable right to affirm and declare that war between nations or classes or races cannot permanently settle conflicts or heal the wounds that brought them into being."

JOHN HAYNES HOLMES
(1879 - 1964)

John Haynes Holmes was one of the most unconventional and courageously vocal preachers in America during the first half of the Twentieth Century. He helped found the Anti-Enlistment League in 1915 and the War Resisters League in 1923, was president of the Unitarian Fellowship for Social Justice from 1908 to 1911, and vice-president of the National Association for the Advancement of Colored People in 1909. He was also one of the initial organizers of the American Civil Liberties Union and a member of the Socialist Party, the League for Industrial Democracy, and the Fellowship of Reconciliation.

Holmes came from a conservative Philadelphia family which could trace its ancestry to settlers at Plymouth in 1630. After graduating from Harvard Divinity School in 1904, he found his conservatism beginning to wear thin and by 1907 was preaching socialism at New York's Church of the Messiah. On the eve of the first World War, Holmes delivered a sermon in which he told his congregation that war is the organized use of physical force to kill wholesale and indiscriminately for national self-interest. "I am opposed to war in general and to this war in particular . . . In this church, if nowhere else in America, the Germans will still be included in the family of God's children." The press denounced him as a traitor but he continued to speak out against the war and made his church New York's unofficial center for conscientious objectors.

From his pulpit Holmes talked about the social gospel which considered personal redemption within the context of social concern. After 1917, he made Gandhi's work in India the text for countless sermons and articles which argued that people could follow their highest ideals and still be politically effective. He also encouraged within his listeners a transnational humanism which he called "the will to peace." In keeping with his understanding of "the unity of all men in the spirit," Holmes left the Unitarian ministry in 1921, changed the name of his church to the Community Church, and removed all Unitarian and Christian implications from its covenant. Thereafter, the Community Church welcomed American Indians, Chinese, Jews, Catholics and Hindus as well as Protestants.

In the spring of 1933, after the first large-scale demonstration in the U.S. against Hitlerism and in support of European Jews, Holmes called on the American people to pressure the Roosevelt Administration to deny

> I am Unalterably Opposed to the Teaching of Military Tactics— the Science of Killing Human Beings— in Civilian Institutions of Learning, and Training Adults for War in Citizens Military Training Camps.

trade relations and cultural courtesies to the dictator. Holmes worked hard throughout the late Thirties with other leading pacifists to gain public support for a commission of neutral nations, including the United States, to arrange an armistice in Europe. Again and again he pointed out that because of the greed incorporated in the Treaty of Versailles, the United States and other Western powers were as responsible for the war as Hitler. When the U.S. entered the war, Holmes maintained his absolute pacifism and became a leading opponent of the idea that an Allied victory alone would make real peace possible. War might stop Hitler, he said, but would it stop Hitlerism?

Throughout his life, Holmes challenged the logic that violence can defend and liberate. The fallacy, he said, is contained in the fact that such force actually brings new forms of conflict and is the ultimate foundation of tyranny. Early in the Twentieth Century, he popularized the thesis that nonviolence is a practical alternative to war as well as a religious obligation, and he continuously articulated the basic tenet that the end is determined by the means.

Rev. John Haynes Holmes speaks at a "No More War" rally at Madison Square Garden, New York City, May 19, 1934. Wide World.

refugees, and said, "America is big enough to find a refuge for persecuted Jews." By closing its doors to Jewish immigration, the United States helped seal the fate of the millions of Jewish victims of the Nazi furnaces. "I learned first hand," Norman Thomas, once executive secretary of the FOR, was to say later, "how many Americans preferred to fight or have their countrymen fight for the rights of Jews in Europe than to give them asylum in America."

The Spanish Civil War also tore at pacifist loyalties. The left, of course, gave ardent support to the Spanish Loyalists whose attempt to set up a Republican government was thwarted by the fascist Franco, with the support of Germany and Italy. The Socialist Party, which had a long anti-militarist tradition, organized the Eugene V. Debs column which served with the Lincoln Brigade. Party leader Norman Thomas explained that the socialists would "use to the uttermost nonviolent methods

"No More War" parade, which included 10,000 people, on Fifth Avenue, New York City, May 19, 1934. Wide World.

Peace demonstration at the University of Chicago, April 22, 1937. Wide World.

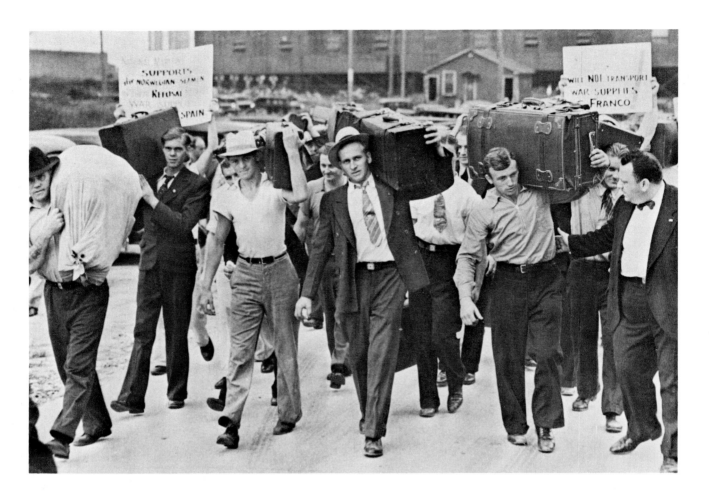

consistent with true democracy. But . . . it will not yield to fascism anywhere without a struggle."

As it turned out, the Loyalist cause was compromised by the support given it by the Soviet Union which fought as hard against the anarchists and other non-Stalinists on the government side as it did against the fascists.

FAILURE OF THE ANTI-WAR MOVEMENT

The experience of Spain mirrored the tragic efforts of the American left to create an independent anti-fascist and anti-militarist alternative to the Roosevelt policy of appeasing Germany when it suited him and then preparing the country for war when the Nazi monster it had tolerated threatened to swallow up first Europe and then the world.

The pacifists, for the most part, remained independent of the various leftist peace organizations which changed their positions on Germany and war with every new development in the foreign policy of the Soviet Union. The American Peace Mobilization, for instance, opposed American entry into the

Refusing to transport war supplies to Franco's Spain, crewmen leave the freighter *Titanian* on the dock at Baltimore, Maryland, September 2, 1938. Wide World.

"If the Nations Used Donkey Sense!," cartoon published in the Emergency Peace Campaign's *No Foreign War Crusade,* 1937.

Photo Courtesy of Abe Kaufman

JESSIE WALLACE HUGHAN
(1876 - 1955)

Jessie Wallace Hughan's overriding concern during her forty years as an outstanding pacifist organizer was to unite all those who agreed on political, humanitarian, or philosophical grounds that war was a crime against humanity. She helped found the Anti-Enlistment League in 1915 and, as an active member of the Fellowship of Reconciliation, was also a driving force in founding the War Resisters League in 1923. Jessie Hughan wrote prolifically about pacifism, socialism, and world government, and was an important theorist about organized war resistance and nonviolent national defense. She directed her total commitment and inexhaustible energy to drawing people into the ranks of organized pacifism.

By Hughan's definition, a pacifist might use personal violence in self-defense but would refuse to participate in any and all wars. She drew an analogy to dueling, a custom which had been eliminated although its causes still remained, and she argued that pacifists could and should organize war resistance to such an extent that the national government would no longer be able to count on popular support for its war plans. While she encouraged pacifists to work to eliminate the economic, nationalist, and imperialist causes of war, she emphasized that war could be abandoned as a national policy if people would act in concert and refuse to fight.

In the first two decades of her work with the War Resisters League, she laid the groundwork for CO counseling and constantly sought to find a common program in which pacifists of varying opinions could unite. In the early 1930s, she encouraged pacifists and non-pacifists to participate in No More War parades which might not have taken place without her persistence. A high school English teacher, she also formed the Pacifist Teachers League in 1940 whose members refused to register draftees.

During World War II, Jessie Hughan was the first in the

WRL to press for payment of conscientious objectors, opposing Civilian Public Service camps because the objectors worked there without compensation. However, in her efforts to keep the League's primary focus on war resistance and anti-conscription work, she refused to sanction actions not directly relevant to war and the draft, for example, prison hunger strikes against segregation. When a split developed in the WRL as to whether it should support all COs, no matter where they drew the line in cooperating with the government, or instead should concentrate on the absolutists in prison, Hughan as a member of the Executive Committee wanted the League to continue its support of the CPS camp system. After the war, when younger and more radical objectors were elected to the Executive Committee, Hughan differed with them about the direction the League should take. She conceived of the League as an educational, service, and enrollment agency which could not, therefore, afford to alienate the public by radical direct action.

In addition to her pacifist activities, Hughan was also an active Socialist. Her interest in politics and economic change began in 1886 when, as a child of ten, she watched her father manage Henry George's campaign for Mayor of New York. She took a Ph.D. in political science at Columbia and with Jack London, Upton Sinclair and Harry Laidler founded the Inter-collegiate Socialist Society in 1905. She worked with the League for Industrial Democracy and was several times a Socialist candidate for public office, including New York Secretary of State, Lieutenant Governor and U.S. Senator. She was sometimes harassed and consistently bypassed for promotion because she advanced socialist and pacifist ideas and organizations.

Leaflet from Jessie Wallace Hughan's write-in campaign. Swarthmore College Peace Collection.

war against Germany until the Germans attacked Russia. It then transformed itself instantly into the American People's Mobilization, and urged that the United States enter the war with the Soviet Union against Nazi Germany.

As the world mobilized for war, liberal and leftist elements of the anti-war movement abandoned their position to support Roosevelt's policy of preparedness, collective security and finally war. Many pacifists saw military force as the only way to stop Hitler. Rabbi Judah Magnes, a pacifist since World War I, acknowledged that a war with Germany may be immoral, but, he said in despair, "we do not know what else to do." When the Nazis attacked Belgium the scientist Einstein said, "Were I a Belgian, I should not, in the present circumstances, refuse military service; rather I should enter such service cheerfully in the belief that I would thereby be helping to save European civilization." It was Einstein who presented President Roosevelt with the idea to build an atomic bomb. His fear was that Germany had the capability to produce one itself. It was never his intention to use the bomb against Japan. □

Members of the Pennsylvania branch of the Women's International League for Peace and Freedom with "Jingo the Dinosaur" at a disarmament demonstration, 1933. Ellen Brenton/Swarthmore College Peace Collection.

Anti-war postcard, c. 1939. Swarthmore College Peace Collection.

THE CATHOLIC WORKER
(Founded 1933)

The Catholic Worker was founded on New York's Lower East Side to encourage Christian pacifism, forthright defense of those who suffer social injustice, and dedication to "personalist" social action. In its houses of hospitality, soup kitchens, farms, and direct actions, the Catholic Worker movement has articulated and demonstrated the radical nonviolence inherent in genuine Christianity. The Worker's political and economic theory came from Peter Maurin, an itinerant French peasant and social philosopher, but it was the insight and practical experience of Dorothy Day, a journalist and convert to Catholicism, which helped to build a movement around Maurin's ideas.

In the midst of the Depression, Maurin emphasized the need for worker ownership of the means of production, agrarian-based communities, institutions of mutual aid, and voluntary poverty so that people could get away from dependence on the state. His vision of a "personalist

revolution" presented in short, simple essays, called for a synthesis of "cult, culture, and cultivation." He encouraged people to take responsibility for bringing the new social order themselves by gathering in urban communities to serve the unemployed with food and shelter, by establishing farming communities to aid a return to the land for those being squeezed out of the urban capitalist economy, and by engaging in roundtable discussions to clarify how persons might live the revolution in their daily situations. Maurin pointed out, "Lenin said, 'There can be no revolution without a theory of revolution,' so I am trying to give the theory of a green revolution."

Peter Maurin was born in 1877, one of 23 children, and grew up in communal life in St. Julien, France. After five years with the Christian Brothers in Paris, he joined a Catholic social action movement called the Sillon which organized young Catholics into a network of hospitality centers, working people's study clubs, and mutual aid

Catholic Worker soupline at 115 Mott Street, New York City, c. 1936. Catholic Worker.

groups. He was a laborer in Canada for seven years, then taught French in Chicago and Woodstock before moving to New York City.

Maurin was a short and stocky man who loved to talk with people, often going out into the highways and byways to find them. A great pamphlet distributor, he spoke from Union Square soapboxes as well as at parish halls and college auditoriums. He enjoyed wandering around the country, speaking at schools and seminaries, or just traveling, sleeping in bus stations or in dormitory flophouses, rarely changing his clothes, always urging individuals to practice the corporal and spiritual works of mercy. He lived in voluntary poverty, believing that there was plenty of money in the world, but what was needed was people absorbed with the right ideas. When he died at a Catholic Worker farm in 1949, he was buried in a donated suit of clothes in a donated grave in Brooklyn.

Maurin's ideas on money and interest harked back to Biblical teachings and the tradition of the Christian church. "The Prophets of Israel," he wrote, "and the Fathers of the Church forbid lending money at interest. Lending money at interest is called usury by the Prophets of Israel and the Fathers of the Church." In another "Easy Essay" he wrote, "Money is by definition a means of exchange and not a means to make money." He often alluded to the fact that the Church never formally lifted its centuries-old ban on interest-taking or usury.

Maurin focused on the collision of capitalism with the teaching of Jesus, a collision which occurs in the use to which surplus money and possessions are put. In the capitalistic code, exemplified in the Puritan ethic, surplus money is to be invested for profit. In the society which Maurin conceived, people would channel their surplus money to those in need. "Money given to the poor," he said, "is functional money, money that fulfills its function. Money used for investment is prostituted money, money that does not fulfill its function." Instead of capital formation for profit, surplus funds and resources would be channeled into small industries producing for peoples' needs. The right of the producer to human work would be considered in contrast to modern society's concentration on the consumer.

He reminded people who took interest for granted that it had only been legalized at a certain point in history, the point at which the take-off of capitalist enterprise had occurred. "When Calvin legalized money-lending at interest," he wrote, "he made the bank account the standard of values. Because John Calvin legalized money-lending at interest, the State has legalized money-lending at interest."

Maurin always maintained that he was far more radical than Marx since Marx did not analyze in depth the anti-human aspects of work under the industrial system, whether capitalist or not. Maurin phrased his idea of revolution in pithy maxims: "The future will be different only if the present is different" and "Be the person you want the other person to be." He always sought concordances, even with social ideas that seemed diametrically opposed to his own, and echoed the Wobblies in aiming to build "the new society in the shell of the old." This, he felt, could not be done by violence but by example and by helping to change the minds of men through "clarification of thought." He wanted to help form a society "in which it would be easier for people to be good."

It was these ideas that Peter Maurin brought to Dorothy Day, a woman with an intimate knowledge of the American social order and the radical Left. She was 35 years old when they met, with long experience in radical politics and in reporting social conditions for the Socialist *Call* in New York, the *New Masses,* and after her conversion to Catholicism, for a lay-edited Catholic magazine, *Commonweal.* She wanted something more to do besides simply reporting social conditions. "I wanted to change them, not just report on them," she wrote, "but I had lost faith in revolution. I wanted to love my enemy, whether Capitalist or Communist."

She first met Peter Maurin in 1932 and they exchanged ideas for several months before deciding to start a monthly newspaper. Day later wrote:

I had been a Catholic only about four years, and Peter, having suggested that I get out a paper to reach the man in the street, started right in on my education; he was a born teacher, and any park bench, coffee shop counter, bus or lodging house was a place to teach. He believed in starting on a program at once, without waiting to acquire classroom or office or meeting hall. To reach the man in the street, you went to the street. Peter was literal.

Peter Maurin at Maryfarm, Easton, Pennsylvania, c. 1938. Catholic Worker.

The first issue of *The Catholic Worker* was sold for a penny a copy at the 1933 May Day celebration in Union Square, New York City. The first issue dealt with black workers exploited by the War Department as cheap labor on the levees in the South. It also contained articles on women and children in industry, and on the spread of unemployment. Subsequent issues carried news of strikes and working conditions throughout the country and news and analyses of developments abroad.

The people affiliated with *The Catholic Worker,* including many workers, students, and poor who come to volunteer, felt that they could not write about issues without participating in them. In 1935 they picketed the German consulate to protest the treatment of European Jews. Catholic Workers acted as a roving strike support team during the organizing days of the CIO. They went to Arkansas to support the Tenant Farmers Union and helped with the formation of the National Maritime Union in 1936.

The editorial position of *The Catholic Worker* was consistently pacifist throughout class war, race war, the Ethiopian War, the Spanish Civil War, all through the second World War, the Korean War, and the war in Indochina. The paper ran countless articles challenging the Catholic thesis of a "just war" and supported the position that Catholics can and should be conscientious objectors. Pacifism was popular in the early Thirties and the paper soon had a circulation of over 110,000; over 30 houses of hospitality were established by enthusiastic followers and nine farming communes followed. During the Depression, the New York Catholic Worker house served meals to as many as 3000 people a day.

In 1935, members organized a branch of the English PAX movement to study Catholic teachings on the morality of war. After the introduction of conscription, this became the Association of Catholic Conscientious Objectors. Having struggled for the right of Catholics to be COs, the Worker supported several Civilian Public Service camps for a time during the war for the fortunate ones who had won CO recognition from their draft boards. With most male members in prison or camps, however, many of the houses of hospitality were forced to close.

After the war, Robert Ludlow, editor of the paper, wrote lucidly and frequently of the need for a nonviolent revolution and the Worker became the center for a unique

brand of anarchist pacifism. In the early Fifties, Ammon Hennacy led the Worker into a new period of activism and established a liaison with the larger peace movement, especially the War Resisters League. It was Hennacy's idea to refuse to take shelter during the New York City Civil Defense air raid drills. The Worker was also strongly influenced by the monk, writer, and poet Thomas Merton, whose theological writings helped to develop a new theology of peace by clarifying the Catholic pacifist stand and encouraging nonviolent resistance. Activist priests Daniel and Philip Berrigan and socialist writer Michael Harrington also shared in Catholic Worker efforts.

During the Cold War, Catholic Workers opposed the use or testing of nuclear weapons and condemned the growing militarism of the United States. In the late Fifties and early Sixties, they were active participants in various Committee for Nonviolent Action projects and founded the Catholic Peace Fellowship and the second American PAX association, which later merged with Pax Christi, the International Movement for Peace founded in Europe after World War II. As an active sponsor of PAX, Dorothy Day spoke at the organization's annual meetings, held at the Catholic Worker farm in Tivoli, New York, on the application of gospel nonviolence to modern war and modern life.

In the mid-Sixties, Catholic Workers were in the forefront of the anti-Vietnam war protests where they worked in concert with other nonviolent groups. In August 1963, the Worker called what may have been the first U.S. demonstration against the war in Vietnam, a picket outside the residence of the South Vietnamese observer to the United Nations. By 1967, most of the young men of the Worker were either in jail or on their way to jail for resisting the war. In the Seventies, the Worker continued to encourage noncooperation with the draft and war taxes and actively supported the United Farm Workers Union.

The Catholic Worker movement has had much influence on the development of active nonviolence in the U.S. Some of the 47 communities associated with it are no more than storefronts. Others are like the Los Angeles house, which conducts an extensive program and publishes a monthly newspaper, *The Catholic Agitator.* Throughout the country, all continue their daily work of direct service to the poor and their witness to the ideals of voluntary poverty, personal action, and community.

Illustration by Ade Bethune. *Catholic Worker.*

CHAPTER 5

WORLD WAR II AND THE PACIFIST COMMUNITY

PACIFISTS STAND ALONE

As the second World War began to seem inevitable, the anti-war movement started to dissolve, leaving a small hard core group of pacifists to oppose the war in isolation. Evan Thomas, now chairman of the War Resisters League, saw history repeating itself. In 1939 he summed up the abortive efforts of politicians the world over to avoid a repetition of the first World War:

> During the past few years we have seen the most frantic efforts to preserve peace. Individuals, organizations and movements that had little in common except a momentary desire to help stop Hitler shouted for a united front and hoped that that would turn the trick. Conservatives who desired only the status quo thought they could have peace by appeasing Hitler. Communists shouted for peace and democracy and practiced just the opposite. The only point on which all these varied move-

Street-speaking about pacifism at one of the War Resisters League's weekly street corner meetings during World War II, New York City. Harry Patton/Swarthmore College Peace Collection.

Prison drawing by Lowell Naeve from *A Field of Broken Stones*.

ments agreed was that, if all else failed, militarism must be met with militarism. The result was war. How could it have been otherwise? War was the inevitable answer to such a setup.

Numerous coalitions of pacifist organizations were created, often under the leadership of A. J. Muste who, in 1940, became executive secretary of the FOR, but they had little effect on public opinion. The Rev. John Haynes Holmes stated the pacifist position against the waning anti-war tide:

See the multitudes of men and women, thousands of them, boys and girls in the colleges, who were against all war in 1930 and 1931 and 1932-37; and then began to hem and haw in 1938 and 1939; and today at last are full fledged supporters of the present war! Yesterday, they were rapturously taking the Oxford Oath; today they are as rapturously taking the oath to King and Country. What has happened? The same thing that happened in the last war. Propaganda has worked its miracle of changing an imperialist war into a holy crusade for no other reason than it is being fought now and therefore can be made to seem one more crisis in the course of civilization. To such propaganda the genuine pacifist is immune. He had thought his problem through . . . He knows that war solves no problems; that war destroys victors along with vanquished; that war is murder and therefore wrong.

When the Japanese attacked Pearl Harbor, December 7, 1941, only Jeannette Rankin voted in Congress against the declaration of war. The War Resisters League, in a statement from the executive

committee to the membership, expressed its reluctant acquiescence to the war:

> *Our country is now at war. However faulty our government's foreign policies may have been, we recognize that the Japanese attack, followed by the war declarations of Germany and Italy, left no choice for those who believe in military defense. We also recognize that the vast majority of Americans are now determined to prosecute this war with energy and steadfastness. This leaves pacifists with a peculiarly difficult responsibility. Under no circumstances, regardless of cost to ourselves, can we abandon our principles, our faith, in methods that are the opposite to those demanded by war. Likewise, under no circumstances do we have any intention of obstructing or interfering with the civil or military officials in carrying out the will of the government. We respect the point of view of those of our fellow citizens to whom war presents itself as a patriotic duty, and we wish to cooperate with them in all community affairs to the limit of our principles as defined by conscience.*

A JUST WAR

If any war could be called a "Just War," then World War II seemed it. The pacifist community, recognizing the threat of fascism long before the U.S.

government, had protested the persecution of the Jews at a time when the Roosevelt government feigned ignorance of its happening. Much of the early anti-Hitlerism was later called "premature anti-Nazism." Many pacifists, even absolutists like Evan Thomas, recognized the moral dilemma that pacifism presented against a regime like that of Hitler. Speaking of his friends who abandoned nonviolence to fight fascism in Europe, Thomas wrote, "Emotionally, I can understand fully why they did this, and I have felt myself that evil such as Hitler represents must be resisted." But how, Thomas asked? "Following the last war," he continued, "I saw enough actual discrimination and brutality in this country to realize that people like Hitler were not unique. I had to make up my mind at that time what I considered to be the best form of resistance to that sort of thing. . . . I came to the conclusion . . . that violence is no answer to tyranny, exploitation or brutality."

Many pacifists, including A. J. Muste, argued that the war was more a cause of the extermination of the Jewish population of Eastern Europe than a help in avoiding it. Certainly, by the time the Allied armies liberated the concentration camps, it was too late. As early as 1942 pacifists were aware of the survival prospects of European Jewry. At a time when the death camps were still only rumors, Jessie Wallace Hughan wrote that extermination, as a government policy, would be "natural" considering the pathological point of view of the Nazis. "It seems that the only way to save thousands and perhaps millions of Jews from destruction," she continued, "would be for our government to broadcast the promise" of an "armistice on condition that the European minorities are not molested any further. . . . It would be very terrible if six months from now, we should find that this threat has literally come to pass without our making even a gesture to prevent it."

When, during the next year, it became known that at least two million Jews had already been killed, she urged the State Department to declare a cease fire. She urged that German military defeats would only invite reprisals on the Jewish scapegoats and thus hasten their extermination and that an Allied "victory will not save them for dead men cannot be liberated." Her prophecy turned out tragically to be true. Until late in the war, the State Department denied Hitler's persecution and the U.S. military made no effort to rescue Jews or liberate concentration camps except as they were encountered during the conquest of Germany.

Representative Jeannette Rankin in a telephone booth surrounded by reporters after voting against the declaration of war with Japan, Washington D.C., December 8, 1941. Wide World.

Bottom right: Anti-conscription cartoon from *The Conscientious Objector*. Swarthmore College Peace Collection.

A PROPHETIC WITNESS

Such pacifist arguments seemed specious at the time; the overwhelming majority of Americans considered the war a necessity. Many pacifists probably agreed with Jim Peck, who recollected after serving his term in Danbury, "I was convinced that a second World War was coming and I knew that when it did, I would refuse to kill and would be imprisoned as a result. I knew that my action and that of other COs would not stop the war. Yet I thought that setting an example was worthwhile."

The individual witness of the thousands of pacifists who refused to serve during this war proved more prophetic than possibly they had hoped. They alone addressed themselves to the future, to the problem, as Niccolo Tucci expressed it in 1945, of "not how to get rid of the enemy, but rather how to get rid of the last victor. For what is a victor but one who has learned that violence works? Who will teach *him* a lesson?"

Who, indeed, but the hard core pacifists who hoped against all odds "to set an example"? Sure enough, the victors of this war became the aggressors in the next wars, cold and hot. The United States, France and the Soviet Union were invaders in Cuba, Santo Domingo, Indochina, Algeria,

Mock test tribunal for prospective conscientious objectors, New York City, September 23, 1940. Roger Baldwin, of the American Civil Liberties Union, Dr. Evan Thomas, of the War Resisters League, and Herman Reissig act as draft board judges while Rev. Francis Hall, a Methodist ministerial student, plays the role of the conscientious objector. Wide World.

Hungary and Czechoslovakia. The two superpowers expended their resources in creating a delicate balance of power that split the world into two opposing camps. Both sides justified militarism to keep the other in check. The war years provided an opportunity for the military in both countries to indoctrinate millions of civilian conscripts in the authoritarian values of military life. As Lawrence S. Wittner wrote, "The veterans of World War II, like those of previous wars, showed a strong proclivity toward militarism in the postwar period; the major difference seems to have been that after 1945 there were more of them."

THE PACIFIST COMMUNITY

Of all the people of the United States, only the pacifists were immune to the war fervor and the growing belief of most Americans that the security of the nation depended on military power. The isolation of the pacifist movement, in prisons and Civilian Public Service (CPS) camps, helped create the feeling of a separate community. Pacifists had their own support organizations and their own publications. *The Conscientious Objector*, a monthly paper edited by Jay Nelson Tuck, gave thorough coverage to the movement as a whole, while Julius Eichel's *The Absolutist* advanced the argument for noncooperation. Eichel fought for the rights of COs inside prison. He also organized the Families & Friends of Imprisoned COs, which helped keep up the morale of COs' relatives and friends and at the same time conveyed a better understanding of why their sons, husbands or friends were doing time for their principles.

Eichel, himself, had been imprisoned as a CO in World War I. In September 1942 he became the only CO to be imprisoned in both World Wars when he was arrested for nonregistration and placed under bail of $25,000. Though technically within the age bracket for registration, men who had been of draft age during the first World War were not being drafted in the second, and he was released. Pacifist organizations counseled COs, intervened with the government in their behalf and gave publicity and support to the noncooperators protesting prison conditions and CPS injustice. The WRL, especially, earned a reputation for sticking up for the radical pacifists whose growing militancy, as the

Back page of a leaflet from the People's Peace Now Committee distributed during a demonstration against the war, Washington D.C., 1943. Dave Dellinger.

Julius Eichel's Notice of Arraignment for refusing to cooperate with the draft during World War II. Julius Eichel Collection.

war ground on, continually got them into trouble with government authorities.

World War II COs had something else going for them that their World War I counterparts lacked: the beginning of a theoretical study of Gandhian nonviolence as a positive force for social change. Gandhi's brand of nonviolence emphasized building decentralized communities grounded in truth, justice and mutual aid, and encouraged the use of mass civil disobedience and noncooperation when the state interfered with the constructive program. Gandhi's work in India was popularized in the United States by Richard Gregg, A. J. Muste, Jessie Wallace Hughan, Reinhold Niebuhr, and others, and by the 1940s, pacifists had begun to implement American versions of Gandhi's program. They started with communities, variously called colonies or ashrams, and by the end of the war, they had gained more experience with organized direct action techniques.

Two of the communities inspired by Gandhi's example were the Harlem Ashram (1940-47) and the Newark, New Jersey, Communal Colony. Jay Holmes Smith, the leading spirit of the Harlem

Ashram, was a U.S. missionary recalled from India because of his open solidarity with the Gandhian movement for independence. A half dozen pacifists formed the core of the community; they shared all possessions and a disciplined, Christian-oriented way of life, including living at a near poverty level. During the war, the Harlem Ashram sponsored Gandhian-type walks, the "Food for Europe Pilgrimages," to press the U.S. government to send food and clothes to starving citizens in German-occupied Europe. The Newark Commune (1939-1944), founded by Dave Dellinger and others from Union Theological Seminary, included over sixty people. Located in the heart of the Newark ghetto, the commune served as a cultural center for the children of the neighborhood, black and white. It also organized a cooperative buying program and later purchased a farm in Chester, N.J., which was worked communally. After the war some of the Newark Commune's members helped organize the Glen Gardner, N.J., Commune and the Libertarian Press, a workers' cooperative where *Liberation* magazine and numerous other publications were printed.

Chester Farm, Newark, New Jersey communal colony, c. 1942. Swarthmore College Peace Collection.

Leaflet from the War Resisters League, August 1944. War Resisters League.

Vol. I   JUNE 11, 1943   No. 1

THE PACIFIST REVOLUTION

PACIFISM is the revolutionary movement of the twentieth century. It is revolutionary because pacifists are now beginning to realize that successful opposition to war depends upon a far-reaching social program that will offer other means than war for the adjustment of international differences.

There is little agreement among pacifists as to what their program ought to involve, but all—excepting only the groups whose pacifism is little more than a refusal to endanger their personal salvation by the sin of killing—perceive that the entire structure and momentum of modern society must undergo a great change before peace can be assured. Eighteenth century revolutionists saw this need for reconstituting the social order, but they used means which destroyed the ends they had in view. The progress they achieved was because of the ideals they believed in and spread through education, and in spite of the violent means they adopted.

The pacifist revolutionaries of the twentieth century have learned their lesson—they know that it is utterly useless to try to force human progress. The old formula, "Kill the tyrants, write a constitution, and establish a new educational system," doesn't work. Every tyrannicide is himself a potential Caesar; he has already acknowledged the superiority of the tyrant's method by using it.

Legalism Fails

But what about the rest of the revolutionary formula? How about a new constitution? Americans have profound faith in legal documents. Nineteenth century visitors to America returned to Europe with the discovery that we are "a nation of lawyers." It is natural that, having had marked success with our own constitution, we should now seek a legal pattern for world government, in order to assure peace.

We forget, however, that the Constitution of the United States simply codified and gave unity to attitudes and convictions which already existed in the minds of many of the people. The Constitution was shaped by political realists who were able to give concise expression to a state of mind that had grown up through a century or more of experience and education.

No such common ground for world government exists today. To write a grandiose constitution "uniting" the nations, and then to make the peoples of the world believe that the establishment of this international institution will usher in an epoch of peace would be the greatest and most tragic deception in history. The failure of the constitution to unite the nations would convince almost everyone that the Nazis were right—that internationalism is visionary folly. The price paid for unintelligent optimism is always cynical disillusionment.

"Unexamined Beliefs"

History shows that successfully functioning institutions are effects, not causes. We cannot create the legal fiction of world government and then sit back and wait for the miracle to take place. First there must be the will of peoples to live in order and peace, and, in the words of à Kempis, they must want "those things that make for peace."

An English sociologist, David Fryd, has pointed out:

A war like the present one or that of 1914-18 could never occur—whatever the interests of the ruling caste involved—unless the mass of the people on each side held certain beliefs about the State, the government, the Fatherland, freedom, democracy, and so on. It may be argued that people can always be stirred by propaganda; but this is true only if that propaganda is directed towards the deep-seated and largely unexamined beliefs that the mass of the people actually hold.

(Turn to page 2)

In addition to being the locus for theoretical discussions about nonviolence, these communities also began to use nonviolent tactics. The Harlem Ashram was a center for nonviolent activity for racial justice, against British imperialism in India and against U.S. rule in Puerto Rico. The Newark Commune organized the Essex County Equality League which picketed and sat-in at restaurants and movie houses that discriminated against blacks. The Commune also engaged in direct action for improved welfare, neighborhood improvement, an end to police brutality, free hot lunches in the schools, and community participation in decisions that affected it.

The Newark colony also sparked organization of a People's Peace Now Committee which picketed the U.S. Capitol in Washington, leafleted at factory gates, and held poster walks in half a dozen major cities during the war. The Committee energetically protested the saturation bombing of German cities, the U.S. refusal to open its doors to Jewish refugees, and the Unconditional Surrender policy that prolonged the war. The Commune, Dave Dellinger wrote, "along with the Catholic Worker and other small but ambitious centers of communal economics, local organizing, and national actions, served as a bridge from the Old Left radicalism of the Thirties to a complex of ideas and actions that later gained prominence in the civil rights movement, the New Left" and other movements in later years. These and other communities became centers for COs during the war and many resisters passed through on their way to and from prison.

In 1942, Jessie Wallace Hughan wrote "Pacifism and Invasion" which described how a nation could nonviolently resist an invasion by even as ruthless an aggressor as Nazi Germany. The writings of Aldous Huxley and Bertrand Russell and reports of the nonviolent resistance of the Norwegians and Danes to Nazi occupation also gave pacifists further hope for the idea of nonviolence as an effective social force. By the end of the war, there emerged a radical pacifist community of nonviolent activists with the experience and an evolving program to challenge the status quo.

THE SELECTIVE SERVICE ACT

The Selective Service Act of 1940 was an improvement over the Conscription Law of 1917. Although only religious objectors were recognized as sincere by the government, the definition of religion was broadened considerably by subsequent court rulings. Those who would not serve as noncombatants in the military had the option of serving time in Civilian Public Service (CPS) camps doing work in the national interest. Though the CPS camps were under the authority of the government, the three traditional peace churches, Friends, Brethren and Mennonite, were given financial and administrative responsibility. In addition, the National Service Board for Religious Objectors (NSBRO) was created, with the AFSC, FOR, WRL and other pacifist organizations as sponsors, to oversee the direction of the camps.

There were an estimated 52,000 government classified COs during the second World War. Of this number, 25,000 men were classified 1-A-O to do noncombatant service within the military and

Cover of *Pacifica Views*, the weekly journal of CPS and imprisoned conscientious objectors, June 11, 1943. Institute for the Study of Nonviolence.

*"IMPRACTICAL MEN, MY BOY— ANY OTHER
FORCE THAN A FORCE OF ARMS IS
IMPRACTICAL ! IM-M-PRACTICAL !"

11,996, classified IV-E, were assigned to civilian service in one of the 151 CPS camps. There, COs did back-breaking labor without pay planting trees, reclaiming rural areas for agriculture, and assisting farmers in soil conservation. Others volunteered for special projects, working as attendants in mental hospitals, training as "smoke jumpers" to fight forest fires in mountain areas, and being human guinea pigs in medical and research experiments.

In addition, 6,086 men refused to cooperate with the draft to the point of serving prison sentences, a jump in number from 450 in the previous war. Three-fourths of the imprisoned COs during World War II were Jehovah's Witnesses. The others were more traditional pacifists and included those who refused to register for the draft, those who refused to apply for CO status, those who refused governmental orders to perform alternative service, and those who grew into more intransigent positions. As the war progressed, there was a growing awareness that legal recognition was at least as much a military convenience as an acknowledgment of conscience.

Free India Committee demonstration outside the British Embassy, Washington D.C., c. 1943. Swarthmore College Peace Collection.

Cartoon from *The Conscientious Objector.* Swarthmore College Peace Collection.

WAR RESISTERS LEAGUE
(Founded 1923)

The War Resisters League, (WRL) founded to support non-religious conscientious objectors, has served for over 50 years to unite political, humanitarian, and philosophical objectors to war. The League helped to move pacifism from its traditional emphasis on individual resistance to war towards an organized and active revolutionary movement against the complex causes of war. After the second World War, the War Resisters League took the lead in advocating fundamental political, economic, and social change by nonviolent means and was of major importance in the peace, civil rights, student and personal liberation movements of the Sixties and Seventies.

The League began largely through the efforts of Jessie Wallace Hughan, Tracy Mygatt, and Frances Witherspoon and with the help of the Fellowship of Reconciliation. Evelyn Hughan and Abraham Kaufman worked in the early years to establish the League as a national organization and Dr. Evan Thomas and Rev. John Haynes Holmes were also important figures in the movement. During its first decade, the League lobbied for peace and secured signatures to its pledge: "War is a crime against humanity.

We therefore are determined not to support any kind of war and to strive for the removal of all causes of war."

By the mid-Thirties, over 12,000 Americans, many of them socialists, anarchists, and independent radicals, had signed the War Resisters League pledge.

The League soon outgrew its role as a register of COs and became deeply involved in anti-war education in the Thirties, still particularly emphasizing individual resistance to war. Activities included parades and demonstrations on particular issues, street meetings and lectures, testimony before. Congressional committees, annual conferences and dinners, and attempts to influence others through letter writing, literature, and petitions.

During the second World War, the League centered its work around maintaining the morale of COs and helping them through the intricacies of draft board and court procedures. Field Secretary Frank Olmstead personally visited 18 prisons and some 100 camps and CPS units, lending support and encouragement to war resisters, reporting ill treatment, and helping with hardship cases. The League published the monthly paper *The Conscien-*

Pacifists at the 1941 War Resisters League conference. Paul Limbert is standing third from left; Evan Thomas is at the center rear; Jewish leader Isidor Hoffman is standing fourth from right; Lillian Mosesco, founder of *The Conscientious Objector*, is standing second from right; and Jessie Wallace Hughan is on the far right. Photo courtesy of Abe Kaufman.

tious Objector and actively supported those COs who went to prison rather than cooperate with the war-making government.

After the war, resisters like Dave Dellinger, Jim Peck, Ralph DiGia, Igal Roodenko, Bayard Rustin, George Houser, and Roy Finch brought a new militancy to the League. Together with militant pacifists like A.J. Muste, Roy Kepler, and George Reeves, they began to organize projects through the League which reached out to treat the root causes of war. WRL organized a number of street demonstrations to protest nuclear bomb tests, to urge a general amnesty for war objectors, and to oppose universal conscription. They organized mass demonstrations against Civil Defense drills and protested the official actions of the American, and many foreign, governments. League members also participated in the civil rights movement from the first Freedom Ride in 1947, during which all three of the men who were jailed were WRL members, to the voter registration drives and anti-poverty campaigns of the Sixties and Seventies. The League was instrumental in founding *Liberation* magazine, the Committee for Nonviolent Action, and the Student Peace Union in the Fifties.

With the advent of the Vietnam war, the WRL grew in size and influence. It co-sponsored the first nationwide anti-war demonstration in 1964 and continued in the forefront of coalition protests and national and local demonstrations throughout the war years. The major thrust of its program was at the grass roots: by 1973, the membership had grown from 3,000 to 15,000, with some thirty local and four regional offices. The League has also been affiliated, since its early days, with the War Resisters International, formerly headquartered in London and now in Belgium, which includes sections in 23 countries and maintains contacts in at least 40 others.

The League was especially active in promoting draft resistance during the war in Vietnam. It co-sponsored the first draft card burning to protest the war and in 1967 initiated a campaign of noncooperation that led thousands of young men to risk felony indictments by returning their draft cards to the government. That same year, the League sponsored a Stop the Draft Week in New York and the San Francisco Bay Area which received substantial national publicity when hundreds were arrested for their nonviolent obstruction of induction centers. In 1971, WRL produced the tactical manual for, and was the only national organization endorsing, the week-long Mayday demonstrations.

WRL helped publish *WIN* magazine, an outgrowth of the New York Workshop in Nonviolence, and continued to promote war tax resistance, amnesty, and disarmament after the end of the war. A founder of the Coalition on the Economic Crisis, WRL also initiated the Continental Walk for Disarmament and Social Justice during the United States' bicentennial year.

OUR ATTITUDE TOWARD PRISON PROBLEMS

(Adpoted by the Executive Committee of the War Resisters League November 15, 1943)

In presenting authentic news about conscientious objectors in prison the War Resisters League has no desire to embarrass the Bureau of Prisons nor does it have any animosity against any individual in the prison system. The League is well aware of the difficulties presented by C.O.s in prison and it can sympathize with officials who have to be responsible for their welfare.

Conscientious objectors do not belong in prison. However great the desire of C.O.s to identify themselves with other prisoners for the good of all, it still is a fact that C.O.s in prison represent a unique problem which can only be solved by their unconditional release. Their presence in prison should be a national scandal. However successful or unsuccessful our prison system may be in the social rehabilitation of others, it was not created, as officers of the Bureau of Prisons freely admit, for people like C.O.s. From a sociological point of view the weak or vicious individual who is anti-social in his thinking and conduct presents a problem which is at the opposite pole from the conscientious objector. To ignore this fact is unrealistic and is certain to cause trouble. Any prison system which is so inflexible as to be unable to make this distinction and act accordingly is open to legitimate criticism.

Granted that the only solution of the C.O. problem in prison is to get C.O.s out of prison, it is still imperative that pacifists and all Americans should know the facts about conditions in prison and that C.O.s should be able to present those facts as well as their opinions to the outside world. Isolated brutalities or injustices whether suffered by C.O.s or other prisoners cannot be ignored by decent people because they are relatively infrequent. If this is done, mistreatment soon becomes the rule. Above all, pacifists cannot afford to look the other way or excuse specific charges of cruelty or injustice, however thankful they may be for tolerable conditions and past reforms.

Consequently the WRL considers itself morally bound to present to its members and the public all charges and complaints made by C.O.s in prison. Every effort is made to check on the truth of these charges or complaints through the Bureau of Prisons and other sources. In all circumstances it is committed to giving the facts about injustices as far as this is possible.

W A R   R E S I S T E R S   L E A G U E
2 STONE STREET • NEW YORK 4, N. Y.

265   5M 12 43

Leaflet from the War Resisters League, 1943. War Resisters League.

Office of *The Conscientious Objector* at 2 Stone Street, New York City c. 1940. Bruce Brown and Ida Kaufman are in the foreground. Photo courtesy of Abe Kaufman.

A Call To...
A DAY OF NATIONAL MOURNING

OCTOBER 16, 1940

The President has proclaimed October 16, 1940 to be Registration Day for conscription for military service.

We declare Registration Day to be a Day of National Mourning!

For on this day—

Free men lose their freedom, their jobs, their home environment.

War is brought nearer by the creation of a military state.

Youth are regimented in military camps for involuntary service to the state.

The existence of free trade unions is threatened.

America's resources are turned to destruction, not to the conquest of suffering and poverty.

CONSCRIPTION CAN BE REPEALED!

On Registration Day demonstrate against this act which gives fascism its first major victory in America! Demonstrate to repeal conscription!

Mourn the death of liberty by wearing the traditional black, a solemn warning that we will still act to prevent mourning for the death of American youth in war.

Fight for free speech, free thought, and free action which are violated so flagrantly by this measure.

Carry on the struggle against war and involvement in war.

Build the security of peace-time plenty, and avert the false prosperity of armament spending.

By every democratic means, work to blot this law from the statute books.

BLACK-OUT CONSCRIPTION

SPONSORS:

- CATHOLIC WORKER
- KEEP AMERICA OUT OF WAR CONGRESS
- LABOR ANTI-WAR COUNCIL
- PROGRESSIVE STUDENTS LEAGUE
- NATIONAL COUNCIL OF METHODIST YOUTH
- WAR RESISTERS LEAGUE
- WOMEN'S INTERNATIONAL LEAGUE FOR PEACE AND FREEDOM
- YOUNG PEOPLES SOCIALIST LEAGUE
- YOUTH COMMITTEE AGAINST WAR

Additional Copies of this Call may be obtained from any of the above organizations or the YOUTH COMMITTEE AGAINST WAR, 22 East 17th Street, New York City.

FIRST NONREGISTRANTS

The first act of resistance to the second World War took place on October 16, 1940, the first day of registration under the new draft law. Pacifist organizations organized counter-activities to mark this day as A Day of National Humiliation. Its highlight was the announcement by eight students at the Union Theological Seminary in New York, all eligible for ministerial deferments, and one Socialist, that they would refuse to register for the draft. These nine — Donald Benedict, Joseph J. Bevilacqua, Meredith Dallas, David Dellinger, George Houser, William H. Lovell, Howard E. Spragg, and Richard J. Wichlei, and Stanley Rappaport — were sentenced to a term of one year and a day; and some of them, including Dellinger, were reindicted after their release and forced to serve a second term in jail.

The statement of the eight seminarians read to the court on the day of their sentences said, in part:

> We do not contend that the American people maliciously choose the vicious instrument of war. In a very perplexing situation, they lack the imagination, the religious faith, and the precedents to respond in a different manner. This makes it all the more urgent to build in this country and throughout the world a group trained in the techniques of nonviolent opposition to the encroachments of militarism and fascism. Until we build such a movement, it will be impossible to stall the war machine at home. When we do build such a movement, we will have found the only weapon which can ever give an effective answer to foreign invasion. Thus in learning to fight American Hitlerism we will show an increasing group of war-disillusioned Americans how to resist foreign Hitlers as well.

The eight theological students joined with eight other COs in the first prison strike of the war, April 23, 1941, at Danbury. The issue was whether the COs could abstain from lunch as a demonstration against war. With permission denied, the COs began to noncooperate. According to a report in *The Conscientious Objector*:

> Employing the principles of nonviolent direct action, the strikers refused to move from their dormitories the morning of April 23 and, throughout the day,

Leaflet from anti-draft protest on the first day of registration, October 16, 1940. Julius Eichel Collection.

Eight divinity students who refused to cooperate with the draft are taken away to jail, New York City, November 14, 1940. Left to right: William Lovell, Richard Wichlei, Meredith Dallas, David Dellinger, Joseph Bevilacqua, George Houser, Donald Benedict, and Howard Spragg. UPI.

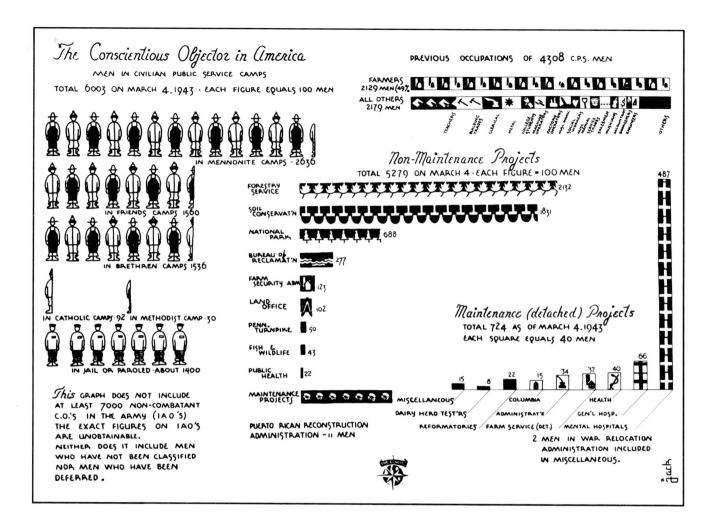

refused to eat, work or cooperate with the prison routine. Prison authorities retaliated and the men were locked up in solitary for two days and, thereafter, deprived of recreation and confined to their cells for thirty days, with the exception of mealtimes and working hours.

CPS CAMPS

Pacifist groups initially supported the CPS camps as a reasonable way of dealing with COs in wartime, especially since the war was a popular one and the camps represented a marked improvement over the way COs were treated during the first World War. The ambiguous division of authority between the Selective Service System and the peace churches which administered and financed the program through the NSBRO invited trouble. The majority of the COs, especially those whose paci-

Chart of Conscientious Objectors in America during the second World War, 1943. *The Compass.*

Civilian Public Service Camp #37, run by the Society of Friends, at Coleville, California (elevation 5800'). Photo courtesy of John Lewis.

fism was purely religious, served their time quietly, even though the work was often meaningless. Politically-oriented COs soon grew restless under the authoritarian nature of the camps, the lack of pay, and absence of socially useful work. These protesters wanted to witness against war, not serve their time tucked quietly away in the countryside.

The first CO to walk out of a CPS camp was Alex Stach. On February 16, 1942, he left the camp at Merom, Indiana, and hitchhiked to the Twin Cities of Minnesota to inform the federal attorney of his action. On leaving the camp he issued a statement to explain his position:

> *A person cannot create a voluntary society in the permanent framework of an involuntary society. A pacifist society must be voluntary, for involuntary service implies the use of force or violence to personality, by definition. The CPS*

"men · · we are all in the same boat.". . .

> *program is an involuntary society that cannot free itself as long as it continues on its same basic assumptions, namely; 1) that a nation can tightly conscript human lives even for apparently good use, and 2) that it is satisfactory and moral for fellow pacifists to act as agents in enforcing involuntary servitude for the Selective Service Act and the United States government.*

Evan Thomas, WRL chairman, was one of the few pacifist leaders to oppose CPS camps, and he urged their abolition at a time when the WRL as a group still supported the system. "Privilege loves to fool itself," Thomas wrote. "Because of its nature, it is unable to face issues squarely or to think in terms of principle. The CPS camps are privilege bought with pacifist money. They represent a weak and ineffectual attempt to skirt the issue of conscription and not to meet it." Thomas felt that if the government wanted a conscription law, it was its duty to provide alternatives for COs. Similarly, it was the duty of the CO who was opposed to the principle of conscription, to protest it in all of its forms. The

Conscientious objectors in a Brethren-run Civilian Public Service camp build a road to a fire lookout at Cascade Locks, Oregon, c. 1942. Swarthmore College Peace Collection.

Bayard Rustin of the Fellowship of Reconciliation, speaking with conscientious objectors at Civilian Public Service camp #152, Powellsville, Maryland, before his arrest for refusing to cooperate with the draft. Swarthmore College Peace Collection.

CPS camps, Thomas felt, were an illogical compromise for they were pacifist financed and thus gave legitimacy to the idea of conscription and to the idea that government has the right to define qualifications for CO status.

The controversy over CPS split the pacifist movement into opposing sides. The militants in the camps and in the prisons felt that their organizations and leaders had compromised and abandoned them. The traditionalists felt that their job was aiding COs, even if this meant critically supporting the CPS experiment, and not in supporting troublemakers whose noncooperation was beside the point. The WRL and leaders like A. J. Muste, who was then executive secretary of the FOR, eventually came over to the absolutist view. This radicalization was the beginning of major changes in the pacifist movement as the militants, coming out of prison and camp, swelled the ranks of many of the nonviolent groups and turned them into more activist and radical organizations.

A. J. Muste reflected the changing view of the

CPS camps during the war:

I had always had great respect for the absolutist position of refusing to register for the draft and refusing to accept any alternative service. I had always backed up those who had taken that position. I did believe at the beginning of the war, however, that the Civilian Public Service Camps, as they had originally been planned, were a major improvement over the brutality toward conscientious objectors in the First War. The work was to have offered a special kind of pacifist witness and was to have been creative social work planned in large part by the religious groups administering the camps. It soon became evident that government control of the camps was quite real, not nominal, and that the creative work was in the line of raking leaves . . . Moreover, the original concept was for the CO to work freely under no disci-

Conscientious objectors protest the Civilian Public Service system of unpaid, forced labor, Minersville, California, Summer 1943. Left to right: John Lewis, Phil Teogue, Clifford Lang, Roy Kepler, Norman Lawson, and Leo Kekoni. Photo courtesy of John Lewis.

Upper left: Cover of *The CPS G.I.*, the mimeographed newsletter put out by men in Civilian Public Service camp #111 at Mancos, Colorado. Drawing by Budd Steinhilber/Courtesy of Roy Kepler.

pline but that of the religious organizations administering the camps. We wound up, however, simply administering conscription for the government. Selective Service retained full control and laid down the rules.

Muste and the FOR withdrew support of CPS in 1944 and he then personally adopted and advocated the absolutist position. The WRL had resigned from the NSBRO in March 1943, causing a few members of its executive committee, including the Rev. John Haynes Holmes and Rabbi Isadore Hoffman, to resign.

THE MURPHY-TAYLOR STRIKE

The most significant walk-out occurred on October 16, 1942, the second anniversary of the Day of National Humiliation. On that day, Stanley Murphy, Louis Taylor and George Kingsley walked out of CPS camp number 46 at Big Flats, N.Y., to protest the camp system as a form of conscription of which they wanted no part. The men were recog-

nized leaders at the camp and their decision was major news. *The Conscientious Objector* reported:

Two nights before they left they read their statements to a camp council meeting, at which a number of the men wept openly. On the day they left the musicians of the camp brightened the farewell scene by striking up Auld Lang Syne *and* For He's A Jolly Good Fellow. *A camper at Big Flats, who reported the walkout for* The Conscientious Objector *commented: "While the views expressed by these men may not be shared by the entire camp, all of the men admire them for taking the stand they did."*

At their trial, in January 1943, at which they were each given two and one half years, Kingsley articulated the absolutist attitude towards the CPS camps. "I felt for a long time," he said, "that a pacifist who accepts work of 'national importance' unwittingly condones the principle of military conscription, and it is the conscription of men, women and labor that I stand in opposition to. . . . CPS is a definite compromise with the war system."

Confined at Danbury Prison, Murphy and Taylor were immediately tossed into solitary for refusing to work. There they began a hunger strike which, in the words of Evan Thomas, "served to wake up the pacifist movement." The hunger strike lasted 82 days. After the seventeenth day the prisoners were removed to the hospital for forced feeding. The promise of reforms in the granting of parole to COs led them to end the strike, but they themselves refused parole on the grounds that that, too, was cooperating with the system.

In retaliation, prison authorities sent the two men to the federal prison hospital in Springfield, Mo., where they were placed in strip cells and beaten by guards. An editorial in *The Conscientious Objector* protested this treatment.

Springfield has been used as a dumping ground for rambunctious COs and the strikers now at Lewisburg fear that fate. At least one CO prisoner – and there are other reports of others who were perfectly sane – has been dumped into a strip cell there. This strip cell, by the way, which the Bureau of Prison officers regard as a 'recognized necessity' for mental patients, is a relic of the Middle Ages. It is bare of all furniture and toilet equipment – literally stripped – and

Leaflet from the Committee for Non-Violent Revolution, c. 1946. Margaret Finch.

prisoners are kept there naked till they become more amenable. . . .

Letters smuggled out of prison by Taylor describing the brutality at Springfield and documenting the fatal beating of at least one prisoner created an uproar in pacifist circles that was taken up by the national press. As a result, investigations of the prison system were begun and reforms made. But of even greater importance, the example of Murphy and Taylor inspired COs throughout the prison system so that by 1943 hardly a month went by where there was not at least one fast, strike or other form of noncooperation somewhere in the prison system. The artist Lowell Naeve, who had already served one term in prison, became convinced "that their hunger strike was doing more for the men in prison than anything else." Back in prison for a second term in 1943, Naeve reported a militant spirit among COs: "nearly everyone . . . wanted to strike back and protest," he said.

Our ultimate aim is a decentralized society. Prison drawing by Lowell Naeve.

EVAN THOMAS
(1890 - 1974)

Evan Thomas championed the cause of war resistance through two World Wars and encouraged the development of militant nonviolence in the post-war period. Imprisoned during the first World War, he became a leader during the second for his opposition to war, conscription, and the Civilian Public Service camps and for his support of war resisters in prison. He defended the rights of COs for half a century and argued that there were political and philosophical reasons for objecting to war which were just as legitimate as the legally-recognized religious basis.

Seeing the rise of totalitarianism throughout the world, Thomas put his whole political trust in individual responsibility and insistence upon freedom. Since conscription was the clearest form through which the state claimed authority over a person's life, Thomas insisted that absolute refusal to cooperate with the draft was the first duty of a person truly in the service of democracy. He expressed his ideas in his war-time essay *The Positive Faith of Pacifism*:

Conscription for war purposes is one of the fundamental manifestations of political absolutism. Without it modern war would be impossible and without war or the threat of war, political absolutism itself would be an anomaly. Therefore, one cannot compromise with conscription for war purposes and accomplish anything positive for freedom or the values on which liberty rests. . . . Unlike war, the refusal to cooperate with tyranny can never destroy the values of democracy. On the contrary, it is a positive contribution to liberty because it is the only way we have of implementing our values in the face of an organized attempt to destroy them. True, the success of non-cooperation with tyranny and exploitation depends on the number of people accepting this method of resistance, but minorities must lead the way. If the appeal of moral integrity to the conscience and reason of mankind fall

Evan Thomas speaking at the War Resisters League Conference, Boundbrook, New Jersey, 1942. Bayard Rustin is on the left. Photo by Sidney Moritz/Courtesy of Margaret Finch.

completely on deaf ears there is no hope anywhere.

Thomas was sentenced to life imprisonment for his refusal to fight in World War I. He wrote that his refusal was "a gesture of protest and an effort to preserve some personal integrity. This can be called self-righteous but to object to war on moral grounds is no more self-righteous than to wage war on moral grounds." So thorough was his rejection of conscription that he would not eat or work under military authority, and eventually he was sent to Leavenworth federal prison. There, in solitary confinement, he was chained to the bars of his cell and forced to remain standing for eight to ten hours a day. His sentence was commuted in 1919.

After his release from prison, Thomas travelled around the country doing odd jobs, including selling encyclopedias door to door, to earn enough money to go to medical school. He received his M.D. in 1930 and, as a professor at New York University Medical College, gained professional renown as a pioneer in the treatment of venereal diseases. As a physician in private practice, he also worked with various public health services and devoted his last ten years to work with retarded children.

During World War II, as chairperson of the War Resisters League, Thomas became the leading spokesperson for the rights of conscientious objectors. He opposed compulsory camps for COs as an enforcement of "slave labor" and encouraged COs in prison to struggle against racial segregation, censorship and brutality. Thomas met often with prison and other government officials to protest treatment of COs. His support of resisters in prison helped draw them into the WRL after the war and he served as the link between them and the older, more service-oriented members of the Executive Committee.

Like his brother Norman, Evan Thomas fought to preserve democracy during the war and articulated the concerns which would lead to a revitalized peace movement after the war.

> *No political program can remove entirely the causes of war nor can any form of social organization make men free in spite of themselves. The very meaning of freedom implies freedom of choice which recognizes human differences and conflicting interests. Any utopia which could remove all causes of conflict is inconceivable and in practice undesirable. . . . The value of democracy consists in its refusal to demand complete conformity and in its ability to keep the struggle of life dynamic rather than static. Thus at best, political democracy is a compromise which seeks*

politics

25¢ a copy   May, 1945

VICTORY !!!

VICTORY. Comes, lights up the horizon and the hearts, and before you know it, it's gone; you have just the ashes and the dead, and instead of ambush, hostage-killing, fight and vengeance, a good chance to grieve, to starve, to see your children die in peace. Makes me sad for those soldiers who are there, in the line, with ideals all theirs, reserved to the military, "requisitioned for the exclusive use of our boys", and forbidden to everybody else at home or abroad. Their job is that of transforming a torture-chamber into a cemetery; a place of terror and of hope into a place without terror and without hope. VICTORY.

(Niccolo Tucci in "Politics", November, 1944.)

to avoid the absolutism of organization. Its goal is not government as an end in itself but the withering away of the state through voluntary cooperation. It must move either in one direction or the other.

With the rise of the Cold War and nuclear weapons in the late Forties, Thomas grew discouraged that pacifists could ever unite effectively to bring about a just social order. He wrote that "ideal peace must be achieved by individuals who are determined to live with as little power over others as possible." However, he saw no clear alternative to meeting the needs of modern civilization other than forms of organization which exercised great power over people. He left the WRL board in 1951, but remained connected to the League, attending its 50th anniversary conference — and picketing with the United Farm Workers Union — in California in 1973 shortly before his death.

Cover of *Politics*, an independent radical journal, May 1945. Institute for the Study of Nonviolence.

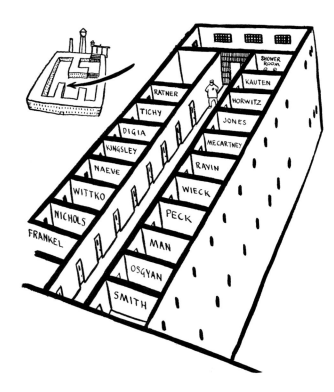

THE DANBURY STRIKE

The most notable prison strike began at Danbury in August 1943 over the policy of racial segregation in the dining hall. Risking loss of good time release and parole, 19 COs, including Naeve, Ralph DiGia, Jim Peck and David T. Wieck, began a work strike that led to their being separated from the prison population, confined to their cells with only 40 minutes a day for exercise, and reduced visiting privileges. The strike lasted 135 days and gained new adherents as it progressed. To pass the time, the men circulated a contraband newspaper and Lowell Naeve made a guitar out of paper maché. Publicity outside the prison, organized by Ruth MacAdam and encouraged by Wieck's parents and absolutists like Evan Thomas and Julius Eichel, brought pressure on the prison system. On December 23, 1943 the warden agreed to end segregation in the dining hall and the strike ended.

Writing of this experience, Peck noted its importance:

> Danbury thus became the first federal prison to abolish Jim Crow seating. COs in several other prisons made similar attacks on segregation, with varying results. It seems to me that the campaigns against racial discrimination may be counted as one of the most important accomplishments of COs in

Front page of *The Conscientious Objector*, August 6, 1943. Roy Kepler.

Forcefeeding during hunger strike. Drawing by Lowell Naeve from *A Field of Broken Stones*.

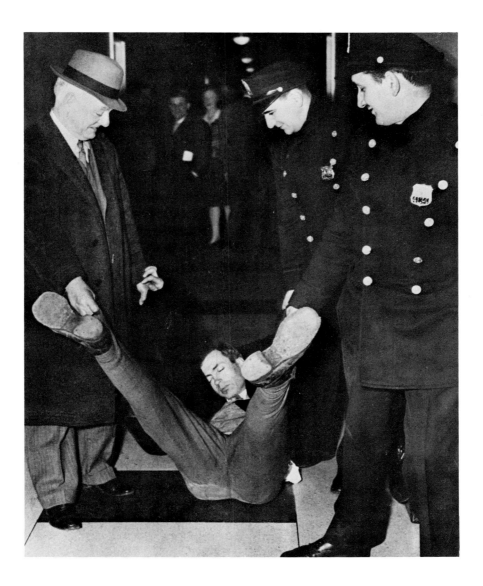

World War II. . . . Within six months Jim Crow was dead and decayed. Danbury being a short term prison, the turnover is fast. Most of the new inmates never heard about the former segregation and the veterans gradually forgot it.

CORBETT BISHOP

The most remarkable act of individual non-cooperation was that of Corbett Bishop who, during three separate prison terms, went a total of 426 days without taking food or water and for 337 of those days maintained a policy of absolute non-cooperation. After his arrest for walking out of a CPS camp in 1944, Bishop said, "The authorities have the power to seize my body; that is all they can do. My spirit will be free." To back this position, Bishop refused to stir from his cot even to use the toilet for the period of his noncooperation. He made the prison officials totally responsible for his body to the point where, if they wanted to move him, they had to carry him themselves.

Bishop was sentenced to four years in prison; but his resistance proved too much for the authorities to bear. He won his unconditional release, extralegally, less than one year after sentencing. Even then he refused to recognize the authority of his jailers. They had to carry him out of the prison to freedom.

Commenting on Bishop's victory, *The Conscientious Objector* said,

> *Nonviolent resistance, applied in a small sphere today, tomorrow can be the bright, strong means of defeating – without war – imperial oppression and aggression throughout the world. . . . Corbett Bishop is a forerunner.* □

Corbett Bishop is carried out of federal court by police after beginning his complete noncooperation with the war effort, Philadelphia, Pennsylvania, February 20, 1945. Wide World.

Upper left: Cells of war resisters during the 135-day work strike against racial segregation at Danbury Federal Prison, 1943. Drawing by Lowell Naeve from *A Field of Broken Stones.*

CHAPTER 6

TOWARDS REVOLUTIONARY NONVIOLENCE

Thermonuclear test explosion, 1952. U.S. Air Force.

NUCLEAR PACIFISM

Postwar pacifism was marked by a sense of urgency brought about by the atomic bombing of the Japanese cities, Hiroshima and Nagasaki, by United States war planes in August 1945. The advent of the nuclear age led many to re-evaluate their views towards war. Humankind seemed at the crossroads. An editor of *The Conscientious Objector* wrote:

> *The one thing that the atomic bomb has achieved, besides the horror of Hiroshima, is a decided simplification of the issues before us, our choice now being a regenerative humanity or literal extinction.*

Fear that the next war would be a nuclear war and that such a war would have neither victors nor survivors turned many people to nuclear pacifism. The nuclear pacifist opposed war on the not impractical grounds that nuclear weapons made war suicidal for all. For others, and this was the argument of government supporters of nuclear weapons, the bomb became the guarantor of peace: the threat of its use would make nations think twice before sending their citizens off to war. As one atomic scientist recalled, "It was not an altogether unrealistic hope

BECAUSE THE PEOPLE OF THE WORLD
ARE TIRED OF THIS

THE RULERS HAVE

THERE CAN BE NO PEACE IN A WORLD IN WHICH

Imperialist Nations such as the United States, Britain, and Russia hold huge sections of the earth in subjection, either as outright colonies or as economic and political dependencies.

The Factories, Mines, Railroads, Shops, and Land are in the hands of profit-seeking private owners or State bureaucrats, while the majority of the people are dispossessed wage-workers who suffer regimentation, insecurity, slums, and depressions.

People rely on physical power to impose their wills on others. The machines of war are kept in readiness (and used for bargaining purposes) through armament factories, atom bombs, armed forces, and conscription.

THESE ARE CAUSES OF WAR. THE UNO CANNOT PREVENT WAR BECAUSE IT PROTECTS THESE CAUSES OF WAR.

EVEN IN "PEACE TIME" THESE EVILS CAUSE UNTOLD FRUSTRATION, DESTRUCTION, AND DEATH.

CONCOCTED THE UNO

PRIVATE INTERESTS WHO PROFIT FROM THESE EVILS OF CAPITALIST OWNERSHIP, COLONIAL DEPENDENTS, STATE DICTATORSHIP, AND WAR ARE PUSHING THE UNO AS AN ALTERNATIVE TO REVOLUTION.

They want to divert the people from winning their full freedom and social equality. Therefore they stage the UNO as a 3-Nation circus in which the other nations are allowed to appear. Already a proposal to outlaw conscription has been quietly shelved; disarmament is not even on the agenda; and the United States continues to manufacture and display atom bombs.

THE MEMBER-STATES SHOW THEIR REAL INTENTIONS BY WHAT THEY ARE DOING IN INDIA, IRAN, PUERTO RICO, CHINA, PALESTINE, JAVA, THE BALTIC STATES, AND OCCUPIED EUROPE.

WE MUST NOT BE SIDETRACKED!
WE MUST ATTACK WAR AND INEQUALITY DIRECTLY:

1. *By refusing to manufacture the tools of murder.* We can demand that our unions go on strike against all manufacture and transportation of the implements of war. As individuals we must refuse to accept any work in munitions plants, no matter what we are offered in the way of higher "blood wages".

2. *By refusing to accept induction into any branch of the armed forces.* We can work against conscription and enlistments. Promote a general strike against war. Begin by refusing to accept military service even if, like the anti-Nazis in Hitlerite Germany, we are subjected to governmental action.

3. *By asserting our solidarity with all people by sending food and clothing to Europe and by insisting on economic equality and independence for all oppressed peoples.*

4. *By taking the factories, mines, shops, and other economic enterprises away from private profiteers and turning them over to the democratic operation of the workers and the public.*

DO NOT ALLOW YOUR FACTORIES TO BE MISUSED FOR ATOM BOMBS, PRIVATE WAGE-SLAVERY, AND WAR. UNDER WORKER-PUBLIC OWNERSHIP WE CAN WORK TOGETHER IN FREEDOM FOR PEACE AND PLENTY FOR ALL.

COMMITTEE FOR NON-VIOLENT REVOLUTION
NEW YORK GROUP
Address inquiries to: Box 327, Newark 1, N. J.
Printed by voluntary labor

Leaflet from the Committee for Non-Violent Revolution, c. 1946. Roy Kepler.

and after the war, say in the bombing of Hiroshima and Nagasaki, has made it clear that to provide scientific information is not a necessarily innocent act. I do not expect to publish any future work of mine which may do damage in the hands of irresponsible militarists.

Albert Einstein commented, "Noncooperation in military matters should be an essential moral principle for all true scientists." The Society for Social Responsibility in Science, founded at Haverford College in 1948, was one of the expressions of this principle.

POSTWAR ACTIONS

Meanwhile, radical pacifists, fresh out of prison and CPS camps, took to the streets with a series of theatrical demonstrations that anticipated guerrilla theater, a style that the Provos and Yippies made good use of many years later. Probably the first postwar demonstration was carried out by some of the veterans of the Danbury strike against segregation in the prison. Their picketing with signs attacking Jim Crow in the federal prison system at a meeting of the American Prison Association was reported by the newspapers the next day. Because of the excellent press coverage, Jim Peck noted, "we considered the demonstration a success."

Other demonstrations followed for a list of reasons: for amnesty for COs, against the bomb, against a permanent conscription law, against racial discrimination, against militarism in general. "These demonstrations," Peck remembers, "constituted attempts to apply effectively on the outside the nonviolent methods of protest which we had used in prison. Somehow it seemed a continuation of the same struggle — a struggle against what we believed to be injustice."

The demonstrators had little trouble finding an audience. "A small number of COs," Peck explains, "totaling not more than 30, could get national and international publicity for pacifism by means of well-timed public demonstrations of such an unusual nature that the press could hardly ignore them." The demonstrators visited taxidermy and theatrical costume shops for their props. A typical demonstration took place in Times Square, New York, in the summer of 1946 on the occasion of the first Bikini atomic bomb test explosion. Because goats

that mankind could be reasoned — or frightened — into entering a new, peaceful world." Many pacifists mistrusted a kind of pacifism based on fear and a hope of peace dependent on the threat of annihilation. "If atomic warfare would be a catastrophe, then why prepare for it?" asked Milton Mayer.

A. J. Muste challenged the atomic physicists, many of whom expressed personal guilt for their work on the bomb, to refuse to continue to work on atomic weapons. In late 1946 Robert Hutchins told Muste that "a movement is gaining ground among scientists . . . against working on anything that looks like a weapon." Norbert Weiner, the father of cybernetics and a missile expert for the U.S. government during the war, stated that:

The policy of government . . . during

Christmas Amnesty demonstration, Washington D.C., December 22, 1946. Julius Eichel Collection.

Amnesty demonstration outside Danbury Federal Prison organized by the Family and Friends of Imprisoned COs, February 12, 1946. Julius Eichel Collection.

CONSCRIPTION MEANS:

Preparation for
    Atomic War

Aggressive
    Foreign Policies

Military
    Strike-Breaking

Army Regimentation
    for American Youth

WHETHER IT'S CALLED 'UNIVERSAL SERVICE,' OR 'CITIZENSHIP TRAINING,'
OR ANY OTHER NAME---

Conscription is the Road to Death

BUT THE MILITARISTS AND WALL STREETERS DON'T CARE WHAT WE THINK
ABOUT CONSCRIPTION--AS LONG AS WE SUBMIT TO IT. AND SUBMISSION CAN
LEAD US INTO A DICTATORSHIP AS BAD AS RUSSIA'S. IF WE'RE GOING TO
PREVENT PERMANENT CONSCRIPTION, WE'VE GOT TO ACT NOW.

ON FEBRUARY 12, THROUGHOUT THE COUNTRY, MEN ARE TAKING ACTION
TO SHOW THEIR OPPOSITION TO CONSCRIPTION.

IN NEW YORK CITY, WE ARE BURNING OUR DRAFT CARDS. THIS IS OUR WAY
OF SAYING: WE'RE THROUGH WITH CONSCRIPTION. WE WON'T FIGHT IN
ANOTHER WAR.

Join with us!   **Break conscription!**

Destroy your draft cards!

Break-with-Conscription Committee
2929 Broadway, New York City

PRINTED BY VOLUNTARY LABOR

were being used on the atoll as guinea pigs to measure the effects of a nuclear blast, the demonstrators rented a stuffed goat, placed it on wheels, and led it through the streets with a sign reading, "Today Me, Tomorrow You." According to Jim Peck, one of the participants, this was probably the first public demonstration against nuclear testing. Later in the year, the same group of pacifists took their message to the Pentagon, but the goat, returned to the taxidermist, remained at home.

Amnesty was the focal point for two demonstrations at the White House, on Christmas Day 1946 and 1947. This time the protesters wore black and white striped prison suits to attract attention to their message. In 1948, another demonstration at the White House to protest President Truman's failure to grant amnesty to COs, had people dressed in funeral attire, marching behind a coffin marked "Justice." The government responded by pardoning only a small number of selected COs, about 10% of the total number. The rest of the World War II COs continue legally classified as felons which deprives them of certain political rights.

In 1947 the wartime draft was permitted to die and the Pentagon was pressing for universal conscription. Opposition by a coalition of church, labor

Amnesty demonstration in front of the White House included more than 150 conscientious objectors, relatives of imprisoned conscientious objectors, and war veterans, Washington D.C., May 11, 1946. Mrs. Edith Neubrand and her daughter Nancy are on the left. The couple behind them are Marjorie and Robert Swann, behind them are David Dellinger, Robert Swink, and Seymore Eichel, who was imprisoned a few years later for opposing the draft. Julius Eichel Collection.

Leaflet from the Break With Conscription Committee, c. 1947. Roy Kepler.

Larry Gara

JAMES PECK
(Born 1914)

A radical activist for over 40 years, Jim Peck gave active life to the fundamental principles of revolutionary nonviolence. With courage and dedication, he put his body on the line repeatedly in support of trade unionism, peace, civil rights in the U.S. and political freedom abroad. He involved himself in countless nonviolent campaigns, large and small demonstrations, weekly vigils, picket lines, civil disobedience actions, and routine office and publicity tasks. He was among the war resisters who gave new breath and insight to the nonviolent movement following the second World War and reflected the unfailing commitment of rank and file workers in the important social movements of the time.

A native of New York City, Peck dropped out of Harvard University after his freshman year and rejected the affluent life in which he had been raised. He got a job as a shipping clerk and then deckboy on a steamship bound for Australia. As a seaman, he worked to help build what became the National Maritime Union, and while organizing in Pensacola, Florida, was jailed for "vagrancy" and then kicked out of town. In 1936 he was brutally beaten by New York police for taking part in a seaman's strike. On the advice of Roger Baldwin of the ACLU, Peck began to work as a newspaperman for the Federated Press, a news syndicate serving the union weeklies, and continually supported union activities.

During the Thirties, he was moved by the depiction of the "enemy" soldiers in *All Quiet on the Western Front* as human beings unwillingly trapped in the war machine and was shocked by the exposé of the big munitions makers in *Merchants of Death*. He declared himself a conscientious objector in 1940 on the first day of registration and worked with the War Resisters League before the war, writing a labor column for *The Conscientious Objector* and speaking against war at street meetings.

Peck was jailed for over 28 months for opposing the war, and while in Danbury prison helped to organize the successful 135-day strike against racial segregation in the messhall. He wrote, "Being in jail, to me, was like working on a big ship which never hits port." During the war he also voluntarily contracted yellow jaundice as a "guinea pig" to help find a cure for the disease, losing 20 pounds during the experiment. Immediately after his release from prison, he wrote an exposé of the preferential treatment given business executives who were in prison for defrauding the government on war contracts.

After the war, Peck continued to give special attention to publicizing the struggles he believed in. He edited publications of the Congress of Racial Equality and the War Resisters League and used the income from his late father's estate to enable him to take full-time, non-paying jobs with groups whose work he believed in. He organized and participated in demonstrations for amnesty, against bomb tests and Civil Defense drills, and in support of racial equality and COs imprisoned for resisting the peacetime draft. In February 1947, he was one of a group who burned their draft cards in front of the White House. He wrote:

Outlawing war becomes more urgent in an era in which nuclear weapons could mean total destruction. And to me, the most effective way for an individual to start outlawing war is simply to refuse to take part in it. Eventually, the mass murder which war is will be recognized as a crime just as individual murder in peacetime is today.

A member of CORE's national action committee and editor of the *CORElator* for 17 years, Peck participated in the 1947 Journey of Reconciliation and countless other civil rights protests and demonstrations. As a member of the 1961 Freedom Ride, he was nearly killed when a Birmingham mob attacked him when he tried to enter a bus terminal lunchroom with a black man. After the beating, with 53 stitches in his face and head, he used the international publicity generated by the attack to further highlight the nonviolent civil rights struggle. He was suddenly ousted from CORE in 1965 when, with the rise of black power, the organization reversed its traditional interracial policy.

During the war in Vietnam, working with the War Resisters League, Peck counseled young men about the draft and helped to organize protest demonstrations. "If I had not been overage and were faced with the alternative of jail or Canada," he wrote, "I would have chosen jail because I feel an obligation to pursue the struggle for peace in my native land throughout my lifetime." He was arrested over a dozen times as a participant in actions such as the Assembly of Unrepresented People, the confrontation at the Pentagon, Mayday, the Daily Death Toll, Tiger Cage Vigil, and other civil disobedience demonstrations against the war.

The father of two sons, Peck received threats on his life and family but maintained his sense of purpose and dedication to a strenuous ideal which he felt had to be fully lived to be real.

and peace forces this time was enough to stop the militarists. On February 12 the first draft card burnings took place, one in front of the White House in Washington, and the second that evening at the Labor Temple in New York. Dwight Macdonald, who shared the speaker's platform with Muste and Dave Dellinger, said, "We have decided to attack conscription by the simplest and most direct way possible: that is, by refusing . . . to recognize the authority of the state in this matter." Of this demonstration, its organizer, George Houser, reported that "it had been planned to burn the cards in a kettle, but the fire department objected, so the torn cards were taken to an outdoor incinerator and burned. One CO ex-con, having no draft card, burned his parole papers instead." Altogether, from 400 to 500 men destroyed their draft cards or mailed them to the President during this series of demonstrations.

Another demonstration at the White House had the demonstrators goose-stepping in rented Uncle Sam costumes. "The Draft Means A Goose-Stepping Uncle Sam," read their placards. Peck recalls that goose-stepping was tiring on the legs but the

Demonstration against universal conscription in front of the White House, Washington D.C., February 12, 1947. World War I resister Julius Eichel is in the center carrying the pot in which draft cards were burned. Julius Eichel Collection.

Leaflet from the Break With Conscription Committee, 1947. Courtesy of Roy Finch.

WE ARE FOUR AMERICANS BICYCLING FROM PARIS TO MOSCOW

We have come to tell you of « another U.S.A. », a U.S.A. which says that the people of the world should lay down their arms.

The U.S. you hear of most often is the U.S. of far-flung military bases, of atom bombs, of American dollars to bribe Europe into rearmament. We are from another United States, a U.S. of persons who want peace and friendship and economic equality throughout the world.

We ourselves have served prison sentences in the U.S. up to four years for opposition to militarism. Like us, more than 25,000 Americans have been sent to prison or detention camps since 1940 for refusal to make or bear arms.

Millions of others go along with American armaments only under stress of a propaganda which says that otherwise the U.S. will be invaded by Soviet Countries. It is difficult to combat this propaganda so long as the building of mass armies and the suppression of political opposition within the Soviet sphere give substance to it. That is why peace-loving Americans look anxiously for concrete evidence that the people of Communist countries will not support a war.

We want to establish contact with « another Europe ». We want to unite with people of both blocs who know that:

1. « defensive armaments » on any side always lead to further rearmament on the other side — and to war.
2. modern war cannot possibly save or defend anything — not « peace », not « democracy », not « socialism », not one's family, or one's self.
3. if these things are true we have a higher obligation than just to grumble about them privately. We must begin to act in accord with what we know by refusing to make or bear arms.

Let us join together in non-violent resistance to war and injustice

Non-violent resistance is the carrying out in practice of the basic insight of all international working class movements and of all great religions — that all men are brothers who will eventually free themselves from artificial hostilities and divisions. Tolstoi in Russia, Gandhi in India, and the American anti-slavery fighter, William Lloyd Garrison, are among the early pioneers of non-violent resistance.

Non-violent resistance uses strikes, boycotts, demonstrations, and civil disobedience to attack militarism, totalitarianism, and injustice. At the same time those who embrace non-violent resistance treat every individual as a friend. They steadfastly refuse to hate or kill anyone, including opponents both in their own country and in the so-called « enemy » countries.

For some the sacrifices will be great — but unlike the sacrifices of war, they can help mankind to find a creative way out of the present hopelessness. Only the self-giving love of total non-violence can sweep away the present fears and bring closer the day when all people will live together as brothers.

LET US SAY « NO » TO REARMAMENT AND WAR	LET US SAY « YES » TO ECONOMIC EQUALITY AND BROTHERLY LOVE.
1. Refuse to serve in the armed forces.	1. Work to equalize the standard of living throughout the world. In the U.S. we advocate contributing the 56 billion dollar arms budget to a world peace budget for this end.
2. Refuse to transport or make weapons of war.	2. Organize communal groups and enterprises where people may live and work together as equals. Work for communal ownership of existing enterprises.
3. Organize a collective non-violent resistance movement.	3. Live and act as members of the world community whose first loyalty is to the people of the world rather than to any national government.
4. Refuse to hate or kill anyone.	

The people of the world must refuse to be enemies.
LET US REACH ACROSS THE ARTIFICIAL BOUNDARIES AND MAKE PEACE

DAVID DELLINGER, Printer, member of World Citizens Community. — RALPH DIGIA, Bookkeeper, former union organizer, member World Citizens Community. — ARTHUR EMERY, Dairy farm worker, Quaker, World Citizen. — BILL SUTHERLAND, Writer, World Citizen.

PEACEMAKERS, 2013 Fifth Avenue, New York City, New York, (UNITED STATES)

demonstration got good publicity. Universal Conscription was prevented, but the Pentagon came back the following year with a refurbished draft law, the Selective Service Act of 1948. Pacifists responded with demonstrations at high schools urging noncooperation, but these had little impact.

MILITANT PACIFISM

It was not until the late 1950s, when a series of direct action projects touched the heart of the public's fear of nuclear weapons, that pacifism reached outward to the community at large. In the interim, the Cold War and the McCarthy Era cast a pall over American life and frightened liberals and much of the left into silence.

In isolation, individual pacifists and pacifist organizations continued to serve COs and to undergo a series of changes that would put them into the forefront of radical action when the climate of fear and complacency cleared. The major change was the radicalization of traditional peace organizations, a result of the influx of thousands of war resisters.

Peacemakers leaflet which was printed in English, French and Russian and distributed by peace cyclists in Europe in 1951. After being refused visas to the USSR, the war resisters illegally visited Boden, the headquarters of the Soviet occupation forces in Austria, and leafleted soldiers who received the leaflets with friendliness. Ralph DiGia.

The WRL was the obvious place for the more militant COs to go because it had given the most support to the absolutist position during the war. By 1948, the young militants had a majority on the executive committee and Abe Kaufman, who had guided the League as an educational and supportive organization for nineteen years, resigned. League policy came more and more under the control of resisters like Dellinger, Peck, George Houser, Roy Finch and Igal Roodenko, who viewed pacifism and nonviolence as the most radical and effective way of creating meaningful change.

At the same time, a number of smaller groups and publications were being organized which sought for themselves the role of cutting edge in the movement at large. The first concrete manifestation of this oncoming wave of militant nonviolence was publication of the magazine *Direct Action* in December 1945, with Dellinger as one of the editors. Subtitled "a magazine devoted to an American Revolution by nonviolent methods," it called for a declaration of "total war" against the American way of life, a way of life which, in producing the atomic bomb, perpetrated "the worst atrocity in history." The editors continued:

> *The war for total brotherhood must be carried on by free men who use methods worthy of the ideals they seek to serve. . . . Every act we perform today must reflect the kind of human relationships we are fighting to establish tomorrow. There must be strikes, sabotage and seizure of public property now being held by private owners. There must be civil disobedience of laws which are contrary to human welfare. But there must always be an uncompromising practice of treating everyone, including the worst of our opponents, with all the respect and decency which they merit as fellow human beings.*

In February 1946 one hundred war resisters met in Chicago and formed the Committee for Nonviolent Revolution (CNVR), a loosely structured organization that attempted to synthesize anarchism and socialism on a pacifist basis. The Committee took an absolutist position towards militarism and all future wars, and looked forward to a democratic, decentralized form of socialism. CNVR held a few small demonstrations, calling for the

close of the Big Flats CPS camp in New York and protesting the United Nations as an attempt by the great powers to restructure the world for their own benefit. On the whole, CNVR did not approach the ambition of its name except, perhaps, in the numerous theoretical papers members circulated and commented upon dealing with nonviolence, revolution and related subjects.

PEACEMAKERS

Two years later, in April 1948, another Chicago conference was held for "a more disciplined and revolutionary pacifism." This conference led to the creation of Peacemakers largely through the efforts of Ernest and Marion Bromley and Wally and

Peacemakers Bill Sutherland, Ralph DiGia, David Dellinger, and Art Emery in Vienna during their attempt to bicycle from Paris to Moscow to urge disarmament and nonviolent resistance, October 15, 1951. War Resisters League.

Anti-apartheid demonstration in front of the Union of South Africa consulate to protest "free elections" in which only one-fifth of the adult population could vote, New York City, April 15, 1953. Fellowship of Reconciliation.

law, to oppose it now. We call on youths to refuse to register or render any service under this iniquitous law and on all others to support youth in their nonviolent noncooperation. . . . We are opposed to nationalism, totalitarianism and violence when practiced in Russia and by Communists, as we are opposed to such practice anywhere by anybody. . . . We have to choose between giving leadership in atomic, bacterial war and preparation therefore, or giving leadership in renouncing war and resisting tyranny by nonviolence. Neither way will be cheap or painless but the way of war is the way of certain destruction. The way of brotherhood and nonviolence is the way to peace and general well-being.

A number of different publications helped to inform and stimulate pacifist thinking throughout the war and post-war years. *The Progressive* and *Common Sense* were popular journals whose integrity and editorial breadth made them important to pacifists during the war. Other socialist or radical papers of value included *Politics*, an influential monthly review edited by Dwight Macdonald, *Enquiry*, issued by a Chicago group, and *Retort*, published in Bearsville, New York, by Holley R. Cantine, Jr. *Fellowship, The Conscientious Objector, Compass* (published by men in CPS), and the English *Peace News* were the principal pacifist publications. *Pacifica Views*, edited on the West Coast by Henry Geiger and others, printed some of the most cogent pacifist writing during the war years.

After the war, *Resistance*, an anarchist review edited by the Resistance Group and David Wieck, and *Alternative*, begun in 1948 as successor to *Pacifica Views* and *Direct Action*, were both published out of New York. Among the editors of *Alternative* were David Dellinger, Roy Kepler, Ralph DiGia, Albert Eichel, Roy Finch, Anne Moffett, and Margaret Rockwell. The Pacifist Research Bureau, set up in 1942, also encouraged research on the problems of reframing a world pattern that would be consistent with pacifist principles. The Bureau pioneered in peace research, publishing numerous pamphlets on peace, nonviolence, and international affairs.

Juanita Nelson. About half the membership of CNVR took part in the conference, along with Dwight Macdonald, A. J. Muste and Milton Mayer. Peacemakers was more Gandhian than it was Marxist and rejected much of the rhetoric of CNVR in favor of small direct action projects. It was organized as a network of local radical pacifist cells, participants in its local activities being deemed members. During the following ten years, until the formation of the Committee for Nonviolent Action (CNVA), Peacemakers was the most active nonviolent direct action group and the initiator of organized war tax resistance. With the passage of the conscription act of 1948, Peacemakers called on

all American citizens, and especially on all who denounced it before it became

Mounted police break up a peace demonstration near Union Square, New York City, August 2, 1950. Wide World.

Harold Fackert and Ralph DiGia in the office of the War Resisters League at 5 Beekman Street, New York City, in the late 1950's. Harold Fackert, a retired railway worker and Socialist in the Debsian tradition, tirelessly performed routine work as a volunteer with the WRL and similar groups. Ralph DiGia was co-secretary of the League with Bayard Rustin. War Resisters League.

The Central Committee for Conscientious Objectors (CCCO) also grew out of the prisons and CPS camps of World War II. Founded in 1948 as a response to the passage of the Selective Service Act of that year, CCCO has served as both mentor and model to hundreds of local draft counseling agencies throughout the land.

On the West Coast, the Pacifica Foundation developed out of the efforts of war resisters Lewis Hill, Denny Wilcher, E. John Lewis and others starting in 1946. Pacifica links four listener-owned, non-profit radio stations: KPFA in Berkeley, KPFK in Los Angeles, KPFT in Houston and WBAI in New York City. KPFA, the first radio station in America to base its operation on listener sponsorship instead of advertisements, went on the air in April, 1949. Immediately it became a living conduit tying together intellectuals, artists, musicians and political activists. Perhaps more than anything else, it transformed the Bay Area into a cultural and

Cover of the radical pacifist magazine *Alternative*, June 1950. Ralph DiGia.

Page from *Alternative*, 1948. Ralph DiGia.

War resisters Roy Kepler, Dave and Betty Dellinger, their sons Patch and Raymond at the Glen Gardner, New Jersey, community, c. 1949. Photo courtesy of Roy Kepler.

PEACEMAKERS
(Founded 1948)

Peacemakers was one of the first organizations to be formed after World War II by radical activists inspired by the growing theory and accomplishments of nonviolence throughout the world. There was a growing conviction among many that the times called for a grass-roots movement, no matter how small in its beginnings, which was committed to a vigorous and unmistakable disassociation from military power. Although it never became a large organization, Peacemakers did have an important effect on many of the people and organizations which came to make up the modern nonviolent movement.

Peacemakers attempted to build a decentralized and self-disciplined movement which stressed local initiative and group coordination along the lines of the nonviolent revolutionary movement in India. Emphasis was put on building intentional communities which practiced communal living. "Groups or cells are the real basis of the movement," Peacemakers announced, "for this is not an attempt to organize another pacifist membership organization, which one joins by signing a statement or paying a membership fee." Instead, Peacemakers emphasized a living program which included resistance to the draft and war taxes, personal transformation, and group participation in work for political and economic democracy.

Uniquely non-organizational, Peacemakers has no national office, paid staff or membership list; decisions are made at yearly Continuation Committee meetings. The major connecting link between individuals and groups considering themselves Peacemakers is *The Peacemaker,* published since 1949 as a forum for letters, announcements, and accounts of the experiences of radical pacifists.

Peacemakers initiated organized work against war taxes and since 1949 a number of its members have been imprisoned for refusing to pay for war. Peacemakers at the Ohio cell organized a land trust to remove property from the market place and established the Peacemaker Sharing Fund, a mutual aid plan designed to insure aid to dependents of imprisoned Peacemakers and to help finance group projects. During the Vietnam war, the sharing fund became the main vehicle for donations to meet the needs of war resisters' families. When the government seized the land trust home where Peacemakers Marion and Ernest Bromley lived, in 1974, allegedly to collect taxes on the "income" to the sharing fund, Peacemakers exposed the fraud and persuaded the government to withdraw its case.

Peacemakers organized a number of direct action projects in the late Forties and Fifties, including demonstrations in Puerto Rico against U.S. colonialism and a disarmament bicycle trip across Europe by four pacifists which preceded the San Francisco to Moscow Walk by nearly ten years. Peacemakers also sponsored the "Walk for Survival" in 1958, the first large post-war peace walk in the U.S., and set up Operation Freedom, a fund to aid people in Tennessee and Mississippi who had been deprived of home or job for seeking their civil rights.

Peacemakers lost some of its initial impetus by the mid-Fifties as it encountered the difficulty of maintaining a decentralized and largely anarchist program and at the same time keeping a disciplined and well organized radical group functioning. Some Peacemakers went on to join or form other nonviolent groups which incorporated the radical view Peacemakers helped to germinate, while others in the organization gave more emphasis to life style and nonviolent principles. Peacemakers published a "Handbook on the Nonpayment of War Taxes," and has also offered summer training and orientation programs in nonviolence since 1957, often organized and led by long-time resisters and Peacemakers Wally and Juanita Nelson.

Leaflet from the Third Camp Conference, 1953. Roy Kepler.

political community. When, after 15 months, KPFA was forced off the air because of insufficient funds, the listeners raised money, collected equipment and re-established the station with a salaried staff and improved programs.

The West Coast attracted a number of other COs coming out of the camps and prisons in the late 40s. From the CPS camp specializing in the arts at Waldport, Oregon, came poets, artists, designers and writers, including Bill Everson, later to gain recognition as poet Brother Antoninus, and Martin Ponch, who helped form the San Francisco theater group Interplayers, recruited in good part from COs, their wives and woman friends.

ECONOMICS

In addition to growing militarism, economics also grew as an important pacifist concern in the years following World War II. Always aware of the heavy burden which an inflated military budget puts on an economy, and conscious of the control played by large corporations and arms manufacturers, pacifists still had not given economic form to their hopes for a nonviolent society. In 1927, Reinhold Niebuhr pointed out this ignorance of economic realities on the part of not just pacifists, but millions of Americans "who are passionate in their espousal of world peace and disarmament."

> *They want America to trust the world and are sure that the world will in turn trust America. Their faith is too naive. They do not realize that a nation cannot afford to trust anyone if it is not willing to go to the length of sharing its advantages. Love which expresses itself in trust without expressing itself in sacrifice is futile. It is not thorough-going enough to be creative or redemptive.*

Many early pacifists recognized the need to actively apply love to economic relations, just as they tried to do in other areas, and had traditionally set up cooperatives and intentional communities to implement their principles and meet their immediate needs. These received renewed attention in the 1940s as more work went into formulating a broader economic program based on nonviolence.

Pacifist thinking was strongly influenced by the theories of Henry George, William James, and Richard Gregg, the proposals of Ralph Borsodi and Arthur Morgan, and the work of Mohandas Gandhi and Vinoba Bhave in India. Arthur Morgan, who was appointed by Roosevelt as head of the Tennes-

R E S I S T A N C E

VOLUME 8 - NO.4
MARCH, 1950

KPFA INTERIM

PROGRAM FOLIO

JUNE 5 - 18, 1949

100.1 MC   CHANNEL 261

On Being "Live".....

In its first six weeks on the air KPFA's programs were almost 50 per cent "live"—not recorded or transcribed, but produced and broadcast directly from the studios. The station has a goal of at least two-thirds "live" programing, to provide a genuinely *active* center of broadcasting. But almost 50 per cent "live" is more than listeners in the Bay Area are used to—from any source. It is not bad.

During these six weeks 48 different musicians performed in the KPFA studios. That is one reason there was so much "live" programing. Another was that 67 different persons participated in Public Affairs broadcasts. If Children's and Drama programs are included, a total of 165 artistically talented, unusually informed or otherwise well-qualified individuals appeared on the station. That number is apart from the 19 persons carrying out staff assignments. KPFA's first six weeks, in short, brought to the microphone directly the skills of 184 individuals, and indirectly the imaginitive and technical effort of many more who were not heard in broadcasts.

There are two things we do not imply in reciting these statistics: that statistics about radio indicate anything of its quality; or that recorded or transcribed programs are necessarily bad.

Recorded music on the radio, if it is properly programed and accompanied by some enlightened intention, can be as valuable as anything else. But nothing can supplant the significance of the radio station's direct use of the cultural resources around it. It is an unfortunate fact that radio management in general has the sole object of purchasing listeners as cheaply as possible. Recorded and "packaged" programs, the (Continued on Page Eight)

Cover of *Resistance,* an anarchist review, 1950. Institute for the Study of Nonviolence.

Cover of program folio for radio station KPFA, 1949. E. John Lewis.

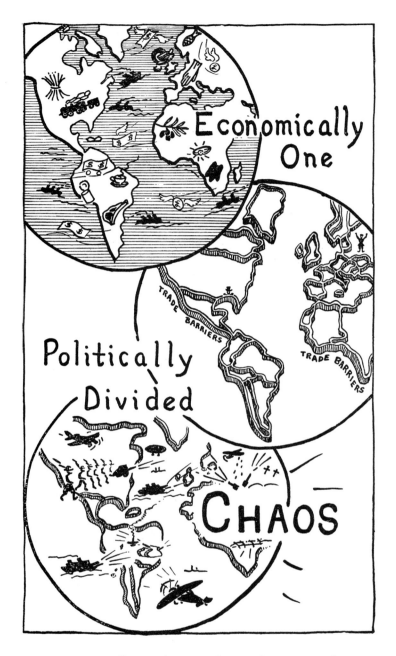

county, state, nation, and world, or in more natural groupings – individual, family, community, society, world.

Realizing that "society" is an abstraction, he substituted a more functional group between the community and the world: the geographic region, where the topography makes it a unified system. He stressed the need for decentralized, regional groups with regional authorities to eliminate nations, and a global understanding which allowed the earth's resources to be used equally by the earth's inhabitants.

With the growth of revolutionary nonviolence, many activists felt the need for stronger, self-sufficient communities and non-competitive lifestyles which freed them from the exploitative practices of modern capitalism and the threat of economic reprisal. In the early Forties, Ralph Templin, who had been active with the *Kristagraha* (Christian Nonviolence) movement in India, became director of the School of Living in Suffern, New York, a nonviolent community founded by Ralph Borsodi which lived and encouraged "decentralist living" as the nearest possibility in America to a nonviolent way of life. Partly through the school's efforts, the idea of nonviolent economics and the implications of a simple life style began to be seriously explored by pacifists and nonviolent groups in the following years. The AFSC sent Templin to speak with COs in CPS camps and the Brethren Service Committee made interest in and study of cooperatives a major free time emphasis at one of the camps it administered.

After the war, a group of COs settled at the Macedonia Cooperative Community in Georgia where they farmed and built a small woodworking

see Valley Authority, advocated economic alternatives based on the idea that the small community (rather than sprawling cities) is the firmest and most satisfying foundation for modern society. Ralph Borsodi also emphasized decentralism as a means towards a richer and more independent life and saw the need to organize principles based in economic justice on a much wider scale:

> Proper organization of families and communities comes first. As we proceed to larger groups, we can go in either of two directions: the political – into ward,

Virginia Cooperative store, Virginia, Minnesota, c. 1941. Fellowship of Reconciliation.

Drawing from the Pacifist Research Bureau's pamphlet, *The New Economics and World Peace*, November 1944. Institute for the Study of Nonviolence.

factory, discarding the wage system and running the whole operation on a communal, subsistence basis. At the Glen Gardner Community in New Jersey, where the worker-controlled Libertarian Press operated, Dave Dellinger wrote:

> *I think the need is not only to be sensitive to new ways of withdrawing our support from the war machine . . . but also to develop new ways of living in brotherhood. . . . It seems to me that the current growing edge of pacifism is the development of communities of sharing, and that those of us who want to attack the causes of war should begin in our own lives.*

Peacemakers, with its emphasis on local communities and personal regeneration, was a direct expression of these concerns and tied together many of the urban and rural communities settled by COs. The Catholic Worker farms and houses of hospitality had earlier made efforts in the same direction and received renewed energy after the war.

In 1942, a rural community was founded on a farm near Americus, Georgia, by Clarence Jordan, a farmer and theologian, and a number of COs. Called Koinonia, meaning "fellowship in Christ," the community lived together in witness to the Christian teachings on economic sharing, racial justice, and pacifism, and assisted local farmers by introducing scientific farming methods. Koinonia practiced economic communism whereby they held all things in common, as was true in the early Christian church, and worked towards being self-sufficient. The community became the object of mounting hostility because of their witness against race prejudice, and for years withstood shootings, beatings, bombings, burnings, and an economic boycott. When local business firms refused to sell the farm necessary supplies, the residents set up a pecan processing plant and a mail order business to replace their roadside market and egg production. In the late Sixties, realizing that "what the poor need is not charity but *capital,* not case-workers but *co-workers,* Koinonia Partners was formed to develop partnership industries and to train local people in management responsibilities.

Further work towards defining a nonviolent economics was done by Robert Swann, a CO who had been imprisoned during the war, who recognized that land and control of natural resources hold a central position within any economic system.

Drawing inspiration from Native American traditions and Gandhi's work in India, Swann began to develop and promote the concept of trusteeship of land as a substitute for ownership. He described the trusteeship concept, which bases ownership of land on use and safeguards natural resources for future generations, as an activist approach to the problem of redistributing resources. In 1969 he helped establish New Communities, a land trust consisting of 5,700 acres run by and for ex-sharecroppers in southwest Georgia.

Swann, in his work with the International Independence Institute, stressed the need for local control and local participation in economic decision making. He proposed a three fold strategy, based on the regional approach popularized by Borsodi, to decentralize economic affairs and insure local control in planning and development. It included community land trusts, which would hold land in stew-

Volunteers working in the fields of New Communities land trust, Georgia, 1970. Photo courtesy of Robert Swann.

Meeting of the board of New Communities Institute, Georgia, 1969. Marion King, James Mays, Robert Swann, L.B. Johnson and Charles Sherrod are facing the camera. Photo courtesy of Robert Swann.

ardship for the common good, Community Development Corporations, which would develop businesses and provide services for a region, and community money, which would establish a currency within a semi-closed economy where production was primarily for local consumption. He also reflected the growing realization of many that economics is not limited to national boundaries but must include the whole world and not proceed from an assumption of nationalism.

NEW DRAFT LAW

The new draft law had no allowance for non-religious COs and by February 1949, 87 men had been arrested for not registering and 42 were in prison serving sentences ranging from sixty days to four years. One of the most important cases of this period was that of Larry Gara who had already served two separate sentences during World War II as a CO. A professor of history at an Ohio college, Gara was found guilty of having "counseled, aided and abetted" Charles Rickert, a student, in failing

Fifty conscientious objectors, protesting the start of the peace-time draft, stage a poster walk through downtown Los Angeles, 1948. Fellowship of Reconciliation.

Ad from the pacifist magazine *Alternative*, c. 1948. Ralph DiGia.

to register. The judge, in his charge to the jury, defined "aid and abet" to mean "support and encourage." Thus, in effect, he made it illegal even to advocate draft resistance. Gara was the object of a protest demonstration at the White House and a publicity campaign that protested the abridgement of free speech. He served seven months of an eighteen month sentence.

THE McCARTHY YEARS

In February 1950, Senator Joseph McCarthy introduced the McCarthy Era with a speech in Wheeling, W. Va. accusing the State Department of employing 205 known Communists. In June of that year, the Korean War broke out. By winning United Nations approval for armed intervention, President Truman successfully squelched opposition to the war from everyone but pacifists and the fractured Communist Party, which, by this time, was isolated by government repression, greatly infiltrated by government agents, and forced to operate underground.

Pacifist dissent was ineffectual. In July 1950 Dave and Betty Dellinger, Bill and Janet Lovett, and Bill Kuenning, all living at the Glen Gardner

community in New Jersey, went on a two week fast. In the same month, Jim Peck, Igal Roodenko, Bill Worthy and Marvin Katz distributed leaflets at the UN calling for mediation rather than intervention. Peck managed to get into the Security Council meeting and personally delivered a leaflet to the delegates before being hauled away by UN guards. There were other small demonstrations against the war but they had little publicity or public response. The Cold War and the McCarthy Era made dissent risky. Distributing leaflets in public was a courageous act, and a difficult one because people were afraid even to accept them. The most noteworthy nonviolent action of this time was an attempt by Dellinger, DiGia, Art Emery and Bill Sutherland to bicycle from Paris to Moscow urging individual noncooperation against the warmaking powers of the states along their route.

While most of the liberal-left joined the U.S. government in its anti-Communist crusade, some pacifists, notably A.J. Muste, attempted to maintain a dialogue with Communists. While pacifists opposed united front activity, many of them continuously insisted that the Communists' view must be heard and their civil rights protected.□

Jim Peck is carried out of the United Nations Security Council after leafleting against war in Korea, July 7, 1950. War Resisters League.

Demonstration protesting the "witch hunts" of the House Un-American Activities Committee, meeting in the San Francisco City Hall, May 13, 1960. Nearly 50 persons were arrested and several injured after police tried to disperse the demonstrators with fire hoses. Wide World.

CHAPTER 7

DIRECT ACTION FOR DISARMAMENT

Twenty-eight people are arrested in City Hall Park, New York City, for refusing to take shelter during the Civil Defense drill, June 15, 1955. Participants in the civil disobedience action included A.J. Muste, visible inside the paddy wagon, Dorothy Day and Ammon Hennacy, just outside of it, and Jim Peck holding the sign. Fellowship of Reconciliation.

CIVIL DEFENSE PROTESTS

In June 1955 twenty-eight participants in a protest against a nationwide civil defense alert were arrested for refusing to take shelter in City Hall Park, N.Y. This demonstration, organized by a coalition of New York pacifist groups including the Catholic Worker, the WRL, Peacemakers and the FOR, was the beginning of a direct action phase of the anti-war movement. The rejuvenated peace movement, coupled with the civil rights movement which began in 1956 with the Montgomery Bus Boycott, fostered the radical movement as we know it today.

The 1955 civil disobedience action against the compulsory air raid drills was led by Dorothy Day,

Ammon Hennacy and other Catholic Workers, Ralph DiGia of the WRL, A.J. Must and others. Their protest got front-page newspaper publicity since the Civil Defense test, which also involved Canada and Mexico, was a major story. Demonstrations also took place in Philadelphia, Chicago, and Boston, and some whole cities, like Peoria, Illinois, considered the entire affair ridiculous and refused to cooperate at all with the drills. Others arrested in the New York action included Kent Larrabee, Eileen Fantino, Jim Peck, Jackson MacLow, Bayard Rustin, Henry Maiden, and a shoe shine man innocently drinking at a water-fountain at the time. In their statement, the demonstrators said:

The kind of public and highly publicized drills held on June 15 are essentially a part of war preparation. They accustom people to the idea of war, to acceptance of war as probably inevitable and as somehow right if waged in 'defense' and 'retaliation'. . . . They create the illusion that the nation can devote its major resources to preparation for nuclear war and at the same time shield people from its catastrophic effects. Whatever anyone's intentions may be, this is perpetrating deceit. . . . We should instead remove the causes of war, devoting our material, intellectual and spiritual resources to combatting poverty and disease throughout the world. . . .

The protestors were herded into a police wagon and taken to jail where they were arraigned before Magistrate Louis Kaplan. There, in a speech which might have come out of George Orwell, he called the pacifists "murderers" who "by their conduct and behavior contributed to the utter destruction of these three million theoretically killed in our City." He then set bail at $1500 each, an exorbitant sum as the crime with which they were charged was only a misdemeanor. A defense committee was formed and the case was appealed, staying in the courts four years before the Supreme Court refused to hear it. As A.J. Muste pointed out:

The fact that Eisenhower used his speech to the nation at the conclusion of

Leaflet from the Civil Defense Protest Committee, 1961. Institute for the Study of Nonviolence.

his three-day sojourn in a 'hide-out' to urge everybody to pressure Congress to adopt the Administration's Reserve Forces Bill, which is Universal Military Training only slightly disguised, gives strong support to the pacifist contention that the major aspect of the demonstration was its contribution to war preparation.

The protests continued and civil disobedience against the civil defense drills became an annual affair. Usually no more than 35 people ever took part in the civil disobedience or served jail sen-

tences longer than five days. In 1960, however, a new spirit was afloat, and the effects of pacifist disarmament agitation began to be more visible. David McReynolds and Bradford Lyttle joined the Civil Defense Protest Committee and helped to organize a more public demonstration that year, offering varied levels of participation to those who wished to protest the drills. People could demonstrate their objection to the drills but leave when the sirens sounded, leave only when ordered to do so, or refuse to leave at all and thus risk arrest. The May 3 protest drew a thousand participants, half of them refusing to take shelter when the air raid alert sounded. The police arrested 26 people randomly picked from the crowd of demonstrators.

The next year, the Civil Defense Protest Committee organized public meetings, picketing and discussions at civil defense offices, building up to city-wide demonstrations on the day of the alert, "to make it finally clear to the authorities that the people overwhelmingly demand an end to this 'cruel deception.'" This time, nearly all of the 2000 people

Leaflet from the Committee for Nonviolent Action/West, 1963. Sam Tyson.

Catholic Workers Eileen Egan and Ammon Hennacy refuse to leave City Hall Park during civil defense drill, New York City, April 28, 1961. Howard Everngam.

School children bury their heads and nuns silently pray during a civil defense drill at St. Joan of Arc parochial school, New York City, November 28, 1951. Bill Stahl/Fellowship of Reconciliation.

Diana Davies

DOROTHY DAY
(Born 1897)

Dorothy Day exerted an influence on her time equalled by few women in American history. For over 50 years, she articulated the need for and elements of active nonviolence and gave personal leadership to the struggles for peace, justice, and human rights. Through her life, her writing, and the work of the Catholic Worker, she applied the teachings of Jesus to modern conditions and actively promulgated a theology of peace. This was in direct contrast to the so-called "just war" theory which dominated Christian thinking since the Fifth Century.

Born in Brooklyn, Day moved with her family to California when she was six, and then to Chicago after the San Francisco earthquake destroyed the newspaper where her father had worked. She received a scholarship to the University of Illinois and her experiences as a needy student, together with her wide reading, led her to join the Socialist group in Urbana. She had completed two years of college when her family moved back to New York, and instead of resuming school, she found a job on the New York Socialist daily, the *Call,* and later wrote for the *New Masses.* Her friends were political activists and writers and she found herself in the middle of the radical world where the debates of socialists, doctrinaire Marxists, anarchists and Wobblies were constantly in the air.

During the suffrage campaigns in 1917, she joined in picketing the White House with a group upholding the rights of women recently jailed to be treated as political prisoners, and when arrested, she went on a ten-day hunger strike in prison. She decided to become a Catholic in 1928 after years of free-lance writing, a common-law marriage, and the birth of a daughter. The difficulties of her decision to give up physical love for the love of God she described in her book, *The Long Loneliness.*

In 1933, with Peter Maurin, Day launched the Catholic Worker movement, which combined religious, radical and anarchist concerns and stressed the importance of direct mutual aid as a way of remaking society. The Catholic Worker took literally the Christian injunction to feed the hungry, clothe the naked, and shelter the homeless, and applied Christ's message to a time of economic depression when faith in capitalism had ebbed.

Day edited *The Catholic Worker* newspaper and helped in setting up houses of hospitality for the poor and a series of farming communes. She wrote of the immorality of war and conscription and provided the leading voice in American Catholic circles for militant pacifism. When conscription was instituted in the U.S. in 1941, Day went to Washington to speak before a Congressional committee on behalf of the right to conscientious objection. *The Catholic Worker* printed articles throughout World War II on such subjects as "The Immorality of Conscription," "Catholics Can Be Conscientious Objectors," "The Weapons of the Spirit," and "The Gospel of Peace."

She wrote movingly about the events and social conditions of the Twentieth Century in her columns, books, and articles, and spoke widely of the Catholic Worker's principles and the need for a decentralist and nonviolent social order. Her philosophy of service and voluntary poverty, and her sustaining vision of nonviolence as a means of bettering society, inspired countless thousands and helped change the thinking of the Catholic community in the U.S. and throughout the world. She was arrested for refusing to take shelter during the civil defense drills in New York City during the Fifties and strongly opposed the testing and proliferation of nuclear weapons.

During the war in Vietnam, her leadership helped catalyze resistance actions and strongly influenced the growth of a radical Catholic Left. She publicly opposed the war, encouraged noncooperation with conscription and war taxes, and spoke at the November 1965 draft card burning in Union Square where two of the five men to burn their draft cards were Catholic Workers. Day also supported the nonviolent struggle of the farmworkers from the first days of the Delano strike, and in the summer of 1973, at the age of 75, she spent twelve days in a California jail for picketing with Cesar Chavez and the United Farm Workers Union. In 1975 she wrote:

> The peace movement knows that there is something fundamentally evil about this society. Kent State and the killing of students. All the years of killing in Vietnam. All the murderous weapons being sold throughout the world. All the endured violence of Civil Rights struggles and freedom rides and sit-ins. Through all this one comes to know the seriousness of the situation and to realize it's not going to be changed just by demonstrations. It's a question of risking one's life. It's a question of living one's life in drastically different ways.

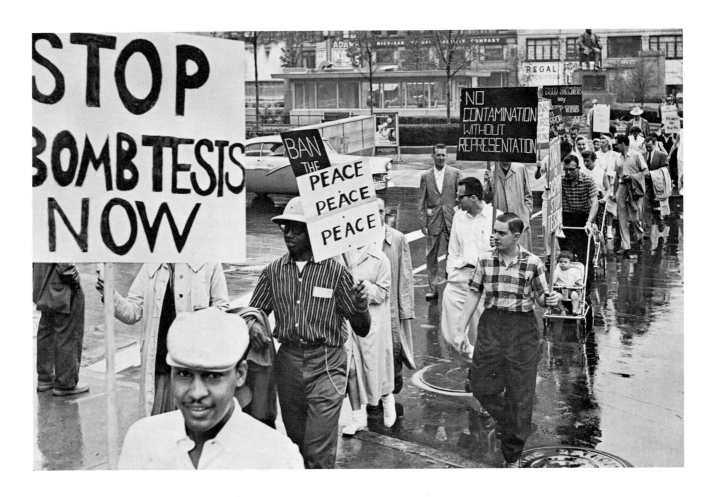

who took part in the City Hall Park demonstration refused to take shelter when ordered. Fifty-two people were arrested, including four leaders of the protest, Ralph DiGia, Robert Gilmore, David McReynolds, and Mrs. Tjader Harris. Following the arrests, 1000 people completely ringed the Criminal Courts Building and picketed until 6 p.m. The demonstrations generated enormous press and television publicity, and marked the last time that New Yorkers were ever required to take shelter during a defense drill.

BAN-THE-BOMB

The growth of the Ban-the-Bomb movement which led to this successful civil disobedience action was primarily due to the influence of *Liberation* magazine, Committee for Nonviolent Action (CNVA) and the Committee for A Sane Nuclear Policy (SANE), all of which were outgrowths of the radical pacifist movement.

Liberation started in 1956 with support from the WRL, and had an editorial staff that included at one

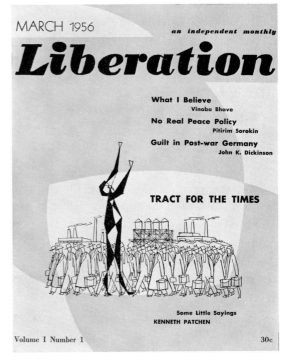

Ban-the-Bomb demonstration, Detroit, 1958. B. Mehrling/Fellowship of Reconciliation.

Cover of the first issue of *Liberation*, March 1956. Institute for the Study of Nonviolence.

time or another Muste, Dellinger, Sid Lens, Bayard Rustin, Charles Walker, Roy Finch, Paul Goodman, Staughton Lynd and Barbara Deming. The magazine took up the cause of civil rights, anarchism, decentralism, nonviolent direct action, unilateral disarmament and a Third Camp foreign policy. Third Camp radicalism rejected the power politics of the Soviet Union and the United States. It looked towards a third way, a path that rejected the centralism, nationalism and the dependence on military power for security that both superpowers shared. "We do not conceive the problem of revolution or the building of a better society as one of accumulating power," the editors said. "The national sovereign, militarized and bureaucratic State and a bureaucratic and collectivist economy are themselves evils to be avoided or abolished." Rather than seize the state, the new radicalism would seek "the transformation of society by human decision and action." Faith in technology, industrialization, and centralization for the sake of efficiency were rejected in favor of "politics of the future." *Liberation* emphasized "the possibilities for decentralization, . . . direct participation of all workers or citizens in determining the conditions of life and work, and . . . the use of technology for human ends, rather than the subjection of man to the demands of technology."

CNVA brought together representatives of all the major pacifist groups. Its purpose was to conduct nonviolent direct action campaigns that local groups could not carry out on their own. It began, under the leadership of a Quaker activist, Lawrence Scott, as an ad-hoc committee called Nonviolent Action Against Nuclear Weapons, which conducted a civil disobedience demonstration during a nuclear bomb test at the atomic proving grounds in Nevada. On August 6, 1957, eleven pacifists crossed over into a prohibited area and were arrested. In 1958 CNVA became a permanent committee and a series of spectacular civil disobedience actions against nuclear weapons were undertaken in the following years. These actions marked CNVA as the cutting edge of a growing movement and as an example of what a few dedicated and committed individuals could achieve with a crucial issue and at the proper time. CNVA never became a membership organization; rather, it planned demonstrations and sought individuals to become full-time participants.

SANE was also formed in 1957, under the leadership of Lawrence Scott, Homer Jack, Norman

A TIME TO WEEP?

A. J. MUSTE

Poster walk for disarmament, Long Beach, California, Armed Forces Day, 1955. Fellowship of Reconciliation.

Cover of pamphlet on the Berlin Crisis published by the War Resisters League, 1961. Institute for the Study of Nonviolence.

AMERICAN FRIENDS
SERVICE COMMITTEE
(Founded 1917)

Since its beginnings in the Seventeenth Century, the Society of Friends has repudiated all wars and refused to participate in them, believing that violence suppresses love, truth and freedom, and at the same time breeds fear, hatred and prejudice. Friends founded the American Friends Service Committee (AFSC) as the corporate expression of the Quaker faith to carry on the traditional peace witness in a constructive and diversified manner. The AFSC, now one of the oldest and largest peace organizations in the world, ministers to the victims of war and injustice on every continent of the world while at the same time searching for new ways to remove the causes of war. By its very nature, the Service Committee has lent a unique definition to organized nonviolence and has often served as the backbone of the ongoing struggle for peace and social justice in the U.S. Three weeks after the U.S. entered the war in 1917, fourteen members of the Religious Society of Friends met to discuss what specific acts Quakers might take to alleviate the agony of war-torn Europe. Rufus Jones echoed the Friends' traditional sentiments when he wrote, "The alternative to war is not inactivity and cowardice. It is the irresistible and constructive power of goodwill." With Jones, Henry Cadbury and James A. Babbitt at its nucleus, the AFSC was formed to provide "a service of love in wartime." Within six months, 116 men

and women were trained and sent to France to do civilian relief work. AFSC greatly expanded its relief work after the war and created a social order committee with study groups on labor conditions and the causes of poverty, the democratization of industry, the distribution of wealth, and the traditional Quaker concepts of simplicity. This increased social concern, arising from the Friends' experiences in the war years, was formalized in the reorganization of AFSC into a permanent organization in 1924 with four sections: foreign service, home service, interracial work, and peace work.

Under Clarence Pickett, who served as Executive Secretary from 1929 until 1950, AFSC extended its activities throughout the world. In the U.S., AFSC fed the starving children of striking Appalacian miners and organized craft cooperatives and homestead farms among sharecroppers and victims of the Depression. The Committee's work with Mennonites and Brethren stimulated unity and social concern among the peace churches and thus set an example of constructive pacifism. In keeping with its non-partisan philosophy, AFSC sent relief aid to both Loyalists and Nationalists during the Spanish Civil War and worked among refugees and prisoners during the second World War. In 1947, AFSC and its British counterpart were awarded the Nobel Peace Prize after sending $7,000,000 worth of relief aid to

Over 1000 silent Quakers surround the Pentagon in testimony to their belief in the futility of war, November 13, 1960. Friends came from across the country for the Peace Witness which marked the 300th anniversary of the first Quaker protest of war (made to King Charles II of England). Theodore Hetzel.

battle-scarred Europe and Japan.

Although AFSC has earned worldwide respect for its relief work, it is not primarily a relief organization. AFSC workers see their primary purpose to be reconciling conflict situations, seeking out areas of tension and misunderstanding in order to bridge the confusions between people and nations. AFSC maintains an active peace program which is directed towards bringing about the day when relief programs will be unnecessary.

In the Thirties, the Service Committee stimulated discussion and action on international issues through its Institutes of International Relations, workcamps, peace caravans, publications and other projects. Beginning in 1926, and continuing over the next 15 years, college students were sent out in pairs in peace caravans, driving from town to town, particularly in the rural Midwest, distributing peace literature and talking to clubs and churches in an effort to build a popular base for the peace movement. In 1936, AFSC participated actively in the Emergency Peace Campaign in the attempt to forestall World War II.

During the war, AFSC administered some 20 CPS camps and 30 smaller units which included 3400 conscientious objectors. On the West Coast, AFSC helped resettle Japanese-Americans who were put into relocation centers, giving them aid and comfort and helping them handle personal and business problems. After the war, the Service Committee spoke out strongly for unilateral disarmament and extended many of its educational programs, such as seminars, workcamps, and conferences, internationally to promote free discussion and intensive study of world problems. AFSC was also at work on Indian reservations, in Mexican-American communities, on programs of housing integration and rural community development.

In 1949 the Service Committee published *The U.S. and the Soviet Union* foreign policy analysis which dealt realistically and objectively with the Cold War. Subsequent reports, such as *Speak Truth to Power* in 1955, laid out the positive requirements for peace — fundamental attacks on world poverty, an end to colonialism, the development of world organization, and disarmament — and protested the reliance on organized mass violence which blocked their development.

During the Vietnam war, AFSC peace workers demonstrated publicly against American involvement, counseled men about the draft, and joined in direct action projects against the war throughout the country. They helped begin peace study courses, provided research into the military-industrial-educational complex, and initiated programs around the Middle East, U.S. involvement in Third World countries, disarmament and peace conversion, and the encroachment on individual freedom in the U.S.

Friends' social and political involvement has not been limited to the American Friends Service Committee. The Friends Committee on National Legislation was founded in 1943, under the direction of E. Raymond Wilson, as a Washington lobby to deal with national actions of the

federal government affecting issues of peace and social justice. The Friends Peace Committee, formed in 1933, provides peace education for various Friends Yearly Meetings and serves as a center to actively promote Quaker peace concerns. A Quaker Action Group (AQAG) and the Movement for a New Society (MNS) are also distinct from AFSC but include many Quakers.

AQAG, founded in 1966 by Lawrence Scott and others, achieved a certain degree of fame for initiating such transnational nonviolent action projects as the attempt to carry medical supplies by boat into parts of Vietnam and an effort to demilitarize the Puerto Rican island of Culebra where the U.S. Navy carried out target practice. Out of these experiences, the need grew to develop a more comprehensive perspective and framework of action, and to create an organizational structure to promote nonviolent revolution different from the national committees characteristic of the peace movement. With the efforts of Susan Gowan, George Lakey, Bill Moyers, and Dick Taylor, the Movement for a New Society grew out of AQAG in 1971 and set up projects and living centers to encourage a simple lifestyle, to create a source of sustained fellowship and moral support, and to provide a bulwark against repression. MNS encouraged political and economic analysis, community involvement, collective work, and a broader conception of nonviolence which unites political action with responsible and joyful living.

Picket line protesting capital punishment outside the gates of San Quentin prison shortly before Caryl Chessman was put to death in the gas chamber. San Quentin, California, May 2, 1960. Wide World.

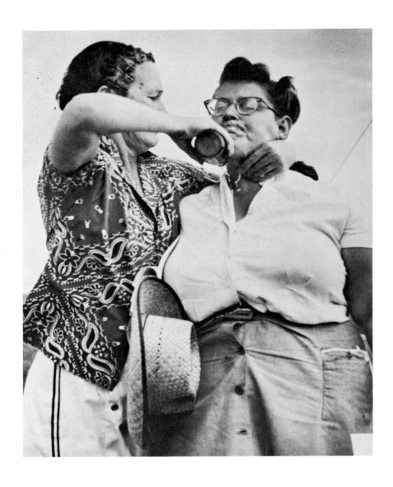

Cousins, Robert Gilmore and others, and was structured as an educational and membership organization to bring pacifists and non-pacifists together in the common cause of bringing the arms race under control. The two organizations effectively complemented one another: CNVA's stirring demonstrations shook people out of their complacency and made them want to do something against the bomb. For the many who were not yet ready to take the risks and make the commitment that CNVA demanded, SANE and the Student Peace Union, organized in Chicago in 1959, were available. Moderate by contrast, both SANE and SPU brought pacifists and non-pacifists into the growing movement against the bomb, the organized movement for peace.

The Nevada demonstration was the first national direct action peace effort since the draft card destruction in 1947. People from the West Coast joined the Eastern contingent which did the planning and three of the eleven people arrested were from a pacifist community in Modesto, California, which was patterned after Peacemaker groups. The

Peninsula Committee for the Abolition of Nuclear Tests was formed in 1957 by Roy Kepler, Ted Roszak, Felix Greene, Aggie Robinson, Al Baez, Ira Sandperl, and Karen Tucker. It joined regionally with AFSC and other groups in supporting the Northern California Committee for the Abolition of Nuclear Tests. A few years later, this sizeable and largely volunteer movement was merged into Acts for Peace, directed by Robert Pickus and initiated by WRL, which later became Turn Toward Peace, a national effort. A West Coast CNVA also grew up in the late Fifties and among its projects were sit-ins at the Lawrence Radiation Laboratory in Livermore, California, home of the H-Bomb, and other demonstrations and acts of civil disobedience at Port Chicago, the Navy's munitions port, the Oakland Naval Base, and the U.S. Federal District Court in San Francisco. Disarmament and anti-war efforts on the West Coast were furthered by WRL/West, which came into existence in 1965, and the Institute for the Study of Nonviolence, which Joan Baez, Ira Sandperl, Roy Kepler, and Holly Chenery organized in Carmel Valley the same year.

Leaflet from Non-Violent Action Against Nuclear Weapons, Las Vegas, Nevada, 1957. Sam Tyson.

An angry Cheyenne woman pours a soda down the blouse of nonresisting Erica Enzer of the Committee for Nonviolent Action while she was picketing the Atlas missile base construction site, Cheyenne, Wyoming, August 28, 1958. Fellowship of Reconciliation.

THE GOLDEN RULE

One of the most successful CNVA projects was the attempted sailing of the *Golden Rule* into the nuclear bomb test area in the South Pacific. The ketch sailed from California to Honolulu on May 2, 1958, with a crew consisting of Albert Bigelow, William Huntington, George Willoughby and Orion Sherwood, and then for Eniwetok, where the United States was planning bomb tests. The Coast Guard intercepted the vessel and the men were arrested and brought to Honolulu where they refused bail while awaiting trial for contempt. The attempt to sail into the test zone caught the attention of the world and with news of their arrest came the announcement of support demonstrations in seven American cities, in Montreal and in London. At the same time, a second group of pacifists including Scott and Bayard Rustin set out for the Soviet Union to appeal to the Russian people to stop their country's bomb testing. Though the pacifists could not get into the Soviet Union, their stops at

London, Paris and Bonn helped spur an international movement against the bomb. As Albert Bigelow wrote in his book *The Voyage of the Golden Rule*:

> *Most of these people had never seen a public demonstration or picket line before. Few would have described themselves as 'pacifists.' Many, in person and by petition . . . tried to share more fully in our actions. : . . In San Francisco alone, 432 persons petitioned the U.S. Attorney to take action against them. They said that if the crew of the* Golden Rule *were guilty, so were they.*

In June, the *Golden Rule* attempted a second sailing, this time without Bigelow who had been arrested for "criminal conspiracy" ten minutes before scheduled sailing, and with Jim Peck having joined the crew. The ketch succeeded in getting out of U.S. territorial waters but the Coast Guard chased after it and arrested the crew, all of whom

The *Golden Rule*, 5 miles out at sea, is pursued by Coast Guard boats while attempting to sail into the nuclear test zone, June 4, 1958. Eight days later, the *Phoenix* sailed. *Honolulu Star-Bulletin.*

were sentenced to sixty days in jail.

A third attempt to sail into the test zone was made by Earle and Barbara Reynolds with their two children and Nick Mikami from Hiroshima. Reynolds, an anthropologist employed by the U. S. Atomic Energy Commission in Japan, was completing an around the world trip when the attempted protest sailings took place. Agreeing with what the *Golden Rule* was doing, he attempted to sail his fifty foot ketch *Phoenix* into the bomb test area and was arrested. The sailings of the *Golden Rule* and *Phoenix* were the most important pacifist demonstrations to that time. Unlike previous actions, they did not occur in a vacuum, but won worldwide publicity and a kind of qualitative support that brought thousands of other people into the street making their disagreement with authority public for the first time. Why did the voyage of the *Golden Rule* attract so much attention and cut through the silence and apathy of the 1950s? "These tiny ships," Bigelow has suggested, "said that here were men who cared enough to become involved . . . to risk everything."

1958 saw other demonstrations for peace. A

Golden Rule skipper Albert Bigelow is sentenced to 60 days in jail after his second attempt to sail into the nuclear test area, Honolulu, Hawaii, June 4, 1958. Fellowship of Reconciliation.

Demonstration outside the federal courthouse, Honolulu, Hawaii in support of the *Golden Rule* , June 4, 1958. *Honolulu Star Bulletin.*

group of pacifists went to Cheyenne to try to gain public support against construction of a missile base and five of them, Ted Olson, Ken and Eleanor Calkins, John White and Erica Enzer, served 104 day prison sentences for trying to halt construction of the base. A group of Peacemakers picketed at Cape Canaveral and walked across Puerto Rico protesting U.S. colonialism. Another Peacemaker, Rev. Maurice McCrackin of Cincinnati, was sentenced to six months in jail for refusing to pay his federal tax, a type of protest that the Peacemakers coordinated on a nationwide basis.

The next year, Lawrence Scott and others initiated the Fort Detrick Vigil, an action which continued for almost two years at the main center for research and development of germ warfare in the country. The major CNVA project was Omaha Action, coordinated by A.J. Muste and Brad Lyttle, which stemmed from the Cheyenne project and from the growing concern about the new delivery

Announcement from the *Livermore* (California) *News*, August 5, 1958. Sam Tyson.

The Easter Walk for Peace, which began in Philadelphia and New Haven, converges on the United Nations, New York City, April 4, 1958. Sam Schulmann/War Resisters League.

systems which escalated the threat of nuclear war. The summer-long campaign was visualized as using a variety of education and nonviolent action techniques, including a vigil throughout the summer months outside the Mead Missile Base near Omaha, Nebraska, walks to the base from Omaha and Lincoln, visitations to churches, organizations, news media, and homes in the whole area, and finally a series of civil disobedience actions in which two or three people at a time attempted to enter the base to protest the construction of the missile silos and urge workers to lay down their jobs.

A. J. Muste, Ross Anderson, Wilmer Young, Karl Meyer, Neil Haworth, Brad Lyttle, Marj Swann, and Arthur Harvey were among the fifteen or so people arrested for "trespassing" and given suspended sentences of 6 months in federal prison and $500 fines. Erica Enzer and John White were sentenced to shorter terms for sitting in the road and attempting to block trucks, and those who returned to the base despite their suspended sentences were re-arrested and sent off to various federal prisons to do their time. While in prison, Brad Lyttle con-

Silent vigil by participants in Omaha Action before civil disobedience at Mead Missile Base, July 1959. Facing from left are: Ross Anderson, Margaret Haworth, A.J. Muste, Karl Meyer, Larry Schumm, Erika Enzer, Neil Haworth, and Wilmer Young. WRL.

A.J. Muste informs army officer of his intention to commit civil disobedience, Omaha, Nebraska, July 1, 1959. War Resisters League.

Signs from CNVA's Omaha Action outside Mead Missile Base, Omaha, Nebraska, July 1959. War Resisters League.

ceived the Polaris Action project as the next step in arousing public, Congressional, and media awareness of the growing risk of nuclear war and the growing danger of the nuclear arms race. He saw the wide-roving Polaris submarines, with their loads of Polaris ICBM missiles targeted on Russian cities and civilian populations, as the keystone of the U.S. nuclear deterrent policy. He also saw the dramatic possibilities of a confrontation between the unarmed bodies of nonviolent "satyagrahis" and the massive Polaris death machines.

WORLD PEACE BRIGADE

Radical pacifists around the world were inspired by these CNVA projects. In December 1959 Muste, Bayard Rustin, Bill Sutherland and British pacifist Michael Scott, who had long been active in the African freedom struggle, journeyed to the Sahara Desert to protest France's nuclear testing program. With a group of Africans they attempted to enter the bomb test zone, but were turned back. However, Africans were introduced to radical nonviolence and in 1961 an experimental World Peace Brigade was established at a conference in Beirut, Lebanon, under the direction of Scott, Muste and an Indian, Jayaprakash Narayan. Also present at Beirut were pacifist activists from many countries, among them the French worker-priest Abbe Pierre, American writers Barbara Deming and Ann Morrissett, and others. The Brigade hoped to establish a nonviolent striking force which would use nonviolent methods to "revolutionize the concept of revolution itself by infusing into the methods of resisting injustice the qualities which insure the preservation of human life and dignity." The Brigade's most important project was a training center for nonviolent action in Dar-es-Salaam, Tanzania. Bill Sutherland settled there, advising the governments of Julius Nyerere and of Kenneth Kaunda of Zambia, both advocates of Gandhian nonviolence.

A.J. Muste climbs the fence of Mead Missile Base in an act of civil disobedience to protest U.S. missile policy, Omaha, Nebraska, July 1, 1959. Ross Anderson, another member of Omaha Action, awaits his turn at right. Swarthmore College Peace Collection.

Upper left: Leaflet from the Vigil at Fort Detrick, Maryland Chemical Warfare Center, 1960. Sam Tyson.

Maury Englander

A.J. MUSTE
(1885 - 1967)

Abraham Johannes Muste, a radical activist all his adult life, was a major figure in the pacifist community in the U.S. throughout much of the Twentieth Century. He was an astute analyst of the social, political, and economic problems of this country and the world, and worked prominently in the American labor movement in the Twenties and Thirties. Convinced of the revolutionary implications of Christian ideals, he sought strategies to implement religious and humanitarian principles as the political norm. He took the lead in organizing resistance to U.S. military involvements throughout the world and concentrated on turning American pacifism into a mass, direct action movement based on the philosophy and techniques of active nonviolence.

Muste came to the U.S. from The Netherlands at the age of six and settled with his parents in Michigan. He was ordained a minister of the Dutch Reformed Church (Calvinist) in 1909 and four years later graduated from Union Theological Seminary in New York. During the first World War, he was forced to resign as minister of the Central Congregational Church in Newtonville, Massachusetts, because he refused to abandon or silence his religious pacifist convictions. After moving to Boston in 1918 with his wife Anna Huizinga Muste, with whom he raised three children, A.J. led a nonviolent strike of textile workers at Lawrence and became General Secretary of the Amalgamated Textile Workers of America. From 1921 to 1933 he directed the Brookwood Labor College, where many future organizers of the CIO were trained. He also chaired the Fellowship of Reconciliation from 1926 to 1929 and the Conference for Progressive Labor Action from 1929 to 1933. Muste was a key figure in a number of labor strikes during the Thirties and was one of the first to popularize the tactic of the sit-down strike.

In his essay "Pacifism and Class War," written in 1927, he wrote that, "In a world built on violence, one must be revolutionary before one can be a pacifist."

There is a certain indolence in us, a wish not to be disturbed, which tempts us to think that things are quiet, all is well. Subconsciously, we tend to give the preference to "social peace," though it be only apparent, because our lives and possessions seem then secure. Actually, human beings acquiesce too easily in evil conditions; they rebel far too little and too seldom. There is nothing noble about acquiescence in a cramped life or mere submission to superior force.

Muste demanded focused thought from pacifists and called on them "to denounce the violence on which the present system is based . . . So long as we are not dealing honestly and adequately with this ninety percent of our problem, there is something ludicrous, and perhaps hypocritical, about our concern over the ten percent of violence employed by the rebels against oppression."

For a brief period in the Thirties, Muste was one of the outstanding leaders of the Trotskyist movement in the United States. He resigned from the orthodox Left in 1936, again convinced of the importance of a radically active nonviolence, and became Executive Secretary of the Fellowship of Reconciliation. "There is no way to peace," he wrote, "peace is the way."

A prolific lecturer and writer, Muste articulated a vision of nonviolent revolution which included a democratic political order, a socialist economic system, world government, and a nonviolent method of national civil defense. He helped establish and edit *Liberation* magazine and was active in Peacemakers, the War Resisters League, and many other nonviolent groups and committees. He was arrested repeatedly for his work on behalf of labor, civil liberties, and peace.

In 1940, Muste stood up at a Quaker meeting and testified, "If I can't love Hitler, I can't love at all." Later he made similar statements about Communists and American racists. During the darkest days of the McCarthy Era, Muste was one of the few non-Communists to keep a dialogue open with the Communists. In 1956 he wrote:

> *As Christians – or on other grounds – in our personal and other relations, Communists are to us human beings, members of the one human family, children of God. We are to love them, but I do not take this to mean that we have to work with them politically or be sentimental and naive about certain aspects of their behavior and strategy. To love a fellow man does not require that we cooperate with him in lying or exploiting others or some other evil thing. It requires the opposite, that we do not let him live, if he is so living, under the delusion that these things are good. It means that we love him even while he does evil, believe that he is capable of redemption, try to call to "that God in him." To love, to be truly human, is always to deal with others on the basis of reality.*

As Executive Secretary of the FOR, Muste had a profound effect on the initiation of the nonviolent civil rights movement which matured in the late Fifties and early Sixties. CORE was founded and led by FOR staff members working in close consultation with Muste. Two of these, James Farmer and Bayard Rustin, became major leaders of the civil rights movement in its period of greatest growth and impact. Other leaders, including Martin

Luther King, Jr., and groups such as SNCC and SCLC were greatly influenced by Muste in their adoption of nonviolence as a tactic and a way of life. Impressed by the political success of Gandhi in India, Muste took the Gandhian concept of Satyagraha — "Soul force" — and placed it in an American context.

In the late Fifties and early Sixties, Muste devoted his attention to the development of a radical, politically relevant nonviolent movement. When the Committee for Nonviolent Action was formed in 1957, Muste served as chairperson, helped to plan and participated in many direct action campaigns. It was largely through his diplomacy that the San Francisco to Moscow peace walkers were able to enter and demonstrate in Poland and the Soviet Union. He also refused to pay war taxes and was one of the principal figures in starting the campaign against Civil Defense drills in New York City.

With the escalation of the Vietnam war in the early Sixties, Muste took a leading role in organizing rallies, vigils and marches to protest expanding U.S. involvement. As dean of American pacifists and one of the few radicals held in esteem by all members of the multifactioned Left, he was propelled into the national leadership of the American anti-war movement. He led the peace movement in New York City as chairperson of the Fifth Avenue Peace Parade Committee and helped lend that broad coalition a degree of openness, honesty, and integrity that had long been absent in the American Left. In May 1966, Muste went with a CNVA group to South Vietnam to make successful contact with Vietnamese dissenters and was deported for demonstrating against the war in the streets of Saigon. In January 1967, at age 81, he met with Ho Chi Minh in Hanoi in an effort to find possible ways to end the war. Muste died seventeen days later, widely honored and respected as a genuine American revolutionary who committed his whole life to the struggle for peace, economic justice, human dignity, and liberation.

A.J. Muste with peace walkers, New York City, August 1963. Neil Haworth/War Resisters League.

CNVA

THIS IS
POLARIS ACTION

ACT NOW FOR PEACE

Americans acting to prevent thermonuclear war and preserve freedom.

WATCH FOR
• **Satyagraha,** a sloop sailing the coast from Florida to Maine; sailing for world peace.
• **Automobile Floats** bearing the message: Polaris Action, Join nonviolent action against missile subs.
• **Leaflets,** like the one you're reading.

OUR PURPOSE
• To alert our fellow Americans to the facts and realities of the suicidal arms race.
• To protest
  — Development of Polaris missile launching sub.
  — The absurd, self-destructive and inhuman policies of deterence and massive retaliation.
• To propose a moral and practical foreign policy, including
  — Defense by nonviolent resistance. We believe that variations of the techniques of resistance used by Ghandi to help free India could defend liberty against totalitarianism.
  — Unilateral disarmament.
  — Massive nonmilitary U.N. foreign aid to "have not" nations.
• To explain and demonstrate the **practicality of nonviolent resistance.**

OUR PROGRAM
Positive action by land and sea using: signs, leaflets, literature, and including: voyages, walks, public meetings, vigil, civil disobedience.

POLARIS ACTION

Polaris Action was started in 1960 and the San Francisco to Moscow Walk for Peace in 1961, both coordinated by Bradford Lyttle. Polaris Action tried to bring nonviolence to a single community, New London, Conn., that was dependent on the construction of nuclear submarines for much of its economy. Most of its actions were routine: leafleting workers, trying to break down their initial hostility and begin communications with them.

There were numerous difficult encounters with sailors, workers and other members of the community. "But worse than the isolated and occasional incidents of violence," reported David McReynolds, "was the constant tension, the realization that at any moment there might be an attack made on the office or the staff." One of the lessons to be learned, he continued, was "that pacifists, established in a hostile community, and unwilling to call upon the police for protection, can defend themselves without resorting to violence."

The emphasis of Polaris Action, like all CNVA projects, was direct action. On numerous occasions, pacifists tried to enter the docks where the submarines were being constructed or to interfere with their launching by paddling boats carrying peace messages into restricted areas or, as on a number of occasions, actually trying to swim out to the submarines to board them. In November 1960 Bill Henry and Don Martin succeeded in swimming

Leaflet from CNVA Polaris Action, 1960. Committee for Nonviolent Action.

CNVA member Don Martin climbs aboard the newly-launched nuclear submarine *Ethan Allen* during CNVA's Polaris Action in Groton, Connecticut, November 22, 1960. Martin was arrested and sentenced to 19 months in jail for his well-publicized protest action. Wide World.

New England CNVA workshop on Latin America, Voluntown, Connecticut, November 1968. Father Blaise Bonpane, a Maryknoll priest expelled from Guatemala, led the workshop which was attended by over 100 participants. Brad Lyttle/Committee for Nonviolent Action.

out to the submarine *Ethan Allen* and climbing on board.

At the end of the summer of 1960, Bob and Marj Swann became concerned about the pattern of summer projects which stirred up a community and engendered intensive action, only to have everything die down and return to "normal" in the fall. With a few others, they decided to move to the New London area and continue Polaris Action, and so New England CNVA came into being, an autonomous committee and staff which related closely to the national organization in New York. From the beginning, New England CNVA was a residential community and located, in the summer of 1962, on an old farm at Voluntown, Connecticut. There, for almost 12 years, New England CNVA, with a volunteer staff of from 6 to 20 people receiving only their maintenance, carried out a constant round of demonstrations, walks, vigils, fasts, and caravans all over New England. They ran a continuous series of nonviolence training programs and conferences on a variety of topics at the farm and engaged in draft and military counseling, sanctuary for deserters and draft refugees, tax resistance, training for big Washington demonstrations, draft card burnings, peace conversion programs, and military base conversion projects.

A constant flow of visitors, students, and resource people from all over the world kept New England CNVA in a constant state of creative ferment and turmoil. Continuously harassed by local young men, by the FBI, state police, and sometimes local officials, CNVA staff gradually developed good relations with many townspeople, nearby merchants, and even public officials. Its consistent adherence to nonviolence and to complete openness (except for work with deserters)

Nonviolent training and role playing at a New England CNVA conference, Voluntown, Connecticut, c. 1967. Brad Lyttle/CNVA.

CNVA member Bill Henry is thrown to the ground during Polaris Action demonstration at the Electric Boat Company, Groton, Connecticut, August 18, 1962. Brad Lyttle, already arrested, peers out a police car window in the rear. Photo courtesy of Barbara Deming.

New England CNVA farm in Voluntown, Connecticut, Summer 1969. Ted Polumbaum/CNVA.

Brad Lyttle

MARJORIE SWANN
(Born 1921)

Through her involvement in civil rights, community relations, and international peace activities, Marjorie Swann helped clarify and encourage the growth of active nonviolence after World War II. She and her husband Bob Swann were among the war resisters who emerged to give radical pacifist leadership to the movements of the postwar years. In her work with the Committee for Nonviolent Action, she inspired other activists and focused national attention on the arms race and the need for fundamental nonviolent change. She engaged extensively in nonviolent training and direct action and was arrested many times in the course of her work for disarmament, equal rights and peace.

Born on a farm in Cedar Rapids, Iowa, Swann moved with her parents to Chicago and did the housework, shopping, and caring for the younger children while both her parents worked. She went to Northwestern University on a scholarship, worked as a typist, dental assistant, waitress and clerk, and joined a Methodist Young People's Fellowship whose minister was a pacifist. She picketed for freedom for India in the early Forties and was arrested for the first time during a demonstration outside the British Embassy in Washington D.C.

During World War II, she worked as administrative secretary of the National Committee on Conscientious Objection and during the Fifties was active with the American Friends Service Committee and the Minnesota Council Against Peacetime Conscription. A charter member of the Congress of Racial Equality, she was also active in Peacemakers, the War Resisters League, NAACP, FOR, and the war tax resistance movement.

In 1959, she was arrested for trespassing during the civil disobedience Omaha Action and was sentenced to six months in federal prison. The following year, she and her husband founded the New England Committee for Nonviolent Action, and for nearly 12 years, they helped guide CNVA's program of nonviolent direct action, development of constructive program, and training in nonvio-

lent action. With Garrisonian vigor, Marj Swann led direct action campaigns against nuclear submarines and nuclear weapons and dramatically popularized the techniques of nonviolent resistance. She challenged pacifists to tackle some of the really formidable, basic problems facing society.

Although advocates of nonviolence talk about the necessity of both direct action – protest – and of constructive program, we do not yet really see the union of these two aspects in a clear workable form. More important, perhaps, is the fact that most of us either do not realize, or have not accepted, the reality that disarmament and peace and the development of a "nonviolent world" call for some startling changes in economic, social and political structures.

Recognizing the lack of overall blueprints and unified direction within the peace movement in the mid-Sixties, she called for continued experimentation and the disciplined application of nonviolence to practical problems.

In the practice of nonviolence, be it on a personal scale, in nonviolent action for civil rights or peace, or on an international level, we cannot expect immediately visible results, and we cannot be disappointed if the response is not mechanically proper according to theory.

With New England CNVA, she organized protests, fasts, vigils and demonstrations against U.S. involvement in Vietnam, and wrote:

Constantly on my mind was the policy I have always understood to have been advocated by Gandhi: "It is better to resist oppression by violent means than to submit, but it is best of all to resist by nonviolent means." Therefore, I understood clearly my own role: to oppose the massive violence and oppression of the U.S. government and that of the Saigon government if possible, by nonviolent resistance – education, direct action, civil disobedience.

With unswerving commitment and revolutionary spirit, she called for activists to keep alive the struggle for nonviolent solutions to conflict, to practice nonviolent resistance to injustice, and to consciously develop and spread a total philosophy of nonviolence. The mother of four children, she wrote:

As a woman, I certainly experience a kind of rage and frustration similar to that which Third World people do, and as a woman working on women's liberation issues, I advocate and practice aggressive nonviolence to deal with the injustices I feel as a woman.

She worked as coordinator of the Harrisburg Pilgrimage in New England in 1972 and was appointed Executive Secretary of the AFSC's New England Regional Office in 1975.

saved CNVA from any of the frame-ups or police raids practiced on many movement centers in the later Sixties. However, two serious attacks by the right-wing paramilitary Minutemen resulted in a serious fire in 1966 and in an armed attack on the farm in 1968. The state police, who engaged in a shoot-out with the Minutemen, had known about the planned attack in advance but did not inform CNVA. This incident so shocked local people that there was never again any harassment, and the changing political climate led to friendly visits by local young people seeking information and draft counseling.

SAN FRANCISCO TO MOSCOW WALK FOR PEACE

During the Polaris Action, CNVA demonstrators were often told to take their ideas about peace to the Russians, and so Brad Lyttle, Scott Herrick, Julius Jacobs, and others took up the challenge. On December 1, 1960, eleven pacifists left San Francisco on a walk that would take them across the United States and Europe to Moscow. After ten months and 6000 miles of walking, a combined

San Francisco to Moscow peace walkers in Pennsylvania, May 21, 1961. Theodore Hetzel.

Call for walkers for CNVA's San Francisco to Moscow Walk for Peace, 1960. Institute for the Study of Nonviolence.

WE ARE WALKING TO MOSCOW

Some of us have walked from San Francisco, almost 4,000 miles, to the Capital of the United States — **WASHINGTON D.C.**

For we are equally opposed to the armaments of the East and West. We are marching for unconditional disarmament NOW.

The most effective way to any disarmament today, we believe, is for some nation to start scrapping its weapons. When one country disarms first, it opens the way for others to do the same. Some nation must find the courage to act first.

In each country we pass through we are calling on the government to give up nuclear weapons unconditionally and to discard military pacts based on them. These pacts intensify the Cold War.

H-bombs and missiles are totally evil. They can kill millions of people outright, destroy thousands more slowly from burns and radiation sickness, and harm future generations. We cannot without protest let our own governments use these weapons in our name. And any country which has H-bombs and missiles, for whatever reason, is in fact willing to use them.

In the nuclear age war is outdated. It cannot deal effectively with major conflicts, and any war is likely to become a nuclear war. Dependence on arms must therefore be rejected.

In this new situation we believe that non-violence — such as Gandhi used for the freedom of India, and the Norwegian teachers used in resisting Hitler — can best defend and enlarge freedom and justice.

All governments should therefore end conscription, start to do away with armed forces and turn to Gandhian non-violence to defend freedom and resist tyranny and oppression.

BREAD NOT BOMBS

The world is full of hunger, disease and poverty. We believe that the Soviet Union and the United States with other countries should pool their resources to remove such suffering — by using the money now wasted on weapons of destruction.

We are appealing above all to the ordinary people in every country we walk through to take personal action and to work for the unconditional renunciation of arms by their own country. In Moscow and in every capital city on our route we shall say what the American Marchers have already said in Washington, D.C., the capital of the United States :

" At this stage disarmament can be achieved if one nation is prepared to take a first step in giving up its arms as an example for others to follow."

WE CANNOT BE SILENT

Some of us act out of religious conviction, others out of commitment to ethical values, and we are united in opposing modern war. Because humanity is in such grave danger of destruction, we are determined to speak what we believe to be true. In our own countries we have all urged the renunciation of mass violence. And we shall continue to do this. Some of us have joined demonstrations for disarmament. Others have refused to pay taxes for war, or have refused military service, or have protested at missile bases and atomic plants, or refused to work in industries making arms. As a result some of us have been arrested in our own countries and have spent time in prison.

WE SHALL SPEAK

This is our record. These are our beliefs. We hope to be able to speak out freely wherever we go. Within each country we will insist on distributing our literature, holding our banners and talking with the people. Because we believe the discussion of our ideas is vital, we are prepared to go to prison if prevented from carrying out our march of spreading our beliefs.

We believe that peace can only come when nations give up dependence on military force and turn to the kind of power Gandhi used in India. We therefore urge you, *according to your convictions,* to

ACT FOR PEACE NOW !

Printed by Goodwin Press Ltd. (T.U.), 135 Fonthill Road, Finsbury Park, N.4

МЫ ИДЕМ В МОСКВУ.

Некоторые из нас прошли пешком почти 7.000 километров от Сан Франциско до **ВАШИНГТОНА,** D.C. С.Ш.А.

Мы одинаково против вооружения как Востока, так и Запада. Мы совершаем наш поход во имя разоружения сейчас же и без всяких условий.

Мы верим, что наилучший способ добиться разоружения сегодня это, чтобы какая нибудь страна начала уничтожать свое вооружение. Разоружившись первой, она тем самым откроет путь другим. Какая нибудь одна страна должна найти мужество быть первой.

В каждой стране, через которую мы проходим, мы призываем правительство отказаться безусловно от ядерного оружия и порвать военные соглашения, на нем основанные.

Водородные бомбы и ракеты могут разом уничтожать миллионы людей и привести медленную смерть тысячам других через ожоги, радиацию и заболевания, а также повредить будущие поколения. Мы не можем без протеста позволить нашему собственному правительству пользоваться этим оружием от нашего имени. А всякая страна обладающая водородными бомбами и ракетами, фактически готова ими пользоваться.

В наш атомный век война устарела. Она неможет справляться с крупными конфликтами, причем всякая война может превратиться в атомическую войну. Поэтому надо освободиться от зависимости от вооружений.

В этой новой ситуации мы считаем, что отказ от насилия — тот, который Ганди использовал для освобождения Индии, а норвежские педагоги в своем сопротивлении Гитлеру — лучше всего сможет защитить и распространить свободу и справедливость.

Поэтому все правительства должны были бы положить конец воинской повинности, начать распускать вооруженные силы и перейти к непротивлению, по примеру Ганди, для того чтобы защитить свободу и дать отпор тирании и насилию.

ХЛЕБ, А НЕ БОМБА.

Мир полон голода, болезней и нищеты. Мы считаем, что Советский Союз и США, вместе с другими странами, должны были бч объединить свои средства и употребить на искоренение этих страданий те деньги, которые сейчас тратятся бесполезно на орудия уничтожения.

Мы прежде всего призываем простых людей каждой страны, через которую мы проходим, принять личное деятельное участие и работать на безусловный отказ от вооружения их собственной родины. В Москве, и в каждой столице на нашем пути мы скажем то, что американские участники похода уже сказали в Вашингтоне, столице США :

«При нынешнем положении вещей, разоружение может быть достигнуто, если одно какое нибудь государство готово сделать первый шаг, отказавшись от вооружений, подав пример, которому бы последовали другие».

МЫ НЕ МОЖЕМ МОЛЧАТЬ.

Некоторые из нас действуют по религиозным убеждениям, другие из соображений этики, и мы объединены в своей оппозиции мировой войне. В виду того, что человечество находится под такой серьезной угрозой уничтожения, мы намерены говорить то, что мы считаем правильным. В наших собственных странах мы все призывали к отказу от насилия войны. И мы будем продолжать так говорить. Некоторые из нас принимали участие в демонстрациях во имя разоружения. Другие отказывались платить налоги для войны, либо отказывались отбывать воинскую повинность, либо протестовали против ракетных баз и ядерных заводов, либо отказывались работать в промышленности, изготовляющей вооружение. В результате некоторые из нас подверглись у аресту себя на родине и провели некоттрое время в заключении.

МЫ БУДЕМ ГОВОРИТЬ

Таков отчет нашей деятельности. Таковы наши убеждения. Мы надеемся на возможность говорить свободно всюду где мы будем. В каждой стране мы будем настаивать на распространении нашей литературы, вздымая наши знамена и обращаясь к людям. Поэтому что мы верим, что обсуждение наших идей абсолютно необходимо, мы готовы идти в тюрму, если нам будут препятствовать вести наш поход или распространять наши убеждения.

Мы убеждены, что мир может наступить только тогда, когда народы откажутся от зависимости от военной силы и обратятся к той силе которую, Ганди употребил в Индии. Поэтому мы призываем вас **работать на мир сейчас соответственно с вашимыми убеждениями.**

Printed by Goodwin Press Ltd. (T.U.), 135 Fonthill Road, Finsbury Park, N.4

Американско—Европейский Комитет Похода, Лондонское Бюро: 5 Каледониан Роад, Лондон, N.1.

---

group of American and European peace walkers reached Moscow and demonstrated in Red Square for peace and disarmament. In the U.S., marchers walked 25 to 30 miles a day, and often had to camp out when even churches were too unfriendly to offer hospitality. Once they ran out of money and had to go for weeks on little but boiled potatoes and multi-purpose food. Few projects, however, made so many friends for the American peace movement or made the demand for an end to nuclear bomb tests so public.

After flying to London, the Americans were joined by peace walkers from nine other countries. Wherever they went, the walkers spoke to students, held rallies, and gave the same message in leaflets and on signs in the language of their host country: oppose the militarism of your government, don't join the army of your country, stop the arms race. Probably the main reason that they were admitted to East Germany, Poland and Russia was that they had all opposed war and the arms race in their own countries, and many had gone to prison because of their opposition.

The walkers reached Red Square in Moscow on October 3, 1961, where they conducted a vigil and distributed leaflets urging unilateral disarmament. "I went to jail because I refused to serve in the U.S. Army," Brad Lyttle told the Russians in a speech. "I have protested against American rockets aimed at your cities and families. There are Soviet rockets

Leaflet in English and Russian from CNVA's San Francisco to Moscow Walk for Peace, 1961. Institute for the Study of Nonviolence.

aimed at my city and family. Are you protesting against that?" This was the first time the radical pacifist message had been heard in the Soviet Union and many commentators took the Soviet decision to allow the CNVA walkers to hike to Moscow as an indication of a "thaw in the Cold War." The *New York Herald Tribune* commented editorially that of course pacifism was not realistic, but it had to admit that pacifists were able to do what no other diplomats or journalists were able to do before — demonstrate visible protest in the Soviet capital.

EVERYMAN

In the following years, before the war in Vietnam became a major issue, CNVA used two basic tactics: peace walks that often included civil disobedience and attempts to sail into nuclear test zones to protest nuclear weapons. In 1962 there were two attempts made to sail into the Christmas Island bomb test zone on *Everyman I* and *II* and an attempt by an international crew to reach the Soviet Union by boat on *Everyman III*.

Attempts to sail the trimaran *Everyman I* out of

The Committee for Nonviolent Action San Francisco to Moscow peace walkers demonstrate for disarmament in Red Square, Moscow, USSR, October 3, 1961. A. Stuzhin/UPI.

Leafleting in Russia during the San Francisco to Moscow Walk for Peace, 1961. Swarthmore College Peace Collection.

the San Francisco harbor, first in May and again in July; were thwarted by the Coast Guard, and members of both crews — Hal Stallings, Evan Yoes, Ed Lazar, Walter Chafee, Bob Robbins and Barton Stone — were arrested and imprisoned. Both Stone and Lazar had been on the San Francisco to Moscow Peace Walk. The aborted attempt to launch *Everyman I* in May led to a number of support demonstrations and the decision of Dr. Monte Steadman to give up his post as a department head at the Kaiser Foundation Hospital in San Francisco and fly to Honolulu where he purchased a 28-foot ketch named *Everyman II*. He was joined by a crew consisting of George Benello and Gordon Zahn and they managed to sail into the Johnson Island test zone for four days before being boarded by the Coast Guard and ordered back to Honolulu.

The third *Everyman* sailed from London on September 26 with an international crew of fifteen, skippered by Earle Reynolds and with Neil Haworth as project coordinator. The aim of the project was to sail the *Everyman III* to Leningrad and then via canals and rivers to Moscow to urge immediate cessation of nuclear tests. When the Russians denied the *Everyman* entry, some of the

Russian citizens reach for disarmament leaflets distributed by CNVA peace walkers, Moscow USSR, October 1961. Committee for Nonviolent Action.

Everyman I leaves San Francisco Bay for the Christmas Island nuclear test zone, May 1962. Joseph Rosenthal/ *San Francisco Chronicle* .

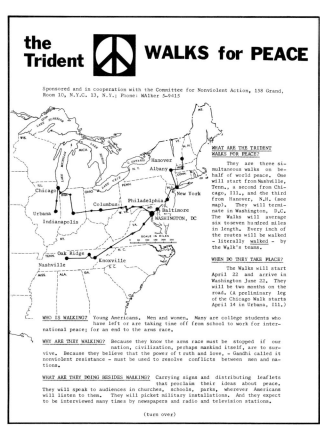

crew jumped overboard and tried to swim to shore. The Russians then tried to tow the boat out to sea, but the pacifists began boring holes in the hull in an attempt to scuttle it. Finally, after holding the participants prisoner on board ship in the harbor, the Soviets repaired the ship and towed it out to sea again, allowing it to sail to Stockholm for the winter.

THE IMPACT OF CNVA

These demonstrations, like the earlier *Golden Rule* and *Phoenix* sailings and the on-going Polaris Action projects in Connecticut, were probably viewed by most people as being somewhat kooky and extreme. But each CNVA action moved some people, led them to change their lives in what seemed at first a small way but which led, in many cases, to a full-time commitment towards peace and justice. Gradually, a cadre of experienced nonviolent activists was being developed for whom nonviolence was a direction for how they wanted to live their lives.

Peace walks achieved the same purpose, getting

Street corner discussion during CNVA peace walk, Philadelphia, May 12, 1961. Matt Herron.

Cover of pamphlet from the Committee for Nonviolent Action, 1963. Institute for the Study of Nonviolence.

Leaflet from the Committee for Nonviolent Action announcing the Trident Walks for Peace, 1962. Institute for the Study of Nonviolence.

We have been asked:

"Are you Peace Walkers or Freedom Walkers?"

WE ARE BOTH. The same belief makes us walk with signs calling for disarmament and with signs calling for Freedom Now. We believe that all men, everywhere, are brothers. We believe that we have not been born to destroy one another, or to exploit one another, or to humiliate one another, but to try to live together in peace, as one human family.

Most Americans, from both North and South, hold a religious faith which assumes the brotherhood of all men. The Fifth Commandment reads: "Thou shalt not kill." Jesus taught a new commandment even more radical: "Love one another." He made it clear that he meant by this even our enemies.

The faith that all men are brothers is also the faith embodied in our Declaration of Independence, which most Americans, in both North and South, think of themselves as cherishing. It asserts that all men are equal, born with certain rights which are not to be taken from them--all men, including those in countries with whom we have strong differences, and those in other countries and in our own whom we have found it convenient to exploit, possess these rights to life and the pursuit of happiness with which we may not interfere.

MOST AMERICANS proudly voice a belief in the teachings of the Bible or in the message of our Declaration of Independence. But--North or South--we still fail to live lives which are consistent with this belief. Now history confronts us with the necessity to be consistent, for if we do not make the most strenuous effort to be, we may well be destroyed. Here at home, the Negro people are demonstrating a new and just impatience for the full citizenship they were promised a hundred years ago. The country cannot withhold what they ask for any longer without doing itself great damage. We have suffered damage enough already, both physical and moral. Abroad, too, we must be consistent. Nations will always have differences with one another, but the nuclear weapons men possess now are so unspeakably destructive that unless we learn the difficult new way of struggling nonviolently for what we believe, we may help the human race to commit suicide.

We hesitate to take new paths, out of fear--fear of what may happen to us if we disarm or if we give exploited people their freedom. But if we would dare to act toward one another as toward brothers--dare to live according to our ideals--we could cast out fear. Love casts it out.

Committee for Nonviolent Action
325 Lafayette St., New York, N.Y. 10012

the peace message across to a large number of people and, more important, influencing a selected few to commit themselves to nonviolent activism as a way of life. In the spring of 1962 CNVA organized three simultaneous walks, beginning in New Hampshire, Chicago and Nashville, Tenn., and designed to converge on Washington on the same day for civil disobedience at the Pentagon. The unique aspect of this project was that the Southern walk was integrated and came during a period when violence against civil rights activists was commonplace throughout the South. The Nashville walk for peace signified to the public what had been true all along: that the nonviolent civil rights movement and the radical peace movement were two aspects of the same struggle.

QUEBEC-WASHINGTON-GUANTANAMO WALK FOR PEACE

The two issues — peace and civil rights — were graphically brought together during the Quebec-Washington-Guantanamo Walk for Peace that began in Quebec City in May 1963. The purpose of the walk was to present to the Cuban people and their leaders the idea of nonviolent resistance and to protest the existence of the US naval base at Guantanamo. Because of the dangers expected to occur as the integrated walk went through the South, only tried nonviolent activists were accepted as participants. One of the members, Bob Gore, an activist with both CORE and CNVA, called it "the most difficult project CNVA ever attempted."

In November the walkers passed through

CNVA peace walkers sit down on Albany, Georgia, sidewalk after being stopped from leafleting by police for the second time, January 27, 1964. Ray Robinson and Ralph DiGia are in the foreground. Connie Kanaga/Courtesy of Barbara Deming.

Leaflet from the Quebec to Guantanamo Walk for Peace, 1963. Institute for the Study of Nonviolence.

Tyrone Jackson, a civil rights worker from Albany, Georgia, and Ray Robinson, a professional boxer from Washington D.C., on the CNVA Quebec to Guantanamo Walk for Peace, December 1963. The walkers served 24 days during the first jail-in and 27 days during the second when they were arrested for trying to leaflet in downtown Albany. Connie Kanaga/Courtesy of Barbara Deming.

Griffen, Ga., and were set upon by police with electric cattle prods. A month later 14 of the walkers were arrested in Albany, Ga., when the racially mixed group insisted on using a main street. Albany was the scene of an intensive civil rights struggle that had been going on for two years. Some of the demonstrators fasted in jail and when more people came to Albany to support the prisoners, they too were arrested. Some of the prisoners then began to noncooperate as the jails filled, a story that is told most eloquently by Barbara Deming in *Prison Notes.* Finally, in February, the walkers got the local police chief to agree to let the integrated group walk through town and they continued to Miami, facing harassment most of the way. When the State Department refused the walkers permission to travel to Cuba, a delegation attempted to sail there on a power-boat, *The Spirit of Freedom.* But, after Albany, this was mostly anti-climactic and, though travel to Cuba became an issue, pacifist concern focused on the civil rights movement and on the then little-known war in Vietnam. □

Protest against the war in Vietnam, organized by the Committee for Nonviolent Action, during the Democratic National Convention, Atlantic City, New Jersey, September 25, 1964. Neil Haworth/Swarthmore College Peace Collection.

Sit-down in front of the Atomic Energy Commission demanding nuclear disarmament, New York City, c. 1962. Karl Bissinger.

CHAPTER 8

THE CIVIL RIGHTS MOVEMENT

EARLY CIVIL RIGHTS ACTIONS

On June 28, 1917, two days after American troops landed in France to fight World War I, 8,000 silent blacks marched down Fifth Avenue in New York City to the beat of muffled drums. At a time when other Americans were caught up in the hoopla of the war to make the world safe for democracy, the marchers' signs bore an ironic message: "Make America Safe for Democracy." Among the leaders of the march were Dr. W.E.B. Dubois and James Wendell Johnson of the National Association for the Advancement of Colored People (NAACP), founded eight years earlier to fight segregation.

By 1917 black Americans still had not achieved the freedom promised them in the Reconstruction Amendments to the U.S. Constitution a half-century earlier. Some 60 blacks a year were being lynched by white vigilante groups. Blacks were poorly educated in segregated public schools and were given only the most menial jobs. They were barred from most restaurants and hotels and were segregated in the Jim Crow sections of buses, trains and theaters. Many expected that things would be better after the war, but they were disappointed.

Then, in the 1920s, frustrated blacks began to read in the newspapers about Gandhi's direct action

Silent Parade in New York City sponsored by the National Association for the Advancement of Colored People in protest against lynching and other forms of racist violence, June 28, 1917. National Association for the Advancement of Colored People.

campaigns in India. A. Philip Randolph, president of the Brotherhood of Sleeping Car Porters, and Howard Thurman, dean of the chapel at Howard University, were among the first to think Gandhi's tactics might work for black Americans. Randolph, head of one of the most powerful black organizations in the country, was in a good position to get the effort started. In 1941, to protest job discrimination in defense industries, he called for a "thundering march on Washington ending in a monster demonstration at Lincoln's Monument." The *Amsterdam News* predicted that 100,000 blacks would respond to the call. Randolph won his objective immediately: President Roosevelt issued an executive order banning job discrimination. The march was called off after the administration capitulated, but the idea of giant marches lived on and became one of the major techniques of the civil rights movement in the 1960s.

Even before 1941, civil rights marches had been organized and carried out by Randolph and another black leader, the Rev. Adam Clayton Powell, Jr., pastor of Harlem's Abyssinian Baptist Church and later a U.S. Congressman. In 1931, after five black

doctors were fired because of their race, 22-year-old Powell set up picket lines at Harlem Hospital and led 6,000 demonstrators to City Hall. Not only were the five doctors reinstated but the entire hospital staff was completely integrated under a black medical director. In 1937, blacks were hired at Woolworths, Grants and other major stores after Powell and Randolph led a boycott of white-owned stores in Harlem. Another Powell campaign got 600 jobs for blacks at the 1939 World's Fair. But Powell was mainly a preacher, Randolph worked for a labor union, and the NAACP usually used lawsuits and educational campaigns, not demonstrations. There was no organization concentrating primarily on civil rights using nonviolent direct action until the Congress of Racial Equality (CORE) filled that gap in 1943.

CONGRESS OF RACIAL EQUALITY

CORE grew out of a bi-racial group in Chicago that began studying Gandhian nonviolence in 1942. Dedicated to confronting racial injustice "without fear, without compromise and without hatred," CORE members — among them Bernice Fisher

Congress of Racial Equality demonstration, Chicago, c. 1945. CORE files/State Historical Society of Wisconsin.

Brooklyn CORE Threatens Sit-In in School Fight
New York Courier

and Jimmy Robinson — pioneered in applying Gandhian methods to oppose discrimination in the U.S. Their first project, to integrate the White City Roller Rink in Chicago through legal means, failed. A bi-racial team of CORE members then sat-in at Jack Spratt, a small eating place in Chicago, and refused to leave until the whole group was served. After some delay and an attempt by the restaurant owner to involve the police, the CORE group was served.

During its early years, CORE was a small organization with no more than a few hundred members. Many of them, including one of its founders and first coordinator, George Houser, were pacifists who had served jail terms as conscientious objectors. Houser was Executive Secretary of CORE from 1943 to 1953 when he left to work for the American Committee on Africa to give aid to African independence movements. James Farmer, another of the founders, also served as Race Relations Secretary for the Fellowship of Reconciliation, then under the leadership of A. J. Muste. In his travels for the FOR, Farmer spread the word about what was

Congress of Racial Equality workshop, Chicago, 1945. CORE files/State Historical Society of Wisconsin.

Sit-in, organized by the Brooklyn chapter of CORE, at the State Commission for Human Rights office demanding admission for a black student to a high school outside his residential area, New York City, June 22, 1953. Wide World.

happening in Chicago and local CORE groups were formed in Detroit, Syracuse and New York. With the FOR's backing, the first national conference of CORE was held in June 1943, at which time 65 people sat-in at Stoners, an expensive, all-white restaurant in Chicago, and succeeded in ending the segregationist policy there.

The actions of the local groups, though they involved small numbers of participants, were often successful. By 1948, CORE had integrated the Palisades Amusement Park in New Jersey, theaters in Denver, restaurants in Detroit, a swimming pool and amusement park in Cleveland and a public bath in Los Angeles. In the course of its work, through its direct actions and summer workshops, CORE trained hundreds of people in the techniques of nonviolent action, instruction that proved to be decisive in later years.

Although the emphasis on local direct action characterized CORE for years, there was also a strong feeling that the issue of racial justice should be addressed at a national level. CORE's first major national demonstration was a Journey of Reconciliation triggered by the 1946 Supreme Court decision outlawing segregation on interstate travel. This first freedom ride was co-sponsored by the FOR and CORE in the spring of 1947. An interracial group, including Bayard Rustin, Igal Roodenko, George Houser, Conrad Lynn, Wally Nelson, Jim Peck and Ernest Bromley rode Greyhound and Trailways buses through the upper South to test the implementation of the decision. The freedom riders met little harassment but some arrests. Rustin, Joe Felmet and Roodenko served thirty-day sentences on segregated North Carolina chain-gangs for sitting together at the front of the bus. The Journey of Reconciliation gave national publicity to CORE and its use of nonviolent direct action to fight racial discrimination. As with the issues of peace and disarmament, however, broader civil rights activity remained dormant for almost a decade.

Participants in the Congress of Racial Equality's Journey of Reconciliation: Worth Randle, Wally Nelson, Ernest Bromley, Jim Peck, Igal Roodenko, Bayard Rustin, Joe Felmet, George Houser, and Andrew Johnson, April 1947. War Resisters League.

morning, every black pulpit in town sounded the call for the boycott. When King drove around town Monday morning from six to seven, when buses were normally packed, he saw only eight blacks riding them. The boycott was a success.

Having demonstrated the power of an organized community, the black leaders formed the Montgomery Improvement Association and elected King as its president. Although at age 26 he was less well known than others, as a newcomer to Montgomery he was an ideal compromise candidate. The Association decided to continue the boycott so as to win some relief from the racist city ordinance. The goal was modest: not complete integration, but only a more flexible color line. People would be seated on a first-come, first-served basis, with blacks filling seats from the rear forward and whites filling seats from the front back, but the

THE MONTGOMERY BUS BOYCOTT

On December 1, 1955, Rosa Parks, a seamstress in a downtown department store, was riding home on a Montgomery, Alabama city bus, sitting toward the front of the section for blacks. When a number of white passengers boarded the crowded bus, the driver ordered her and three other black people to give up their seats, as required by law. The others got up, but Mrs. Parks refused and the bus driver had her arrested. Mrs. Parks was well known and respected in Montgomery's black community. She had been the secretary of E. D. Nixon, a divisional head of the Brotherhood of Sleeping Car Porters, when he was state chairman of the NAACP, and she asked him to bail her out.

The next morning, after Rosa Parks was released, Nixon phoned Ralph Abernathy, pastor of the First Baptist Church of Montgomery, to suggest a one-day boycott of city buses. Abernathy agreed. The Rev. Martin Luther King, Jr., pastor of the Dexter Avenue Baptist Church, made his church basement available for a meeting that evening to discuss the proposal. About 40 black community leaders attended and endorsed the plan for a one-day boycott on the day of Rosa Parks' trial.

Black taxi companies agreed to help by carrying boycotters for ten cents, the normal bus fare. Blacks distributed leaflets explaining the boycott throughout their communities and the conservative *Montgomery Advertiser* inadvertently helped by printing the leaflet on its front page. On Sunday

bus company and the city refused to relax their policies.

The boycott continued several months and the effect of 42,000 black people refusing to ride city buses was felt by the company and the city. Since 65% of their riders had been black, the bus company was forced to raise fares and cut schedules. Downtown stores were also losing business because fewer blacks were going downtown to shop. The bus company decided it would grant the Montgomery Improvement Association's demands if the city would repeal the bus segregation ordinance. The Men of Montgomery, an influential businessmen's club, tried to get the city to agree, but Mayor W. A. Gayle, who was a member of the White Citizen's Council, said he didn't care if a black ever rode a bus again.

Two months into the boycott, the Kings' house

Mrs. Rosa Parks is fingerprinted after refusing to give up her seat for a white passenger on a Montgomery, Alabama, bus, February 1956. "It was a matter of dignity; I could not have faced myself and my people if I had moved," she said. Wide World.

Pin designed by Montgomery women during the 1956 bus boycott. The cross showed that the movement was Christian, the heart represented nonviolence, and the two feet symbolized walking for freedom. *Liberation*

was bombed. The news spread, and soon a thousand blacks, armed with knives, guns, sticks, rocks and bottles, filled the street near the house. King, a student of Gandhi since his days at Crozer Theological Seminary, persuaded his neighbors to return home with the words:

> *We cannot solve the problem through retaliatory violence. . . . We must love our white brothers no matter what they do to us . . . We must meet hate with love . . . What we are doing is just, and God is with us.*

Two nights later, a stick of dynamite exploded on E. D. Nixon's lawn. A third bombing occurred at the home of Robert Graetz, a white pastor and secretary of the Montgomery Improvement Association. Instead of intimidating the movement or provoking a violent reaction, the bombings, in King's words, "further cemented the Negro cause and brought sympathy for our cause from men of good will all over the world."

Meanwhile, the bus segregation law was being challenged in the courts. In June 1956, the federal district court ruled in a case similar to Rosa Parks'

Rev. Martin Luther King, Jr. urges his neighbors to maintain their nonviolent discipline after a bomb exploded at his home in Montgomery, Alabama, February 4, 1956. UPI.

Leaflet announcing meeting to support the Montgomery bus boycott, New York City, 1956. War Resisters League.

bus company instructed its drivers to be courteous. On December 21, 1956, 55 weeks after Rosa Parks' arrest, King and Glenn Smiley, a white Texas minister and FOR official who had come to assist with the boycott, boarded a Montgomery bus and sat side by side without incident.

SOUTHERN CHRISTIAN LEADERSHIP CONFERENCE

On January 10, 1957, King and other black leaders, including C. K. Steele, Fred Shuttlesworth, William Holmes Borders and Bayard Rustin, formed the Southern Christian Leadership Conference (SCLC) to apply the lessons learned in Montgomery throughout the South. A month later, SCLC asked President Eisenhower to call a White House Conference on civil rights and, when he did not, SCLC organized a "Prayer Pilgrimage" on Washington.

The march, which took place on March 17, 1957, was similar to the massive march A. Philip Randolph had proposed in 1941. More than 25,000 people, the vast majority of them black, marched to the Lincoln Memorial for a rally. Among the

that intrastate bus segregation was unconstitutional. The city of Montgomery appealed, saying that it had to take "every step possible to prevent such a drastic change in the habits of the people," but the Supreme Court unanimously affirmed the decision on November 13, 1956. Five weeks later, the decision took effect. Montgomery blacks prepared to sit quietly in the face of white hostility. Mayor Gayle said he would obey the law and the

Black citizens organized a motor pool of church- and privately-owned cars to provide transportation during the Montgomery, Alabama bus boycott., May 31, 1956. Wide World.

Wilson Riles (left), Pacific Coast Regional Secretary of the Fellowship of Reconciliation, conducts a seminar on nonviolence at Moorehouse College, Atlanta, Georgia, May 1956. Fellowship of Reconciliation.

War Resisters International

BAYARD RUSTIN
(Born 1910)

Bayard Rustin, a conscientious objector in World War II, became a leading theoretician and organizer of the civil rights movement in the late Fifties and early Sixties. A close associate of A.J. Muste, A. Philip Randolph, and Martin Luther King, Rustin labored for a more revolutionary nonviolence and helped to unite the peace, civil rights, labor and student movements after the second World War.

Rustin was raised in West Chester, Pennsylvania and, in the Thirties, traveled to New York City where he sang in cafes with Leadbelly and Josh White. In 1938 he became an organizer with the Young Communist League because it strongly opposed war and racism, but when its position shifted, he resigned and joined the Fellowship of Reconciliation. During his 12 years with the FOR, Rustin served first as Field Secretary and then as Race Relations Secretary. In the latter position, he helped to develop the Congress of Racial Equality with A.J. Muste and James Farmer.

In 1942 Rustin wrote his draft board that "conscription for war is inconsistent with freedom of conscience, which is not merely the right to believe, but to act on the degree of truth that one receives." He spent 28 months in prison for his refusal to cooperate with the draft and strongly criticized the pacifist community for cooperating with the government in running the CPS camps. After his release from prison in 1945, he led the Free India Committee and was frequently arrested for sitting-in at the British Embassy in Washington in support of the Gandhian independence movement. In 1948, at the invitation of the Indian Congress party, he spent six months in India studying the Gandhian movement.

From 1953 to 1964, Rustin served as Executive Sec-

retary of the War Resisters League and helped to move the League to a more radical position in the post-war years. Rustin's premise that "the issue of human rights takes many forms: race relations is one such form, and international relations is another, but beneath the formal differences these issues are really inseparable," made him an active member of CORE, Peacemakers, and later the Committee for Nonviolent Action.

Rustin was invited by Martin Luther King to help with organizing the Montgomery bus boycott in 1955 and, on leave from WRL, Rustin served as King's special assistant for the next seven years. He drafted the plan for what became the Southern Christian Leadership Conference and helped bring the civil rights struggle to the attention of a wide cross section of the American people. On his return from Montgomery in 1955, Rustin wrote:

> We in the North should bear in mind that the most important thing we can do to help the Montgomery situation is to press now for total integration in the North. Montgomery is important as it stimulates us to greater action where we are.
>
> Montgomery is also significant because it reveals to a world sick with violence that non-violent resistance has relevance today in the United States against forces that are prepared to use extreme measures to crush it. This is a very real educational factor for all people to utilize who are working for world peace.

In 1963 he organized the massive civil rights March on Washington, and the next year directed a boycott against the racially imbalanced New York City public school system. The boycott, in which 44.8% of the city school children participated, was the largest civil rights action of any kind up to that time. In 1965, Rustin wrote, "Every project we set up, we have set up to reveal truth, not to win minor victories."

As one of the major architects of the civil rights movement along nonviolent lines, Rustin made a substantial contribution to interpreting the Gandhian approach to social struggle. His distinguished manner and skill as an extemporaneous speaker helped to communicate his thorough understanding of nonviolence to a broader public. One of the foremost experienced early black radicals, he gave example and counsel which inspired many young civil rights activists working with SNCC and CORE. He built strong coalitions and was one of the most effective strategists in the early drive for equal rights.

Rustin realized that the problems of black Americans were as much the result of economics as racial prejudice and that the civil rights movement by itself could not win political power. He left WRL in 1964 to become Executive Director of the A. Philip Randolph Institute, where he began to work even more closely with established labor leaders and liberal Democrats and parted politically with many of his former colleagues.

Cover of the Fellowship of Reconciliation comic book about the Montgomery bus boycott. Over a quarter of a million copies of this introduction to nonviolence, illustrated by Al Capp, were published and distributed throughout the country. FOR.

The Prayer Pilgrimage for Freedom, sponsored by the Southern Christian Leadership Conference, Washington D.C., March 17, 1957. *New York Times*

marchers were such celebrities as Jackie Robinson, Sidney Poitier, Harry Belafonte and Sammy Davis, Jr. Up to that time, it was one of the largest demonstrations in American history.

King, Randolph, Powell and Roy Wilkins addressed the rally. Powell urged blacks to use in their struggle such means as boycotts, work stoppages and slow-downs. King drew the loudest applause of the afternoon when he charged that both the Democratic and Republican parties had "betrayed the cause of justice." The *New York Times* expressed surprise and relief that, unlike previous demonstrations of its size (such as Coxey's Army and the Bonus Expeditionary Force), the Prayer Pilgrimage had been orderly and nonviolent.

After the march, CORE in the North and SCLC in the South kept up the pressure with local demonstrations and boycotts. There were successful sit-ins at segregated businesses in Oklahoma City and Wichita in 1957. Thirty-five Southern cities abandoned *de jure* school segregation, in some cases because of demonstrations or threatened demonstrations.

Prodded by these actions, Congress passed the Civil Rights Act of 1957, the first major civil rights bill since 1875. The new law authorized the Justice Department to sue on behalf of blacks denied the right to vote, created the Civil Rights Commission to study discrimination and added an assistant attorney general in charge of civil rights to the Justice Department. Although the right-to-vote section proved ineffective, the Civil Rights Act was the movement's first national legislative victory.

In order to spend full time in the movement, King resigned his Montgomery pastorate and moved to SCLC headquarters in Atlanta early in 1960. Before he moved, he outlined his plans:

> We must not let the present strategic opportunity pass. Very soon our new program will be announced. Not only will it include a stepped up campaign of voter registration, but a full-scale assault will be made upon discrimination and segregation in all forms. We must train our youth and adult leaders in the techniques of social change through nonviolent resistance. We must employ new methods of struggle involving the masses of people.

But while King was putting his plans into motion, the initiative of the civil rights movement was taken up by a new generation.

White students jeer Dorothy Counts, the first black student to attend Harding High School, Charlotte, North Carolina, September 4, 1957. Dr. Edwin Tompkins, a Charlotte professor and family friend, is walking beside her. Wide World.

Bottom left: Congress of Racial Equality demonstration. CORE files/State Historical Society of Wisconsin.

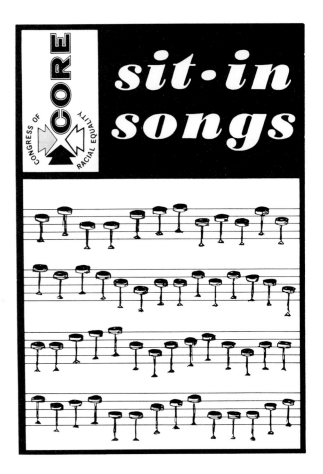

THE SIT-INS

On Sunday, January 31, 1960, Joseph McNeill, a freshman at North Carolina Agricultural and Technical College in Greensboro, tried to get something to eat at the lunch counter of the local bus terminal. "We don't serve Negroes," he was told. That evening, McNeill told his roommate, Exell Blair, Jr., about the incident. Blair had been reading a comic book, "Martin Luther King and the Montgomery Story," published by the Fellowship of Reconciliation. Inspired by the comic book, McNeill, Blair and two other A&T freshmen sat down the next day at the lunch counter of the local Woolworth's. When they were refused service, they stayed seated from 10 a.m. until 12:30 p.m. and returned again on Tuesday and Wednesday. On Thursday, they were joined by white students from the Women's College of the University of North Carolina.

Shortly after the sit-ins began, the students asked the advice of Dr. George Simkins, a local dentist and the president of the NAACP's

Cover of Congress of Racial Equality songbook, produced after CORE's Freedom Highways project in 1962, which challenged segregation in chain restaurants along major highways. Institute for the Study of Nonviolence.

Ronald Martin, Robert Patterson and Mark Martin, students from North Carolina A&T College, sit-in at the Woolworth lunch counter after being refused service, Greensboro, North Carolina, February 2, 1960. UPI.

Congress of Racial Equality demonstrators urge Harlem residents not to patronize Woolworth's until lunch counter discrimination ends in the North Carolina stores, February 13, 1960. Ralph DiGia of the War Resisters League is in the center. UPI.

Greensboro chapter. Simkins, who had just been reading a CORE pamphlet on direct action, called CORE's New York office and Len Holt was sent immediately to Greensboro to conduct training sessions in nonviolence. Martin Luther King was the second experienced civil rights activist to go to Greensboro; others who were involved in nonviolent education during the early days of the sit-ins included James Lawson, Glenn Smiley and Charles Walker of the FOR and Herbert Wright, youth secretary of the NAACP.

The student sit-in movement spread with extraordinary speed. Radio and television spread the news of the Greensboro demonstration and within a week black students from North Carolina Central and white students from Duke University started a lunch counter sit-in in Durham, 50 miles east of Greensboro. Soon students were sitting in at lunch

White Southerners pour sugar, ketchup, and mustard over the heads of civil rights demonstrators during a lunch counter sit-in in Jackson, Mississippi, June 12, 1963. Wide World.

After refusing to move, Mrs. Ruth E. Tinsley is carried away by police from a downtown department store where students and others were protesting segregated lunch counters, Richmond, Virginia, February 23, 1960. UPI.

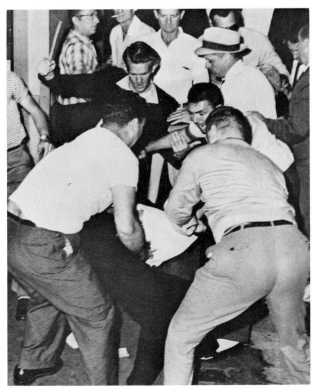

The bus which carried the first Freedom Riders into Alabama is gutted by fire outside Anniston, Alabama, May 14, 1961. Wide World.

Freedom rider Jim Peck is beaten by segregationists as he tries to enter the "White Only" lunchroom in the Trailways bus terminal, Birmingham, Alabama, May 14, 1961. Tom Langston.

Student Nonviolent Coordinating Committee worker, 1964. Diana Davies.

counters in South Carolina, Tennessee and Virginia. For the first time, the nonviolent technique introduced by CORE 15 years earlier was being used on a mass basis.

The first arrests came on Lincoln's birthday, February 12, when 41 students from Shaw University and St. Augustine's College were arrested in Raleigh, North Carolina. The next day, students from Florida A&M were arrested in Tallahassee. The arrests helped publicize the protest, and by the end of March sit-ins had spread to more than 50 cities. In April 1960, SCLC lent $800 and its executive secretary, Ella Baker, to help start the Student Nonviolent Coordinating Committee (SNCC) to support and encourage sit-ins.

Often the older generation joined the students in jail. In October 1960, King and 36 others were arrested while trying to integrate the Magnolia Room, the main dining room in Rich's department store in Atlanta. The others were released, but King was sentenced to four months in jail, technically because he had an earlier offense — driving without

a Georgia driver's license. Atlantans kept on demonstrating downtown and won over stores one by one. Two years later, virtually all public facilities were integrated. Not only in Atlanta, but throughout the South the nonviolent sit-in movement had succeeded in challenging segregation.

FREEDOM RIDES

In December 1960, the Supreme Court extended its 1947 decision that segregation was unconstitutional on interstate transport to include station restrooms, waiting rooms and lunch rooms. CORE decided to test this new ruling with a second freedom ride, only this time the ride would extend into the deep South. On May 4, 1961, thirteen people, seven blacks and six whites, left Washington in two groups.

In Virginia and North Carolina, the freedom riders integrated waiting rooms and lunch counters successfully and usually without incident. In Rock Hill, South Carolina, however, John Lewis and Albert Bigelow were attacked by a white mob, and the next day Henry Thomas and Jim Peck were

The "River Rats" from the Harlem chapter of the Congress of Racial Equality block traffic on the Triboro Bridge to protest slum conditions and racial discrimination, New York City, c. 1964. *New York Times.*

arrested at a lunch room in Winnsboro, South Carolina. After a mob attempted, unsuccessfully, to storm the jail, Thomas and Peck were released unobtrusively at early dawn the following day.

On May 14, a mob armed with chains, sticks and iron rods met the Greyhound bus carrying one group of freedom riders as it pulled into the station in Anniston, Alabama. They attacked the bus, breaking windows and slashing the front tires. Several hours later, the mob intercepted the freedom riders again seven miles out of town and someone threw an incendiary bomb into the bus. The bus burst into flames but the passengers escaped and were treated for smoke inhalation at the local hospital.

Meanwhile, the mob met the second group of freedom riders when they reached Anniston on a

Over 200,000 civil rights demonstrators gather in front of the Lincoln Memorial climaxing the March on Washington for Jobs and Freedom, Washington D.C., August 23, 1963. National Archives.

Police carry out some of the 170 civil rights demonstrators who sat-in at the First National Bank to protest racial bias in hiring, East St. Louis, Illinois, August 15, 1963. Wide World.

Trailways bus. Jim Peck and Walter Bergman were knocked to the floor of the bus and beaten; Bergman subsequently suffered a stroke which paralyzed him. Upon arrival in Birmingham, the riders were again attacked. This time the whites were armed with chains, sticks and iron rods, and they beat Jim Peck so severely that he required 53 stitches in his head. Both groups of freedom riders wanted to continue the trip, but no driver could be found to drive them out of Birmingham.

Six days later, another group, primarily SNCC members, continued the freedom ride, after federal authorities assured the bus company of protection. The new riders were arrested and jailed in Mississippi for trying to integrate bus stations, but civil rights groups sent in more and more people willing to go to jail. By the end of the summer of 1961, hundreds of people from all parts of the country had joined the Freedom Riders and 328 people had been arrested in Jackson, Mississippi.

Spurred by Northern outrage over the beatings and arrests of the freedom riders, Attorney General Robert Kennedy asked the Interstate Commerce Commission to force bus companies and railroads into compliance with the Supreme Court decision. After months of hearings, the ICC issued an order prohibiting segregated facilities in interstate travel. After the order went into effect on November 1, the lunch rooms and waiting rooms were integrated. The 1961 Freedom Rides had abolished segregation in interstate travel, just as the 1960 sit-ins had abolished segregation at lunch counters.

THE MARCH ON WASHINGTON

In the early 1960's, the Southern civil rights movement got increasing support from white sympathizers in the North. Students and clergy came south by the thousands to work on voter registration, to picket and to sit-in with Southern blacks. Sometimes the strategy was successful and sometimes major campaigns failed, but the movement grew. During the 1960 sit-ins, 3600 demonstrators were arrested in eight months, but there were at least four times that many arrests during the same time period in 1963.

Albany, Georgia was the scene of a major campaign launched by SNCC and SCLC to test the difficulty of ending segregation in the smaller cities of the deep South. Hundreds of people were jailed and many ugly incidents occurred but after two years of struggle, no one could discern any real

progress. In Albany and throughout the movement there were many examples of individual courage and sacrifice, such as that of William Moore, a white CORE member from Baltimore. On the night of April 23, 1963, while on a one-man freedom walk to the governor of Mississippi, Moore was shot in the back and killed on an Alabama highway.

Frustrated by failure in places like Albany and encouraged by growing Northern support, the major civil rights groups collaborated in a March on Washington on August 28, 1963 in an attempt to gain federal support for the drive against segregation in the deep South. Bayard Rustin was lent by

Civil rights demonstration in Birmingham, Alabama, is broken up by police and dogs, May 3, 1963. Wide World.

Civil rights demonstrators in the one-room stockade at Leesburg, Georgia, after being arrested in Americus. Some had been there for three weeks. Danny Lyon/Magnum.

Ken Thompson

MARTIN LUTHER KING, JR.
(1919 - 1968)

Martin Luther King, Jr. was a principal leader and theoretician in the nonviolent civil rights movement in the United States. Beginning with his leadership of the year-long Montgomery bus boycott in 1955, through eleven years of non-stop civil rights agitation, he inspired and organized an explicitly nonviolent mass movement to challenge racial discrimination. His campaigns took the offensive in exercising and winning civil rights which had been denied black Americans since their arrival on this continent as slaves. A minister of courage and conviction, King was repeatedly the target of racist violence: he was threatened, harassed and indicted; he was jailed numerous times; his house was bombed with his family inside; he was stabbed and eventually assassinated because he worked for racial equality while making the broader connections to U.S. economic injustice at home and aggression abroad.

Born in Atlanta, Georgia, King was ordained at age 18 in his father's church. He married Coretta Scott in 1954, received a Ph.D. in systematic theology at Boston University the next year, and accepted a post as minister of the 400-member Dexter Avenue Baptist Church in Montgomery, Alabama. There he organized a social and political action committee and urged his congregation to join the NAACP, on whose executive committee he served. When the bus boycott began in 1955, King was chosen head of the Montgomery Improvement Association and gained national recognition for his leadership in the 382-day nonviolent action. "Christ showed us the way," he wrote, "and Mahatma Gandhi showed us it could work."

In an article in *Liberation* magazine shortly after the start of the boycott, King described what was to be the basis for his years of civil rights work:

> *If, in pressing for justice and equality in Montgomery, we discover that those who reject equality are prepared to use violence, we must not despair, retreat, or fear.*

Because they make this crucial decision, they must remember: whatever they do, we will not use violence in return. We hope we can act in the struggle in such a way that they will see the error of their approach and will come to respect us. Then we can all live together in peace and equality.

The basic conflict is not really over the buses. Yet we believe that, if the method we use in dealing with equality in the buses can eliminate injustice within ourselves, we shall at the same time be attacking the basis of injustice – man's hostility to man. This can only be done when we challenge the white community to reexamine its assumptions as we are now prepared to reexamine ours.

Shortly after the bus boycott, King helped found the Southern Christian Leadership Conference, and as president planned the course of many of the major civil rights campaigns. He inspired and encouraged the growth of the sit-ins and student civil rights movement, helped to establish the Student Nonviolent Coordinating Committee, and organized a training school in nonviolence in Montgomery after the Freedom Rides. King led mass protests and civil disobedience demonstrations throughout the South for equal education, integration, voting rights and fair hiring practices. His dramatic campaigns won the movement countless supporters and worldwide publicity and made King a symbol of the suffering, courage and sacrifice of black Americans striving for freedom. He wrote:

The nonviolent resister must often express his protest through noncooperation or boycotts, but he realizes that these are not ends themselves; they are merely means to awaken a sense of moral shame in the opponent. The end is redemption and reconciliation. The aftermath of nonviolence is the creation of the beloved community, while the aftermath of violence is tragic bitterness.

At the center of nonviolence stands the principle of love. The nonviolent resister would contend that in the struggle for human dignity, the oppressed people of the world must not succumb to the temptation of becoming bitter or indulging in hate campaigns. To retaliate in kind would do nothing but intensify the existence of hate in the universe. Along the way of life, someone must have sense enough and morality enough to cut off the chain of hate. This can only be done by projecting the ethic of love to the center of our lives.

King was widely honored for his civil rights work and was awarded the Nobel Peace Prize in 1964. In his acceptance speech in Oslo, Norway, he spoke of the prize as an award to the movement, in recognition that "nonviolence is the answer to the crucial political and moral question of our time — the need for man to overcome oppression and violence without resorting to violence and oppression." He used the $54,000 prize to finance further civil rights activities.

A year before his death, King spoke out publicly against the war in Vietnam, saying:

This war turns the clock of history back and perpetuates white colonialism. The greatest irony and tragedy of it all is that our own nation which initiated so much of the revolutionary spirit in this modern world is now cast in the mold of being an arch anti-revolutionary.

King was killed by an assassin in Memphis, Tennessee, on April 3, 1968.

Rev. Martin Luther King and civil rights marchers kneel to offer a prayer on their way to jail following their mass arrest, Selma, Alabama, February 1, 1965. War Resisters League.

the War Resisters League to help organize the march with A. Philip Randolph. It was the largest demonstration in American history up to that time: 200,000 people, including 150 members of Congress. The speeches were more hopeful than angry. Martin Luther King, Jr., Ralph Abernathy, Rosa Parks, SNCC chairperson John Lewis, Rev. Eugene Carson Blake, A. Philip Randolph, Walter Reuther and others spoke of all that needed to be done. Mahalia Jackson, Odetta, Bob Dylan, Joan Baez, and Peter, Paul and Mary sang.

Not long after the March on Washington, Congress passed the Civil Rights Act of 1964 which outlawed job discrimination on the basis of race, color, religion, sex or national origin; outlawed segregation in public places; created the Equal Employment Opportunity Commission to enforce the job discrimination ban; and created the Community Relations Service to mediate civil rights disputes with local officials. The job discrimination provisions did not have much immediate effect, but the provision requiring the integration of public places worked where place-by-place direct action campaigns had failed. Few motels and restaurants resisted the new federal law openly, even in the rural areas of the deep South, though more establishments tried to discourage black customers with discourteous service.

VOTER REGISTRATION

During the early 1960s the civil rights movement worked most dramatically in the freedom rides, marches and sit-ins, but it also worked on quieter projects such as voter registration. Especially in the South, a variety of legal technicalities were used to discourage blacks from registering to vote. Sometimes educated blacks were told that they had failed the literacy test and, when they demanded to be told where they had erred, they were informed that the results were confidential.

In 1961, the civil rights movement began a massive campaign to register black voters in the deep South. John Hardy, one of the first to work on the project, left college in Nashville to go to Walthall County, Mississippi where none of the 2,500 voting-age blacks were registered. On September 7, 1961, Hardy took Edith Peters and Lucius Wilson to register, but John Q. Wood, the county registrar, pulled a gun and struck Hardy on the head. When he complained to the sheriff, Hardy was arrested for breach of the peace.

People close to the new Kennedy administration

Two Student Nonviolent Coordinating Committee workers are arrested on the steps of the Old Post Office Building during a Freedom Day demonstration, Selma, Alabama, c. 1962. Danny Lyon/Magnum.

told civil rights leaders that liberal foundations would finance a voter registration program if a coalition was formed to administer it. In response, CORE, the NAACP, SCLC, SNCC and the Urban League set up the Voter Education Project (VEP) to make grants to local programs throughout the South. In Mississippi, the state where blacks were most disenfranchised, VEP funded the Council of Federated Organizations (COFO). This coalition of CORE, SNCC, SCLC and NAACP workers sponsored the Mississippi Summer Project in 1964 which brought hundreds of black and white college students to Mississippi to help with voter registration. COFO also organized the Mississippi Freedom Democratic Party (MFDP) which challenged the lily-white regular Democratic Party.

COFO workers faced high risks and terrible odds. Medgar Evers, Mississippi State Secretary of the NAACP, was shot and killed by white terrorists on June 12, 1963. At the beginning of Mississippi Summer, on June 21, 1964, three COFO workers disappeared. Andrew Goodman, a 20-year-old Queens College student, had just arrived in Meridian the previous day, but he had met Michael Schwerner, a New York City social worker, and James Chaney, a black born and raised in Meridian, earlier at a training program for Mississippi Summer. The search for the three activists went on for six weeks before their bodies were found in an earthen dam near Philadelphia, Miss. An investigation revealed that the three had been murdered by white terrorists and that a local deputy sheriff

Newly-registered voter outside Batesville, Mississippi courthouse, Summer 1966. Bob Fitch.

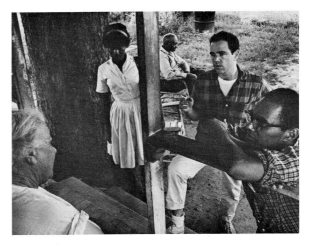

apparently was involved in the crime. The deputy sheriff and six others were found guilty four years later.

The sacrifices of COFO and other civil rights workers did have some immediate results: between 1961 and 1964 the number of black voters in the South increased by 60%. The problem, however, was far from solved. In the South as a whole, blacks constituted 20% of the population but only 8% of the electorate. In Mississippi, they were 35% of the population but only 2% of the electorate. At that rate, ending voter discrimination in the South would have taken a generation.

SELMA

To support legislation that would speed up the process of registering black voters, SCLC planned a 54-mile march in 1965 from Selma, Alabama to the state capital in Montgomery. On Sunday, March 7, Hosea Williams led 525 marchers out of Selma. Just outside the city, they were met by a battalion of state troopers in steel helmets and gas masks, a squad of sheriff's deputies and a company of possemen. The demonstrators stopped but did not turn back. In a moment, they were chased back, trampled by horses, beaten with whips and clubs and gassed as they ran. Sixteen marchers were hospitalized.

King announced from Atlanta that he would lead a march on the following Tuesday over the same route and sympathizers from 30 states poured into Selma. On March 9, 1500 marchers, including 450 clergy, walked with King to the site where the previous march had been stopped.

Civil rights workers in Ruleville, Mississippi. "Come down and try to register. You may lose your job, you may even lose your home. You may be beaten. . . but join us, come down and register to vote." Robert Moses is on the right. Danny Lyon/Magnum.

Over 5000 civil rights demonstrators begin the march from Selma to Montgomery, Alabama, for the third time, March 21, 1965. UPI.

Congress of Racial Equality demonstration in Harlem, March 1965. Diana Davies.

Because a federal court had issued an injunction against continuing the march, King offered a prayer at the site and turned back. That night, Klansmen attacked three white Unitarian ministers who had come to town for the march and the Rev. James Reeb of Boston died from the injuries he received.

The country was shocked. Six days later, on March 15, President Johnson went on television to describe the voting rights bill he was submitting to Congress. He gave credit for civil rights progress to the demonstrators:

> The real hero of this struggle is the American Negro. His actions and protests, his call to risk safety, and even to risk his life, have awakened the conscience of this nation. His demonstrations have been designed to call attention to injustice; designed to provoke change; designed to stir reform. He has called upon us to make good the promise of America. And who among us can say that we would have made the same progress were it not for his persistent bravery and his faith in American democracy.

Meanwhile civil rights activists continued to ask the courts for permission to continue their march to Montgomery. On March 17, a U.S. District Court judge upheld their right to stage an orderly march. The march began March 21 at Brown's Chapel Methodist Church in Selma and ended in front of the state capitol in Montgomery shortly before noon March 25, without serious incidents. At the capitol, King addressed the crowd saying: "We are on the move now . . . . No wave of racism can stop us."

Several hours after the march, Viola Liuzzo, a white 39-year-old civil rights activist from Detroit, was fatally shot as she was driving a car of demon-

---

Civil rights leaders meet during the 1966 Mississippi-Meredith March just after Stokely Carmichael's "Black Power" speech, Greenwood, Mississippi, 1966. Rev. Bernard Lee, Rev. King's assistant with the Southern Christian Leadership Conference, is in the left foreground; on the couch are SCLC members Rev. Andy Young, Robert Green and Rev. Martin Luther King. Stokely Carmichael is on the floor in the front. Bob Fitch.

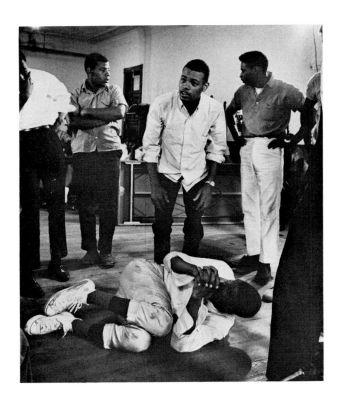

STUDENT NONVIOLENT COORDINATING COMMITTEE
(Founded 1960)

The Student Nonviolent Coordinating Committee grew out of the sit-ins of the early Sixties. Ella Baker, a middle-aged black woman who ran the Atlanta, Georgia, office of the Southern Christian Leadership Conference, was one of the first experienced activists to go to North Carolina to help organize the sit-ins. With financial help from SCLC, she arranged a conference in Raleigh, N.C., in April 1960 which set up a temporary organization to encourage sit-ins and other actions against discrimination throughout the South. That organization later became the Student Nonviolent Coordinating Committee (SNCC).

During 1960 and 1961, SNCC workers helped organize sit-ins all over the South and in 1962 they joined with other civil rights organizations to sponsor voter registration campaigns. In 1963, they began organizing in Selma, Alabama, the site two years later of the historic march to Montgomery for voter registration. SNCC also helped organize the Mississippi Freedom Democratic Party, whose challenge to the lily-white Mississippi delegation to the 1964 Democratic National Convention led to party reforms that increased minority participation four years later.

For several years, SNCC was the most radical and perhaps the most influential civil rights organization in the U.S. SNCC always had a small staff and a low budget; there was no formal membership and a minimum of structure. The organization was committed to making decisions on the basis of participatory democracy with-

out a bureaucracy or hierarchy. SNCC staff members — such as John Lewis, who left divinity school, and Bob Moses, who left graduate school at Harvard to join — worked long hours and under dangerous circumstances for subsistence wages of about $10 a week. The skills and dedication of the 150 or so activists in SNCC — going to jail in town after town to break down the barriers of segregation — captured a great deal of public sympathy and infused the civil rights movement with new life and direction.

For a while, SNCC was highly successful, but the informality of its organization and changes within the movement eventually led to its falling apart. In an all-night meeting held near Nashville, Tennessee, in May 1966, John Lewis, one of the strongest voices in SNCC since its beginning, was replaced as chairman by Stokely Carmichael. At first Lewis had been re-elected, but as the discussion continued on other topics many people left. In the weary hours of the morning, Lewis' election was challenged by a non-member. Another vote was taken and Carmichael, who did not share SNCC's commitment to nonviolence, was elected chairman. Many SNCC activists, including James Foreman and Julian Bond, soon left the organization. Carmichael and his successor a year later, H. Rap Brown, gradually repudiated SNCC's philosophy, eventually changing the group's name to the Student National Coordinating Committee. SNCC rapidly lost supporters and within two or three years, Carmichael and Brown's supporters admitted that SNCC was dead.

SNCC workers demonstrate nonviolent defense tactics during a Danville, Virginia, workshop, June 1963. Danny Lyon/Magnum.

Poor People's Campaign, Washington D.C., 1968. Diana Davies.

strators back to Selma. President Johnson went on television again the following night to denounce Mrs. Liuzzo's murder as the "horrible crime . . . [of] a hooded society of bigots." The national outrage over the murder helped gain Congressional support for the Voting Rights Act.

The Voting Rights Act of 1965, signed into law on August 6, led to the election of a number of black public officials. Previously, in 1964, there had been only 16 black state legislators in the South. By 1966, there were 37 and by 1970 the number had doubled again to 73. Southern voters sent two blacks to Congress in 1972 and a third in 1974, the first to serve there from the South in more than 70 years. White Southern politicians also began to pay attention to black voters.

POVERTY

Economic discrimination became the new focus of the civil rights movement in the late 1960s. Although federal laws now protected the rights of minorities to public facilities, many blacks could not afford to take advantage of the legal victories. Black America's major problem was poverty. The civil rights movement helped to get President Johnson's War on Poverty legislation passed, but most of the programs that resulted were ineffective in making substantial changes in the lives of people who had suffered from generations of being destitute. The government's promises of rapid improvement turned out to be grandiose dreams.

Deeply dissatisfied with the limited progress and the broken promises, many black ghettos turned to violence in the late 1960s. The first major uprising began on August 11, 1965, in the Los Angeles ghetto Watts, where more than 30% of the labor force was unemployed. The violent uprising lasted seven days and left 34 people dead, 1,032 injured and 3,952 arrested. Almost all of the dead and injured were blacks. During the next three years, black anger and frustration led to similar outbursts in poor areas of Chicago, Cleveland, Omaha, Atlanta, Minneapolis, San Francisco, Detroit and a dozen other cities.

Some civil rights workers responded to the violent demands for much needed change by advocating violent action. SNCC abandoned its nonviolent philosophy and modified its name to the Student National Coordinating Committee, but there was more violent talk than violent action. For

Civil rights activist Taylor Washington, 17-year-old high school honor student, is arrested for the eighth time, Atlanta, Georgia. Danny Lyon/Magnum.

Black power demonstration, Marks, Mississippi, c. 1966. Diana Davies.

at the blacks over the heads of police and chased the marchers back to a black neighborhood. The marches for open housing continued, nevertheless, and with growing white support.

To speed up the negotiations that SCLC had undertaken with the city of Chicago, King announced a march into the neighboring city of Cicero, where a job-hunting black man had been beaten to death with a baseball bat a few months before. Chicago's leaders feared that the march to Cicero would result in further white racist violence and, two days before the scheduled demonstration, the city officials promised to work more quickly toward full integration and the elimination of the slums. Black leaders accepted the compromise and King called off the Cicero march. The city of Chicago did not keep its promise however, and later that year Congress rejected a bill to outlaw housing discrimination.

At the end of 1966, King took time out from SCLC to write *Where Do We Go From Here?*, but his book had no solution for the floundering civil rights movement. A year later he began to make plans for a Poor People's Campaign. Beginning in May 1968, mule trains would make their way from Mississippi to a tent colony called Resurrection City in Washington, D.C. There, thousands of blacks, American Indians, Chicanos and poor whites would camp out until Congress acted on a program to eliminate poverty.

During March and April 1968, King took time off from preparations for the campaign to lead demonstrations in Memphis in support of a garbage workers' strike. On April 3 he told a rally he was confident that the civil rights movement would succeed. The next evening, when King stepped out on the balcony of his Memphis motel, he was assassinated.

The nation was shocked and grieved; there were riots in 125 cities and memorial demonstrations throughout the world. Many people took King's death as an opportunity to renew their commitment to win economic justice and racial equality by nonviolence. SCLC decided to proceed with the Poor People's Campaign, but encountered many problems. The shantytown of plywood A-frame shacks near the Lincoln Memorial lasted less than two months before those living there were forcibly evicted. Congress passed the Civil Rights Act of 1968 to eliminate housing discrimination, but the new law did not touch the fundamental problem of poverty.

the most part, SNCC and the Black Panther Party did their utmost to prevent ghetto violence.

Other civil rights organizations responded by trying to re-establish contact with the people in urban ghettos. King moved into the slums of Chicago to see if he could adapt the tactics that had worked in the South to the problems of Northern blacks. SCLC tried to put the unemployed on Chicago's West Side to work fixing up the slums in which they lived. King attempted to renovate a vacant slum building, and the United Auto Workers helped recruit other tenants into a Union to End Slums that would bargain with landlords.

King also began to lead weekly marches into white neighborhoods to demand an open housing program so that blacks could move out of the ghettos. The negotiations necessary to begin this population shift plodded along and the attempt to change the status quo met with violent opposition. On July 31, a mob led by American Nazi Party leader George Lincoln Rockwell assaulted one of King's weekly marches. The mob hurled bricks and rocks

Demonstration in memory of Martin Luther King, Central Park, New York City, April 5, 1968. Diana Davies.

THE IMPACT OF THE MOVEMENT

In 1946, Walter White, the Executive Director of the NAACP, had led a delegation which urged President Truman to sponsor comprehensive civil rights legislation. Truman set up the President's Committee on Civil Rights and included the Committee's recommendations in a civil rights message to Congress on February 2, 1948. He asked for legislation that would create a Civil Rights Division in the Justice Department and a Civil Rights Commission, protect minorities against lynching, protect the rights of minorities to vote, prohibit job discrimination, and prohibit discrimination in interstate transportation. By 1968, after 20 years of direct action, the civil rights movement finally had achieved those goals. During its most intensive years, the 13 years from the Montgomery bus boycott in 1955 to the Poor People's Campaign in 1968, massive direct action transformed the South from a place where "white only" signs were everywhere to a place much like the North, where discrimination is less pervasive and less visible.

And there was an additional gain. Blacks now have many of the tools they need to fight the discrimination that remains in education, employment and housing, in the North and in the South. They have better access than ever before to the political system and the courts, and, if other methods fail, thousands of black leaders know from experience how to organize direct action.

The civil rights movement also left a legacy to other groups everywhere in the world who feel powerless to change their societies. More than any other direct action movement in American history, it demonstrated and popularized the efficacy of nonviolence. Dissidents active in the Soviet Union, such as Nobel Peace Prize winner Andrei Sakharov, remember reading about the marches of the 1950s and 1960s. Chicanos working in the United Farm Workers campaigns remember the civil rights movement. And it was the example of the civil rights workers that made it possible for the anti-Vietnam war movement to be the first direct action campaign in American history to end a protracted war, before the total devastation of either side, through largely nonviolent opposition. □

Rev. Ralph Abernathy leads a march through Resurrection City during the Poor People's Campaign, 1968, Washington D.C. Diana Davies.

CHAPTER 9

UNITED FARM WORKERS UNION

Farm workers on the Delano to Sacramento March, Spring 1966. Strike leader Cesar Chavez is on the right. Photo © George Ballis, all rights reserved.

FARM WORKERS ORGANIZE

On September 8, 1965, the mostly Filipino members of the Agricultural Workers Organizing Committee, AFL-CIO, struck the grape fields of Delano, California. They were joined one week later by the mostly Mexican-American members of the National Farm Workers Association, led by Cesar Chavez. Thus began the first successful strike by farm workers for union recognition in American history.

Giant landowners were in control of much of the agricultural land in California; from the U.S. takeover of the state, land has been owned in huge parcels, first as plantations based on (often fraudulent) Mexican land grants, and later as agricultural components of corporate conglomerates. There had been many attempts by migrant laborers to organize over the years, but all had been systematically and often violently suppressed. Agribusiness sought cheap, expendable labor, available in needy droves for the harvest but no financial burden at any other season. So workers were drawn from those populations too poor to protest: the Chinese, Japanese, Filipinos, "Okies," Chicanos and Mexicans. Their labor won no security, they rarely achieved even the U.S. government's official estimate of a

ROMA WINES • CRESTA BLANCA WINES

I. W. HARPER • SCHENLEY RESERVE • O. F. C. WHISKEY • CUTTY SARK
J. W. DANT • ANCIENT AGE • MELROSE BOTTLED COCKTAILS • DEWARS SCOTCH

DON'T BUY
SCHENLEY
PRODUCTS

FREEDOM NOW
CORE

poverty-level income, and their children were lucky to attain an eighth grade education. They struck against their hardships sporadically, but had never been organized in an on-going union. Migrant farm workers were generally considered to be unorganizable, and that was the way many growers and politicians wanted it to stay.

Chavez' NFWA had built a base among workers over a three year period, while AWOC's Filipinos brought the experience of previous organizing struggles. Together they mounted a 300 mile march from Delano to Sacramento to publicize the strike. The walk ended on Easter Sunday 1966 with the announcement of the first farm worker contract — with Schenley Industries, a wine grape grower. The two union groups merged as the United Farm Workers' Organizing Committee on August 22, 1966, with Cesar Chavez as director.

CESAR CHAVEZ

Chavez was born in Arizona in 1927 and was forced to follow the crops to California when his family lost their small farm ten years later. He stopped his formal education in the seventh grade after attending 37 schools, and became part of the stream of

California farm workers march from Delano to Sacramento for union recognition, Spring 1966. Photo © George Ballis, all rights reserved.

Boycott sign, Delano, California, 1966. Photo © George Ballis, all rights reserved.

farm workers who pulled the beets, picked the lettuce and cotton, and cut the grapes for the large growers in the California valleys. Married in 1948 to Helen Fabela, Chavez became a community organizer with the National Community Service Organization and by 1962 had become its director. After his challenge to the CSO to organize farm workers was rejected, he quit and began to organize on his own.

Chavez brought to farm labor organizing a personal commitment to nonviolence and an insistence that union members subscribe to this discipline at least as a tactic. He brought to nonviolence a new

understanding of the necessity for the hard work of solid organization and a determination to make his efforts a victory for farm workers, rather than merely a witness for justice.

> *I don't think any one event, or any one day, or any one action, or any one confrontation wins or loses a battle. You keep that in mind and be practical about it. It's foolish then to try and gamble everything on one roll of the dice – which is what violence really gets down to. I think the practical person has a better chance of dealing with nonviolence than people who tend to be dreamers or who are impractical. We're not nonviolent because we want to save our souls. We're nonviolent because we want to get some social justice for the workers.*
>
> *If all you're interested in is going around being nonviolent and so concerned about saving yourself, at some*

An organizer with the Agricultural Workers Organizing Committee speaks with other farm laborers during a 1961 organizing meeting. Photo © George Ballis, all rights reserved.

National Farm Workers Association strike line, Delano, California, 1965. Photo © George Ballis, all rights reserved.

Boycott picket line outside Fresno, California supermarket, 1966. Photo © George Ballis, all rights reserved.

point the whole thing breaks down – you say to yourself, 'Well, let them be violent, as long as I'm nonviolent.' Or you begin to think it's okay to lose the battle as long as you remain nonviolent. The idea is that you have to win and be nonviolent. That's extremely important! You've got to be nonviolent – and you've got to win with nonviolence!

What do the poor care about strange philosophies of nonviolence if it doesn't mean bread for them?

The United Farm Workers Union has to be "a real organization" Chavez has said, "a living organization, there has to be people in motion, and they have to be disciplined. I don't mean, like, marching; I mean a trained instinct so that when the moment comes, we just turn around and hit it. If you organize for demonstration, all you have is demonstration. You must demonstrate, and then return right away to the real work."

In boycott offices throughout the country, UFW organizers do that "real work" — 18 to 20 hours a day

United Farm Workers Union members and supporters picket Detroit, Michigan, produce terminal, 1969. Bob Fitch.

Farm worker Marta Rodrigues is arrested during UFW strike, Fresno, California, Summer 1973. Bob Fitch.

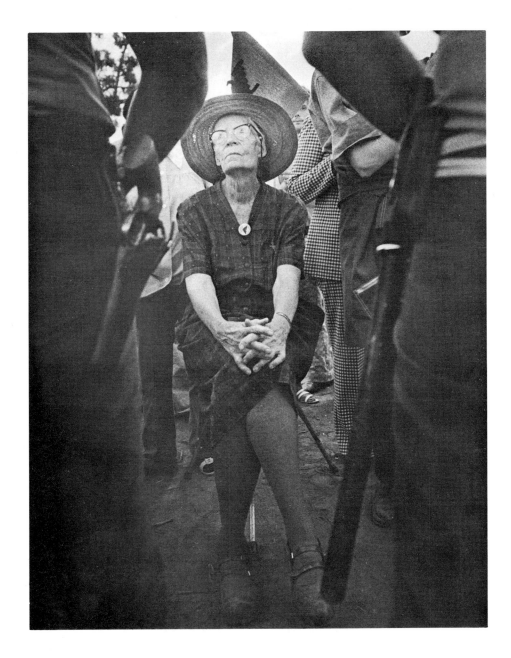

—for the meager material return of room and board and $5 a week. Chavez also insisted, "We have to find some cross between being a movement and being a union." He sought to include any group which might be of help to the farm workers' struggle. So, from the beginning, workers themselves, civil rights activists, AFL-CIO officials, youthful dropouts, old fashioned leftists, and clergy have rubbed shoulders within the movement, not always happily, but learning to subsume differences before the urgency of the worker's needs.

THE GRAPE BOYCOTT

Hungry people cannot sustain a long walkout, as growers and workers knew from previous agricultural strikes. Early in its history, the UFW found the tactic that was to break this stalemate: the boycott. The first boycott, that of Schenley in 1966, was little more than a propaganda tactic, but the International Grape Boycott mounted in 1968 brought disciplined organizers to over 100 cities across the U.S. and Canada. The loss of sales from the boycott, together with strong public pressure, led the growers in 1970 to sign the first wide scale union contracts in California.

Almost immediately, the UFW found itself in new battles. To undercut the militant new union, lettuce growers in Salinas signed "sweetheart" con-

Dorothy Day of the Catholic Worker before being arrested on a farm worker strike line, Lamont, California, August 1973. Bob Fitch.

tracts for their workers with the Teamsters' Union. In September 1970, 10,000 United Farm Workers struck against the phony pacts. A new boycott of head lettuce began. In 1972, the UFW proved its potential stength across the nation by signing a contract with Coca-Cola's Minute Maid subsidiary in Florida which covered the mostly black orange pickers. In 1973, in a desperate effort to destroy the UFW, wine and table grape growers refused to renegotiate their contracts and instead delivered their workers to the Teamsters. Two striking farm workers were killed and over 10,000 workers and supporters were arrested in the wave of protest strikes which swept California that summer. The boycott extended to take in wine and table grapes again.

In June 1975, for the first time in America, the California legislature guaranteed the right of agricultural workers to vote for the union of their choice. Whether the new law will prove a major victory for America's poorest workers, or merely another chapter in the history of collusion between legal authorities and employers, remains to be seen. But already, the dynamic use of nonviolence in the farm workers' struggle has changed the agricultural scene — and the workers and growers themselves — drastically from what they were less than ten years ago. □

United Farm Workers Union solidarity march, Modesto, California, 1975. Bob Fitch.

CHAPTER 10

THE PEACE MOVEMENT

VIETNAM

During the summer of 1963 the War Resisters
League created a peace action committee which
set, as its major focus, the anti-Buddhist terrorism
by the US-supported Diem government of South
Vietnam. On July 25 there was a picketing of the
home of South Vietnam's permanent observer to
the UN and in October, a demonstration to "greet"
Madame Ngo Dinh Nhu during her visit to New
York. In July 1964 Dave McReynolds and A. J.
Muste issued a "Memo on Vietnam" for the War
Resisters League. They reviewed the history of
Vietnam and of the American intervention and
declared:

> Any hope for a US victory is the closest
> thing yet to a military impossibility. . . .
> American policy is at a dead end . . . we

*must not fall into the trap of supporting
the US government 'pending' an agreement on neutralization. US policy
should be totally opposed as a bumbling
fraud, and the withdrawal of US troops
and arms urged as a first step. . . . In
our approach to the public and to opinion leaders . . . It is not enough to
express our moral outrage. We must also
communicate the utter folly of U.S. policy in Southeast Asia in political and
military terms. If we fail to do so – vigorously, now, everywhere – then we shall
continue to drift toward a general war in
Asia.*

In November, McReynolds restated this
position. Speaking for the WRL, he wrote:

Dave McReynolds of the War Resisters League speaks at a demonstration against the war in Vietnam, New York City,
December 19, 1964. War Resisters League.

Declaration Of Conscience
AGAINST UNITED STATES POLICIES
IN VIETNAM AND THE DOMINICAN REPUBLIC

Because the use of the military resources of the United States in Vietnam, the Dominican Republic and elsewhere suppresses the aspirations of the people for political independence and economic freedom;

Because inhuman torture and senseless killing are being carried out by forces armed, uniformed, trained and financed by the United States;

Because we believe that all peoples of the earth, including both Americans and non-Americans, have an inalienable right to life, liberty, and the peaceful pursuit of happiness in their own way, and to freedom from military intervention by any foreign power; and

Because we think that we must go beyond conventional protest to put an end to the threat of nuclear catastrophe and death by chemical or biological warfare, whether these result from accident or escalation --

We hereby declare our conscientious refusal to cooperate with the United States government in the prosecution of the war in Vietnam. We further declare our refusal to cooperate with U.S. military intervention in the Dominican Republic, or the affairs of any other nation.

We encourage those who can conscientiously do so to refuse to serve in the armed forces and to ask for discharge if they are already in.

Those of us who are subject to the draft ourselves declare our own intention to refuse to serve.

We urge others to refuse and refuse ourselves to take part in the manufacture or transportation of military equipment, or to work in the fields of military research and weapons development.

We shall encourage the development of other nonviolent acts, including acts which involve civil disobedience, in order to stop the flow of American soldiers and munitions to Vietnam and other countries.

NOTE: *Signing or distributing this Declaration of Conscience might be construed as a violation of the Universal Military Training and Service Act, which prohibits advising persons facing the draft to refuse service. Penalties of up to 5 years imprisonment, and/or a fine of $10,000 are provided. While prosecutions under this provision of the law almost never occur, persons signing or distributing this declaration should face the possibility of serious consequences.*

NAME   ADDRESS

_____

_____

_____

_____

_____

_____

_____

_____

_____

_____

Some of the more than 5,000 people who signed the original Declaration of Conscience——

J. Malvern Benjamin, Jr.
The Rev. Lloyd A. Berg
Rev. Dan Berrigan, S.J.
Rev. Philip Berrigan, S.S.J.
Julian Bond
Kay Boyle
James Bristol
Emile Capouya
Gordon Christiansen
William C. Davidon
Dorothy Day
David Dellinger
Barbara Deming
Ralph DiGia
Lawrence Ferlinghetti
W. H. Ferry
Maxwell Geismar
Rabbi Everett E. Gendler
Paul Goodman
Robert Brookins Gore
Richard B. Gregg
Margaret Halsey
Ammon Hennacy
Paul Jacobs
Erich Kahler
Roy C. Kepler
Paul Krassner
Irving Laucks
Sidney Lens
John Lewis
Roger Lockard
Staughton Lynd
Bradford Lyttle
Milton Mayer
David McReynolds
Stewart Meacham
Helen Mears
Mary Meigs
Morris R. Mitchell
Mrs. Lucy Montgomery
A. J. Muste
Otto Nathan
Robert B. Nichols
Robert Osborn
Linus Pauling
Jim Peck
Diane di Prima
A. Philip Randolph
Anatol Rapoport
Earle Reynolds
Bayard Rustin
Ira J. Sandperl
Marc Schleifer
Glenn E. Smiley
Monte G. Steadman, M.D.
Harvey Swados
Marjorie Swann
Robert Swann
Ralph T. Templin
Samuel R. Tyson
Denny Wilcher
George Willoughby

Please return signed petitions to one of the sponsoring organizations listed below.

Catholic Worker
175 Chrystie Street
(Att: Tom Cornell)
New York, N. Y. 10002

Committee for Nonviolent Action
5 Beekman Street, Room 1033
New York, N. Y. 10038

Student Peace Union
5 Beekman Street, Room 1029
New York, N. Y. 10038

War Resisters League
5 Beekman Street, Room 1025
New York, N. Y. 10038

Printed by the Grindstone Press

Our position must be absolutely clear. We are for negotiation. We are for neutralization. But first of all, and most of all, we are for the immediate withdrawal of all US military forces and military aid. Not all peace groups have taken this position, but it is safe to predict that they will be forced by events to follow the WRL's lead in this regard.

FIRST NATIONWIDE PROTEST

The first important demonstration against the war took place in New York on December 19, 1964, sponsored by WRL, CNVA, the FOR, Socialist Party and SPU. Fifteen hundred people turned out in subfreezing weather to hear Muste, Norman Thomas and A. Philip Randolph denounce the war. In San Francisco, 100 people heard Joan Baez sing and Roy Kepler speak. Other demonstrations took place in Minneapolis, Miami, Austin, Sacramento, Philadelphia, Chicago, Washington, Boston and Cleveland. A feature of the mobilization was the circulation of "An Appeal to the American Conscience," that urged an immediate ceasefire and the earliest possible withdrawal of US troops.

Declaration of Conscience Against the War in Vietnam, 1965. Institute for the Study of Nonviolence.

THE YEAR OF VIETNAM

1965 was, as the *CNVA Bulletin* declared, "The Year of Vietnam." Picketing and sit-downs across the country marked the announcement of the first US bombing of North Vietnam on February 7. These continued throughout the month and much effort was expended gathering signatures for a new appeal, the Declaration of Conscience, circulated by radical pacifist groups, urging civil disobedience. The Peacemakers group in Cincinnati organized a "No Tax for War in Vietnam Committee" calling for tax resistance. In December 1969 a separate group — War Tax Resistance, coordinated by Bob Calvert — was established and at one time included some 200 local tax resistance centers across the country.

On March 16, 1965, Alice Herz, an 82-year-old widow who had fled Nazism, left a note saying, "I choose the illuminating death of a Buddhist to protest against a great country trying to wipe out a small country for no reason," and set herself afire at a busy Detroit intersection. She died ten days later. On November 2 Norman Morrison, secretary of a Friends Meeting, burned himself to death in front of the Pentagon, and later was honored by the North Vietnamese. One week later Roger La Porte, a young volunteer for the Catholic Worker movement in New York, immolated himself in front of the United Nations.

The first national demonstration against the war was organized by the Students for a Democratic Society on April 17, a March on Washington to end the war in Vietnam. This demonstration was controversial because SDS refused to prohibit Communists from taking part. At first, radical pacifists protested this policy, but they eventually came around to support it and the non-exclusionary policy became a part of the Vietnam protest movement. This represented a deliberate and constructive break with the anti-communist past. The SDS March gave the anti-war movement its first national publicity and led to bitter attacks on it from the

A Vietnamese Buddhist monk burns himself to death on Saigon's Market Square to protest the government's military and anti-religious policies, October 5, 1963. UPI.

Top right: March protesting the war in Vietnam, Berkeley, California, February 23, 1966. Harvey Richards/War Resisters League.

CALL FOR AN ASSEMBLY OF UNREPRESENTED PEOPLE
in Washington, D.C., August 6-9

"I like to believe that the people in the long run are going to do more to promote peace than our governments. I think the people want peace so much that one of these days governments had better get out of their way and let them have it."

--- President Dwight D. Eisenhower, Aug. 31, 1959

WE DECLARE PEACE

IN MISSISSIPPI and Washington the few make the decisions for the many. Mississippi Negroes are denied the vote; the voice of the thirty per cent of Americans now opposed to the undeclared war in Vietnam is not heeded and all Americans are denied access to facts concerning the true military and political situation. We must make it plain to the Administration that we will not be accomplices to a war that we did not declare. There can be no doubt that the great majority of the people of the world do not approve of the presence of American troops in Vietnam. We who will come to Washington on August 6 through 9 cannot in any sense represent this majority, but we can let our voices be heard in a symbolic *Assembly of Unrepresented People to Declare Peace.*

AUGUST 6 is the twentieth anniversary of the dropping of the first atomic bomb on Hiroshima;

August 9 the anniversary of the Nagasaki bomb. Therefore, we choose August 6, 7, 8, and 9 for a new attempt to draw together the voices of nonviolent protest in America; not only those who have for so long been calling for an end to the Cold War, but also those whose protests focus on racial injustice, inquisition by Congressional committees, inequities in labor legislation, the mishandling of anti-poverty and welfare funds and the absence of democratic process on the local level. We invite not only those now active in organized protests but ministers, members of the academic community, teachers, women, professional people, students, people from the newly formed community groups in slums and rural areas, industrial workers, anyone who wishes to symbolically withdraw his support from the war and who wishes to explore the possibilities of inter-action inherent in this community of concerned people.

Norma Becker	Stephen Amdur	Sandra Adickes
Bob Swann	Eric Weinberger	Francis H. Mitchell
Donna Allen	Walter M. Tillow	John Porcelli
Bob Parvis	Carl Oglesby	William Hartzog
Mel McDonald	Ed Hamlett	Barbara Deming
Carl Bloise	Jeffrey Gordon	Mack Smith
Peter Kellman	Jimmy Garrett	Staughton Lynd
Barry Weisberg	Courtland Cox	Dennis Sweeney
Dena Clamager	Dave Dellinger	Russ Nixon
Steve Weissman	Ray Raphael	Florence Howe
		Paul Lauter

Johnson administration and all segments of the press.

On June 16, officials of the Pentagon, confronted with a CNVA-organized civil disobedience demonstration, turned the steps of the Pentagon over to the pacifists for a "speak-out", with talks by Muste, Bill Davidon, Gordon Christiansen and others. The idea of a "speak-out" derived from the "teach-ins," round-the-clock meetings on Vietnam that, beginning at Ann Arbor in March, swept the college campuses for the duration of the school year, and made students aware of the facts about Vietnam for the first time.

The Assembly of Unrepresented People, August 6 to 9, brought the civil rights and peace movements together for the largest civil disobedience demonstration ever held in Washington up to that time. Eric Weinberger, a CNVA activist and CORE field worker, and Robert Parris Moses of SNCC were the coordinators. A march from the Washington Monument to the Capitol ended with a sit-down in which 350 people were arrested.

At the same time, students from Berkeley and other Bay Area schools attempted to stop trains arriving at Oakland with soldiers destined for Vietnam. This demonstration was organized by the Vietnam Day Committee (VDC), a coalition in which pacifists played an important part. The VDC

Leaflet from the Assembly of Unrepresented People, 1965. Sam Tyson.

Dave Dellinger, Staughton Lynd, and Robert Parris Moses lead the Assembly of Unrepresented People to the Capitol to protest U.S. policy in Vietnam, Washington D.C. August 9, 1965. A heckler splattered red paint across their chests. Neil Haworth/WRL.

Printed by the Grindstone Press

WHY BURN DRAFT CARDS?

Drew Pearson quotes Father Hoa, a Vietnamese, anti-Communist Catholic priest, who says: "How can we explain to a mother when her child is burned by napalm? And how can we claim to be for the people when we burn their homes simply because their houses happen to be in Vietcong-controlled territory?" (New York Post, Feb. 26, 1965).

"In London, the Daily Mirror's Saigon correspondent reports an interview (July 4) in which . . . Air Force General Ky, now head of the South Vietnamese government, was asked who his heroes were, 'I have only one,' he replied, 'Hitler.'" (I. F. Stone's Weekly, July 12, 1965).

"So far we have not had any government that is really representative. Americans must accept the egotism and capriciousness of the Vietnamese. The military uprising and dissolution of the High National Council [legislature] is not a great affair for us." (General Nguyen Khanh, former dictator of South Vietnam, quoted in the New York Times, January 22, 1965).

"[American pilots] are given a square marked on a map and told to hit every hamlet within the area." (Washington Post, March 4, 1965).

Gen. Samuel Williams, former U. S. adviser to President Diem, says: "Every non-Communist in such a village [that we bomb] is going to be a darned good Communist by the time we get through." (New York Post, February 26, 1965).

FEDERAL LAW HAS REQUIRED since 1948 that all men over 18 who were born after 1922 carry a draft card. Those failing to comply can be subjected to a prison term of up to five years and/or a $10,000 fine. On August 30, 1965, the President signed into law a new act making those who wilfully destroy their draft cards liable to the same sentence.

CONGRESS AND THE PRESIDENT in effect gave a small piece of paper a symbolic significance it had not previously possessed, making possession of the draft card not only proof of registration but a test of loyalty. The draft card thus became a unique document in American life, the only document tens of millions must either carry or face the courts and a five year maximum sentence—a heavier penalty than suffered by scores of convicted Nazi war criminals. The card is unique in still another way. It is the symbolic link between every young American and the present war.

WHILE WE CANNOT SUPPORT ANY WAR, the war in Vietnam has become a classic example of the unjust war. It is a war which has seen villages reduced to ashes, rice paddies defoliated, prisoners and suspects tortured, innocents and non-combatants killed by the thousands. These crimes are committed in behalf of a series of dictatorships the very support of which is contrary to all American ideals. The leader of the present regime has described Hitler as his number one hero. Each of the many Saigon governments has ignored the rights which we as Americans hold to be self-evident: the right to free expression and a free press, the right to assemble and petition. The present regime in Saigon executes men who advocate negotiations to end the war.

The draft card has thus become something we cannot carry without shame, a document which offends our religious beliefs and our belief in the concept of justice which we were taught in our schools. Further, it is incompatible with the bonds which unite us with our fellow men who bear the burden of that fratricidal jungle war in Southeast Asia.

THE DRAFT HAS BECOME A SYMBOL of our government's will to prosecute this war; we therefore find we must reject that symbol, reject it openly and stand ready to bear the consequences. In doing so we are not rejecting the many Americans who are giving their lives in this conflict, but the system which has placed them there. We are calling on them to turn from war to peace. We have in the past protested against the war in Vietnam in other more familiar ways. We intend to participate in and support all forms of open, responsible opposition to war, ranging from letter writing to conscientious objection.

WHAT WE ARE SAYING TODAY IS THIS: the real crime is not burning this scrap of paper; the crime is burning villages, burning hospitals, burning children. It is bombing the helpless. It is a willingness to strike out at defenseless villages. It is in fact the false belief that violence can determine what men believe. From these crimes, from such beliefs, we hereby disaffiliate ourselves.

also staged a march to the Oakland Army Terminal that was broken up by Oakland city police and Hells Angels. It was this march that led Allen Ginsberg to write a poem entitled "How to Make A March/Spectacle" that urged, among other suggestions

> *Masses of flowers – a visual spectacle – especially concentrated in the front lines. Can be used to set up barricades, to present to Hells Angels, Police, politicians, and press and spectators whenever needed or at parade's end. Masses of marchers can be asked to bring their own flowers. Front lines should be organized and provided with flowers in advance.*

The Assembly of Unrepresented People also produced the National Coordinating Committee to End the War in Vietnam which planned demonstrations for October 15 and 16, 1965, called the Days of International Protest. This led to the formation in New York of the Fifth Avenue Peace Parade Committee, a unique coalition of all groups opposing the Vietnam War, including liberals, pacifists, Communists, and the new and old left. What made such a broad based coalition possible was the personality of A. J. Muste. While few of the groups had ever agreed, worked with or much less trusted one another, they were all united in their respect for A. J. Under his leadership, a walk down Fifth Avenue with over 50,000 participants was achieved and an organizational model for future and nation-wide mobilizations created.

DRAFT CARD BURNINGS

The highpoint of the first International Days of Protest occurred on October 15 at a small demonstration at the Whitehall Street Induction Center in New York City, organized by radical pacifists and attended by about 500 people. One of the speakers, David Miller, a Catholic Worker, decided to burn his draft card instead of giving a speech. The act received enormous publicity, for Miller's was the first draft card burning following a Congressional law, enacted earlier in the summer, making destruction of a draft card a felony equal in seriousness to draft refusal.

Draft card burning had been a traditional way pacifists protested against the draft. The draft card burnings in 1947 have been related earlier. In May 1964, 12 men burned their draft cards in New York City to protest conscription. A few weeks before the Assembly of Unrepresented People, there was another draft card burning in New York which was reported in the national media and caused the patriots in Washington to rush a bill through Congress making it illegal.

On November 6, again in New York City, A. J. Muste presided over a carefully organized draft card burning in which Dave McReynolds, Marc-Paul Edelman, Tom Cornell, Jim Wilson and Roy Lisker took part. The following month, at a SANE rally in Washington, D.C., SDS President Carl Oglesby delivered a speech entitled "Let Us Shape the Future" which called the war in Vietnam a product of "corporate liberalism," and emphasized that the war was not an aberration as liberals thought, but a basic result of American policy at home and abroad.

LOCAL PACIFIST GROUPS

Up to this point there were few local pacifist action groups in the country. CNVA-West was active in

Leaflet produced by the Catholic Worker, CNVA, New York Workshop in Nonviolence, and the WRL for the November 6, 1965 draft card burning, New York City. Institute for the Study of Nonviolence.

the Bay Area and there was a core group of Boston activists — Dave Reed, John Phillips, John Benson, and Dave O'Brien — that existed briefly during the winter of '65 and '66 before going out of existence after a wave of draft card burnings and induction refusals. There was also New England CNVA which, like the Boston chapter, was now concerned mainly with draft resistance.

About this time Maris Cakars and Gwen Reyes, with help from the WRL and CNVA, formed the N.Y. Workshop In Nonviolence which produced *WIN* magazine as one of its major projects. Many of the people connected with *WIN* were new to pacifism and saw themselves more in the bohemian-beat setting, then going through a rejuvenation on New York's Lower East Side, than in the pacifist tradition. Many poets and artists, some in the beat generation and some not, were already involved with radical pacifism: Jackson MacLow, Allen Ginsberg, Tuli Kupferberg, Ed Sanders, and the General Strike for Peace people centered around

Julian Beck and Judith Malina of The Living Theater. In the West there was the pacifist Anarchist Circle in San Francisco with poets Kenneth Rexroth, Robert Duncan, Philip Lamatia, and William Everson (Brother Antoninus) as members.

What *WIN* was most attracted to, however, was the gentle and playful commitment of the Dutch Provos, the Diggers in San Francisco and the pioneer spokesmen for psychedelics. Dissatisfied with the negative connotations of a peace movement that was *anti*-war and in favor of *non*violence, *WIN* tried to bring a positive joy to peace demonstrations, to make them celebrations of a new and different kind of life. The result was the launching of a 10-foot canvas yellow submarine, inspired by the Beatles and Polaris Action, which was marched through the streets of Manhattan with flowers, balloons and music. The Yellow Submarine demonstration was indicative of a new mood in the nation, a new way of living.

Tom Cornell, Marc Paul Edelman, Roy Lisker, Dave McReynolds, and Jim Wilson burn their draft cards at a noon rally in Union Square, New York City, November 6, 1965. Neil Haworth.

*Wherever there is a young man who wakes in the
early morning to face yet another day of prison for
opposition to this war, or to all wars; wherever a
person takes risks on behalf of the vision of a peace-
able kingdom; wherever – to use one of A.J.'s favor-
ite images – a man, like Abraham, leaves behind him
the city of his nativity and turns his face toward the
city of his dreams, A.J. is at his side.*

Staughton Lynd, *Liberation*, September 1967

The Fifth Avenue Peace Parade, New York City, March 26, 1966. Over 50,000 people marched to Central Park in protest of the Vietnam war and gave A.J. Muste, Parade Committee head, a standing ovation when he spoke. Eli Finer/Swarthmore College Peace Collection.

A.J. Muste in North Vietnam shortly before his death, January 1967. Photo courtesy of Barbara Deming.

Float honoring A.J. Muste in the Spring Mobilization to End the War in Vietnam march, New York City, April 15, 1967. John Goodwin.

Diana Davies

DAVID DELLINGER
(Born 1915)

A printer, writer, and organizer, Dave Dellinger was one of the war resisters who emerged from prison after World War II to lead the disarmament, civil rights, and anti-war movements and encourage the development of active nonviolence in the U.S. A radical activist all his adult life, his writing and organizing work helped draw many into the ranks of the organized peace movement, and he was influential in determining the more radical direction taken by pacifists in the post-war years. A socialist and father of five children, he also sought to unite in his personal and family life the nonviolent principles which guided his political work.

Born in Wakefield, Massachusetts, Dellinger attended Yale College and Yale Divinity School. Before the war, he was involved in an unsuccessful campaign to get the U.S. to lower its immigration barriers to provide asylum for Jews and antifascists. In 1939 he helped set up a communal colony in Newark, New Jersey, which included a number of radical pacifists and had strong Christian, Gandhian and socialist influences. He worked as a community organizer in the slums of Harlem and Newark and soon realized "that the United States was an unreliable ally whose goals were not my goals and whose methods were not my methods."

He recognized the collusion of the War Department and Big Business in determining foreign policy and in maintaining an unequal distribution of wealth, power and privilege. "The health of the state conflicts with the health of the citizenry," he wrote, "and the prerogatives of property prevent the fulfillment of the people." He criticized the industrial and commercial interests which were behind World War I and subsequent wars, and condemned capitalism for exalting private ownership, usury and private profit. The American dream, he wrote, has always had two sides: the promises and the reality.

In 1940, while a student at Union Theological Seminary, Dellinger publicly refused to register under America's first peace-time conscription law and was imprisoned for a year and a day. After his release, he refused to accept assignment to a CPS camp and was imprisoned again, for two years. While in Lewisberg Penitentiary, he took part in a 60-day fast protesting racial segregation. Shortly after his release in 1945, he wrote a Declaration of War in which he said:

> The evil of our civilization cannot be combated by campaigns which oppose militarism and conscription but leave the American economic and social system intact. . . . The American system has been destroying human life in peace and in war, at home and abroad, for decades. Now it has produced the crowning infamy of atom bombing. . . . There is no solution short of all-out war.

He called for a "nonviolent war carried on by methods worthy of the ideals we seek to serve," and helped bring radical pacifists and others together after World War II to build a strong nonviolent movement for revolutionary change in America.

Dellinger spent 25 years living and working communally in New Jersey, first in Newark and then at Glen Gardner. He helped edit *Direct Action* and *Alternative* immediately after the war, was active in the War Resisters League, Peacemakers, and the Committee for Nonviolent Revolution, and helped found the Glen Gardner community and the Libertarian Press, a workers cooperative. He organized disarmament and civil rights actions, protested Civil Defense drills, and was active in a number of Committee for Nonviolent Action campaigns. An editor of *Liberation* magazine for many years, he worked with A.J. Muste and others to clearly present the radical pacifist perspective to the public and helped catalyze wider disarmament, civil rights, and anti-war actions.

During the war in Vietnam, he actively led protests and organized resistance to American aggression, serving as co-chairperson of the New Mobilization Committee to End the War in Vietnam after A.J. Muste's death. "The war in Vietnam," he wrote, "is a logical expression of America's profit-oriented economy and self-righteous foreign policy, both of which have been with us from the beginning." He was indicted in 1968 for his role in organizing demonstrations at the Democratic National Convention in Chicago, and as a member of the Chicago Eight, was tried and convicted in the widely-publicized "conspiracy" trial, the conviction later being overturned on appeal.

After the war, he called for "the power of force without violence to wrench concessions from the establishment that weaken the system's mystical authority and strengthen the self-confidence of the people." In the Seventies, he encouraged the growth of the counter-culture, feminist movement, and alternative institutions as means of attacking "the single most destructive aspect of the existing society — the willingness to pursue one's own fulfillment without concern for the fulfillment of one's fellows."

John Goodwin

PAUL GOODMAN
(1911 — 1972)

Paul Goodman's radical common sense and bold inventiveness inspired the radical youth of the Sixties and made him an outspoken advocate of individual and sexual freedom for over 40 years. A writer, teacher, poet, and social critic, often termed the "Father of the New Left," he emphasized the need for a "rational community" where tolerance and respect were the norm and individual initiative were honored. A pragmatic anarchist, he believed that people are essentially creative, loving and communal, but that institutions and behavioral roles alienate them from their natural selves. Once society's organizations become more important than the individuals who comprise them, then humanity is suppressed to suit an inhuman system. He rejected institutional life and advocated decentralizing social functions into smaller units that suit human needs.

> Our abundant society is at present simply deficient in many of the most elementary objective opportunities and worthwhile goals that could make growing up possible. It is lacking . . . in honest public speech . . . in the opportunity to be useful. It thwarts aptitude and creates stupidity. It corrupts ingenuous patriotism. It corrupts the fine arts. It shackles science. It dampens animal ardor. It discourages the religious convictions of Justification and Vocation. It dims the sense that there is a Creation. It has no Honor. It has no Community.

Goodman was born in Greenwich Village, New York, and graduated from the City College of New York in 1931. He continued his formal education by simply walking into classes he liked and, without registering, taking a seat. His criticism and poetry began to be published in the Thirties and rapidly grew to include a substantial body of work. Besides numerous novels, short stories, plays, and articles, Goodman also wrote major works on education, city planning, psycho-therapy and literary criticism.

During the late Forties and Fifties, Goodman was influential among anarchist, bohemian and intellectual circles in New York City. He was a theoretician of the first gestalt therapy groups in America, an associate of the Living Theater (pioneers of off-Broadway), a teacher at Black Mountain College, and a contributor to such germinal publications as *Politics* and later *Liberation,* of which he was an editor. He also taught at the University of Chicago, Manumit School of Progressive Education, the University of Wisconsin, and San Francisco State's Experimental College.

Although much of his work was published during the Fifties, Goodman lived on the periphery of society, with a limited following and close to failure and poverty. His talents gained recognition and his fortune rose dramatically with the publication of *Growing Up Absurd* in 1960. In it he gave a bristling indictment of American society and a spirited defense of the young who were beginning to drop out of it. He toured the nation's campuses in the early Sixties, speaking publicly and privately to a generation of students who instinctively rejected the values of American society.

Goodman's message was not so much ideology as a challenge to celebrate life and love, and to reject the American norms of military violence, sexual conformity, and racial hatred. The spontaneous defiance of the student movement of the late Sixties grew partly from his influence. "In a society that is cluttered, overcentralized, and overadministered," he wrote, "we should aim at simplification, decentralization, and decontrol."

When, in October 1967, he was invited to address the National Security Industrial Association Conference on "Research and Development" at the State Department, Goodman spoke out with typical honesty, insight, and flair:

> You people are unfitted by your commitments, your experience, your customary message, your recruitment, and your moral disposition. You are the military-industrial of the United States, the most dangerous body of men at the present in the world, for you not only implement our disasterous policies but are an overwhelming lobby for them, and you expand and rigidify the wrong use of brains, resources, and labor so that change becomes difficult. Most likely the trends you represent will be interrupted by a shambles of riots, alienation, ecological catastrophies, wars, and revolutions, so that current long-range planning, including this conference, is irrelevant.

The father of three children, he was one of the most committed older-generation supporters of the Resistance movement, and one of the most articulate proponents of a popular, mass-based nonviolent movement against the war in Vietnam. Above all else though, he was a teacher, who viewed the world as an organic whole in which human needs are of central importance and human community the most sought after goal.

BEGINNING OF A COUNTER-CULTURE

Pacifists had long urged people to stop working in war industries and to disassociate themselves from the war-making government. Many young people now came to view the whole society as being part of a war culture and simply dropped out of it; they became non-cooperators with the American way of life which had produced Vietnam. This movement was apolitical in intent but in effect it was a decisive political rejection of militarism and the state. Because it was opposed to violence and addressed itself to life style rather than abstruse rhetoric, radical pacifists found they could relate to it easily. The WIN group in New York, Jim Hayes and friends in New England, the people around WRL-West in San Francisco and a newly formed anarchist-oriented WRL chapter in Los Angeles began addressing themselves to the drop-out community in an attempt to give the new life style political content. The time was ripe for this kind of transformation and, as a result, the peace movement became more than a movement against the war in Vietnam and made changes reaching deeply into the most basic ways that Americans saw themselves and structured their lives.

MAKING PROTEST VISIBLE

This change came gradually, beginning in 1966, peaking in the euphoria of the summer of love of 1967 and crashing with the reality of the Chicago demonstrations of 1968. And the war continued. In the spring of 1966 CNVA sent Muste, Lyttle, Barbara Deming, Karl Meyer, Sherry Thurber and Bill Davidon to Saigon. They met with anti-war Buddhist and Catholic leaders and then picketed the US embassy with placards denouncing the war, for which they were deported. Meanwhile, Vietnamese translated and circulated their message illegally throughout South Vietnam.

Street demonstrations were frequent during 1966. The slightest provocation was enough to bring people into the streets to picket a dinner addressed by Secretary of State Dean Rusk, to block traffic in protest of renewed bombing of North Vietnam, to block military recruiters on campus, to sit-in at the Dow Chemical offices protesting its manufacture of napalm, to distribute anti-draft leaflets in the early morning hours at induction centers urging young men to refuse to be drafted and offering advice on how to stay out — there was a demonstration for every occasion. The main pur-

Leaflet from the New York Workshop in Nonviolence, c. 1966. Marty Jezer.

Poets Gary Snyder and Allen Ginsberg march against the war in Vietnam, New York City, November 5, 1966. Maury Englander.

pose of these demonstrations was to make the anti-war movement visible to the American public and to make the media, which was overwhelmingly in support of the war and opposed to criticism of government policy, acknowledge that an opposition did exist, that it had facts, that it was vocal and could disrupt the status quo if provoked far enough.

Apparently, President Johnson got the message. According to David Halberstam, Pentagon officials advised the President in 1966 that their computers forecast victory if he would authorize the bombing of Hanoi and Haiphong. Johnson refused to allow this escalation. He told the military to ask their computers "how long it will take five hundred thousand angry Americans to climb that White House wall out there and lynch their President." The voice of the peace movement was now being heard.

Draft card burning in Sheeps Meadow, Central Park, New York City, April 15, 1967. Dave McReynolds/WRI.

Drawing from *On the Resistance*, published by the Palo Alto Resistance, 1969. Institute for the Study of Nonviolence.

Upper right: Leaflet from the Palo Alto Resistance, 1968, Palo Alto, California. Christopher Jones.

A CALL TO RESIST MILITARY CONSCRIPTION

WE WILL NOT BE FOOLED BY A DRAFT LOTTERY
WE WON'T BE DETERRED BY CONSPIRACY INDICTMENTS

We are engaged in a struggle for life, building communities of men and women actively shaping their own lives, freeing themselves from political oppression, economic exploitation, and channeling by the draft and other repressive institutions. We see the war our government is waging against Vietnam as a horrible example of its larger policy of grasping for economic, political, and military power in the world. Closely linked with the government, providing its top personnel and shaping its policies, are the giant corporations. These centers of private power control the economic life of our nation and increasingly of the world. We insist that the world's resources should be used responsibly for the benefit of all, and not usurped by a small powerful minority for their own profit.

We are not fooled by changes being made in the draft, such as the lottery system and the calling of nineteen year olds. These make it all the more crucial that we stand together, and not allow our brothers and neighbors—many of whom have not yet had a chance to become aware of the actual purposes of the U.S.

military nor of their own rights and responsibilities—to be isolated from the rest of us and quietly shipped off. Those who are in or who are just leaving high school have difficult and crucial decisions to make. We can work with them, and support those whose respect for life and freedom leads them to insist on their right to serve their communities freely and constructively, and to reject the system of involuntary servitude demanded by the war-makers.

We realize that the draft and other institutions of oppression exist in our society because, through our cooperation with them, we allow them to exist. We stand in solidarity with those who say no to supporting institutions of death and yes to life by returning their draft cards.

We will gratefully accept these cards and publicly return them. We declare our refusal to be intimidated by "conspiracy" indictments and our determination to encourage, support and participate in life-affirming acts.

Robert P. Bair	Robert Dietz	Russell Johnson	Mark Morris
Thompson Bradley	Richard Drinnan	Donald Kalish	Grace Paley
Henry Braun	Michael Ferber	Paul Lauter	Rev. Findley Schaeff
Noam Chomsky	Mitchell Goodman	Sid Lens	Ken Sherman
Norbert Considine	Paul Goodman	Dwight Macdonald	Rick Sterling
Tom Cornell	Rev. David Gracie	Joshua Markel	Natalie Stephens
William Davidon	Michael W. Griefen	David McReynolds	Marjorie Swann
Dorothy Day	Florence Howe	Stewart Meacham	Ron Young

In a demonstration sponsored by Resistance and the New Mobilization Committee to End the War in Vietnam, we will return the draft cards the first day of the Senate Armed Services Committee hearings on the draft in late February. We urge you to collect cards in your community and/or send in your own card. Mail before February 15th to Philadelphia Resistance, 2006 Walnut Street, Philadelphia, Pennsylvania.

Note: Nonpossession of a draft card may be construed to be a violation of the Selective Service Act. Reading this leaflet may make you guilty of conspiracy.

PHILADELPHIA RESISTANCE
2006 WALNUT STREET ♪ PHILADELPHIA ♪ PENNSYLVANIA ♪ (215) 561-5080

THE RESISTANCE

Radical pacifists had always insisted that "wars would cease when men refused to fight." Thus, much of their energy went into organizing draft resistance activities. Throughout the early years of the Vietnam conflict there were numerous instances of men refusing to be inducted or even to register for the draft. Peacemakers published a list of noncooperators which grew in length each month and many activists connected with CNVA burned draft cards or refused induction, but none of these efforts was organized as mass actions.

The first mass anti-draft action took place April 15, 1967, at what was until then the largest peace demonstration in American history, a rally at the Sheeps Meadow in New York's Central Park followed by a walk to the UN with hundreds of thousands of participants. The morning of the march, 175 men burned their draft cards in a joint effort organized by Bruce Dancis and five other Cornell students. After the march, the draft card burners met to organize themselves in a mutual support organization. Non-draftable friends also met and

Leaflet from the Philadelphia Resistance. Institute for the Study of Nonviolence.

Anti-war rally sponsored by the Philadelphia Resistance, May 1, 1969. On the platform are Larry Scott, Jim Bristol, George Willoughby, Bob Eaton (speaking), and Stewart Meecham. Theodore Hetzel.

wín magazine
1 april 1969   30¢

At the grass roots
Resistance & Renewal
April 3 thru 6, 1969

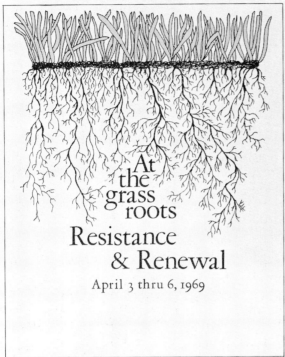

organized support groups that eventually came together as Resist — Support-in-Action.

About the same time, David Harris, Dennis Sweeney, Lenny Heller, Richard Ian Harrison and Steve Hamilton, all of them activists in the Bay Area and Palo Alto, began talking up the idea of The Resistance. They would choose a specific day for young men to gather all across the country and publicly declare their independence by returning their draft cards to the government. The Resistance operated in decentralized local offices throughout the nation. The first turn-in took place on October 3, 1967, and more than 1500 men returned their cards. A second turn-in on December 4 brought forward about 475 new resisters and on April 3, 1968, another 630 began their noncooperation with the draft.

In 1967 CNVA, realizing that its nonviolent direct action tactics and civil disobedience campaigns were being used by everyone, dissolved itself into the WRL. The Resistance then became the cutting edge of the movement, with people willing to put their bodies on the line to confront the government on principle and as directly as possible. The implicit threat of The Resistance was that going to jail was no longer thought cowardly. If an escalated war would enlarge the draft calls, thousands of young men would not go. *The Pentagon Papers* later revealed that this indeed did limit the government's involvement in the land war. But The

Catherine Allsup commits civil disobedience on the steps of the Supreme Court building by burning the draft card given her by another war resister, Washington D.C., June 19, 1968. The demonstration, organized by the Committee for Nonviolent Action, protested the law which made mutilating draft cards a federal crime. Brad Lyttle/CNVA.

Cover of *WIN* magazine, published by the War Resisters League and the New York Workshop in Nonviolence, April 1, 1969.

Draft card turn-in organized by The Resistance, Central Park, New York City, April 3, 1968. Maury Englander.

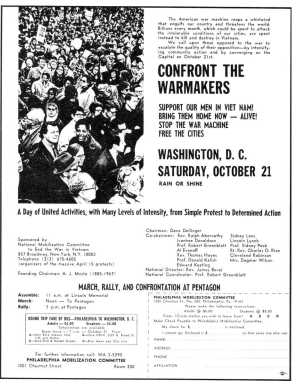

The American war machine reaps a whirlwind that engulfs our country and threatens the world. Billions every month, which could be spent to attack the intolerable conditions of our cities, are spent instead to kill and destroy in Vietnam.

We call upon those opposed to the war to escalate the quality of their opposition—by intensifying community action and by converging on the Capital on October 21st.

CONFRONT THE WARMAKERS

SUPPORT OUR MEN IN VIET NAM!
BRING THEM HOME NOW — ALIVE!
STOP THE WAR MACHINE
FREE THE CITIES

WASHINGTON, D. C.
SATURDAY, OCTOBER 21

RAIN OR SHINE

A Day of United Activities, with Many Levels of Intensity, from Simple Protest to Determined Action

Sponsored by
National Mobilization Committee
to End the War in Vietnam
857 Broadway, New York, N.Y. 10003
Telephone (212) 675-4605
(organizers of the massive April 15 protests)

Founding Chairman: A. J. Muste (1885-1967)

Chairman: Dave Dellinger
Co-chairmen: Rev. Ralph Abernathy   Sidney Lens
Ivanhoe Donaldson   Lincoln Lynch
Prof. Robert Greenblatt   Prof. Sidney Peck
Al Evanoff   Rt. Rev. Charles O. Rice
Rev. Thomas Hayes   Cleveland Robinson
Prof. Donald Kalish   Mrs. Dagmar Wilson
Edward Keating
National Director: Rev. James Bevel
National Coordinator: Prof. Robert Greenblatt

MARCH, RALLY, AND CONFRONTATION AT PENTAGON

Assemble: 11 a.m. at Lincoln Memorial
March: Noon — To Pentagon
Rally: 3 p.m. at Pentagon

ROUND TRIP FARE BY BUS—PHILADELPHIA TO WASHINGTON, D. C.
Adults — $6.00   Students — $5.00
Scholarships are available
Buses leave — 7 a.m. — October 21   From:
A—Farm Rock Subway Stop   B—Core Office, 2229 N. Broad St.
11th and Nedro
C—32nd-33rd & Market Streets   D—Bryn Mawr and City Line

For further information call: WA 2-5295
PHILADELPHIA MOBILIZATION COMMITTEE
1001 Chestnut Street   Room 200

PHILADELPHIA MOBILIZATION COMMITTEE
1001 Chestnut St., Rm. 200, Philadelphia, Pa. 19107
Please make the following reservations:
Adults @ $6.00   Students @ $5.00
From: (Circle station you wish to leave from)   A   B   C   D
Make Check Payable to Philadelphia Mobilization Committee.
My check for $ _____ is enclosed.
I cannot go. Enclosed is $ _____ so that some one else can.
NAME: _____
ADDRESS _____
PHONE _____
AFFILIATION _____

Resistance, though it might have prevented enlargement of the war, failed to bring it to an end. Draft calls never reached that total size and The Resistance never succeeded in reaching those large numbers of men, many of whom never discovered the varying alternatives, legal and illegal, to military service.

CONFRONTING THE WARMAKERS

Noncooperation with the draft was only one facet of The Resistance. In Philadelphia and throughout the country, GI coffee houses were set up, military bases were leafletted and entered, and deserters were given refuge while legal aid was arranged or they were aided in getting out of the country. As important were attempts to apply the spirit of resistance to actions in the streets. The crucial action, and probably the most memorable one, was billed as a "confrontation with the warmakers" and took place at the Pentagon October 21 and 22, 1967. Thousands of people marched on the building and, when it was blocked off by soldiers, sat-down at their feet for an impromptu teach-in that lasted all

Confrontation with the Warmakers demonstration at the Pentagon, October 21, 1967. Maury Englander.

Leaflet from the Philadelphia Mobilization Committee, 1967. Theodore Hetzel.

Saturday night and on into Sunday night. Hundreds of people were arrested, and many were beaten by U.S. marshals who tried to break the morale of the demonstrators by riotous brutality. People brought away different memories. Some remembered the community created among strangers on the steps of the Pentagon, the sharing of food, the refusal to fight back or break ranks in the face of government aggression; others remembered best the feeling of oneness with the soldiers and came away with the idea that soldiers were not the enemy, despite their uniforms, and that they shared many of the move-

ment's values and beliefs and should be approached as brothers. Still others, chafing at the failure to get through the military lines and invade the Pentagon, considered the whole thing a failure and blamed it on the nonviolent tactics.

A second crucial action occurred in the Bay Area the week of the Pentagon confrontation. Stop The Draft Week was structured to close down the Oakland Induction Center. On Monday a pacifist sit-in shut down the Center for three hours and caused 123 arrests. Tuesday was not under a nonviolent discipline and the demonstrators got

Confrontation with the Warmakers demonstration at the Pentagon, Washington D.C., October 21, 1967. Minoru Aoki.

Upper right: Pacifists block the Oakland Induction Center, Oakland, California, December 18, 1967. Bob Fitch.

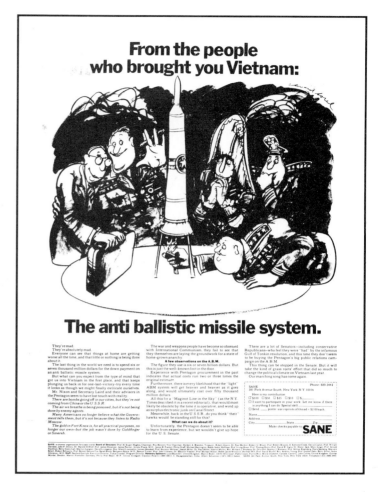

roughed up by the police. Friday they returned for another encounter, with mobile tactics: avoiding static confrontation with the police, but remaining in the streets one step ahead of them and disrupting traffic and the pattern of everyday business. The demonstrators managed to tie up the Center and much of the city of Oakland. Roy Kepler commented:

> Eight or ten thousand people on Friday, milling though the streets and blocking intersections in a mix of "self-defense" and "militant" styles, were little more successful than the 123 of Monday in terms of the amount of time that they prevented access to the Induction Center. But has anyone asked himself what might have been possible Monday (or any other day of the week) if instead of 123 people there had been 500 or 1000 or more people ready to undertake disciplined nonviolent action backed up by the readiness both to absorb any violence on the part of the police and to accept arrest and imprisonment?

But most activists preferred the excitement of skirmishes with the police. Radical pacifists were left with the option of entering into coalitions in an

Advertisement produced by SANE. Institute for the Study of Nonviolence.

Jim Peck, Dr. Benjamin Spock and other anti-war demonstrators in jail after blocking the Whitehall Street induction center during Stop the Draft Week, New York City, 1967. Diana Davies.

effort to bring a nonviolent spirit into the confrontations or of going back to small disciplined demonstrations as in the CNVA days. To many this seemed irrelevant at a time when the movement had grown from a group of dedicated individuals to a movement of millions of people with varying politics and levels of commitment.

For much of 1968 the pacifist movement coexisted with the movement at large, participating in the street actions that climaxed in August 1968 at the Democratic National Convention. By then the tide had swung partially towards violence, peaking with the futility of the Weathermen actions and terrorist bombings. Partly in reaction to this, mass rallies and marches, organized by various Mobilization committees headed by Dave Dellinger, Muste's successor as coalition leader, were organized to keep visible, broad-based public pressure on Washington. On November 15, 1969, more than half a million people came to Washington for the biggest anti-war demonstration in U.S. history. Local Peace Centers were also set up through-

A Vietnam veteran protesting the war throws his combat medals over a temporary fence onto the steps of the Capitol, Washington D.C., April 23, 1971. UPI.

Two soldiers are arrested during a Pray-in for Peace in Vietnam at Fort Jackson, South Carolina, February 13, 1968. *Columbia Record.*

Anti-war rally outside the gates of the Army Presidio in support of soldiers who had been arrested for protesting the war, San Francisco, California, April 6, 1969. Wide World.

out the country to organize people to work for an immediate end to the war. Nonviolent groups like Clergy and Laity Concerned and the Syracuse Peace Council in New York, and local chapters of WILPF, AFSC, and other pacifist groups across the nation continued to educate and demonstrate with each new development in the war.

G.I. RESISTANCE

The Pentagon demonstration of 1967 brought the attention of the movement to the growing number of GI resisters against the war. All during the war, pacifist and other anti-war groups were counseling GI resisters and occasionally helping them find refuge in Canada and elsewhere. In doing this, people regularly sheltered AWOL soldiers and provided for their safety much as abolitionists had established an Underground Railroad for runaway slaves during the Civil War. There were an esti-

Anti-draft demonstration, New York City, March 19, 1970. John Goodwin.

The War Resisters League's New York office after it was broken into and trashed, May 9, 1969. Mary Mayo and Dave McReynolds are on the right. Photo courtesy of Dave McReynolds/War Resisters League.

mated 80-100,000 military deserters and draft evaders, mostly in Canada, but also in Sweden, France, and most other West European countries, in many of which they had been granted legal asylum.

Beginning in 1966, the War Resisters' International, of which the WRL is an American section, began a campaign to encourage GIs to resist the military. Until 1967, individual cases of GI resistance, such as Dr. Howard Levy and the Fort Hood 3, who were the first soldiers to refuse to serve in Vietnam, attracted attention because of their uniqueness. After 1967 a growing GI movement was organized with civilian support that encouraged and supported resistance to the military by men in uniform. This movement, represented best by Vietnam Veterans Against the War and the hundreds of uniformed men in prison was a powerful part of the anti-war movement.

OPPOSITION SPREADS

In the 1970s the anti-war movement as a whole was badly fractured into violent and nonviolent factions

Peace march, San Francisco, April 24, 1971. Bob Fitch.

Pennsylvania State University students during their 53 hour sit-in protesting the school's research on chemical and biological warfare, Philadelphia, April 27, 1967. Bill Wingell/Swarthmore College Peace Collection.

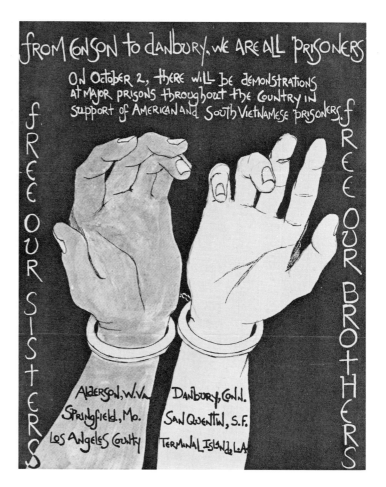

as well as into assorted sectarian political groups. None was able to command the enthusiasm of large numbers of activists as SDS had been able to do before 1969. Part of this, as we now know, was due to the disruptive tactics of the FBI's Cointelpro (Counterintelligence Program) focused on the New Left and the anti-war movement. Nevertheless, the Peoples Coalition for Peace and Justice (successor to the various Mobilization Committees) was able to mobilize scores of thousands of demonstrators for peaceful rallies. The most impressive took place in May 1970 when over 100,000 people came to the capital on a week's notice to protest the invasion of Cambodia and the murder of four students at Kent State University, Ohio, by National Guardsmen, and the police shootout at the black Jackson State College, Miss., where two students were killed.

For pacifists, the early 70s were marked by small nonviolent raids on Selective Service offices and, in one instance, the FBI office at Media, Pa. The first of these raids took place May 17, 1968, when Fathers Dan and Philip Berrigan, John Hogan, Tom Lewis and George Mische removed the draft files from Local Board 33 at Catonsville, Md. and burned them outside with homemade napalm.

An estimated million draft files were subsequently destroyed in a number of widely-spread actions, the participants either destroying the records publicly and courting arrest, or engaging in hit-and-run tactics. Although many were jailed, the raids dramatized and encouraged anti-war feelings. The most celebrated court case — conducted in Harrisburg, Pa., in 1971 — was based on exaggerated charges of conspiring to blow up Washington heating systems and kidnap a presidential

adviser. Only two of the defendants, Fr. Philip Berrigan and Sister Elizabeth McAlister, were found guilty — but only of exchanging contraband letters while the former was in jail.

Also growing out of the anti-war movement was the case of Dan Ellsberg and Tony Russo. Working for a government-subsidized research agency, both first became disillusioned with the methods of the war, and later outraged by its purposes. What to do about this later became clearer when Ellsberg attended a conference of the War Resisters' International, held in Haverford, Pa., in 1969, where he met Randy Kehler, Bob Eaton, and other resisters. Concluding that America was jailing some of its best young people for war resistance and that he was morally obligated to do something as courageous, he decided to publish some of the government documents he had been studying. Publication of *The Pentagon Papers* caused a great public uproar and threatened Ellsberg and Russo with long prison terms before the case was dismissed.

Daniel Ellsberg speaks at a workshop on political prisoners during the War Resisters League's 50th anniversary national conference, Monterey, California, August 1973. With him are Ginetta Sagan, Joan Baez, and Millicent Duncan of Amnesty International. Bob Fitch.

Leaflet from the Harrisburg Defense Committee, 1971. Larry Gara.

WAR TAX RESISTANCE

Nonpayment of war taxes, practiced by Quakers and others, disappeared as a pacifist testimony soon after the Civil War and Thoreau's famous stand against the U.S. foray in Mexico. It first reappeared in World War II when a few widely scattered individuals refused to pay federal taxes on the grounds that there was no way to prevent a significant part of their money from being used for military purposes. One resister, Ernest Bromley, was prosecuted and imprisoned for his refusal. Many others began to inform the Internal Revenue Service that payment violated their principles.

The enactment during World War II of a measure which required employers to withhold taxes from their employees caused particular difficulties for pacifists and led to the formation of Peacemakers in 1948. A Peacemaker committee promoted tax refusal and provided research, literature, action suggestions, and publicity for those in the tax resistance movement. Although many hundreds of people were refusing to pay income taxes during the 15 years following 1948, the government pro-

secuted and imprisoned only six: James Otsuka of Indiana, Maurice McCrackin of Ohio, Eroseanna Robinson of Illinois, Walter Gormly of Iowa, Arthur Evans of Colorado, and Neil Haworth of Connecticut. These imprisonments and the seizure of a few cars and houses by the IRS, served to highlight the tax refusal testimony and establish it as a major nonviolent principle and tactic.

Tax resistance, like other forms of opposition to the military, increased dramatically during the Vietnam War. In 1966 the federal government levied an additional tax on every private telephone, and in a rare moment of candor, admitted that the money would help subsidize the war in Indochina. Peacemakers, the War Resisters League, and other nonviolent groups urged refusal of this tax and in the following years countless thousands heeded their call. Under the leadership of Bob and Angie Calvert, War Tax Resistance was formed in 1969 as a separate organization to investigate all aspects and ramifications of conscientious tax refusal. During the war there were over 200 local war tax resistance centers,

Ernest and Marion Bromley, Peacemakers and tax resisters, outside their land trust house which the government seized and then was forced to return, Cincinnati, Ohio, 1974. Terry Armor.

as well as a number of "alternative life funds" which rechanneled refused tax money back into the local community for constructive purposes. Many of these continued after the end of the war.

The tactic of claiming enough dependents so that no income tax would be withheld became more widespread as the Vietnam war continued. Often the tax refuser would make clear the moral grounds for the protest by listing, for example, "all the Vietnamese" as dependents. Refusing to pay for war by claiming excessive exemptions brought particularly strong response from the government. A number of people were prosecuted and imprisoned: Jim Shea, Karl Meyer, William Himmelbauer, Mark Riley, Ellis Rece, Carole Nelson, John Leininger, and Martha Tranquilli (a 64 year old grandmother and nurse). The tax resistance movement continued after the war and grew to include both pacifists and non-pacifists who could no longer in conscience support the military priorities of the government.

Peace march, New York City, 1971. Diana Davies.

Peacemaker Eroseanna Robinson, an amateur athlete and social worker, is carried into court by U.S. marshals after being arrested for refusing to pay war taxes, Chicago, Illinois, January 27, 1960. She refused to cooperate in any way, was imprisoned indefinitely, and fasted 93 days until her release. Wide World.

"Thoreau Money" leaflet from the Committee for Nonviolent Action, c. 1968. Marty Jezer.

Diana Davies

BARBARA DEMING
(Born 1917)

A writer and activist, Barbara Deming helped connect the radical movements of the Sixties and Seventies and broaden the focus and influence of active nonviolence. Her work for disarmament, civil rights, and peace, together with her feminist analysis and activity in the women's movement, helped clarify the connections of pacifism to issues other than war and was influential in presenting the philosophy of radical nonviolence to new generations of Americans.

Deming was born in New York City, a descendent through her mother of Elihu Burritt, the early pacifist abolitionist. She graduated from Bennington College and Western Reserve University and worked in the theater, taught, and did editorial and secretarial work during the Thirties. She was film analyst for the Library of Congress from 1942 to 1944 and out of this experience came her first book, *Running Away from Myself: A Dream Portrait of America Drawn from the Films of the 40s* (published in 1969). During the Fifties, she wrote short stories, poetry, and essays, particularly about the theater and films, and began to read Gandhi in 1959 after a visit to India.

She joined the Committee for Nonviolent Action in 1960 and became deeply involved in the radical nonviolent movement. Her skills as a writer and teacher aided many CNVA campaigns and she was repeatedly arrested for civil disobedience actions against war and racism. In 1964, she served 24 days in jail with other peace walkers in Albany, Georgia, and wrote movingly about the experience in her book *Prison Notes*. In 1966, she took part in a protest action in Saigon, South Vietnam, with A.J. Muste and three other CNVA members, for which they were deported.

An editor of *Liberation* magazine, she called for "radical and uncompromising action" from pacifists and non-pacifists alike.

> May those who say that they believe in nonviolence learn to challenge more boldly those institutions of violence that constrict and cripple our humanity. And may those who have questioned nonviolence come to see that one's rights to life and happiness can only be claimed as inalienable if one grants, in action, that they belong to all.

In her essay *On Revolution and Equilibrium*, written in response to Frantz Fanon's *The Wretched of the Earth*, she restated classic nonviolent principles and gave original insight to the process of revolution and the work of revolutionaries.

> If greater gains have not been won by non-violent action it is because most of those trying it have . . . expected too much from "the powerful"; and so, I would add, they have stopped short of really exercising their peculiar powers — those powers one discovers when one refuses any longer simply to do another's will. They have stopped far too short not only of widespread nonviolent disruption but of that form of noncooperation which is assertive, constructive — that confronts those who are "running everything" with independent activity, particularly independent economic activity. There is leverage for change here that has scarcely begun to be applied.

Deming's writing and activity as a lesbian-feminist helped connect the members and concerns of the radical nonviolent movement with those of the women's movement in the late Sixties and Seventies. She denounced patriarchy and society's heterosexual emphasis and wrote probingly on the relationship of violence and sexuality, "for imperialist actions do seem to me, more and more clearly, to be patriarchal acts, acts of rape." Her essays spoke eloquently of human sexuality as an expression of communion with the rest of the world and in 1976 she wrote:

> I now put my hopes for real social change above all else in the feminist movement and also my hopes for the further invention of nonviolence. I think the root violence in our society is the attempt by men to claim women and children as their property.

Her personal commitment and political thought encouraged activists after the Vietnam war to reexamine patriarchal assumptions and to reaffirm the nurturing and life-giving emphasis of active nonviolence.

Mayday sit-down, Washington D.C., May 1971. John Goodwin.

RETURN TO NONVIOLENCE

The continuing frustrations in having no direct impact on ending the war led small parts of the anti-war movement to bombings and other acts of violence, but these were no more effective. An incipient return to nonviolence began to develop for some after the ruthless smashing of the demonstrations at the Democratic Party Convention in Chicago in 1968 — although for others, Chicago simply increased their rage. This return was strengthened by growing awareness of the issues by older and more middle class Americans, as exemplified by the presidential campaigns of Eugene McCarthy and George McGovern, and such movements as Common Cause and those associated with Ralph Nader. Movements for greater control by

people over their lives — amongst women, students, homosexuals, blacks, Native Americans, Chicanos and other groups — also led to the realization that courage without wisdom leads to the morgue and to jail more often than to liberation.

In May 1971 The Mayday Tribe, a group composed of both pacifist and nonpacifist activists, organized a week-long demonstration designed to bring the city of Washington to a halt with nonviolent obstruction tactics. More than 13,500 people were arrested in three days of nonviolent action. Charges against virtually every defendent were dropped and the Nixon administration was widely condemned for unconstitutional high-handedness. Through 1971 and 1972 there were also a growing number of direct nonviolent confrontations with

Nonviolence is not a gimmick

Today, we confront our government. After the massacre at Kent State, the murders of Hampton and Clark in Chicago, the killings in Santa Barbara and Berkeley—and the endless murder in Vietnam—many are arguing that the time has come for violence.

This leaflet has two points to make. One is hard tactics. The other is to ask about the kind of society we want to build.

TACTICS: The peace movement is not armed. That is a fact. The government is armed. And, as Nixon would say, that is also a fact. The government is willing to kill people —Black Panthers, student demonstrators, and Vietnamese. If you are talking about the peace movement using violence then you are talking about heroism, courage, "machismo," and **defeat.** You are not talking about revolution.

Trashing windows and property does not hurt Nixon—it helps him by frightening more "middle Americans" into supporting things like the Kent massacre. If our job is revolution, then our job is building the widest possible support, not breaking the largest number of windows. In France, after the dramatic events of May in 1968, De Gaulle won the elections overwhelmingly—partly because students had burned cars in the street, cars that working class Frenchmen had spent years saving to buy.

Chanting "Off the Pigs!" makes one big mistake—it leads people to see the police as the enemy, when they are actually only the agents of the real enemy. There is not that much difference between our troops in the Mekong Delta and the cops patrolling the ghettos or beating on our heads—they are all agents of the war system. Our job is to get them to join our side. The chant "Join Us!" is a lot more revolutionary than "Off the Pigs!"

If you **must** trash, then do it on your own—not from the back of a crowd. When a lot of us are on the front line facing the cops and someone starts throwing bottles from behind us, toward the cops, **we** get clubbed—not the bottle throwers. Getting heads busted is not our bag—it's the government's bag. Government agents in this demonstration will try to provoke violence. Don't play their game.

WHAT KIND OF NEW SOCIETY? Regis Debray, still jailed in Bolivia as a member of Che's guerrilla organization, wrote of violence "Naturally, the tragedy is that we do not kill objects, numbers, abstract or interchangeable instruments, but, precisely, on both sides, irreplaceable individuals, essentially innocent, unique for those who have loved, bred, esteemed them. This is the tragedy of history, of any history, of any revolution. It is not individuals that are placed face to face in these battles, but class interests and ideas; but those who fall in them, those who die, are persons, are men."

The rocks or bottles or bullets we might use, in our rage, will not strike the Pentagon or the corporations—they will strike young national guardsmen, cops with small children. The dead of Vietnam and Kent State will not be restored to life by our becoming brutalized. Che said: "Let me say, at the risk of seeming ridiculous, that the true revolutionary is guided by great feelings of love."

We know we want a new society. Thousands have been jailed in this country struggling for it. Some have died. But what is new about a society where, instead of **their** prisons, we have **our** prisons, and instead of **their** Attorney General Mitchell we have one of our own, **just** as stupid and violent? A new society means more than taking the guns away from one group of cops and giving them to a new group of cops.

But that, of course, is the pacifist line and we won't push it here . . . our main point, one on which all the sponsors are absolutely agreed, is that even if you are not a pacifist, today is a time for risking arrest rather than trashing. A day for nonviolent **action,** rather than violent slogans.

For the revolution to win, it must win the people, not permit itself to be isolated from them. The only ones to gain from violence are Nixon, Agnew and Mitchell—and their agents will be trying to provoke that violence today, as they have tried—and succeeded—in the past.

Rallies are not enough.

After Saturday return home
    to organize draft resistance.

Refuse all military service.

Organize nonviolent actions to close down
    induction, recruiting, and draft centers.

- -

      WAR RESISTERS LEAGUE   339 Lafayette Street, New York 10012

☐ Send me information on draft resistance   ☐ Enclosed is 25¢ for a sample copy of WIN Magazine—
                                          published by a group of hard core dissidents, effete intel-
☐ Send me information on tax resistance   lectuals, professional anarchists, and impudent snobs, and
                                                which is a hippy type magazine.

Name

Address   Zip

demonstrators placing themselves bodily in front of government and military offices. The Daily Death Toll at the White House resulted in several hundred arrests over a three-week period. Flotillas of canoes and rowboats maintained symbolic blockades of naval vessels in San Diego, Ca., Leonardo, N.J., Norfolk, Va., and elsewhere, also leading to frequent arrests. Confrontations of this sort, nonviolent but frequently leading to arrest, were formerly engaged in only by committed pacifists and often considered too "symbolic" by other activists. Now they were being practiced by growing numbers in the anti-war movement, many of whom would not consider themselves pacifists in any formal sense.

ENDING THE WAR

On January 20, 1973, thousands of demonstrators converged on Washington to protest Richard Nixon's inauguration and the Christmas attempt to terrorize North Vietnam into submission with 36,000 tons of bombs. When the Paris Peace Agreements were concluded, most Americans felt relieved that the Vietnam War, finally, was over. They were unaware that, in effect, the war would continue for over two more years, with Vietnamese casualties mounting progressively. It

Fr. Philip Berrigan and eight other Catholic activists burn draft board files in Catonsville, Maryland, May 17, 1968. Wide World.

Leaflet from the War Resisters League, 1970. Institute for the Study of Nonviolence.

Anti-war rally, New York City, 1969. Maury Englander.

was to be a war-by-proxy, conducted by the U.S. through its puppet government in South Vietnam under the leadership of Nguyen Van Thieu.

The total of Thieu's political prisoners had mounted to about 200,000 and, despite the Paris Agreements, he refused to release them. Freeing these political prisoners became the focus of protest in the U.S. The symbol became replicas of the notorious tiger cages, manufactured in the U.S. and used for holding prisoners in South Vietnam.

The first such demonstration, two days of international protest, took place February 28 to March 1, 1973 under the sponsorship of the Emergency Project for Saigon Civilian Prisoners. Thereafter, tiger cage demonstrations took place frequently in many American cities. When Thieu came to Washington in April, he was "greeted" with a tiger cage and placards asking: "Why Do You Violate the Truce?" Throughout the summer of 1974, a tiger cage was mounted on the Capitol steps and protestors came from all parts of the country to leaflet, fast and vigil there.

Linking the Watergate scandal to the war-by-proxy in Southeast Asia, some 2,500 demonstrators, with placards focusing on the Cambodia bombing, marched from the Watergate Hotel to the White House in mid-June 1973. Ten months later, on

Pacifist comedian Dick Gregory after 22 days of fasting in protest against the war in Vietnam, December 14, 1967. WRL.

Anti-war demonstration in Washington D.C., April 24, 1971. Theodore Hetzel.

Committee for Nonviolent Action demonstrators Dan Baty and Bob Greene try to block the battleship *U.S.S. New Jersey* after its commissioning at the Philadelphia Navy Yard, April 6, 1968. *Philadelphia Enquirer.*

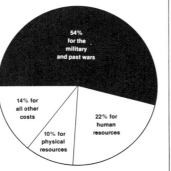

DO YOU KNOW WHAT YOUR TAX DOLLAR BUYS?

54% for the military and past wars

14% for all other costs

22% for human resources

10% for physical resources

Where Do Your Taxes Go?

You work hard for your money. But much of your tax dollar goes to pay for wars — past, present and future: 54% in the Fiscal Year 1976 budget proposed by the Administration.*

In fact, the U.S. has spent $1.5 trillion on the military since the end of World War II.

The Administration is asking Congress for $254.2 billion in Federal funds for Fiscal 1976. Of this amount:

Military: 54% — 37% is earmarked for current military expenditures and 17% for the cost of past wars — 6% for veterans benefits (which the Administration includes in "human resources") and 11% for interest on the national debt (four-fifths of which can be conservatively estimated as war-incurred).

Human Resources (education, manpower, social services, health, income security): 22%

Physical Resources (agriculture, community and regional development, natural resources, commerce, transportation, environment, energy): 10%

All Other (international affairs, justice, space, general government, revenue-sharing, and one-fifth of the interest on the national debt): 14%

The figures above have been compiled by the Library of Congress Legislative Reference Service as released by Rep. Les Aspin.

Administration Budget

The Administration, however, presents a far different picture of federal spending priorities. It claims that the federal government will spend more money on "human resources" than on the military. This claim is based on a change in budget accounting, made in 1968, whereby tax revenues from income, inheritance and excise taxes are placed in the same pot as receipts from trust funds such as Social Security, Railroad Retirement and the Highway Trust Fund.

These trust funds were set up years ago to provide specific benefits. They are financed by separate taxes. For example, you pay social security taxes now and receive benefits when you retire. The federal government merely acts as caretaker for these funds. **Neither Congress nor the President can spend the money in the trust funds, except for earmarked purposes.** Therefore, if you want to know what happens to your tax dollars which the federal government can spend, the trust funds should be considered as separate cookie jars, not as part of the federal pie.

The accounting and the rhetoric have changed, but not the reality. Fifty-four percent of the Federal funds budget for Fiscal Year 1976, controllable by the President and Congress, will go to pay for military-related programs.

Based on these budget figures, and an estimated 55 million families in the United States today, the cost to the average American family for military-related programs during Fiscal 1976 will be $2,485. This compares with $301 for health, $258 for education, manpower and social services, and $107 for community and regional development.

Is this how you want YOUR taxes spent?

Are You More Secure?

At the end of World War II, no enemy could attack the United States. Today, in a nuclear war, the U.S. could be wiped out in less than an hour. The Fiscal 1976 Annual Defense Department Report estimated that the U.S. would have 8,500 long-range nuclear weapons in mid-1975, the Soviet Union 2,800. Just 200 to 400 of these weapons could destroy a third of the Soviet population and three quarters of its industrial capacity.

Are you more secure knowing we can "overkill" the Russians more times than they can "overkill" us? Are you more secure knowing the U.S. have over 40 military commitments to other countries and over 2,000 bases and installations around the world? Are you more secure knowing the needs of the American people are being neglected while you pay for more "efficient" and sophisticated weapons — with cost overruns of more than three times the original estimates? Are you more likely to be threatened by Soviet missiles or by crime, polluted air and water, and dishonesty in government?

Does spending over $100 billion a year on the military make you feel secure?

To see how the Administration wants to spend your tax dollars, turn to the other side.

*Federal funds budget: excludes trust funds, which are separately financed.

sane A CITIZENS' ORGANIZATION FOR A SANE WORLD, 318 Mass Ave., N.E., Wash., D.C. 20002

No More Broken Treaties

The Paris Peace Agreement guarantees the right of self-determination to the Vietnamese people through democratic liberties and elections.

Instead, Thieu's Saigon regime holds and torments millions of citizens in prisons, refugee camps and heavily-policed slums; and rains bombs, shells and defoliants on the countryside.

All this depends on American advisors, American equipment, American tax dollars — $1.7 billion in 1974.

Honor the Peace Agreement

This is a TIGER CAGE It holds 3 to 5 people at a time in South Vietnam. They are designed and built by American companies and paid for by your tax dollar. Over ..... are in Saigon jails for having opposed the war or the U.S.-Thieu regime.

WHY DO YOU VIOLATE THE TRUCE?

Leaflet from SANE, 1976.

Tiger cage demonstration protesting South Vietnamese President Thieu's visit to Richard Nixon, Washington D.C., April 5, 1973. Dorothy Marder.

April 27, 1974, some 10,000 people marched down Pennsylvania Avenue demanding Nixon's impeachment. On the fourth of July, Washington was also the scene of the first sizeable demonstration demanding universal and unconditional amnesty for all Vietnam war resisters.

By early fall, Watergate exposures and popular pressure forced Nixon to resign, but foreign policy in general, and Southeast Asia policy in particular, remained unchanged. On January 25 to 27, 1975, over 1,500 anti-war activists from across the U.S., and a number of prominent peace people from abroad, came to Washington for an Assembly to Save the Peace Agreements, climaxed by a candlelight march to the White House. It was two years since the signing of the Paris Agreements, but still there was no peace in Southeast Asia.

Peace finally came in April 1975, but not as a consequence of the Paris Agreements. Despite massive U.S. support, the war effort in South Vietnam and Cambodia became totally demoralized and collapsed. On May 11 at the Sheep's Meadow of New York's Central Park, some 80,000 people turned out to celebrate the end of the war.

On a big banner across the speakers' platform, on placards and on white balloons was painted the slogan "The War Is Over!" It was a joyous celebration, with music and a minimum of speeches. Joan Baez, Pete Seeger, Richie Havens, Phil Ochs and Odetta were among the singers.

The idea that "wars will end when men refuse to fight" always seemed utopian. But never before had resistance to war been so widespread, committed and effective as against U.S. involvement in Southeast Asia. Men and women in and out of uniform and numbering in the tens and hundreds of thousands took risks and interrupted the routine of their lives to say "No" to war. Even more important, growing numbers took to searching for ways of living that could minimize violence in their own lives and militarism in public life.

In these brief sixty years, radical pacifism has become a political and cultural force in American life. No longer an isolated and individualistic attitude towards war, it has become a way of life that holds the promise of a viable political alternative to the militarism and injustice of the past and the present. □

Anti-war veterans, demanding U.S. withdrawal from Southeast Asia, occupy the Statue of Liberty and fly the American flag upside down in the international symbol of distress, New York City, December 27, 1971. Wide World.

Upper left: Poster from the Indochina Peace Campaign, 1974. Public Media Center/Institute for the Study of Nonviolence.

AFTERWORD

By the time the war in Vietnam ended, radical activity in the United States had considerably broadened from the opposition to war, racism, and militarism which had marked the late Fifties and early Sixties. The mass movement against the war, following — even overlapping — the civil rights movement, had an impact on the nation and on nonviolence which has yet to be fully evaluated. Not only were nonviolent ideas and tactics more widely popularized than ever before, but hundreds of thousands of people came to realize that the United States' presence in Indochina, like racism at home, was not an accident or tragic mistake but a necessary result of the prevailing values and structures of "the richest, most powerful country in the world."

In the late Sixties and Seventies, activists began to apply the lessons gleaned from the civil rights and peace movements to the long term needs of society as a whole. Useful ideas and strategies introduced earlier in nonviolent campaigns were picked up by organizations serving a wide diversity of causes. The broadened political arena, in turn, challenged pacifists to show that nonviolence had relevance to critical national and international problems.

Throughout the country, many nonviolent activists worked to establish neighborhood groups for tenants' rights, equal education, community control, child care facilities, and other local needs. Activists also organized to stop the growth of nuclear power plants, protested unemployment and the economic crisis, demanded an end to secret government and grand jury harassment, and tried to halt the exploitation of the environment. Organizers joined with the United Farm Workers and other unions, land reform and research groups, Native American, Third World and other movements to answer immediate needs and prepare for larger changes in society.

As a result of searching for the causes of war and oppression, many radicals began to explore and live out the implications of nonviolence in their family, group, sexual, and work relationships. Activists struggled for truth and consistency in their personal lives as well as their political affairs. They organized hundreds of rural communities and urban living centers both to apply nonviolent communitarian principles to their daily lives and to provide housing and support for political workers.

As many developed nonviolence as a way of life or ethical system, others gave more attention to developing nonviolence as a serious political force. Neil Katz, writing in *Fellowship* in 1976, cautioned advocates of nonviolence not to restrict the potential audience for nonviolent alternatives to "those who *a priori* agree that violence is always immoral and that one must 'love one's enemies' in nonviolent struggle." Such moral imperatives may well be beneficial, Katz maintained, but need not be necessary components of nonviolent struggle. He wrote, "Nonviolent action has often been used in the past

 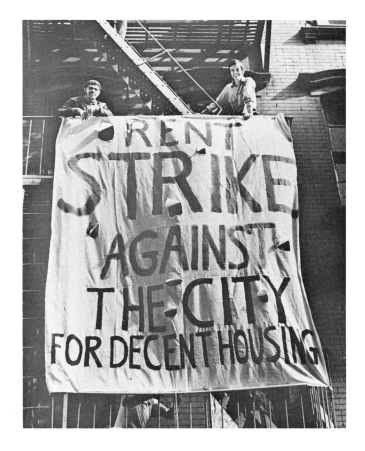

because it seemed to be the most effective struggle technique, not because its practitioners felt morally compelled to adopt its stringent philosophical underpinnings." War resister Gene Sharp's extensive study, *The Politics of Nonviolent Action*, (1973) documented examples of pragmatic nonviolent action and was influential in broadening the discussion about nonviolence.

One of the most significant developments of the Vietnam era was the resurgence of the women's liberation movement and the growth of feminism in the late Sixties. Women throughout the country, many of them already conscious of racial and economic injustice, grew more aware of their own oppression and inferior treatment as women. In increasing numbers they began to expose and challenge sexism in many areas of American society. The feminists' critique of power centered on male dominance and patriarchy, and their analysis of violence and subjugation extended into nearly every corner of society. Activist Andrea Dworkin wrote of the male system of power and privilege:

> *Patriarchy is a system of ownership*
> *wherein women and children are*

owned. Patriarchy is the original authoritarian model, the molecular totalitarian model, and every tyrannical form is derived from it. . . . *The destruction of the psychologies and behaviors which we call dominant (master, male) and submissive (slave, female), or aggressor-victim, demands the destruction of the source of those mental sets and behaviors – patriarchy. Ending forever the war of the powerful against the powerless – and ending the smaller wars of bad men against worse men – means dismantling the machinery of patriarchy.*

Feminists demanded that the psychological, physical and economic violence perpetrated by men against women be recognized and ended, and that social institutions be changed so as to no longer reflect the pattern of dominance and submission. Feminists turned towards encouraging a more humane, nurturing and loving standard of behavior instead of relationships steeped in aggression, competition or exploitation. Since women are so intimately close to their oppressors, feminists have had

Earth Day, New York City, April 22, 1970. John Goodwin.

Lower East Side tenants' rent strike, New York City, 1973. Diana Davies.

to explore new forms of relating and whole new concepts of struggle which are very relevant to nonviolence. Barbara Deming brought her experience in nonviolent direct action campaigns to the women's movement and wrote:

> *The feminist vision . . . abandons the concept of naming enemies and adopts a concept familiar to the nonviolent tradition: naming behavior that is oppressive, naming abuse of power that is held unfairly and must be destroyed, but naming no person one whom we are willing to destroy. If we can destroy a man's power to tyrannize, there is no need, of course, to destroy the man himself. And if the same man who behaves in one sense as a tyrant is in another sense our comrade, there is no need to feel that we have lost our political minds (or souls) when we treat him as a person divided from us (and from himself) in just this way.*

The evolving feminist critique also included an analysis of sexism within the peace movement. "Our experience as women," wrote nonviolent activist Shelley Douglass, "has been one of awakening to a reality that was often harsh: we were welcomed into the movement in lower-echelon positions, as somebody's woman, girl, old lady, wife, as sex objects, as workhorses." She observed that insofar as the movement was patriarchal, it was simply part of the system.

Marita Heller criticized the "stereotypically male organizing patterns" within AFSC's work: "Even our frame for thinking is stereotypically masculine and militaristic rather than in terms of growth, understanding, unity, sharing, people and grassroots orientation — things that may not be measurable, but are nonetheless real. Why must we measure our success by how many people turned up in Washington?" With many others, she demanded an end to male dominance so as to allow everyone the opportunity to contribute and she emphasized more local, person to person political accomplishments as

Women's theater, Central Park, New York City. Sid Sattler/Swarthmore College Peace Collection.

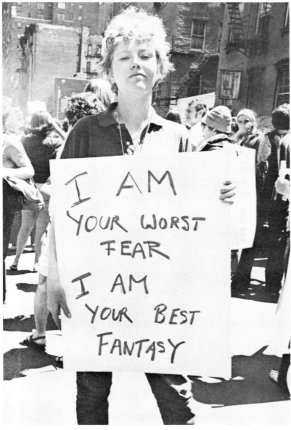

opposed to largely symbolic national actions. The feminist movement's impact on the development and direction of active nonviolence has only begun, but already it has suggested new priorities and approaches which are certain to influence nonviolent work in the future.

After the war, many radical pacifists once again termed disarmament the priority issue. They continued to protest the militarism and war-based economy of the U.S. with direct action projects to halt new weapons systems, resist war taxes, and encourage conversion to a peace-time economy. Repeatedly they emphasized to the public that American priorities in economic and foreign policy remained largely unchanged from those which had originally led the U.S. to make war on Indochina. One of the largest national projects was the Continental Walk for Disarmament and Social Justice, organized by nonviolent groups including the WRL, AFSC, FOR, SCLC, and WILPF, which left Ukiah, California in early 1976 to reach Washington D.C. in mid-October. The Call of the Walk stated in part:

> *Military spending priorities continue*
> *to rob our sisters and brothers on this*
> *planet of dignity and even of life itself,*

Women's contingent in the Continental Walk for Disarmament and Social Justice, San Francisco, California, January 31, 1976. J.C. Stockwell.

Gay Liberation parade, New York City. Diana Davies.

while continuing to fuel the fires of inflation and unemployment. Foreign policies based on fear and mistrust continue to foster ever increasing arms stockpiles. Nuclear arms continue to threaten total destruction. Non-nuclear arms continue to be used to repress social change and to preserve patterns of injustice. . . .

We know that those who control the governments are trapped in the illusion that militarism can defend the interests of their nations and peoples. The last 30 years have shown that, without massive public pressure, governments will not take a single step toward disarmament.

Nonviolent activists continued to be internationalist in their approach, launching educational and direct action projects around conflicts and oppression in the Middle East, Puerto Rico, Northern Ireland, Namibia, Chile and many other countries. Radicals exposed and protested the involvement of the U.S. government and multi-national corporations in the affairs of other countries and formed

defense groups for political prisoners throughout the world. While efforts were underway to help the people of Vietnam rebuild their country, activists in the U.S. pressured for universal and unconditional amnesty for the hundreds of thousands of people who went into exile, were jailed or dishonorably discharged from the military for resisting the war in Indochina.

Nonviolent activists also developed new economic forms to meet such basic human needs as food, shelter, clothing, and health care which were not equally or reasonably available. Nonviolent activists continued to build up cooperatives, working collectives, non-profit businesses, alternative tax funds, land trusts and other decentralized economic experiments as practical expressions of nonviolent principles. There was a growing recognition that the struggle to confront the capitalist system as a whole takes many forms. Staughton Lynd, a veteran of the civil rights and anti-war movements, identified the employer-employee relationship as crucial to capitalism and turned his energies to fostering work democracy and workers' control. He

Marchers protest the murders of Navajos, Farmington, New Mexico, 1974. Bob Fitch.

wrote:

>The vision of what is and what can be that I would like to see broadcast by a new movement would contrast our society's democratic ideology with the undemocratic, arbitrary power which private employers have over those who work for them. . . . Every time an employee straightens his or her back and says "No" at the risk of being fired, capitalism is that much weaker. Every time a worker ceases to seek gratification and promotion from the boss, and seeks approval instead from his or her fellow-workers, a brick in the new society has been laid.

The diversity of issues and activity after the war reflected a rise in commitment and energy among a significant number of Americans who realized that fundamental changes in U.S. society are necessary to insure a decent life for all. As popular awareness of the issues and problems facing the human race grows, the search for nonviolent, life-affirming directions will increase in importance and immediacy. In a world strangling in violence and dishonesty, the further development of nonviolence as a philosophy and effective political force becomes one of the most urgent priorities. □

25th anniversary of the atomic bombing of Hiroshima, Japan. New York City, 1970. Joel Shumer.

READING LIST

This reading list is designed to help readers follow up on some of the ideas, people, groups and movements described in this book. The suggestions are based on bibliographies and/or footnotes of books that were used as resources, bibliographies listed below in the *Bibliographies* section, suggestions of nonviolent activists, and material encountered in the preparation of this book. Books dealing with the religious basis of pacifism, foreign policy and international law, and opposition arguments have been omitted for the most part due to space limitations. (Several of the bibliographies listed below contain extensive entries under these headings.) With a few exceptions, books dealing with nonviolence in countries other than the U.S. and magazine articles have also been omitted.

The list falls in two parts. In the first, books are arranged to cover the events mentioned and people profiled chapter by chapter. We have particularly tried to include first person accounts and, where appropriate, art and photographic books. Some of the titles are out of print or rare pamphlets which may be difficult to find except in university or large public libraries or in archival collections. The second part, following the chapter breakdowns, lists more generally useful bibliographies, histories, anthologies, works by and about Gandhi, and books which help to present a vision of a nonviolent social order. We also recommend that you see the *Research Notes* presented elsewhere in this book.

THE ROOTS OF AMERICAN NONVIOLENCE 1650-1915

Andrews, Edward Deming. *The People Called Shakers.* (New York: Oxford University Press, 1953).

Ballou, Adin. *Autobiography of Adin Ballou.* Edited by William S. Heywood. (Lowell, MA: 1896).

_____. *Christian Non-Resistance In All Its Important Bearings, Illustrated and Defended.* Edited by William S. Heywood. (Philadelphia: J.M. M'Kim, 1846) and (New York: J.S. Ozer, 1972).

_____. *History of the Hopedale Community from its Inception to its Virtual Submergence in the Hopedale Parish.* Edited by William S. Heywood. (Lowell, MA: Thompson & Hill, 1897).

_____. *A Discourse on Christian Non-Resistance in Extreme Cases.* (Hopedale: 1860) (New York: Garland, 1971).

_____. *Non-Resistance in Relation to Human Governments.* (Boston: 1839).

_____. *Practical Christian Socialism: A Conversational Exposition of the True System of Human Society.* (New York: Fowlers and Wells, 1854).

Barksdale, Brent E. *Pacifism and Democracy in Colonial Pennsylvania.* (Stanford, CA: Stanford University Press, 1961).

Beckwith, George C. *The Peace Manual, or War and Its Remedies.* (1847) (New York: Garland, 1971).

Beisner, Robert. *Twelve Against Empire: The Anti-Imperialists, 1898-1900.* (New York: McGraw-Hill, 1968).

Bender, Wilbur J. "Pacifism Among the Mennonites, Amish Mennonites and Schwenkfelders of Pennsylvania to 1783," *Mennonite Quarterly Review* I, no. 1(July, 1927) and no. 4 (Oct. 1927).

Benezet, Anthony. *The Plainness and Innocent Simplicity of the Christian Religion with its Salutary Effects, Compared to the Corrupting Nature and Dreadful Effects of War.* (Philadelphia: 1782).

Bert, Harry. "Notes on Non-resistance in the Brethren in Christ Church to the End of World War I," *Notes and Queries in Brethren in Christ History.* (Grantham, PA) VI, no. 1 (Jan. 1965).

Bestor, Arthur E. *Backwoods Utopias: The Sectarian and Owenite Phases of Community Socialism in America, 1663-1829.* (Philadelphia: University of Pennsylvania Press, 1950).

Bolles, John R. and Anna B. Williams. *The Rogerenes: Some Hitherto Unpublished Annals Belonging to the Colonial History of Connecticut.* (Boston: 1904).

Bowman, Rufus D. *The Church of the Brethren and War 1788-1941.* (1944) (New York: Garland, 1971).

Brailsford, Mabel Richmond. *Quaker Women, 1650-1690.* (London: Duckworth & Co., 1915).

Brinton, Anna C. *Quaker Profiles, 1750-1850.* (Wallingford, PA: Pendle Hill, 1964).

Brock, Peter. *Pacifism in the U.S. from the Colonial Era to the First World War.* (Princeton, NJ: Princeton University Press, 1968).

Bronner, Edwin B. "The Quakers and Non-Violence in Pennsylvania," *Pennsylvania History.* XXXV, no. 1 (Jan. 1968), 1-22.

Brookes, George S. *Friend Anthony Benezet.* (Philadelphia: University of Pennsylvania Press, 1937).

Burritt, Elihu. *Ten-Minute Talks on all Sorts of Topics, with Autobiography of the Author.* (Boston: 1874).

Cartland, Fernando G. *Southern Heroes or the Friends in War Time.* (1895) (New York: Garland, 1971).

Cassel, Daniel K. *History of the Mennonites.* (Philadelphia: 1888).

Chapman, John Jay. *William Lloyd Garrison.* (Boston: Atlantic Monthly Press, 1921).

Child, Lydia Maria. *Letters of Lydia Maria Child.* (Boston: Houghton, Mifflin & Co., 1883).

Climenhaga, A.W. *History of the Brethren in Christ Church.* (Nappanee, IN: 1942).

Cook, Blanche, Charles Chatfield and Sandi Cooper (eds.). *The First American Peace Movement.* (New York: Garland, 1971). Writings by David Low Dodge, James Mott, and Noah Worcester.

_____, Charles Chatfield and Sandi Cooper (eds.). *Sermons on War by Theodore Parker.* (1863) (New York: Garland, 1971).

Crosby, Ernest. *Garrison the Non-Resistant.* (Chicago: Public Publishing Co., 1905) and (New York: J.S. Ozer, 1972).

Crowmell, Otelia. *Lucretia Mott.* (New York: Russell & Russell, 1971).

Curti, Merle Eugene. *The American Peace Crusade, 1815-1860.* (Durham, NC: Duke University Press, 1929).

_____. *The Learned Blacksmith: The Letters and Journals of Elihu Burritt.* (New York: Wilson-Erickson, 1937).

_____. *Peace or War: The American Struggle, 1636-1936.* (New York: W.W. Norton, 1936).

Darrow, Clarence S. *Resist Not Evil.* (Chicago: C.H. Kerr, 1903) and (New York: J.S. Ozer, 1972).

Dodge, David Low. *War Inconsistent with the Religion of Jesus Christ.* Edited by Edwin D. Mead. (Boston: Ginn & Co., 1905).

Doherty, Robert Wesley. "Alfred H. Love and the Universal Peace Union." (Ph.D. dissertation, University of Pennsylvania, 1962).

Dowd, Douglas. *The Twisted Dream: Capitalist Development in the United States since 1776.* (Cambridge, MA: Winthrop, 1974).

Drake, Thomas E. *Quakers and Slavery in America.* (New Haven: Yale University Press, 1950).

Dunn, Mary Maples. *William Penn: Politics and Conscience.* (Princeton, NJ: Princeton University Press, 1967).

Durnbaugh, Donald F. *The Brethren in Colonial America.* (Elgin, IL: Brethren Press, 1967).

Fisher, Sydney G. *The Quaker Colonies.* (New Haven, CT: Yale University Press, 1919).

Flexner, Eleanor. *Century of Struggle: The Woman's Rights Movement in the United States.* (Cambridge: Harvard University Press, 1968).

Garrison, William Lloyd. *Selections from the Writings and Speeches of William Lloyd Garrison.* (New York: New American Library, 1969).

_____. *A House Dividing Against Itself, 1836-1840.* Edited by Louis Ruchanes. (Cambridge: Harvard University Press, 1971).

Grimke, Archibald H. and Frank F. Garrison (comp.). *Garrison Centenary, December Tenth, 1805-1905.* (Philadelphia: E.A.Wright, 1905).

Harrell, David Edwin, Jr. *Quest for a Christian America: The Disciples of Christ and American Society to 1866.* (Atlanta: Publishing Systems, 1966).

Hemmenway, John. *The Apostle of Peace: Memoir of William Ladd.* (Boston: 1872) (New York: J.S. Ozer, 1972).

Hendrick, George. "The Influence of Thoreau's 'Civil Disobedience' on Gandhi's *Satyagraha*" *New England Quarterly* XXIX, no. 4 (Dec. 1956). Documentation of Gandhi's knowledge of Thoreau.

Hinds, William Alfred. *American Communities.* (Chicago: C.H. Kerr, 1902).

Hoblitzelle, Harrison. "The War Against War in the Nineteenth Century: A Study of the Western Backgrounds of Gandhian Thought." (Ph.D. dissertation, Columbia University, 1959).

Holloway, Mark. *Heavens on Earth: Utopian Communities in America, 1680-1880.* (London: Turnstile Press, 1951).

Horsch, John. *The Principle of Nonresistance as Held by the Mennonite Church.* (1927) (New York: Garland, 1971).

Huggard, William Allen. "Emerson and the Problem of War and Peace." (Ph.D. dissertation, University of Iowa, 1938).

Jones, Rufus M. et al. *The Quakers in the American Colonies.* (New York: Macmillan, 1923) and (New York: W.W. Norton, 1966).

Kelsey, Rayner Wickersham. *Friends and the Indians 1655-1917.* (Philadelphia: Associated Executive Committee of Friends on Indian Affairs, 1917).

Kline, John. *Life and Labors of Elder John Kline the Martyr Missionary.* Edited by Benjamin Funk. (Elgin, IL: Brethren Publishing House, 1900).

Kraditor, Aileen S. *Means and Ends in American Abolitionism: Garrison and His Critics on Strategy and Tactics, 1834-1850.* (New York: Pantheon, 1968).

Ladd, William. *An Essay on a Congress of Nations for the Adjustment of International Disputes without Resort to Arms.* (1840) Edited by James Brown Scott. (New York: Oxford University Press, 1916).

_____. *The Essays of Philanthropos on Peace and War.* (1827) (New York: Garland, 1971).

Lerner, Gerda. *The Grimké Sisters from South Carolina: Rebels Against Slavery.* (Boston: Houghton, Mifflin, 1967).

Loughborough, J.N. *Rise and Progress of the Seventh-Day Adventists.* (Battle Creek, MI: 1892).

Lutzker, Michael A. "The Practical Peace Advocates, 1898-1917." (Ph.D. dissertation, Rutgers University, 1969).

Lynd, Staughton (ed.). *Nonviolence in America: A Documentary History.* (Indianapolis: Bobbs-Merrill, 1966).

MacDonald, Clyde Winfield, Jr. "The Massachusetts Peace Society 1815-1828: A Study in Evangelical Reform." (Ph.D. dissertation, University of Maine, 1973).

McPherson, James M. *The Struggle for Equality: Abolitionists and the Negro in the Civil War and Reconstruction.* (Princeton, NJ: Princeton University Press, 1964).

Mabee, Carlton. *Black Freedom: The Nonviolent Abolitionists from 1830 through the Civil War.* (New York: Macmillan, 1970).

Madden, E.H. *Civil Disobedience and Moral Law in Nineteenth Century American Philosophy.* (Seattle: University of Washington Press, 1968).

Marchand, C. Roland. *The American Peace Movement and Social Reform, 1898-1918.* (Princeton, NJ: Princeton University Press, 1972).

Martin, James J. *Men Against the State.* (DeKalb, IL: Adrian Allen Assoc., 1953).

Meltzer, Milton. *Bread and Roses: The Struggle of American Labor 1865-1915.* (New York: Knopf, 1967).

Moritzen, Julius. *The Peace Movement of America.* (1912) (New York: Garland, 1971).

Nordhoff, Charles. *The Communistic Societies of the United States.* (New York: Harper, 1875).

Norris, Marjorie Mae. "Nonviolent Reform in the United States, 1860-1915." (Ph.D. dissertation, University of Maryland, 1970).

Noyes, John Humphrey. *History of American Socialisms.* (1870) (New York: Hillary House, 1961).

_____. *Strange Cults and Utopias of 19th Century America.* (New York: Dover, 1966).

Parker, Robert A. *A Yankee Saint: John Humphrey Noyes and the Oneida Community.* (New York: G.P. Putnam's Sons, 1935).

Patterson, David S. "The Travail of the American Peace Movement, 1887-1914." (Ph.D. dissertation, University of California, Berkeley, 1968).

Peare, Catherine Owens. *William Penn.* (Philadelphia: Lippincott, 1957).

Perkins, William Rufus and Barthinius L. Wick. *History of the Amana Society or Community of True Inspiration.* (Iowa City, IA: University of Iowa, 1891).

Pillsbury, Parker. *Acts of the Anti-Slavery Apostles.* (Concord, NH: 1883).

Pringle, Cyrus. *The Civil War Diary of Cyrus Pringle.* (New York: Macmillan, 1918).

Pritchard, H.O. "Militant Pacifists: A Study of the Militant Pacifists of the Restoration Movement," *World Call* (Indianapolis, IN) XVIII, no. 3 (March 1936).

Raybeck, Joseph G. *A History of American Labor.* (New York: Macmillan, 1964).

Reuben, Odell Richardson. "Peace Against Justice: A Nineteenth Century Dilemma of Quaker Conscience." (Ph.D. dissertation, Duke University, 1970).

Sappington, Roger E. *Courageous Prophet: Chapters from the Life of John Kline.* (Elgin, IL: Brethren Press, 1964).

Schlissel, Lillian D. (ed.). *Conscience in America: A Documentary History of Conscientious Objection in America, 1757-1967.* (New York: Dutton, 1968).

Schuster, Eunice Minette. *Native American Anarchism: A Study of Left-Wing American Individualism.* (Northampton, MA: Smith College, 1932).

Seibert, Russell Howard. "The Treatment of Conscientious Objectors in War Time, 1775-1920." (Ph.D. dissertation, Ohio State University, 1936).

Sharpless, Isaac. *Political Leaders of Provincial Pennsylvania.* (New York: Macmillan, 1919).

_____. *A Quaker Experiment in Government.* (Philadelphia: A.J. Ferris, 1898).

Sokolow, Jayme A. "Revivalism and Radicalism: William Lloyd Garrison, Henry Clarke Wright and the Ideology of Nonresistance." (Ph.D. dissertation, New York University, 1972).

Spalding, Arthur Whitefield. *Origin and History of Seventh-Day Adventists.* (Washington, DC: 1961).

Tolis, Peter, *Elihu Burritt: Crusader for Brotherhood.* (Hamden, CT: Shoe String Press, 1968).

Tolles, F.B. *Quakers and the Atlantic Culture.* (New York: Macmillan).

Villard, Fanny Garrison. *William Lloyd Garrison on Non-Resistance.* (New York: Nation Press Printing Co., 1924).

Walker, Amasa. *Le Monde: Or in Time of Peace Prepare for War.* (London: 1859).

Ware, Henry, Jr. *Memoirs of the Rev. Noah Worcester.* (Boston: 1844).

Whipple, Charles K. *Evils of the Revolutionary War.* (Boston: 1839).

_____. *Non-Resistance Applied to the Internal Defense of a Community.* (Boston: 1860).

_____. *The Non-Resistance Principle: With Particular Application to the Help of Slaves by Abolitionists.* (Boston: R.F. Wallcut, 1860).

Whitney, Janet. *John Woolman, American Quaker.* (Boston: 1942).

Wilcox, Francis McLellan. *Seventh-Day Adventists in Time of War.*

(Washington, DC: Review and Herald Publ. Assn., 1936).

Woolman, John. *The Journal of John Woolman and a Plan for the Poor: A Spiritual Autobiography.* (Secaucus, NJ: Citadel, 1973).

Wright, Edward Needles. *Conscientious Objectors in the Civil War.* (Philadelphia: University of Pennsylvania Press, 1931).

Wright, Henry C. *Ballot Box and Battle Field. To Voters Under the United States Government.* (Boston: 1842).

_____. *The Natick Resolution: Or, Resistance to Slaveholders, The Right and Duty of Southern Slaves and Northern Freemen.* (Boston: 1859).

_____. *Declaration of Radical Peace Principles.* (Boston: 1866).

Yellen, Samuel. *American Labor Struggles, 1877 - 1934.* (New York: Harcourt, Brace & Co., 1936).

WORLD WAR I AND AMERICAN OPPOSITION

Addams, Jane. *New Ideals of Peace.* (New York: Macmillan Co., 1907).

_____. *Forty Years at Hull-House: Being Twenty Years at Hull-House and the Second Twenty Years at Hull-House.* With afterword by Lillian Wald. (New York: Macmillan, 1935).

_____. *Peace and Bread in Time of War.* (New York: King's Crown Press, 1945).

_____, Emily Green Balch and Alice Hamilton. *Women at the Hague: The International Congress of Women and Its Results.* (New York: Macmillan Co., 1915).

Balch, Emily Greene. *Occupied Haiti.* (1927) (New York: Garland, 1971).

Baldwin, Roger. "Recollections of a Life in Civil Liberties," *The Civil Liberties Review,* Vol. 2, no. 2 (1975), 39-72.

Beales, A.C.F. *The History of Peace.* (New York: Dial Press, 1931).

Bourne, Randolph S. *War and the Intellectuals: Collected Essays, 1915-1919.* (New York: Harper Torchbooks, 1964).

_____. *Untimely Papers.* Edited by James Oppenheim. (New York: B.W. Huebsch, 1919).

Brookes, Arle and Robert J. Leach. *Help Wanted: The Experiences of Some Quaker Conscientious Objectors.* (Philadelphia: Pendle Hill, 1940).

Brown, Kenneth I., (ed.). *Character "Bad": The Story of a Conscientious Objector as Told In the Letters of Harold Studley Gray.* (New York: Harper & Bros., 1934).

Burns, Edward M. *David Starr Jordan: Prophet of Freedom.* (Stanford, CA: Stanford University Press, 1953).

Bussey, Gertrude and Margaret Tims. *The WILPF, 1915-1965: A Record of Fifty Years Work.* (London: George Allen & Unwin, Ltd., 1965).

Chaplin, Ralph. *Wobbly, The Rough-and-Tumble Story of an American Radical.* (Chicago: University of Chicago Press, 1948).

_____. *Bars and Shadows, The Prison Poems of Ralph Chaplin.* Introduction by Scott Nearing. (New York: The Leonard Press, 1922).

Conlin, Joseph R. "The IWW and the Question of Violence," *Wisconsin Magazine of History,* LI (1968), 316-326.

Cook, Blanche. "Woodrow Wilson and the Anti-Militarists, 1914-1918." (Ph.D. dissertation, John Hopkins University, 1970).

_____ (ed.). *Jane Addams on Peace and Freedom 1914-1935.* (New York: Garland, 1971).

_____. *Max and Crystal Eastman on Peace, Revolution and War.* (New York: Garland, 1971).

_____. *The Organized American Peace Movement in War Time 1914-1919.* (New York: Garland, 1971).

_____. *Oswald Garrison Villard: The Dilemmas of the Absolute Pacifist in Two World Wars.* (New York: Garland, 1971).

_____, Charles Chatfield and Sandi Cooper (eds.). *Reminiscences of War Resisters in World War I.* (New York: Garland, 1971).

Curti, Merle Eugene. *Bryan and World Peace.* (1931) (New York: Garland, 1971).

Debs, Eugene Victor. *Walls and Bars.* (Chicago: Socialist Party, 1927).

Degen, Marie Louise. *The History of the Women's Peace Party.* (Baltimore: John Hopkins Press, 1939) and (New York: Garland, 1971).

Drinnon, Richard. *Rebel in Paradise: A Biography of Emma Goldman.* (Chicago: University of Chicago Press, 1961).

Dubofsky, Melvyn. *One Shall Be All: A History of the Industrial Workers of the World.* (Chicago: Quadrangle, 1969).

Duffus, Robert L. *Lillian Wald, Neighbor and Crusader.* (New York: Macmillan Co., 1938).

Fainsod, Merle. *International Socialism and the World War.* (New York: Octagon Books, 1966).

Farrell, John C. *Beloved Lady: A History of Jane Addams' Ideas on Reform and Peace.* (Baltimore: John Hopkins Press, 1967).

Fitzgerald, Richard. *Art and Politics: Cartoonists of the Masses and Liberator.* (Westport, CT: Greenwood Press, 1973).

French, Paul Comly. *We Won't Murder, Being the Story of Men Who Followed Their Conscientious Scruples and Helped Give Life to Democracy.* (New York: Hastings House, 1940).

Ginger, Ray. *The Bending Cross: A Biography of Eugene Victor Debs.* (New Brunswick: Rutgers University Press, 1949).

Goldman, Emma. *Living My Life.* (New York: Knopf, 1931).

Grubbs, Frank L., Jr. *The Struggle for Labor Loyalty: Gompers, the A.F.of L. and the Pacifists, 1917-1920.* (Durham: Duke University Press, 1967).

Hillquit, Morris. *Loose Leaves From a Busy Life.* (New York: Macmillan Co., 1934).

Johnson, Donald. *The Challenge to American Freedoms: World War I and the Rise of the American Civil Liberties Union.* (Lexington: University of Kentucky Press, 1963).

Jordan, David Starr. *War and the Breed: The Relation of War to the Downfall of Nations.* (Boston: Beacon Press, 1915).

_____. *Days of a Man.* (New York: World Book Co., 1922).

Kellogg, Walter. *The Conscientious Objector.* (New York: Boni & Liveright, 1919) and (New York: Garland, 1971).

Kerr, Eby. *War.* (New York: Garland, 1971).

Kornbluh, Joyce L. (ed.). *Rebel Voices: An IWW Anthology.* (Ann Arbor: University of Michigan Press, 1964).

Linn, James Weber. *Jane Addams: A Biography.* (New York: D. Appleton-Century Co., 1937).

Meyer, Ernest L. *"Hey! Yellowbacks!": The War Diary of a Conscientious Objector.* (New York: John Day Co., 1930).

Mitchell, John Ames. *The Silent War.* (New York: Life Publishing Co., 1906).

Nearing, Scott. *The Making of a Radical: A Political Autobiography.* (New York: Harper-Row, 1972).

_____. *War: Organized Destruction and Mass Murder by Civilized Nations.* (1931) (New York: Garland, 1971).

Peterson, H.C. and Gilbert C. Fite. *Opponents of War, 1917-1918.* (Madison: University of Wisconsin Press, 1957).

Preston, William J. *Aliens and Dissenters: Federal Suppression of Radicals, 1903-1933.* (New York: Harper and Row, 1966).

Rand School of Social Science. *The Trial of Scott Nearing and the American Socialist Party, from the 5th to the 19th February 1919.* (1919) (New York: Garland, 1971).

Randall, John Herman, Jr. *Emily Green Balch of New England: Citizen of the World.* (n.p.: Women's International League for Peace & Freedom, 1946).

Randall, Mercedes M. *High Lights in W.I.L.P.F. History: From the Hague to Luxembourg, 1915-1946.* (Philadelphia: Women's International League for Peace & Freedom, 1946).

_____. *Improper Bostonian: Emily Greene Balch.* (New York: Twayne Publishers, 1964).

Russell, Bertrand. *Justice in Wartime.* (1917) (New York: Garland, 1971).

Seidler, Murray B. *Norman Thomas: Respectable Rebel.* (Ithaca, NY: Cornell University Press, 1961).

Shannon, David. *The Socialist Party of America.* (New York: Macmillan Co., 1955).

_____. "Anti-War Thought and Activity of Eugene V. Debs, 1917-1921." (MA thesis, University of Wisconsin, 1946).

Thomas, Norman. *War's Heretics: A Plea for the Conscientious Objector.* (New York: Civil Liberties Bureau of the American Union Against Militarism, 1917).

————. *The Christian Patriot.* (Philadelphia: W.H. Jenkins, 1917).

————. *The Conscientious Objector in America.* (New York: B.W. Huebsch, 1923).

Trachtenberg, Alexander. *The American Socialists and the War.* (New York: Rand School of Social Science, 1917).

Villard, Oswald Garrison. *Fighting Years: Memoirs of a Liberal Editor.* (New York: Harcourt, Brace and Co., 1939).

Wald, Lillian D. *Windows on Henry Street.* (Boston: Little, Brown, & Co., 1934).

Weinstein, James. *The Decline of Socialism in America, 1912-1925.* (New York: Monthy Review Press, 1967).

————. *Ambiguous Legacy: The Left in American Politics.* (New York: New Viewpoints, 1975).

Whitfield, Stephen J. *Scott Nearing: Apostle of American Radicalism.* (New York: Columbia University Press, 1974).

Wreszin, Michael. *Oswald Garrison Villard, Pacifist at War.* (Bloomington, IN: Indiana University Press, 1965).

WOMAN'S SUFFRAGE

Blackwell, Alice Stone. *Lucy Stone: Pioneer of Woman's Rights.* (Norwood, MA: A.S. Blackwell Committee, 1930).

Blatch, Harriet Stanton and Alma Lutz. *Challenging Years: The Memoirs of Harriet Stanton Blatch.* (New York: G.P. Putnam's Sons, 1940).

Brittain, Vera. *Lady Into Woman: A History of Women from Victoria to Elizabeth II.* (New York: Macmillan, 1953).

Flexner, Eleanor. *Century of Struggle: The Woman's Rights Movement in the United States.* (Cambridge: Harvard University Press, 1959).

Fulford, Roger. *Votes for Women: The Story of a Struggle.* (London: Faber and Faber, 1957).

Hays, Elenor. *Morning Star: A Biography of Lucy Stone, 1818-1893.* (New York: Harcourt, Brace & World, 1961).

Irwin, Inez Haynes. *Uphill with Banners Flying: The Story of the Woman's Party.* (New York: Harcourt, Brace, 1921).

Kraditer, Aileen. *The Ideas of the Woman Suffrage Movement, 1890-1920.* (New York: Columbia University Press, 1965).

Lakey, George. "The Sociological Mechanisms of Nonviolent Action." (MA thesis, University of Pennsylvania, 1962).

————. "Technique and Ethos in Nonviolent Action: The Woman Suffrage Case," *Sociological Inquiry.* 38 (Winter, 1968), 37-42.

O'Neill, William L. *Everyone Was Brave: The Rise and Fall of Feminism in America.* (Chicago: Quadrangle, 1969).

Seifert, Harvey J.D. "The Use by American Quakers of Nonviolent Resistance as a Method of Social Change." (Ph.D. thesis, Boston University, 1940).

Stanton, Elizabeth Cady and Susan B. Anthony et al (eds.). *History of Woman Suffrage.* (New York: Fowler and Wells, 1881-1922).

Stevens, Doris. *Jailed for Freedom.* (New York: Boni and Liveright, 1920).

Tremain, Rose (ed.) *The Fight for Freedom for Women.* (New York: Ballantine, 1973).

Zimmerman, Loretta Ellen. "Alice Paul and the National Woman's Party, 1912-1920." (Ph.D. dissertation, Tulane University, 1964).

THE LABOR MOVEMENT

Ameringer, Oscar. *If You Don't Weaken.* Foreword by Carl Sandberg. (New York: Holt & Co., 1940).

Barton, Betty Lynn. "The Fellowship of Reconciliation: Pacifism, Labor, and Social Welfare, 1915-1960." (Ph.D. dissertation, Florida State University, 1974).

Boyer, Richard O. and Herbert M. Morais. *Labor's Untold Story.* (New York: United Electrical, Radio and Machine Workers of America, 1972).

Cannon, James P. *The History of American Trotskyism: Report of a Participant.* (New York: Pioneer Publishers, 1944).

Chatfield, Charles (ed). *Devere Allen and a Radical Approach to War.* (New York: Garland, 1971).

Cleghorn, Sarah N. *Threescore: The Autobiography of Sarah N. Cleghorn.* (New York: Harrison Smith & Robert Haas, 1936).

Dos Passos, John. *USA.* (New York: Modern Library, 1937).

————. *Facing the Chair: The Story of the Americanization of Two Foreignborn Workmen.* (Boston: Sacco-Vanzetti Defense Committee, 1927).

Fine. Sidney. *Sit-Down: The General Motors Strike of 1936-37.* (Ann Arbor: University of Michigan Press, 1969).

Frankfurter, Marion and Gardner Jackson (eds.). *Letters of Sacco and Vanzetti.* (New York: E.P. Dutton, 1960).

Hentoff, Nat (ed.). *The Essays of A.J. Muste.* (Indianapolis: Bobbs-Merrill, 1967).

Lens, Sidney. *Left, Right and Center, Conflicting Forces in American Labor.* (Hinsdale, IL: H. Regnery, 1949).

————. *The Labor Wars from the Molly Maguires to the Sitdowns.* (Garden City, NY: Doubleday, 1973).

Lynd, Alice and Staughton Lynd (eds.). *Rank and File: Personal Histories by Working Class Organizers.* (Boston: Beacon Press, 1973).

Meltzer, Milton. *Brother Can You Spare a Dime: The Great Depression, 1929-1933.* (New York: Knopf, 1969).

Pettingill, George E. *Sit-Down Strikes: A Reading List.* New York Public Library Bulletin, New York, 1937. V. 41, 480-484.

Schnapper, Morris Bartel. *American Labor: A Pictorial Social History.* (Washington: Public Affairs Press, 1972).

THE ANTI-WAR MOVEMENT

Allen, Devere. "Bring the Peace Movement to Socialism!" *Eighteenth Convention of the Socialist Party of America (1934).*

————. "Pacifism and Its Critics," *American Socialist Monthly.* IX (Feb. 1937), 25-31.

————. "The Peace Movement Moves Left," *Annals of the American Academy of Political and Social Science,* CLXXV (Sept. 1934), 150-155.

————. *Pacifism in the Modern World.* (New York: Doubleday, Doran & Co., 1929).

————. *The Fight for Peace.* (New York: Macmillan Co., 1930).

Baber, Zonia. "Peace Symbols," *Chicago Schools Journal.* XVIII (1937), 151-158.

Boechel, Florence Brewer. *The Turn Toward Peace.* (Washington DC: National Council for the Prevention of War, 1930).

Bowers, Robert Edwin. "The American Peace Movement, 1933-1941." (Ph.D. dissertation, University of Wisconsin, 1949).

Brittain, Vera. *Rebel Passion: A Short History of Some Pioneer Peace Makers.* (Nyack, NY: Fellowship, 1964).

Chamberlain, William Joseph. *Fighting for Peace: The Story of the War Resistance Movement.* (1929) (New York: Garland, 1971).

Chatfield, Charles (ed). *Kirby Page and the Social Gospel: Pacifist and Socialist Aspects.* (New York: Garland, 1971).

————. *Norman Thomas: Social Realism Through Peace and Democratic Justice.* (New York: Garland, 1971).

Detzer, Dorothy. *Appointment on the Hill.* (New York: Henry Holt & Co., 1948).

Eddy, Sherwood. *A Pilgrimage of Ideas, or the Re-Education of Sherwood Eddy.* (New York: Farrar & Rinehart, 1934).

————. *Eighty Adventurous Years, An Autobiography.* (New York: Harper & Bros., 1955).

Einstein, Albert. *The Fight Against War.* Edited by Alfred Lief. (New York: John Day Company, 1933).

Englebrecht, Helmuth C. *One Hell of a Business.* (New York: Harper & Bros., 1934).

———— and F.C. Hannighan. *Merchants of Death: A Study of the International Armament Industry.* (New York: Dodd, Mead & Co., 1934).

Floyd, William. *War Resistance.* (New York: Arbitrator Press, n.d.).

Fosdick, Harry Emerson. *The Living of These Days: An Autobiography.* (New York: Harper & Bros., 1956).

Harris, Ted Carlton. "Jeannette Rankin: Suffragist, First Woman Elected to Congress and Pacifist." (Ph.D. dissertation, University of Georgia, 1972).

Holloway, Vernon Howard. "American Pacifism Between Two Wars,

1919-1941." (Ph.D. dissertation, Yale University, 1949).

Holmes, John Haynes. *New Wars for Old.* (New York: Dodd, Mead & Co., 1916).

_____. *Patriotism Is Not Enough.* (New York: Greenberg Publ., Inc., 1925).

_____. *I Speak for Myself.* (New York: Harper & Bros., 1959).

Hughan, Jessie Wallace. *American Socialism of the Present Day.* (New York: John Lane Co., 1911).

_____. *The Beginnings of War Resistance.* (New York: War Resisters League, 1935).

_____. *The Facts of Socialism.* (New York: John Lane Company, 1913).

_____. *A Study of International Government.* (New York: T.Y. Crowell Co., 1923).

Johnpoll, Bernard K. *Pacifist's Progress: Norman Thomas and the Decline of American Socialism.* (Chicago: Quadrangle Books, 1970).

Josephson, Hannah. *Jeannette Rankin, First Lady In Congress: A Biography.* (Indianapolis: Bobbs-Merrill, 1974).

Kuusisto, Allan. "The Influence of the National Council for the Prevention of War on United States Foreign Policy, 1935-1939." (Ph.D. dissertation, Harvard University, 1950).

Lansbury, George. *My Pilgrimage for Peace.* (New York: Henry Holt & Co., 1938).

Lash, Joseph P. *The Campus Strikes Against War.* (New York: Student League for Industrial Democracy, 1935).

Lewinsohn, Richard. *The Profits of War Through the Ages.* Translated by Geoffrey Sainsbury. (New York: E.P. Dutton, 1937).

Lewis, John. *The Case Against Pacifism.* (1940) (New York: Garland, 1971).

Libby, Frederick. *The American Peace Movement.* (Washington DC: National Council for the Prevention of War, 1930).

_____. *To End War.* (Nyack, NY: Fellowship Publication, 1969).

Nall, Gary Lynn. "The Ludlow War Referendum." (MA thesis, University of Texas, 1959).

Niebuhr, Reinhold. *Does Civilization Need Religion?* (New York: Macmillan Co., 1927).

_____. *Moral Man and Immoral Society.* (New York: Macmillan Co., 1927).

_____. *Christianity and Power Politics.* (New York: Charles Scribner's Sons, 1940).

_____. *Why the Christian Church Is Not Pacifist.* (Toronto: Macmillan Co., 1940).

Page, Kirby. *A New Economic Order.* (New York: Harcourt & Brace, 1930).

_____. *Individualism and Socialism: An Ethical Survey of Economic and Political Forces.* (New York: Farrar & Reinhart, 1933).

_____. *The Abolition of War.* (New York: George H. Doran Co., 1924).

_____. *What Shall We Do About War?* (New York: Eddy & Page, 1935).

_____. *War: Its Causes, Consequences and Cure.* (New York: George H. Doran Co., 1923).

_____. *National Defense: A Study of the Origins, Results and Prevention of War.* (New York: Farrar & Rinehart, 1931).

_____. *How to Keep America Out of War.* (Philadelphia: AFSC *et al.*, 1939).

_____. *Must We Go To War?* (New York: Farrar & Rinehart, Inc., 1937).

Rankin, Jeannette. "Suffragists Oral History Project," Berkeley, CA, n.d. Interview conducted by Malca Chall and Hannah Josephson. Afterword by John Kinkley.

Rodin, Doris Galant. "The Opposition to the Establishment of Military Training in Civil Schools and Colleges in the United States, 1914-1940." (MA thesis, American University, 1949).

Russell, Bertrand. *Which Way to Peace?* (London: Michael Joseph, 1936).

Schaffer, Ronald. "Jeannette Rankin, Progressive Isolationist." (Ph.D. dissertation, Princeton University, 1959).

Seldes, George. *Iron, Blood and Profits: An Exposure of the World-Wide Munitions Racket.* (New York: Harper & Bros., 1934).

Szegedi Szuts, Istvan. *My War.* (London: John Lane, 1931).

Thomas, Norman. *As I See It.* (New York: Macmillan Co., 1932).

_____. *The Choice Before Us: Mankind at the Crossroads.* (New York: Macmillan Co., 1934).

_____ and Bertram D. Wolfe. *Keep America Out of War: A Program.* (New York: Frederick Stokes Co., 1939).

_____. *War: No Glory, No Profit, No Need.* (New York: Frederick Stokes Company, 1935).

Voss, Carl Herman. *Rabbi and Minister: The Friendship of Stephen S. Wise and John Haynes Holmes.* (New York: World Publishing Co., 1964).

Waldman, Seymour. *Death and Profits: A Study of the War Policies Commission.* (New York: Brewer, Warren & Putnam, 1932).

Why They Cannot Go To War. (Philadelphia: American Friends Service Committee and Women's International League for Peace & Freedom, 1940).

Wiltz, John E. *In Search of Peace: The Senate Munitions Inquiry, 1934-36.* (Baton Rouge: Louisiana State University Press, 1963).

Wise, Stephen. *Challenging Years.* (New York: Putnam's Sons, 1949).

CATHOLIC WORKER MOVEMENT

Coles, Robert. *A Spectacle Unto the World: The Catholic Worker Movement.* (New York: Viking Press, 1973).

Cornell, Thomas C. and James H. Forest. *A Penny a Copy: Readings From the* Catholic Worker. (New York: Macmillan Company, 1968).

Day, Dorothy. *The Long Loneliness.* (Garden City, NY: Image Books, 1959).

_____. *Loaves and Fishes.* (New York: Curtis Books, 1972).

_____. *On Pilgrimage: The Sixties.* Dedication by Daniel Berrigan and Introduction by Stanley Vishnewski. (New York: Curtis Books, 1972).

_____. *Meditations.* (Paramus, NJ: Paulist Press, 1975).

Hennacy, Ammon. *The One Man Revolution.* (Salt Lake City: Author, 1970).

_____. *The Book of Ammon.* (Salt Lake City: Author, 1964).

Hugo, John J. *Weapons of the Spirit.* (New York: Catholic Worker Press, 1943).

Gray, Francine Du Plessix. *Divine Disobedience: Profiles in Catholic Radicalism.* (New York: Knopf, 1969).

LeBrun, John Leo. "The Role of the Catholic Worker Movement in American Pacifism, 1933-1972." (Ph.D. dissertation, Case Western Reserve University, 1973).

McNeal, Patricia F. "The American Catholic Peace Movement 1928-1972." (Ph.D. Dissertation, Temple University, 1974).

Maurin, Peter. *Easy Essays.* (London: Sheed and Ward, 1938).

_____. *Catholic Radicalism: Phrased Essays for the Green Revolution.* (New York: Catholic Worker Books, 1949).

Merton, Thomas. *Blessed Are the Meek: The Christian Roots of Nonviolence.* (Nyack, NY: Catholic Peace Fellowship, n.d.).

_____. *Faith and Violence.* (Notre Dame, IN: University of North Dakota Press, 1968).

_____. *Thomas Merton on Peace.* Introduction by Gordon Zahn. (New York: McCall Publishing Co., 1971).

_____. *Conjectures of a Guilty Bystander.* (Garden City, NY: Doubleday, 1966).

Miller, William. *A Harsh and Dreadful Love.* (New York: Liveright, 1972).

O'Toole, George Barry. *War and Conscription at the Bar of Christian Morals.* (New York: Catholic Worker, 1941).

Sheehan, Arthur. *Peter Maurin: Gay Believer.* (Garden City, NY: Hanover House, 1959).

Thomas, Joan. *The Years of Grief and Laughter: A "Biography" of Ammon Hennacy.* (Phoenix: Hennacy Press, 1974).

WORLD WAR II AND THE PACIFIST COMMUNITY

American Civil Liberties Union. *The Bill of Rights in War: A Report on*

American Democratic Liberties in Wartime. (New York: ACLU, 1942).

American Friends Service Committee. *The Experience of the American Friends Service Committee In Civilian Public Service*. (Philadelphia: AFSC, 1945).

_____. *An Introduction to Friends Civilian Public Service*. (Philadelphia: AFSC, 1945).

_____. *Peacetime Conscription: A Problem for Americans*. (Philadelphia: AFSC, 1944).

Cantine, Holley and Dachine Rainer (eds.). *Prison Etiquette: The Convict's Compendium of Useful Information*. (Bearsville, NY: Retort Press, 1950).

Chatfield, Charles (ed.). *The Radical "No": The Correspondence and Writings of Evan Thomas on War*. (New York: Garland Publishing, Inc., 1974).

_____. (ed.). *International War Resistance Through World War II*. (New York: Garland, 1971).

Cornell, Julien. *The Conscientious Objector and the Law*. (New York: John Day Company, 1943).

Emanuel, Cyprian. *The Morality of Conscientious Objection to War*. (Washington DC: Catholic Association for International Peace, 1941).

Fleischman, Harry. *Norman Thomas: A Biography*. (New York: W.W. Norton & Co., 1944).

Gingerich, Melvin. *Service for People: A History of Civilian Public Service*. (Akron, PA: Mennonite Central Committee, 1949).

Goodman, Jack (ed.). *While You Were Gone: A Report on Wartime Life in the United States*. (New York: Simon and Schuster, 1946).

Goodman, Paul. *Drawing the Line*. (New York: Random House, 1962).

Gregg, Richard. *Pacifist Program in Time of War, Threatened War or Fascism*. (Wallingford, PA: Pendle Hill, 1939).

_____. "How Can Hitler Be Stopped?" *Fellowship*. V (Oct. 1939), 6.

Hassler, R. Alfred. *Conscripts of Conscience*. (New York: Fellowship of Reconciliation, 1942).

_____. *Diary of a Self-Made Convict*. (Chicago: Henry Regnery Company, 1954).

Hughan, Jessie Wallace. *If We Should Be Invaded*. (New York: War Resisters League, 1938).

_____. "What About the Jews in the Ghettos?" *Pacifica Views*, I (Sept. 3, 1943), 1.

_____. *New Leagues for Old: Blueprints or Foundations?* (New York: Plowshare Press, 1945).

Jacob, Philip E. *The Origins of Civilian Public Service*. (Washington DC: National Service Board for Religious Objectors, 1946).

Mayer, Milton. *Conscience and the Commonwealth*. (New York: Plowshare Press, 1944).

_____. *They Thought They Were Free*. (Chicago: University of Chicago Press, 1966).

Muste, A.J. *Nonviolence in an Aggressive World*. (New York: Harper & Bros., 1940).

_____. *The World Task of Pacifism*. (Wallingford, PA: Pendle Hill, 1941).

_____. *What Would Pacifists Have Done About Hitler?* (Nyack, NY: Fellowship of Reconciliation, 1949).

_____. *Wage Peace Now*. (New York: Fellowship of Reconciliation, 1942).

_____. *War Is the Enemy*. (Wallingford, PA: Pendle Hill, 1942).

Naeve, Lowell. *Phantasies of a Prisoner*. (Denver: Swallow, 1958).

_____ in collaboration with David Wieck. *A Field of Broken Stones*. (Glen Gardner, NJ: Libertarian Press, 1950).

National Service Board for Religious Objectors (ed.). *Congress Looks at the Conscientious Objector*. (Washington DC: NSBRO, 1943).

_____. *The Conscientious Objector Under the Selective Training and Service Act of 1940*. (Washington DC: NSBRO, 1942).

Olmstead, Frank. *They Asked for a Hard Job: COs At Work in Mental Hospitals*. (New York: Plowshare Press, 1943).

Pacifica Studies on Conscientious Objectors. (Glendora, CA: Pacifica Library Associates, 1942).

Richards, Edward C.M. *They Refuse To Be Criminals: Parole and the Conscientious Objector*. (n.p.: Nur Mahal, 1946).

Sargent, Porter. *War and Education*. (Boston: Author, 1943).

Sharp, Gene. *Tyranny Could Not Quell Them*. (London: Housmans, 1959).

Sibley, Mulford Q. and Ada Wardlaw. *Conscientious Objectors in Prison 1940-1945*. (Philadelphia: Pacifist Research Bureau, 1945).

_____ and Philip E. Jacob. *Conscription of Conscience: The American State and the Conscientious Objector, 1940-47*. (New York: Doubleday and Co., 1952).

Thomas, Evan. *Why We Oppose Military Conscription*. (New York: War Resisters League, 1944).

Unarmed Against Fascism. (*Peace News* Pamphlet).

West, Dan. *What Ought a Conscript Do?* (Elgin, IL: Brethren Service Committee, 1940).

TOWARDS REVOLUTIONARY NONVIOLENCE

Calhoun, Don. "Non-Violence and Revolution," *Politics*. III (Jan. 1946).

Hersey, John. *Hiroshima*. (New York: Knopf, 1946).

Jones, Ashton. *After Prison What?* (Vista, CA: Author, n.d.).

Mabee, Carlton. "Evolution of Non-Violence," *Nation*. CXCII (Aug. 12, 1961), 78-81.

Macdonald, Dwight. *Discriminations: Essays and Afterthoughts, 1938-1974*. (New York: Grossman Pub., 1974).

_____. *Memoirs of a Revolutionist: Essays in Political Criticism*. (New York: Farrar, Straus and Cudahy, 1957).

Masters, Dexter and Catherine Way (eds.). *One World or None: A Report to the Public on the Full Meaning of the Atomic Bomb*. (New York: McGraw-Hill Book Company, 1946).

Muste, A.J. *Gandhi and the H-Bomb*. (New York: Fellowship Publications, 1950).

_____. *Not By Might: Christianity, the Way to Human Decency*. (New York: Harper & Bros., 1947) and (New York: Garland, 1971).

_____. *Of Holy Disobedience*. (1952) (New York: Garland, 1971).

"The Non-Violent Revolutionists," *Politics*. III (April 1946), 118-19.

"The Pacifist Revolution," *Pacifica Views*. I (June 11, 1943), 1-2.

Page, Kirby. *Now Is the Time to Prevent a Third World War*. (La Habra, CA: Author, 1946).

Peacemakers. *A Declaration to the American People*. (Glen Gardner, NJ: Libertarian Press, 1948).

Peck, James. *We Who Would Not Kill*. (New York: Lyle Stuart, 1958).

"Report of Chicago Conference on More Disciplined and Revolutionary Pacifism," *Fellowship*. XIV (May 1948), 26.

Young, Michael David. "Wars Will Cease When Men Refuse to Fight: The War Resisters League 1925-1950." (Thesis, Brown University, 1975).

DIRECT ACTION FOR DISARMAMENT

Alsop, Joseph and Stuart Alsop. *We Accuse! The Story of the Miscarriage of American Justice in the Case of J. Robert Oppenheimer*. (New York: Simon and Schuster, Inc., 1954).

Batz, William George. "Revolution and Peace: The Christian Pacifism of A.J. Muste." (Ph.D. dissertation, University of Minnesota, 1974).

Barnet, Richard. *Who Wants Disarmament?* (Boston: Beacon Press, 1960).

Benoit, Emile and Kenneth E. Boulding (eds.). *Disarmament and the Economy*. (New York: Harper & Row, 1963).

Bigelow, Albert. *The Voyage of the Golden Rule: An Experiment with Truth*. (Garden City: Doubleday, 1959).

Boulding, Kenneth. *Conflict and Defense, A General Theory*. (New York: Harper & Bros., 1962).

Boulton, David (ed.). *Voices From the Crowd Against the H-Bomb*. (Philadelphia: Dufour, 1964).

Braden, Anne. *The Wall Between*. (New York: Monthly Review Press, 1958).

Brown, Harrison and James Real. *Community of Fear*. (Santa Barbara, CA: Center for the Study of Democratic Institutions, 1960).

Deming, Barbara. *Prison Notes*. (New York: Grossman Publishers, 1966).

Fellowship of Reconciliation. *How To Hide From an H-Bomb: A Brief Manual Designed to Inform the American Public of the Meaning and Purposes of "Operation Alert" and Similar Civil Defense Exercises.* (New York: FOR, 1956).

_____. *How Will You Look In a Concrete Pipe?* (New York: FOR, 1955).

_____. *A Sane Man's Guide to Civil Defense: Being a Glossary of Terms Useful for the Citizen Hoping to Remain Unvaporized After the Bombs Drop.* (New York: FOR, 1955).

Henthoff, Nat. *Peace Agitator: The Story of A.J. Muste.* (New York: Macmillan Co., 1963).

Jungk, Robert. *Brighter Than a Thousand Suns: A Personal History of the Atomic Scientists.* (New York: Harcourt Brace, 1958).

Katz, Milton Steven. "Peace, Politics, and Protest: SANE and the American Peace Movement, 1957-1972." (Ph.D. dissertation, Saint Louis University, 1973).

Katz, Neil H. "Radical Pacifism and the Contemporary American Peace Movement: The Committee for Nonviolent Action, 1957-1967." (Ph.D. dissertation, University of Maryland, 1974).

Lehmann, Jerry. *We Walked to Moscow.* (Canterbury, NH: Greenleaf Books, 1966).

Lifton, Robert Jay. *Death in Life: Survivors of Hiroshima.* (London: Weidenfeld & Nicolson, 1968).

Lilienthal, David E. *Change, Hope and the Bomb.* (Princeton: Princeton University Press, 1963).

Lyttle, Bradford. *You Come With Naked Hands: The Story of the San Francisco To Moscow March For Peace.* (Raymond, NH: Greenleaf Books, 1966).

Mayer, Milton. *What Can a Man Do?* (Chicago: University of Chicago Press, 1964).

Melman, Seymour (ed.). *Disarmament: Its Politics and Economics.* (Boston: American Academy of Arts & Sciences, 1962).

Nathan, Otto and Heinz Norden (eds.). *Einstein on Peace.* (New York: Simon and Schuster, 1960).

Pauling, Linus. *No More War!* (New York: Dodd, Mead, & Co., 1958).

Reynolds, Earle L. *The Forbidden Voyage.* (New York: McKay, 1961).

Swann, Marjorie. *Decade of Nonviolence: Through the Years with New England CNVA.* (n.p.: New England Committee for Nonviolent Action, 1970).

Teller, Edward and Allen Brown. *The Legacy of Hiroshima.* (Garden City, NY: Doubleday, 1962).

Thomas, Norman. *The Prerequisites for Peace.* (New York: W.W. Norton & Co., 1959).

Waskow, Arthur. *A Worried Man's Guide to Peace.* (Garden City, NY: Anchor Books, 1963).

SOCIETY OF FRIENDS

American Friends Service Committee. *In Place of War: An Inquiry Into Nonviolent National Defense.* (New York: Grossman, 1967).

_____. *Struggle for Justice: A Report on Crime and Punishment in America.* (New York: Hill & Wang, 1971).

_____. *Speak Truth to Power: A Quaker Search for an Alternative to Violence.* (Philadelphia: AFSC, 1955).

_____. *Uncommon Controversy: Fishing Rights of the Muckleshoot, Puyallup, and Nisqually Indians.* (Seattle: University of Washington Press, 1970).

_____. *To See What Love Can Do.* (Philadelphia: AFSC, 1967).

_____. *Who Shall Live: Man's Control over Birth and Death.* (New York: Hill & Wang, 1970).

Brinton, Anna Cox (ed.). *Then and Now: Quaker Essays, Historical and Contemporary by Friends of Henry Cadbury on his Completion of 22 Years as Chairman of AFSC.* (Plainview, NY: Books for Libraries, 1960).

Brinton, Howard. *Friends for 300 Years: The History and Beliefs of the Society of Friends Since George Fox Started the Quaker Movement.* (New York: Harper, 1952).

Cadbury, Henry. *Quakerism and Early Christianity.* (London: Allen & Unwin, 1957).

Democratizing the Workplace. (AFSC Working Paper, 1973).

Experiment Without Precedent: Some Quaker Observations on China Today. (AFSC Working Paper, 1972).

Forbes, John. *The Quaker Star Under Seven Flags, 1917-1927.* (Philadelphia: University of Pennsylvania Press, 1962).

Fox, George. *The Journal of George Fox.* (New York: Capricorn Books, 1963).

Greenberg, David F. *The Problem of Prisons.* (Philadelphia: AFSC, 1970).

Hinshaw, David. *Rufus Jones, Master Quaker.* (New York: G.P. Putnam & Sons, 1951).

Hirst, Margaret Esther. *The Quakers in Peace and War: An Account of Their Peace Principles and Practice.* (1923) (New York: Garland, 1971).

Jones, Gerald. *On Doing Good: The Quaker Experiment.* (New York: Scribners, 1971).

Jones, Marie Hoxie. *Swords Into Plowshares: An Account of the American Friends Service Committee, 1917-1937.* (New York: Macmillan Co., 1937).

Jones, Rufus M. *The Later Periods of Quakerism.* (London: Macmillan Co., 1921).

_____. *A Service of Love in War Time: American Friends Relief Work in Europe, 1917-1919.* (New York: Macmillan Co., 1920).

_____. *The Church, the Gospel, and War.* (1948) (New York: Garland, 1971).

Pickett, Clarence. *For More Than Bread: An Autobiographical Account of Twenty-Two Years Work with the American Friends Service Committee.* (Boston: Little, Brown & Co., 1953).

Seifert, Harvey J.D. "The Use by American Quakers of Nonviolent Resistance as a Method of Social Change." (Ph.D. dissertation, Boston University, 1940).

Sims, Nicholas A. *Disarmament: An Analysis for Quakers.* (London: Friends Peace and International Relations Committee, n.d.).

Thierman, Stephen. *Welcome to the World.* (San Francisco: AFSC, 1968).

Thomas, Trevor. *This Life We Take: A Case Against the Death Penalty.* (San Francisco: Friends Committee on Legislation, 1970).

Violence and Oppression: A Quaker Response. (London: Friends Peace and International Relations Committee, 1972).

West, Jessamyn (ed.). *The Quaker Reader.* (New York: Viking Press, 1962).

Wilson, E. Raymond. *Uphill for Peace: Quaker Impact on Congress.* (Richmond, IN: Friends United Press, 1975).

Witney, Norman. *Spectator Papers.* Edited by Adele Rickett. (Philadelphia: AFSC, 1971).

CIVIL RIGHTS

Aptheker, Herbert. *A Documentary History of the Negro People in the U.S.* (New York: Citadel Press, 1968).

Bell, Inge Powell. *CORE and the Strategy of Nonviolence.* (New York: Random House, 1968).

Brooks, Thomas R. *Walls Come Tumbling Down: A History of the Civil Rights Movement: 1940-1970.* (Englewood Cliffs, NJ: Prentice-Hall, 1974).

Conant, Ralph W. *The Prospects for Revolution: A Study of Riots, Civil Disobedience, and Insurrection in Contemporary America.* (New York: A Harper's Magazine Press Book, 1971).

Editors of *Ebony. Ebony Pictorial History of Black America.* (Chicago: Johnson Publishing Company, Inc., 1971).

Educational Book Publishers. *Afro-American Encyclopedia.* (North Miami, FL: Educational Book Publishers, 1974).

Fager, Charles. *Selma 1965: The Town Where the South Was Changed.* (New York: Scribner's, 1974).

Farmer, James. *Freedom, When?* (New York: Random House, 1966).

Forman, James. *Sammy Younge, Jr.: The First Black College Student to Die in the Black Liberation Movement.* (New York: Grove Press, Inc., 1968).

Franklin, John Hope. *From Slavery to Freedom: A History of Negro*

Americans. (New York: Alfred A. Knopf, 1974).

Freedman, Jill. *Old News: Resurrection City.* (New York: Grossman, 1970).

Grant, Joanne. *Black Protest.* (Greenwich, CT: Fawcett Publications, 1968).

Griffin, John Howard. *Black Like Me.* (Boston: Houghton Mifflin, 1962).

Hansberry, Lorraine. *The Movement: Documentary of a Struggle for Equality.* (New York: Simon & Schuster, 1964).

Houser, George M. *CORE: A Brief History.* (New York: CORE, 1949).

_____. *Erasing the Color Line.* (New York: Fellowship Publications, 1945).

_____ and Bayard Rustin. *We Challenged Jim Crow! A Report on the Journey of Reconciliation, April 9-23, 1947.* (New York: Fellowship of Reconciliation, 1947).

Kellogg, Charles Flint. *NAACP: A History of the National Association for the Advancement of Colored People.* (Baltimore: John Hopkins Press, 1967).

King, Martin Luther, Jr. *Where Do We Go From Here: Chaos or Community?* (New York: Bantam Books, 1967).

_____. *Why We Can't Wait.* (New York: A Signet Book, 1964).

_____. *Strength to Love.* (New York: Harper & Row, 1963).

_____. *The Trumpet of Conscience.* (New York: Harper & Row, 1967).

_____. *Stride Toward Freedom.* (New York: Harper & Brothers, 1958).

Lester, Julius. *Search for the New Land.* (New York: Dell Publ. Co., 1970).

Lewis, Anthony and the *New York Times. Portrait of a Decade: The Second American Revolution.* (New York: Bantam Books, 1971).

Lewis, David L. *King: A Critical Biography.* (New York: Praeger, 1970).

Lomax, Louis E. *The Negro Revolt.* (New York: A Signet Book, 1962).

Louis, Debbie. *And We Are Not Saved: A History of the Movement As People.* (New York: Doubleday, 1970).

Meier, August and Elliott Rudwick. *CORE: A Study in the Civil Rights Movement.* (New York: Oxford University Press, 1973).

Miller, William R. *Martin Luther King, Jr.: His Life, Martyrdom, and Meaning for the World.* (New York: Avon Books, 1968).

National Commission on the Causes and Prevention of Violence. *Violence in America.* (Washington DC: U.S. Government Printing Office, 1969).

New South: A Quarterly Review of Southern Affairs. (Atlanta: Southern Regional Council).

Peck, James. *Cracking the Color Line: Nonviolent Direct Action Methods of Eliminating Racial Discrimination.* (New York: CORE, 1962).

_____. *Freedom Ride.* (New York: Simon & Schuster, 1962).

Rustin, Bayard. *Down the Line.* (Chicago: Quadrangle Books, 1971).

_____. *Interracial Primer.* (New York: Fellowship of Reconciliation, 1943).

Schulke, Flip. *Martin Luther King, Jr. A Documentary . . . Montgomery to Memphis.* (New York: Norton, 1976).

Smith, Kenneth and Ira G. Zepp, Jr. *Search for the Beloved Community: The Thinking of Martin Luther King, Jr.* (Valley Forge, PA: Judson Press, 1974).

Student Nonviolent Coordinating Committee, San Francisco Office. *Key List Mailing: Selected Documents of Current and Lasting Interest in the Civil Rights Movement.* (Published biweekly by SNCC from 1965 to 1967).

Walton, Hanes. *The Political Philosophy of Martin Luther King, Jr.* Introduction by Samuel Du Bois Cook. (Westport, CT: Greenwood Publ. Corp., 1971).

Zinn, Howard. *SNCC: The New Abolitionists.* (Boston: Beacon Press, 1965).

THE UNITED FARM WORKERS UNION

Basta: The Tale of Our Struggle. Photos by George Ballis. (Delano, CA: Farm Worker Press, 1966).

Chavez, Cesar. "Letter from Delano." *Christian Century.* 86 (April 23, 1969), 539-540.

_____. "Nonviolence Still Works." *Look.* 33 (April 1, 1969), 52-57.

_____. "Nonviolence on the Line." Interview conducted by Jim Forest. *WIN.* IX, no. 25 (Sept. 6, 1973), 4-8.

Day, Mark. *Forty Acres: Cesar Chavez and the Farm Workers.* Introduction by Cesar Chavez. (New York: Praeger, 1971).

Dunne, John Gregory. *Delano: The Story of the California Grape Strike.* (New York: Farrar, Straus & Giroux, 1967).

Fusco, Paul and George D. Horowitz. *La Causa: The California Grape Strike.* (New York: Collier Books, 1970).

Galarza, Ernesto. *Merchants of Labor: The Mexican Bracero Story: An Account of the Managed Migration of Farm Workers in California, 1942-1960.* (Santa Barbara: McNally & Loftin, 1964).

_____. *Spiders in the House and Workers in the Field.* (South Bend, IN: University of Notre Dame Press, 1970).

Kushner, Sam. *Long Road to Delano.* (New York: International Publishers, 1974).

Levy, Jacques. *Cesar Chavez: Autobiography of La Causa.* (New York: W.W. Norton Co., 1975).

London, Joan and Henry Anderson. *So Shall Ye Reap.* (New York: Crowell, 1970).

McWilliams, Carey. *Factories in the Field: The Story of Migratory Farm Labor in California.* (Boston: Little, Brown and Co., 1939. Revised edition, Hamden, CT: Shoe String Press, 1969).

"March of the Migrants." *Life.* 60 (April 29, 1966), 93-94.

Matthiessen, Peter. *Sal Si Puedes: Cesar Chavez and the New American Revolution.* (New York: Random House, 1970).

Nelson, Eugene. *Huelga: The First Hundred Days of the Great Delano Grape Strike.* (Delano, CA: Farm Worker Press, 1966).

Taylor, Ronald B. *Sweatshops in the Sun.* (Boston: Beacon Press, 1973).

_____. *Chavez and the Farm Workers.* (Boston: Beacon Press, 1975).

THE PEACE MOVEMENT

American Friends Service Committee. *Peace in Vietnam: A New Approach in South East Asia.* (New York: Hill and Wang, 1966).

Baez, Joan. *Daybreak.* (New York: Dial Press, 1968).

Barger, Robert Newton. *Amnesty: What Does It Really Mean?* (Available from National Committee for Universal and Unconditional Amnesty, 339 Lafayette St., New York, NY 10012).

Berrigan, Daniel. *America is Hard to Find.* (Garden City, NY: Doubleday, 1972).

_____. *The Geography of Faith: Conversations Between Daniel Berrigan, When Underground, and Robert Coles.* (Boston: Beacon Press, 1971).

_____. *The Trial of the Catonsville Nine.* (Boston: Beacon Press, 1970).

_____. *Absurd Convictions, Modest Hopes: Conversations After Prison with Lee Lockwood.* (New York: Random House, 1972).

Berrigan, Philip. *Prison Journals of a Priest Revolutionary.* Compiled and edited by Vincent McGee. Introduction by Daniel Berrigan. (New York: Holt, Rinehart and Winston, 1970).

_____. *Widen the Prison Gates: Writings from Jails, April, 1970 – December, 1972.* (New York: Simon & Schuster, 1973).

CADRE (Chicago Area Draft Resistance). *A Prison Anthology.* (Available from the Fellowship of Reconciliation).

Calvert, Robert (ed.). *Ain't Gonna Pay for War No More.* (Kansas City: War Tax Resistance, 1971).

Central Committee for Conscientious Objectors. *The Non-Cooperator and the Draft.* (Philadelphia: CCCO, 1963).

Chomsky, Noam. *American Power and the New Mandarins.* (New York: Pantheon Books, 1969).

Daly, James and Lee Bergman. *A Hero's Welcome.* (Indianapolis. Bobbs-Merrill, 1975).

Dellinger, David. *More Power Than We Know: The People's Movement Toward Democracy.* (Garden City, NY: Anchor Press, 1975).

_____. *Contempt: Transcript of the Contempt Citations, Sentences and Responses of the Chicago Conspiracy 10.* (Chicago: Swallow Press, 1970).

_____. *Revolutionary Nonviolence.* (New York: Bobbs-Merrill, 1970).

Ellsberg, Daniel. *Papers on the War.* (New York: Simon & Schuster, 1972).

Erikson, Erik H. (ed.). *The Challenge of Youth.* (New York: Doubleday, 1965).

Feiffer, Jules. *Pictures at a Prosecution: Drawings and Text from the Chicago Conspiracy Trial.* (New York: Grove Press, 1971).

Ferber, Michael and Staughton Lynd. *The Resistance.* (Boston: Beacon Press, 1971).

Fitch, Bob. *My Eyes Have Seen.* (San Francisco: Glide Publications, 1971).

FitzGerald, Frances. *Fire in the Lake: The Vietnamese and the Americans in Vietnam.* (Boston: Little, Brown, 1972).

Front Lines: Soldiers' Writings From Vietnam. (Indochina Curriculum Group, 11 Garden St., Cambridge, MA 02138).

Galloway, K. Bruce and Robert Bowie Johnson. *West Point: America's Power Fraternity.* (New York: Simon & Schuster, 1973).

Gaylin, Willard. *In the Service of Their Country: War Resisters in Prison.* (New York: Viking Press, 1970).

Gettleman, Marvin E. (ed.). *Vietnam: History, Documents and Opinions on a Major World Crisis.* (Greenwich, CT: Fawcett Publ., 1965).

_____ and S.L. Silverman (Compilers). "Bookmarks: Vietnam Guide," *Nation.* 205 (Sept. 11, 1967), 215-217. Annotated list of 31 books on Vietnam.

Gold, Gerald, Allan M. Siegal and Samuel Abt (eds.). *Pentagon Papers.* (New York: Bantam Books, 1971).

Goodell, Charles. *Political Prisoners in America.* (New York: Random House, 1973).

Goodman, Mitchell. *The Movement Toward a New America.* (Philadelphia: Pilgrim Press, 1970).

Goodman, Paul. *Utopian Essays and Practical Proposals.* (New York: Random House, 1962).

_____. *Like a Conquered Province: The Moral Ambiguity of America.* (New York: Random House, 1967).

Gregory, Dick. *Write Me In.* Edited by James R. McGraw. (New York: Bantam Books, 1968).

Harris, David. *Goliath.* (New York: Richard W. Baron, 1970).

_____ and Joan Baez. Photos by Bob Fitch. *Coming Out.* (New York: Pocket Books, 1971).

Hassler, Alfred. *Saigon USA.* (New York: Richard Baron, 1970).

Helmer, John. *Bringing the War Home: The American Soldier in Vietnam and After.* (New York: Free Press, 1974).

Horowitz, David. *From Yalta to Vietnam: American Foreign Policy in the Cold War.* (Harmondsworth: Penguin, 1967).

Jacobs, Paul and Saul Landau. *The New Radicals.* (New York: Random House, 1966).

Karlin, Wayne et al (eds.). *Free Fire Zone: Short Stories by Vietnam Veterans.* (New York: McGraw, 1973).

Keniston, Kenneth. *Young Radicals: Notes on Committed Youth.* (New York: Harcourt, Brace & World, Inc., 1968).

Kerry, John and Members of Vietnam Veterans Against the War. *New Soldier.* (New York: MacMillan, 1971).

Lasch, Christopher. *The Agony of the American Left.* (New York: Random House, 1969).

Levine, Mark L., George C. McNamee and Daniel Greenberg (eds.). *The Tales of Hoffman.* Introduction by Dwight Macdonald. (New York: Bantam Books, 1970).

Liberation. "The American Resistance." 12 (Nov. 1967), entire.

_____. "Special Issue on A.J. Muste." (Sept.-Oct. 1967), entire.

Lifton, Robert Jay. *Home from the War: Vietnam Veterans, Neither Victims Nor Executioners.* (New York: Simon & Schuster, 1974).

Long, Priscilla (ed.). *The New Left: A Collection of Essays.* (Boston: Porter Sargent, 1969).

Lynd, Alice (ed.). *We Won't Go: Personal Accounts of War Objectors.* (Boston: Beacon, 1968).

McReynolds, Dave. *We Have Been Invaded by the 21st Century.* (New York: Praeger, 1970).

Mailer, Norman. *Armies of the Night.* (New York: New American Library, 1968).

_____. *Miami and the Siege of Chicago: An Informal History of the Republican and Democratic Conventions of 1968.* (New York: World Publishing Co., 1968).

Mantell, David Mark. *True Americanism: Green Berets and War Resisters: A Study of Commitment.* (Columbia, NY: Teachers College Press, 1974).

Middleton, Neil (ed.). *The I.F. Stone's Weekly Reader.* (New York: Random House, 1973).

Miller, David and Howard Levy. *Going to Jail: The Political Prisoner.* (New York: Grove Press, 1970).

Mungo, Raymond. *Famous Long Ago: My Life and Hard Times with Liberation News Service.* (Boston: Beacon Press, 1970).

Nhat-Hanh, Thich. *Vietnam: Lotus In a Sea of Fire.* Foreword by Thomas Merton and afterword by Alfred Hassler. (New York: Hill & Wang, 1967).

Oglesby, Carl and Richard Shaull. *Containment and Change.* (New York: Macmillan, 1967).

Peck, James. *Underdogs v. Upperdogs.* (Canterbury, NH: Greenleaf Books, 1969).

Prasad, Devi. *They Love It But Leave It.* (London: War Resisters International, 1971).

_____ and Tony Smythe (eds.). *Conscription: A World Survey: Compulsory Military Service and Resistance to It.* (London: War Resisters International, 1968).

Raskin, Marcus and Bernard Fall (eds.). *Vietnam Reader: Articles and Documents.* (New York: Vintage, 1967).

Roszak, Theodore. *The Making of a Counter Culture: Reflections on the Technocratic Society and Its Youthful Opposition.* (Garden City, NY: Doubleday, 1969).

Rottman, Larry, Jan Barry and Basil T. Paquet (eds.). *Winning Hearts and Minds: War Poems by Vietnam Veterans.* (First Casualty Press).

Russell, Bertrand and Russell Stetler. *War and Atrocity in Vietnam.* (London: Bertrand Russell Peace Foundation, 1964).

Sale, Kirkpatrick. *SDS: Ten Years Toward a Revolution.* (New York: Random House, 1973).

Scott, Peter Dale. *The War Conspiracy.* (New York: Bobbs-Merrill, 1972).

Stone, I.F. *The Killings at Kent State.* Including Justice Department secret summary of FBI findings. (New York: New York Review, Dist. by Vintage, 1971).

_____. *Polemics and Prophecies, 1967-1970.* (New York: Random House, 1970).

Teodori, Massimo (ed.). *The New Left: A Documentary History.* (New York: Bobbs-Merrill, 1969).

Useem, Michael. *Conscription, Protest and Social Conflict: The Life and Death of a Draft Resistance Movement.* (New York: John Wiley & Sons, 1973).

Wirmark, Bo. *The Buddhists in Vietnam.* (Available from the Fellowship of Reconciliation).

Woito, Robert. *Vietnam Peace Proposals.* (Berkeley, CA: World Without War Council, 1967).

Zahn, Gordon C. *War, Conscience and Dissent.* (New York: Hawthorn Books, 1967).

Zinn, Howard. *Vietnam: The Logic of Withdrawal.* (Boston: Beacon Press, 1967).

BIBLIOGRAPHIES

(In addition to the topics noted, these bibliographies contain sections on Gandhi; international relations, including world law; religious treatments and histories; and anti-militarism, including conscientious objection and draft resistance.)

Carter, April, David Hoggett and Adam Roberts. *Nonviolent Action: A Selected Bibliography.* (London: Housmans, 1970). Listings of resistance movements involving use of nonviolent action; aspects of nonviolent social order.

Cook, Blanche Wiesen (ed.). *Bibliography of Peace Research in History.* Bibliography and Reference Series, no. 11. (Santa Barbara, CA: American Bibliographical Center Clio Press, 1969). Listings include bibliographical aids and organizations providing material for the peace researcher; histories of peace organizations; autobiographies, memoirs and biographical studies of leaders.

Hoggett, David. *Nonviolence and Peacemaking.* (Cheltenham, Glos., England: Commonweal Trust, 1963).

Hyatt, John. *Pacifism: A Selected Bibliography.* (London: Housmans, 1972).

Lakey. George. *Exploring Nonviolent Action: A Guide to Research.* (London: Housmans, 1970).

Miller, William Robert. *Bibliography of Books on War, Pacifism, Nonviolence and Related Studies.* (Nyack, NY: Fellowship, 1965). The related studies section is extensive.

Nonviolence: An Annotated Bibliography. Cornell University Libraries Bibliography Series, no. 4, 1971. Listings include works on training for nonviolent action; the tradition of nonviolence in America; the Civil Rights Movement.

Pickus, Robert and Robert Woito. *To End War: An Introduction; Ideas, Books, Organizations, Work That Can Help.* (New York: Harper and Row, 1970). Probably the best overall bibliography; carefully annotated and currently being revised.

Weaver, Anthony. *Committee of 100: Schools for Nonviolence.* (London: Committee of 100, 1961). Listings include works on industrial action and the economics of disarmament.

HISTORIES

Allen, Devere. *The Fight for Peace.* (New York: Macmillan Co., 1930).

Brock, Peter. *Pacifism in the United States: From the Colonial Era to the First World War.* (Princeton, NJ: Princeton University Press, 1968).

_____. *Twentieth Century Pacifism.* (New York: Van Nostrand Reinhold Co., 1970).

Chatfield, Charles. *For Peace and Justice: Pacifism in America 1914-1941.* (Knoxville, TN: University of Tennessee Press, 1971).

_____. *Peace Movements in America.* (New York: Schocken Books, 1973).

Curti, Merle. *Peace or War: The American Struggle, 1636-1936.* (New York: W.W. Norton & Co., 1936).

_____. *The American Peace Crusade: 1815-1860.* (Durham, NC: Duke University Press, 1929).

Hughan, Jessie Wallace. *Three Decades of War Resistance.* (New York: War Resisters League, 1942).

Wittner, Lawrence. *Rebels Against War: The American Peace Movement, 1941-1960.* (New York: Columbia University Press, 1969).

ANTHOLOGIES

Allen, Devere (ed.). *Pacifism in the Modern World.* (New York: Doubleday, Doran & Co., 1929). Essays by leading liberals who addressed themselves to nonviolent forms of social change.

Estey, George and Doris Hunter. *Nonviolence: A Reader in the Ethics of Action.* (Xerox College Publishing, 1971). Readings from ancient to modern.

Finn, James (ed.). *Protest: Pacifism and Politics.* (New York: Random House, 1968). Interviews with 38 leading nonviolent activists.

Freeman, Harrop (ed.). *Peace Is the Victory.* (New York: Harper, 1944). Essays by John Haynes Holmes, A.J. Muste, Clarence Pickett and others.

Goodman, Paul (ed.). *Seeds of Liberation.* (New York: George Braziller, 1964). Nonviolent technique and theory are discussed in articles from *Liberation* magazine.

Guinan, Edward (ed.). *Peace and Nonviolence.* (Paramus, NJ: Paulist-Newman Press, 1973). Basic writings from a religious perspective.

Hare, A. Paul and Herbert H. Blumberg (eds.). *Nonviolent Direct Action, American Cases: Social-Psychological Analyses.* (Washington DC: Corpus Books, 1968). Social-psychological analyses and first person accounts.

Hunter, Allan A. (ed.). *Courage in Both Hands.* (New York: Ballantine, 1962). Fifty-six incidents in which nonviolence was used.

Lynd, Staughton (ed.). *Nonviolence in America: A Documentary History.* (Indianapolis: Bobbs-Merrill, 1966). Selections from colonial writers to recent civil rights and anti-war activists.

Mayer, Peter (ed.). *The Pacifist Conscience.* (Chicago: Henry Regnery Co., 1967). Selections from ancient to contemporary.

Miller, William Robert (ed.). *Nonviolence: A Christian Interpretation.* (New York: Schocken Books, 1966). History, politics, theory and cases, emphasizing religious basis for nonviolence.

Schlissel, Lillian (ed.). *Conscience in America: A Documentary History of Conscientious Objection in America, 1757-1967.* (New York: Dutton & Co., Inc., 1968). Legal documents, diary excerpts and statements by conscientious objectors.

Sibley, Mulford Q. (ed.). *The Quiet Battle: Writings on the Theory and Practice of Nonviolent Resistance.* (New York: Beacon Press, 1968). Pacifist writings throughout history arranged in such a way as to suggest the increasingly self-conscious and political use of nonviolent action.

Weinberg, Arthur and Lila Weinberg (eds.). *Instead of Violence: Writings by the Great Advocates of Peace and Nonviolence Throughout History.* (New York: Grossman Publishers, 1963). While some selections touch on nonviolence, most of these short pieces are anti-war with a humanistic emphasis.

GANDHI

Ashe, Geoffrey. *Gandhi.* (New York: Stein and Day, 1968).

Black, Jo Ann, Nick Harvey and Laurel Robertson. *Gandhi The Man.* (San Francisco: Glide Publ., 1973).

Chatfield, Charles (ed.). *The Americanization of Gandhi.* (New York: Garland, 1971).

Datta, Dhirendra Moham. *The Philosophy of Mahatma Gandhi.* (Madison: University of Wisconsin Press, 1961).

Erikson, Erik. *Gandhi's Truth: On the Origins of Militant Nonviolence.* (New York: W.W. Norton & Co., 1969).

Fischer, Louis. *The Life of Mahatma Gandhi.* (New York: Harper, 1950).

_____. *Gandhi and Stalin: Two Signs at the World's Crossroads.* (New York: Harper, 1947).

Fülöp-Miller, René. *Lenin and Gandhi.* (1927) (New York: Garland, 1971).

Gandhi, Mohandas K. *Gandhi on Nonviolence.* Introduction by Thomas Merton. (New York: New Directions, 1965).

_____. *All Men Are Brothers.* (Paris: UNESCO, 1958).

_____. *Nonviolent Resistance (Satyagraha).* (New York: Schocken Books, 1963).

_____. *Gandhi, An Autobiography: The Story of My Experiments with Truth.* Translated by Mahadev Desai. (Boston: Beacon Press, 1970).

_____. *Constructive Programme: Its Meaning and Place.* (Ahmedabad: Navajivan Publ., 1945).

Homer, A. (ed.). *The Gandhi Reader: A Sourcebook of His Life and Writings.* (Bloomington, IN: Indiana University Press, 1956).

Horsburgh, H.J.M. *Nonviolence and Aggression: A Study of Gandhi's Moral Equivalent of War.* (New York: Oxford University Press, 1968).

Iyer, Raghavan. *The Moral and Political Thought of Mahatma Gandhi.* (New York: Oxford University Press, 1973).

Kumar, Satish. *Non-Violence or Non-Existence.* (London: Christian Action, n.d.).

Mashruwala, K.G. *Gandhi and Marx.* (Canterbury, NH: Greenleaf Publications, 1951).

Orwell, George. "Reflections on Gandhi," *A Collection of Essays.* (Garden City, NY: Doubleday, 1954).

Ostergaard, Geoffrey and Melville Currell. *Gentle Anarchists: A Study of the Leaders of the Sarvodaya Movement for Nonviolent Revolution in India.* (Oxford: Clarendon Press, 1971).

Ramachandran, G. and T.K. Mahadevan (eds.). *Gandhi: His Relevance To Our Times.* (Berkeley, CA: World Without War Council, 1971).

Shridharani, Krishnalal. *War Without Violence: A Study of Gandhi's Methods and Its Accomplishments.* (New York: Harcourt, Brace & Co., 1939).

NONVIOLENT ACTION

(See also Anthologies)

Boserup, Anders and Andrew Mack. *War Without Weapons: Nonviolence in National Defense.* (New York: Schocken, 1975).

Carter, April. *Direct Action.* (London: *Peace News* Pamphlet, 1962).

Friends Peace Committee. *A Perspective on Nonviolence.* (Philadelphia: Friends Peace Committee, 1957).

_____. *Public Witness.* (Philadelphia: Friends Peace Committee, 1962).

Gregg, Richard. *The Power of Nonviolence.* (Philadelphia: J.B. Lippincott Co., 1934).

_____. *Training for Peace: A Program for Peace Workers.* (Philadelphia: J.B. Lippincott Co., 1937).

_____. *The Value of Voluntary Simplicity.* (Wallingford, PA: Pendle Hill, 1936).

_____. *A Discipline for Nonviolence.* (Philadelphia: Pendle Hill, n.d.).

_____. *What's It All About and What Am I?* (New York: Grossman, 1968).

James, William. *The Moral Equivalent of War.* (London: Peace News, 1963).

Lakey, George. *Strategy for a Living Revolution.* (New York: Grossman Publishers, 1973).

Lyttle, Bradford. *National Defense Through Nonviolent Resistance.* (Chicago: Author, 1958).

McKay, Bidge. *Training for Nonviolent Action for High School Students.* (Philadelphia: Friends Peace Committee, 1971).

Madden, E.H. *Civil Disobedience and Moral Law in 19th Century American Philosophy.* (Seattle: University of Washington Press, 1968).

Noell, Chuck and Bob Levering. *Crisis: Nonviolent Direct Action as a Strategy for Social Change.* (Available from the War Resisters League.)

Olson, Theodore and Lynne Shivers. *Training for Nonviolent Action.* (Available from the War Resisters League.)

Oppenheimer, Martin and George Lakey. *A Manual for Direct Action.* (Chicago: Quadrangle Books, 1965).

Quaker Action Group. *Resistance in Latin America: The Pentagon, Its Oligarchies, and Nonviolent Action.* (Philadelphia: American Friends Service Committee, 1970).

Roberts, Adam (ed.). *Civilian Resistance as a National Defense.* (Harrisburg, PA: Stackpole Books, 1968).

Sharp, Gene. *Nonviolent Action.* (London: Friends Peace Committee, 1963).

_____. *The Politics of Nonviolent Action.* (Boston: Porter Sargent, 1973).

_____. *Exploring Nonviolent Alternatives.* (Boston: Porter Sargent, 1971).

Walker, Charles C. *Organizing for Nonviolent Direct Action.* (Cheney, PA: Author, 1961).

War Resisters International. *Training in Nonviolence: A Full Documentation of the WRI Study Conference, 1966.* (Available from War Resisters International).

Zietlow, Carl. *Nonviolent Strategy Manual.* (Available from Fellowship of Reconciliation).

NONVIOLENT THEORY

(See also Anthologies)

American Friends Service Committee. *Speak Truth to Power: A Quaker Search for an Alternative to Violence.* (Philadelphia: AFSC, 1955).

_____. *In Place of War.* (New York: Grossman, 1967).

Arendt, Hannah. *On Violence.* (New York: Harcourt, Brace & World, 1970).

Bainton, Roland. *Christian Attitudes Toward War and Peace: A Historical Survey and Critical Re-Evaluation.* (New York: Abingdon Press, 1960).

Bedau, Hugo (ed.). *Civil Disobedience: Theory and Practice.* (New York: Pegasus, 1969).

Bloomfield, Lincoln P. *The Power to Keep Peace.* (Berkeley, CA: World Without War Council, 1971).

Bondurant, Joan V. *Conquest of Violence: The Gandhian Philosophy of Conflict.* (Princeton: Princeton University Press, 1958).

_____ and Margaret Fisher (eds.). *Conflict, Violence and Nonviolence.* (Chicago: Aldine-Atherton, Inc., 1971).

Buhner, John Collin. "The Political Theory of Nonviolence." (Ph.D. dissertation, University of Wisconsin, 1963).

Camus, Albert. *Neither Victims Nor Executioners.* Translated by Dwight Macdonald. (New York: Liberation, 1960).

Case, Clarence Marsh. *Nonviolent Coercion.* (New York: Century, 1923) and (New York: Garland, 1971).

Cohen, Carl. *Civil Disobedience: Conscience, Tactics and the Law.* (New York: Columbia University Press, 1971).

Dalmolen, Albert. "War, Peace and Pacifist Thought: A Critical Analysis of A.J. Muste and Aldous Huxley." (Ph.D. dissertation, American University, 1972).

deLigt, Barthelemy. *The Conquest of Violence: An Essay on War and Revolution.* (New York: E.P. Dutton, 1938) and (New York: Garland, 1971).

Dellinger, David. *Revolutionary Nonviolence.* (Indianapolis: Bobbs-Merrill Co., 1970).

del Vasto, Lanza. *Return to the Source.* (New York: Schocken, 1972).

_____. *Principles and Precepts of the Return to the Obvious.* (New York: Schocken, 1974).

_____. *Gandhi to Vinoba: The New Pilgrimage.* (New York: Schocken, 1974).

_____. *Warriors of Peace: Writings on the Technique of Nonviolence.* (New York: Alfred A. Knopf, 1974).

_____. *Make Straight the Way of the Lord.* (New York: Knopf, 1974).

Deming, Barbara. *Revolution and Equilibrium.* (New York: Grossman, 1971).

Douglass, Jim. *The Nonviolent Cross: A Theology of Religion and Peace.* (New York: Macmillan, 1968).

_____. *Resistance and Contemplation: The Way of Liberation.* (Garden City, NY: Doubleday, 1972).

Duvakar, R.R. *Satyagraha.* (Chicago: Regnery, 1948).

Ellul, Jacques. *Violence: Reflections from a Christian Perspective.* Translated by Cecelia Gaul Kings. (New York: Seabury, 1969).

Freeman, Harrop A., Bayard Rustin, et al. *Civil Disobedience.* (Santa Barbara, CA: Center for the Study of Democratic Institutions, 1966).

Goodwin, Robert A. (ed.). *On Civil Disobedience: Essays Old and New.* (Chicago: Rand McNally & Co., 1969).

Gregg, Richard. *The Power of Nonviolence.* (Nyack, NY: Fellowship of Reconciliation, 1959).

Gunn, John. *Violence.* (New York: Praeger, 1973).

Harvey, Arthur. *Theory and Practice of Civil Disobedience.* (Canterbury, NH: Greenleaf Books, 1961).

Hentoff, Nat (ed.). *The Essays of A.J. Muste.* (Indianapolis: Bobbs-Merrill, 1967).

Hoblitzelle, Harrison. "The War Against War in the Nineteenth Century: A Study of the Western Background of Gandhian Thought." (Ph.D. dissertation, Columbia University, 1959).

Howard, Michael. *Studies in War and Peace.* (New York: Viking Press, 1971).

Huxley, Aldous. *Ends and Means: An Enquiry into the Nature of Ideals and into the Methods Employed for their Realization.* (New York: Macmillan, 1968).

Kraus, Karl. *The Last Days of Mankind.* Translated by Alexander Gode and Sue E. Wright. (New York: Ungar, 1975).

Macgregor, G.H.C. *The New Testament Basis of Pacifism.* (Nyack, NY: Fellowship Publ., 1936).

Marrin, A. (ed.). *War and the Christian Conscience: From Augustine to Martin Luther King, Jr.* (Chicago: Regnery, 1971).

Morgan, Arthur. *Search for Purpose.* (Yellow Springs, OH: Antioch, 1955).

Murphy, Jeffrie G. (ed.). *Civil Disobedience and Violence.* (Belmont, CA: Wadsworth Publishing Co., 1971).

Naess, Arne. *Gandhi and the Nuclear Age.* (Totowa, NJ: Bedminster

Press, 1965).

Olson, Theodore. "Forcing Social Change: Gandhi and Guevara." no. 4 Monograph Series, Nonviolent Action Research Project of the Center for Nonviolent Conflict Resolution, Haverford College, Haverford, PA.

Paullin, Theodore. *Introduction to Nonviolence*. (Philadelphia: Pacifist Research Bureau, 1944).

Pelton, Leroy H. *The Psychology of Nonviolence*. (Elmsford, NY: Pergamon Press, 1975).

Sampson, Ronald Victor. *The Psychology of Power*. (New York: Pantheon Books, 1966).

Seifert, Harvey. *Conquest by Suffering: The Process and Prospects of Nonviolent Resistance*. (Philadelphia: Westminster Press, 1965).

Sibley, Mulford Q. *The Political Theories of Modern Pacifism*. (Philadelphia: Pacifist Research Bureau, 1944).

Stanage, S.M. *Reason and Violence*. (Totowa, NJ: Littlefield, Addams, & Co., 1974).

Swomley, John. *Liberation Ethics*. (New York: Macmillan, 1972).

Templin, Ralph. *Democracy and Nonviolence*. (Boston: Porter Sargent, 1965).

Thoreau, Henry David. "Civil Disobedience," *Walden and Other Writings*. (New York: Modern Library, 1950). Also other editions.

Tolstoy, Leo. *The Kingdom of God is Within You and Peace Essays*. (London: Oxford University Press, 1936).

_____. *The Law of Love and the Law of Violence*. (New York: Rudolf Field, 1948).

_____. *Tolstoy's Writings on Civil Disobedience and Nonviolence*. (New York: Bergman Publishers, 1967).

Walzer, Michael. *Obligations: Essays on Disobedience, War and Citizenship*. (New York: Simon and Schuster, 1970).

Waskow, Arthur I. *From Race Riot to Sit-In, 1919 and the 1960's*. (Garden City, NY: Doubleday & Co., 1967).

Wertham, Frederic. *A Sign for Cain: An Exploration of Human Violence*. (New York: Doubleday & Co., 1967).

Zinn, Howard. *Disobedience and Democracy: Nine Fallacies on Law and Order*. (New York: Random House, 1968).

Zwisohn, Van, Jim Forest and David McReynolds. *1776 or 1984*. (New York: War Resisters League, 1975).

TOWARDS A NONVIOLENT SOCIAL THEORY

Adams, Frank with Myles Horton. *Unearthing Seeds of Fire*. (John F. Blair Publ. 1406 Plaza Dr., Winston-Salem, NC 27103).

Aronowitz, Stanley. *False Promises: The Shaping of American Working Class Consciousness*. (New York: McGraw Hill, 1974).

Artin, Tom. *Earth Talk: Independent Voices on the Environment*. (New York: Grossman, 1973).

Atkinson, Ti-Grace. *Amazon Odyssey*. (New York: WIN Books, 1975).

Beauvoir, Simone de. *The Second Sex*. Translated by H.M. Parshley. (New York: Knopf, 1953).

Benello, George C. and Dimitrios Roussopoulos (eds.). *The Case for Participatory Democracy: Some Prospects for a Radical Society*. (New York: Grossmans, 1971).

Bernikow, Louise. *The World Split Open – Four Centuries of Women Poets in England and America*. (New York: Vintage, 1974).

Berry, Wendell. *A Continuous Harmony: Essays Cultural and Agricultural*. (New York: Harcourt, Brace & Jovanovich, 1972).

_____. *Long Legged House*. (New York: Harcourt, Brace & World, 1969).

Bhave, Vinoba. *Swarajya Sastra: The Principles of Nonviolent Political Order*. Translated by Bharatan Kumarappa. (Bombay: Padma, 1945).

_____. *School of Nonviolence*. (London: Housmans, 1969).

_____. *Revolutionary Sarvodaya: Philosophy for the Remaking of Man*. (Bombay: Bharatiza Vidya Bhavan, 1964).

Black Elk (Oglala) as told through John G. Neihardt. *Black Elk Speaks*. (Lincoln, NB: University of Nebraska Press, 1961).

Blum, Fred H. *Work and Community*. (London: Routledge and Kegan Paul, 1968).

Blumberg, Paul. *Industrial Democracy: The Sociology of Participation*. (New York: Schocken, 1974).

Bookchin, Murray. *Post-Scarcity Anarchism*. (Berkeley, CA: Ramparts Press, 1971).

_____. *The Limits of the City*. (New York: Harper & Row, 1974).

_____. *Our Synthetic Environment*. (New York: Knopf, 1962).

Borsodi, Ralph. *Education and Living*. (Melbourne, FL: Melbourne University Press, 1948).

_____. *Flight from the City: An Experiment in Creative Living on the Land*. (New York: Harper Colophon Books, 1972).

_____. *Seventeen Problems of Man and Society*. (Anand: Charotar Book Stall, 1968).

Boulding, Kenneth E. *Beyond Economics*. (Ann Arbor: University of Michigan, Ann Arbor Paperbacks, 1970).

_____ (ed.). *Peace and the War Industry*. (New York: Transaction, 1970).

Brown, J.A.C. *The Social Psychology of Industry*. (New York: Pelican).

Buber, Martin. *Paths in Utopia*. Translated by R.F.C. Hull. (New York: Macmillan, 1950).

Calverton, Victor. *Where Angels Dared to Tread*. (Freeport, NY: Books for Libraries Press, 1969).

Camara, Helder. *The Desert Is Fertile*. Translated by Dinah Livingstone. (Maryknoll, NY: Orbis Books, 1974).

_____. *Spiral of Violence*. Translated by Della Couling. (London: Sheed and Ward, 1971).

_____. *Revolution Through Peace*. (New York: Harper Row, 1972).

Carnoy, Martin. *Education as Cultural Imperialism*. (New York: McKay, 1974).

Carter, April. *Direct Action and Liberal Democracy*. (London: Routledge & K. Paul, 1973).

The Case Against Capital Punishment. (Washington, DC: Washington Research Project, 1971).

Coates, Ken and Wyn Williams. *How and Why Industry Must Be Democratised*. (Nottingham: Institute for Workers Control, 1969).

Cohen, Benjamin J. *The Question of Imperialism: The Political Economy of Dominance and Dependence*. (New York: Basic Books, 1973).

Cohn-Bendit, Daniel and Gabriel Cohn-Bendit. *Obsolete Communism*. Translated by Arnold Pomerans. (New York: McGraw-Hill, 1968).

Comfort, Alex. *Authority and Delinquency in the Modern State: A Criminological Approach to the Problems of Power*. (London: Routledge and Kegan Paul, 1950).

Comstock, Margaret. *Building Blocks for Peace*. (Philadelphia: Jane Addams Peace Assn., 1973). Peace curricula.

Cordova, Jeanne. *Sexism: It's A Nasty Affair*. (New Way Books, 5850 Hollywood Blvd., Hollywood, CA 90038).

Council on Interracial Books for Children. *Chronicles of American Indian Protest*. (Greenwich, CT: Fawcett Publ., 1971).

Daly, Mary. *Beyond God the Father: Toward a Philosophy of Women's Liberation*. (Boston: Beacon Press, 1973).

Danforth, Art. *Cooperatives: Direct Economic Action*. (Ann Arbor: American Student Cooperative Organization, 1971).

Davis, Elizabeth Gould. *The First Sex*. (New York: Penguin, 1972).

Deloria, Vine. *We Talk, You Listen: New Tribes, New Turf*. (New York: Macmillan, 1970).

_____. *Behind the Trail of Broken Treaties: An Indian Declaration of Independence*. (New York: Delta, 1974).

_____. *Custer Died for Your Sins: An Indian Manifesto*. (New York: Macmillan, 1969).

Deming, Barbara. *We Cannot Live Without Our Lives*. (New York: Grossman, 1974).

Dennison, George. *Lives of Children*. (New York: Random House, 1969).

Dolci, Danilo. *The Man Who Plays Alone*. (New York: Pantheon, 1968).

_____. *A New World in the Making*. (London: Macgibbon & Kee, 1965).

_____. *Poverty in Sicily*. (London: Macgibbon & Kee, 1959).

_____. *Report from Palermo*. (n.p.: Orion Press, 1959).

_____. *The Outlaws of Partinico*. (London: Macgibbon & Kee, 1960).

Dolgoff, Sam (ed.). *The Anarchist Collectives*. (New York: Free Life Editions, 1974).

Domhoff, William. *Who Rules America*. (Englewood Cliffs, NJ: Prentice Hall, 1967).

_____. *The Bohemian Grove and Other Retreats: A Study in Ruling Class Cohesiveness*. (New York: Harper-Row, 1975).

Duberman, Martin. *Black Mountain: An Exploration in Community*. (New York: Dutton, 1972).

Dworkin, Andrea. *Woman Hating*. (New York: E.P. Dutton, 1974).

Ferguson, Charles Wright. *The Male Attitude*. (Boston: Little, Brown, 1966).

Firestone, Schulameth. *Dialectic of Sex: The Case for Feminist Revolution*. (New York: W. Morrow, 1970).

Freire, Paolo. *Pedagogy of the Oppressed*. Translated by Myra Bergman Ramos. (New York: Herder and Herder, 1970).

Fritz, Leah. *Thinking Like A Woman*. Afterword by Barbara Deming. (New York: WIN Books, 1976).

Garson, Barbara. *All the Livelong Day: The Meaning and Demeaning of Routine Work*. (New York: Doubleday, 1975).

Georgakas, Dan and Marvin Surkin. *Detroit: I Do Mind Dying*. (New York: St. Martin's Press, 1975).

George, Henry. *Progress and Poverty*. (New York: Robert Schalkenbach Foundation, 1966).

_____. *Social Problems*. (New York: Robert Schalkenbach Foundation, 1963).

Goldsmith, Edward G. *Blueprint for Survival*. (Boston: Houghton Mifflin, 1972).

Goldstein, Herb. *A Compendium of Legal Documents Relating to Land Trusts*. (Available from Author, Downhill Farm, Rt. 1, Box 177, Hancock, MD 21750).

Goodman, Paul. *Drawing the Line*. (New York: Random House, 1962).

_____. *Growing Up Absurd: Problems of Youth in the Organized System*. (New York: Random House, 1960).

_____. *People or Personnel: Decentralizing and the Mixed System*. (New York: Random House, 1965).

_____ and Percival Goodman. *Communitas*. (New York: Vintage Books, 1960).

Gowan, Susan, George Lakey, William Moyer and Richard Taylor. *Moving Toward a New Society*. (Philadelphia: New Society Press, 1976).

Greer, Germaine. *The Female Eunuch*. (New York: McGraw-Hill, 1971).

Hauser, Richard and Hephzibah Hauser. *The Fraternal Society*. (New York: Random House, 1963).

Heilbrun, Carolyn. *Toward a Recognition of Androgyny*. (New York: Knopf, 1973).

Hirsch, Sherry et al (eds.). *Madness Network News Reader*. (San Francisco: Glide Publications, 1974). (Available from Network Against Psychiatric Assault, 2150 Market St., San Francisco, CA 94114).

Holt, John. *How Children Fail*. (New York: Pitman, 1964).

Horkheimer, Max and Theodor W. Adorno. *Dialectic of Enlightenment*. (New York: Herder and Herder, 1972).

Illich, Ivan. *Energy and Equity*. (New York: Harper & Row, 1974).

_____. *Tools for Conviviality*. (New York: Harper & Row, 1973).

_____. *Deschooling Society*. (New York: Harper & Row, 1971).

Infield, Henrik F. *The American Intentional Communities*. (Glen Gardner, NJ: Community Press, 1955).

International Independence Institute. *Community Land Trust: A Guide to a New Model for Land Tenure in America*. (Cambridge: Community for Community Economic Development, 1972).

Jenkins, David. *Job Power: Blue and White Collar Democracy*. (Garden City, NY: Doubleday, 1973).

Jensen, Oliver. *The Revolt of the American Women*. (New York: Harcourt, Brace, Jovanovich, 1971).

Jerome, Judson. *Families of Eden: Communes and the New Anarchism*. (New York: Seabury, 1974).

Kagawa, Toyohiko. *Brotherhood Economics*. (Ann Arbor: North American Student Cooperative Organization, 1971).

Kagan, Paul. *New World Utopias: A Photographic History of the Search for Community*. (New York: Penguin, 1975).

Kanter, Rosabeth Moss. *Communes: Creating and Managing the Collective Life*. (New York: Harper, 1973).

_____. *Commitment and Community: Communes and Utopias in Sociological Perspective*. (Cambridge: Harvard University Press, 1972).

Knapp, Joseph G. *The Rise of American Cooperative Enterprise 1620-1920*. (Danville, IL: Interstate Printers & Publishers, Inc. 1969).

_____. *The Advance of American Cooperative Enterprise 1920-1945*. (Danville, IL: Interstate Printers & Publishers, Inc., 1973).

Kohl, Herbert. *36 Children*. (New York: Signet Books, 1968).

_____. *Half the House*. (New York: Dutton, 1974).

Kohr, Leopold. *The Breakdown of Nations*. (New York: Rinehart, 1957).

Kotler, Milton. *Neighborhood Government: The Local Foundations of Political Life*. (New York: Bobbs-Merrill, 1969).

Kriyananda. *Cooperative Communities: How to Start Them and Why*. (Nevada City, CA: Ananda Publ., 1968).

Kropotkin, Peter. *Fields, Factories and Workshops*. (New York: G.P. Putnam's Sons, 1904).

_____. *Mutual Aid*. (New York: New York University Press, 1972) and (New York: Knopf, 1922).

Kumar, Satish. *School of Nonviolence*. (London: Housmans, 1969).

Lao Tzu. *The Way of Life*. Translated by Witter Byner. (New York: John Day, 1944).

Lappe, Frances Moore. *Diet for a Small Planet*. (New York: Ballantine, 1975).

Lee, Dorothy. *Freedom and Culture*. (Englewood Cliffs, NJ: Prentice Hall, 1959).

Lipsky, Michael. *Protest in City Politics: Rent Strikes, Housing and the Power of the Poor*. (Chicago: Rand McNally & Co., 1970).

McHarg, Ian. *Design with Nature*. (Garden City, NY: Natural History Press, 1969).

Macdonald, Dwight. *The Root is Man*. (Alhambra, CA: Cunningham Press, 1953).

Manas Editors. *The Manas Reader*. (New York: Grossman, 1971).

Mangione, Jerre. *A Passion for Sicilians: The World Around Danilo Dolci*. (New York: William Morrow, 1968).

Mayer, Milton. *If Men Were Angels*. (New York: Atheneum, 1972).

_____. *The Nature of the Beast*. Edited by W. Eric Gustafson. (Amherst, MA: University of Massachusetts Press, 1975).

Merton, Thomas. *Zen and the Bird of Appetite*. (New York: New Directions, 1968).

Millett, Kate. *Sexual Politics*. (Garden City, NY: Doubleday, 1970).

_____. *Flying*. (New York: Ballantine, 1974).

Mishan, Edward. *The Costs of Economic Growth*. (London: Staples, 1967).

Mitchell, Juliet. *Psychoanalysis and Feminism: Freud, Reich, Laing & Women*. (New York: Pantheon, 1974).

Mitford, Jessica. *Kind and Usual Punishment: The Prison Business*. (New York: Knopf, 1975).

Morgan, Arthur. *Nowhere was Somewhere: How History Makes Utopias and How Utopias Make History*. (Chapel Hill, NC: University of North Carolina, 1946).

_____. *The Long Road*. (Washington DC: National Home Library Foundation, 1936).

_____. *The Community of the Future and the Future of the Community*. (Yellow Springs, OH: Community Service, 1957).

_____. *Small Community Economics*. (New York: Fellowship Publ., 1943).

Morris, David and Karl Hess. *Neighborhood Power: The New Localism*. (Boston: Beacon Press, 1975).

Morris, William. *News From Nowhere*. (New York: Longmans, Green & Co., 1906).

Mumford, Lewis. *The Myth of the Machine/The Pentagon of Power*. (New York: Harcourt, Brace & World, 1974).

Murray, D. Stark. *Blueprint for Health: A Multinational Portrait of the Costs and Administration of Medical Care in the Public Interest*.

(New York: Schocken Books, 1974).

Narayan, Jayaprakash. *Socialism to Sarvodaya.* (Madras: Socialist Book Centre, 1956).

_____. *Socialism, Sarvodaya and Democracy.* Edited by Devi Prasad. (New York: Taplinger, 1964).

Nearing, Helen. *The Good Life Album of Helen and Scott Nearing.* (New York: Sunrise Books, E.P. Dutton, 1974).

_____ and Scott Nearing. *Living the Good Life: How to Live Sanely and Simply in a Troubled World.* (New York: Schocken Books, 1970).

Neill, A.S. *Summerhill.* Foreword by Erich Fromm. (New York: Hart Publ. Co., 1960).

Nordhoff, Charles. *The Communistic Societies of the United States.* (New York: Schocken Books, 1965).

Nyerere, Julius. *Ujamaa: Essays on Socialism.* (Dar es Salaam: Oxford University Press, 1968).

Osgood, R.E. and R.W. Tucker. *Force, Order and Justice.* (Baltimore: John Hopkins University Press, 1967).

Paley, Grace. *Enormous Changes at the Last Minute.* (New York: Farrar, Strauss and Giroux, 1974).

Papanek, Victor. *Design for the Real World: Human Ecology and Social Change.* Introduction by R. Buckminster Fuller. (New York: Pantheon Books, 1972).

The Peckham Experiment: A Study in the Living Structure of Society. (London: Pioneer Health Center, 1945).

Pleck, Joseph and Jack Sawyer (eds.). *Men and Masculinity.* (Englewood Cliffs, NJ: Prentice-Hall, 1974).

Prasad, Devi (ed.). *Gramdan: The Land Revolution of India.* (London: War Resisters International, n.d.).

Reed, Evelyn. *Woman's Evolution: From Matriarchal Clan to Patriarchal Family.* (New York: Pathfinder Press, 1975).

Revel, Jean-Francois. *Without Marx or Jesus: The New American Revolution has Begun.* (New York: Doubleday, 1971).

Rich, Adrienne. *Diving Into the Wreck.* (New York: Norton, 1973).

_____. *Poems: Selected and New, 1950-74.* (New York: Norton, 1975).

Richard, Jerry. *The Good Life.* (New York: New American Library, 1973).

Ronco, William. *Food Co-ops: An Alternative to Shopping in Supermarkets.* (Boston: Beacon Press, 1974).

Roszak, Theodore (ed.). *Sources: An Anthology of Contemporary Materials Useful for Preserving Personal Sanity While Braving the Great Technological Wilderness.* (New York: Harper & Row, 1972).

_____. *Where the Wasteland Ends: Politics and Transcendance in Postindustrial Society.* (Garden City, NY: Doubleday, 1972).

_____. *Unfinished Animal.* (New York: Harper Row, 1975).

Rowbotham, Shelia. *Woman's Consciousness, Man's World.* (Gretna, LA: Pelican, 1973).

_____. *Women Resistance and Revolution: A History of Women and Revolution in the Modern World.* (New York: Pantheon, 1973).

Sahlins, Marshall. *Stone-Age Economics.* (Chicago: Aldine, 1972).

Sampson, Anthony. *The Sovereign State of ITT.* (New York: Fawcett World, 1974).

Sandperl, Ira. *A Little Kinder.* (Palo Alto, CA: Science & Behavior Books, 1974).

Sanford, Nevitt and Craig Comstock (eds.). *Sanctions for Evil.* (San Francisco: Jossey-Bass, 1971).

Scheer, Robert. *America After Nixon.* (New York: McGraw, 1974).

Schonborn, Karl. *Dealing with Violence: Police and Other Peacekeepers.* (Springfield, IL: Charles C. Thomas Publ., 1975).

Schumacher, Ernst Friedrich. *Small is Beautiful: Economics as if People Mattered.* (New York: Harper & Row, 1973).

Seherak, Emil and Art Danforth. *Consumer Cooperation: The Heritage and the Dream.* (Palo Alto, CA: Consumers Cooperative Publishing Assn., n.d.).

Sennet, Richard. *The Uses of Disorder: Personal Identity and City Life.* (New York: Knopf, 1970).

Seymour, John and Sally Seymour. *Farming for Self Sufficiency: Independence on a Five Acre Farm.* (New York: Schocken, 1973).

Sherman, Susan. *With Anger/With Love.* (Amherst, MA: Mulch Press, 1974).

Smedley, Agnes. *Daughter of Earth.* (Old Westbury, NY: Feminist Press, 1973).

Smith, Eve. *Worker and Environment.* (South Island, BC, Canada: 1973).

Snyder, Gary. *Earth House Hold: Technical Notes and Queries to Fellow Dharma Revolutionaries.* (New York: New Directions, 1969).

_____. *Turtle Island.* (New York: New Directions, 1974).

Source Collective. *Organizing for Health Care.* (Boston: Beacon Press, 1974).

Spring, Joel. *A Primer of Libertarian Education.* (New York: Free Life Editions, 1975).

Swomley, John. *American Empire: The Political Ethics of Twentieth Century Conquest.* (New York: Macmillan, 1970).

Taylor, Richard K. *Economics and the Gospel.* (Philadelphia: United Church Press, 1973).

Tolley, Howard. *Children and War: Political Socialization to International Conflict.* (Columbia, NY: Teachers College Press, 1973).

Turner, John F. and Robert Fichter (eds.). *Freedom to Build: Dweller Control of the Housing Process.* (New York: Macmillan, 1972).

Van Dresser, Peter. *A Landscape for Humans: A Case Study of the Potentials for Ecologically Guided Development in an Uplands Region.* (Albuquerque: Biotechnic Press, 1972).

Veysey, Lawrence. *The Communal Experience: Anarchist and Mystic Counter Cultures in America.* (New York: Harper, 1973).

Ward, Colin. *Anarchy in Action.* (London: Allen & Unwin, 1973).

_____. *Tenants Take Over.* (London: Architectural Press, 1974).

Waters, Frank. *Book of the Hopi.* (New York: Viking Press, 1963).

Weil, Simone. *The Need for Roots.* (New York: Harper & Row, 1971).

Weissman, Steve and Members of Pacific Studies Center and the North American Congress on Latin America. *The Trojan Horse: A Radical Look at Foreign Aid.* (San Francisco: Ramparts Press, 1974).

Wertham, Fredric. *A Sign for Cain.* (New York: Macmillan, 1966).

Wilken, Folkert. *The Liberation of Work.* (New York: Roy Publ., 1969).

Williams, William Appleman. *Roots of the American Empire: A Study of the Growth and Shaping of a Social Consciousness in a Marketplace Society.* (New York: Random House, 1969).

Williams, William Carlos. *In the American Grain.* (New York: A&C Boni, 1925).

Wilson, Edmund. *To the Finland Station.* (Garden City, NY: Doubleday, 1940).

Woolf, Virginia. *Three Guineas.* (London: Hogarth Press, 1938).

_____. *A Room of One's Own.* (New York: Harcourt, Brace, Jovanovich, 1929).

Yee, Min S. *The Melancholy History of Soledad Prison: In Which Utopian Dream Turns Bedlam.* (New York: Harper's Magazine Press, 1973).

Young, Nigel. *On War, National Liberation and the State.* (Peace News pamphlet).

Zablocki, Benjamin. *The Joyful Community.* (New York: Penguin, 1971).

Zinn, Howard. *Justice in Everyday Life.* (New York: William Morrow, 1974).

NONVIOLENT ORGANIZATIONS IN THE UNITED STATES

The following groups are working toward substantive social change in the United States although they do not all have a mutual agreement about nonviolence. Generally, only the national (*) and regional offices of organizations are listed; we suggest that you contact one of these offices for the addresses of groups in your area. (They might also be able to provide leads to other local groups, ad hoc committees, etc.) Many of these organizations have newsletters and literature available and provide other services such as films, study groups, and speakers. Nearly all are supported by public contributions. If you send for literature, it would be good to enclose some money to help offset the costs of printing and postage. Following the group list is a list of current periodicals relating to nonviolence.

ALABAMA

AFSC
310 Sengstak St.
Mobile, AL 36603

ARIZONA

Arizonans for Peace
1414 S. McAllister
Tempe, AZ 85281

CALIFORNIA

* National WTR
3359 Canyon Crest Rd.
Altadena, CA 91001

Los Angeles WRL
3359 Canyon Crest Rd.
Altadena, CA 91001

Los Angeles WSP
5899 W. Pico Blvd.
Los Angeles, CA 90019

Ammon Hennacy
House (CW)
605 N. Cummings
Los Angeles, CA 90033

Another Mother for Peace
407 N. Maple Dr.
Beverly Hills, CA 90210

South Bay WSP
c/o Mollie Siegel
434 26th Place
Manhattan Beach, CA 90266

Los Angeles FOR
605 N. Marengo
Pasadena, CA 91101

AFSC
980 N. Fair Oaks
Pasadena, CA 91103

South California CALC
980 N. Fair Oaks
Pasadena, CA 91103

Inland FOR
2460 First Ave.
San Bernardino, CA 92405

Humanitas Foundation
892 Camino del Sur
Goleta, CA 93017

Santa Barbara WSP
Box 2103
Santa Barbara, CA 93102

War Tax Resistance
1836 N. Lincoln
Santa Maria, CA 93454

* United Farm Workers
Box 62
Keene, CA 93531

San Francisco WSP
50 Oak St.
San Francisco, CA 94102

WRL West
1380 Howard St., 2nd Floor
San Francisco, CA 94103

Martin de Porres
House (CW)
2826 23rd St.
San Francisco, CA 94110

Agape Foundatin
660 York St., #204
San Francisco, CA 94110

Episcopal Peace Fellowship
409 Clayton St.
San Francisco, CA 94117

Amnesty International
3618 Sacramento St.
San Francisco, CA 94118

AFSC
2160 Lake St.
San Francisco, CA 94121

CCCO
1251 Second Ave.
San Francisco, CA 94122

Mid-Peninsula
Nonviolent Library
667 Lytton
Palo Alto, CA 94302

Mt. Diablo Peace Center
1809 Sharpe Ave.
Walnut Creek, CA 94596

East Bay Women for Peace
2302 Ellsworth
Berkeley, CA 94704

World Without War Council
1730 Grove St.
Berkeley, CA 94709

Ecumenical Peace Institute
P.O. Box 9334
Berkeley, CA 94709

Greenpeace America
Box 476
Bolinas, CA 94924

Islandia, Inc. (WRL)
P.O. Box 1207
Felton, CA 95018

Resource Center
for Nonviolence
P.O. Box 2324
Santa Cruz, CA 95063

Bay Area FOR
160 S. 14th St.
San Jose, CA 95112

Catholic Worker House
201 N. 5th
San Jose, CA 95112

Modesto Peace Center
631 15th St.
P.O. Box 2124
Modesto, CA 95354

Casa de Vida
Catholic Worker Community
432 First St.
Eureka, CA 95501

Davis Women
for Peace (WSP)
c/o Judith Reynolds
813 Sycamore Lane
Davis, CA 95616

Friends Committee
on Legislation
1107 9th St.
Sacramento, CA 95814

Sacramento Peace Center
1021 R Street
Sacramento, CA 95814

COLORADO

Institute Mountain West
(MNS)
2096 Emerson St.
Denver, CO 80205

Denver CALC
935 Garfield
Denver, CO 80206

AFSC
1428 Lafayette St.
Denver, CO 80218

CCCO Rocky Mountain
Military Project
1764 Gilpin
Denver, CO 80218

Catholic Peace Center (CW)
508 El Paso
Colorado Springs, CO 80903

CONNECTICUT

New England Committee
for Nonviolent Action
RFD #1, Box 430
Voluntown, CT 06384

AFSC
Box 494
Voluntown, CT 06384

Promoting Enduring Peace
P.O. Box B 103
Woodmont, CT 06460

DELAWARE

Pacem in Terris (AFSC)
1106 N. Adams St.
Wilmington, DE 19801

DISTRICT OF COLUMBIA

* Friends Committee
on National Legislation
245 Second St., N.E.
Washington, DC 20002

Council for a Dept. of Peace
110 Maryland Ave., N.E.
Washington, DC 20002

Women Strike for Peace
120 Maryland Ave., N.E.
Washington, DC 20002

White House Daily Meeting
120 Maryland Ave., N.E.
Washington, DC 20002

* SANE
318 Massachusetts
Avenue N.E.
Washington, DC 20002

Ad Hoc Coalition
for a New Foreign Policy
110 Maryland Ave., N.E.
Washington, DC 20002

National Association
for the Advancement
of Colored People
422 First St., N.E.
Washington, DC 20003

Community for
Creative Nonviolence (CW)
1335 N St., N.W.
Washington, DC 20005

National Interreligious
Service Board for
Conscientious Objectors
550 Washington Bldg.
15th & New York Ave., N.W.
Washington, DC 20005

Greenpeace
#616 - 910 17th St.
Washington, DC 20006

World Peace Tax Fund
2111 Florida Ave., N.W.
Washington, DC 20008

Source Collective
Box 21066
Washington, DC 20009

AFSC
1822 R St., N.W.
Washington, DC 20009

Corporate Action
  Project (CALC)
1500 Farragut St.
Washington, DC 20011

Catholic Peace Fellowship
Emmaus House
3619 12th St., N.E.
Washington, DC 20017

WSP
2141 P St.
Washington, DC 20036

Cooperative League
  of the USA
1828 L St., N.W., Suite 1100
Washington, DC 20036

FLORIDA

Miami CALC
Temple Israel
137 N.E. 19th St.
Miami, FL 33132

Miami Peace Center (AFSC)
3005 Byrd Ave.
Coconut Grove, FL 33133

Cedar Bend Nursery (MNS)
Norma & Jim Payne
P.O. Box 212
State Rd. #595
Aripeka, FL 33502

Tampa Bay Area AFSC
5709 29th Ave. S.
St. Petersburg, FL 33707

GEORGIA

Southern Christian
  Leadership Conference
334 Auburn Ave., N.E.
Atlanta, GA 30303

CCCO
Suite 303
848 Peachtree N.E.
Atlanta, GA 30308

WRL/Southeast
Box 7477
Atlanta, GA 30309

King Center
  for Social Change
671 Beckwith St., S.W.
Atlanta, GA 30314

Koinonia Partners
Rt. 2
Americus, GA 31709

HAWAII

AFSC
2426 Oahu Ave.
Honolulu, HI 96822

Women for Peace
3645 Woodlawn Terrace
Honolulu, HI 96822

Hawaii WRL/Catholic Action
1918 University Ave.
Honolulu, HI 96822

ILLINOIS

North Shore CALC
810 Forest Ave.
Wilmette, IL 60091

DeKalb MNS
c/o DeKalb Learning
  Exchange
157½ E. Lincoln Highway
DeKalb, IL 60115

Brethren
  Service Commission
1451 Dundee Ave.
Elgin, IL 60120

North Shore CALC
828 Ingleside Place
Evanston, IL 60201

Northshore FOR
c/o George Hitt
1429 Washington St.
Evanston, IL 60202

Oak Park WRL
806 Carpenter
Oak Park, IL 60304

West Suburban FOR
3912 Woodland
Western Springs, IL 60558

World Without War Council
110 S. Dearborn St.
Chicago, IL 60603

Chicago Peace Council
524 S. Dearborn St.
Chicago, IL 60605

Nonviolent Training
  and Action Center
542 S. Dearborn
Chicago, IL 60605

AFSC
407 S. Dearborn St.
Chicago, IL 60605

Metro Chicago CALC
542 S. Dearborn Ave.
Chicago, IL 60605

Beacon Fraternity (CW)
4617 N. Beacon St.
Chicago, IL 60610

Women for Peace (WSP)
2440 N. Lincoln Ave.
Chicago, IL 60614

CCCO
5615 S. Woodlawn Ave.
Chicago, IL 60637

Chicago WRL
c/o David Finke
1152 E. 52nd St.
Chicago, IL 60615

The Catholic Worker
4652 N. Kenmore
Chicago, IL 60690

Omega House (CW)
3826 7th Ave.
Rock Island, IL 61201

AFSC
Central Illinois
  Area Committee
RR 3, Box 34
Decatur, IL 62526

INDIANA

Ephesus House (CW)
342 N. Arsenal
Indianapolis, IN 46201

Hoosiers for Peace (CALC)
c/o Indiana Council
  of Churches
1100 W. 42nd St.
Indianapolis, IN 46208

Harbor House (CW)
3212 Guthrie St.
East Chicago, IN 46312

AFSC
8 N. Washington St.
Valparaiso, IN 46383

IOWA

AFSC
4211 Grand Ave.
Des Moines, IA 50312

Catholic Worker House
806 W. 5th St.
Davenport, IA 52802

KANSAS

Shalom House (CW)
40 S. 13th St.
Kansas City, KS 66102

WRL/Midwest
3950 Rainbow Rd.
Kansas City, KS 66103

WRL
9606 Outlook Dr.
Overland Park, KS 66207

KENTUCKY

Louisville FOR
c/o A.C. Cuppy
4019 Hillbrook Dr.
Louisville, KY 40220

MAINE

AFSC
280 Concord St. West
Portland, ME 04103

MARYLAND

Heathcote School of Living
Rt. 1, Box 129
Freeland, MD 21053

Jonah House
1933 Park Ave.
Baltimore, MD 21217

AFSC Peace Collective
319 E. 25th St.
Baltimore, MD 21218

Annapolis CALC
144 Conduit St.
Annapolis, MD 21401

MASSACHUSETTS

Woolman Hill
Deerfield, MA 01342

Western Mass. CALC
24 Churchill St.
Amherst, MA 01002

AFSC
3 Langworthy Rd.
Northampton, MA 01060

International
  Independence Institute
West Road, Box 183
Ashby, MA 01431

House of Ammon (CW)
69 Elm St.
Hubbardstown, MA 01452

Central Mass. CALC
111 Park Ave.
Worcester, MA 01609

Voice of Women (WSP)
811 Washington St.
Newtonville, MA 02106

Greenpeace
14 Beacon St.
Boston, MA 02108

Haley House (CW)
23 Dartmouth St.
Boston, MA 02116

Vocations for Social Change
353 Broadway
Cambridge, MA 02139

New England
  War Tax Resistance
Box 174, MIT Branch P.O.
Cambridge, MA 02139

AFSC
48 Inman St.
Cambridge, MA 02139

Boston WRL
40 Highland Ave.
Somerville, MA 02143

Boston Area CALC
474 Centre St.
Newton, MA 02158

MICHIGAN

Peace & National
  Priorities (CALC)
Center for Oakland County
P.O. Box 5194
Orchard Lake, MI 48033

Internal Communication
  Collective (MNS)
1910 Hill St.
Ann Arbor, MI 48104

AFSC
1414 Hill St.
Ann Arbor, MI 48104

North American Student
  Cooperative Organization
Box 1301
Ann Arbor, MI 48106

Interfaith Council
  for Peace (CALC)
604 E. Huron
Ann Arbor, MI 48108

Detroit WRL
692 West Forest
Detroit, MI 48201

Center for Teaching
  About Peace & War
Wayne State University
5229 Cass Ave.
Detroit, MI 48202

St. Martha &
  St. Francis Houses (CW)
1818 Leverette St.
Detroit, MI 48216

Detroit CALC
19760 Meyers
Detroit, MI 48235

East Lansing
  Peace Education Center
1118 S. Harrison
East Lansing, MI 48823

Michigan CALC
205 W. Saginaw
P.O. Box 206
Lansing, MI 48901

Ammon Hennacy
  House (CW)
241 Charles S.E.
Grand Rapids, MI 49503

West Michigan AFSC
1503 Lake Dr., S.E.
Grand Rapids, MI 49506

MINNESOTA

Minnesota FOR
1563 Fairmount Ave.
St. Paul, MN 55105

AFSC
1925 Nicollet Ave.
Suite 207
Minneapolis, MN 55403

Minnesota CALC
122 W. Franklin Ave.
Minneapolis, MN 55404

Twin Cities WRL
2005 Vincent Ave. North
Minneapolis, MN 55411

FOR
c/o Michael Johnson
320 13th Ave., S.E. #7
Minneapolis, MN 55414

MISSISSIPPI

St. Francis of
Assisi Church (CW)
310 Cleveland St.
New Albany, MS 38652

MISSOURI

Institute for the
Study of Peace
3700 W. Pine Blvd.
St. Louis, MO 63108

St. Louis CALC
3753 W. Pine
St. Louis, MO 63108

St. Louis WRL
6199 Waterman
St. Louis, MO 63112

AFSC
438 N. Skinker
St. Louis, MO 63130

Nonviolent Studies Institute
912 East 31st St.
Kansas City, MO 64109

Holy Family House (CW)
912 East 31st St.
Kansas City, MO 64109

Kansas City FOR
3406 Wyoming
Kansas City, MO 64111

Columbia FOR
4K University Terrace
Columbia, MO 65201

Columbia WRL
813 Maryland Ave.
Columbia, MO 65201

NEBRASKA

Omaha Center
for the Pursuit of Peace
1715 Izard St.
Omaha, NB 68102

Catholic Worker
4718 N. 28th St.
Omaha, NB 68111

Lincoln/Omaha WRL
P.O. Box 80675
Lincoln, NB 68501

Nebraskans for
Peace (CALC)
430 S. 16th St.
Lincoln, NB 68506

NEVADA

AFSC
500 Cranleigh Dr.
Reno, NV 89502

NEW HAMPSHIRE

AFSC
298½ N. State St.
Concord, NH 03301

NEW JERSEY

New Jersey SANE
324 Bloomfield
Montclair, NJ 07042

Not by Bread Alone/FOR
c/o Clare Damio
101 Highland Ave.
Jersey City, NJ 07306

Fisher Folk (MNS)
641 York St.
Camden, NJ 08102

Princeton FOR
Box 185
Princeton, NJ 08534

Moorestown CALC
Center for
Cultural Awareness
62 E. 2nd St.
Moorestown, NJ 08057

NEW MEXICO

Albuquerque WRL
5021 Guadalupe Trail, N.W.
Albuquerque, NM 87107

NEW YORK

Episcopal Peace Fellowship
61 Gramercy Park N.
New York, NY 10001

AFSC
15 Rutherford Place
New York, NY 10003

Center for
War/Peace Studies
218 E. 18th St.
New York, NY 10003

FOR
c/o Ann Slavitt
One University Place
New York, NY 10003

* Catholic Worker
36 E. First St.
New York, NY 10003

WSP
799 Broadway
New York, NY 10003

* World Without War Council
175 Fifth Ave.
New York, NY 10010

* WRL
339 Lafayette St.
New York, NY 10012

A.J. Muste Memorial Inst.
339 Lafayette St.
New York, NY 10012

Committee on New Alterna-
tives in the Middle East
339 Lafayette St.
New York, NY 10012

Catholic Peace Fellowship
339 Lafayette St.
New York, NY 10012

* American Civil Liberties
Union
22 E. 40th St.
New York, NY 10016

The Christophers Center
12 E. 48th St.
New York, NY 10017

Jane Addams Peace Assn.
345 E. 46th St.
New York, NY 10017

* Clergy & Laity Concerned
235 E. 49th St.
New York, NY 10017

Council on Religion &
International Affairs
170 E. 64th St.
New York, NY 10021

* Amnesty International
200 W. 72nd St.
New York, NY 10023

Institute for World Order
1140 Avenue of the Americas
New York, NY 10036

Peace Studies Institute
Manhattan College
Bronx, NY 10471

Westchester CALC
People's Action Coalition
11 Forest Blvd.
Ardsley, NY 10502

Westchester Women
for Peace
36 Manchester Rd.
East Chester, NY 10709

Jewish Peace Fellowship
Box 271
Nyack, NY 10960

* FOR
Box 271
Nyack, NY 10960

Northeast Regional
Organizing
Collective (MNS)
248 Dean St.
Brooklyn, NY 11217

Peace Shelter
44 Bellhaven Road
Bellport, NY 11713

Assn. for World Education
3 Harbor Hill Dr.
Huntington, NY 11743

Day House (CW)
37 First St.
Troy, NY 12180

Arbor House (CW)
100 Clinton Ave.
Albany, NY 12210

FOR
c/o Robert Zeuner
530 Franklin St. #207
Schenectady, NY 12305

Schenectady Area CALC
405 Hulett St.
Schenectady, NY 12307

Catholic Worker Farm
Box 33
Tivoli, NY 12583

Unity Kitchen (CW)
243 W. Adams St.
Syracuse, NY 13202

Syracuse Peace Council
924 Burnett Ave.
Syracuse, NY 13203

AFSC
821 Euclid Ave.
Syracuse, NY 13210

Unity Acres (CW)
Orwell, NY 13426

Buffalo CALC
25 Calumet Place
Buffalo, NY 14207

Western NY Peace Center
243 Leroy Ave.
Buffalo, NY 14214

Maranatha (CW)
2115 10th St.
Niagra Falls, NY 14305

Rochester CALC
Peace & Justice
Education Center
713 Monroe Ave.
Rochester, NY 14607

St. Joseph's House (CW)
402 South Ave.
Rochester, NY 14620

NORTH CAROLINA

AFSC
Box 2234
High Point, NC 27262

Chapel Hill WRL
108-B Purefoy Rd.
Chapel Hill, NC 27514

Institute for Nonviolent
Study & Action
Box 4752 Duke Station
Durham, NC 27708

NORTH DAKOTA

CALC
602 9th Ave., S.E.
Jamestown, ND 58401

CALC
Lutheran Campus Ministries
North Dakota State College
Fargo, ND 58102

OHIO

Columbus FOR
1563 Genessee Ave.
Columbus, OH 43211

Cleveland CALC
10912 Magnolia Dr.
Cleveland, OH 44106

Thomas Merton House (CW)
1703 W. 32nd St.
Cleveland, OH 44113

Women Speak Out (WSP)
P.O. Box 18138
Cleveland, OH 44118

N.E. Ohio WRL
550 S. Lincoln St.
Kent, OH 44240

AFSC Humanity House
475 W. Market St.
Akron, OH 44303

Peacemakers
1255 Paddock Hills Ave.
Cincinatti, OH 45229

AFSC
915 Salem Ave.
Dayton, OH 45406

Bluffton FOR
First Mennonite Church
119 Church St.
Bluffton, OH 45817

OKLAHOMA

Oklahoma City CALC
2221 N.W. 22nd St.
Oklahoma City, OK 73107

OREGON

World Without War Council
1838 S.W. Jefferson
Portland, OR 97201

Main Street
 Gathering (MNS)
5124 N.E. Cleveland Ave.
Portland, OR 97211

Ammon Hennacy
 House (CW)
1225 S.E. Oak
Portland, OR 97214

Oregon FOR
2032 S.E. 11th St.
Portland, OR 97214

Portland CALC
2032 S.E. 11th Ave.
Portland, OR 97214

AFSC
4312 S.E. Stark St.
Portland, OR 97215

Greenpeace
Box 135
Portland, OR 97231

Eugene CALC
1414 Kincaid
Eugene, OR 97401

Eugene Life Center (MNS)
1059 Hilyard St.
Eugene, OR 97401

PENNSYLVANIA

Thomas Merton Center (CW)
1223 East Carson St.
Pittsburgh, PA 15203

Friends Peace Center
4836 Ellsworth Ave.
Pittsburgh, PA 15213

Peace & Conflict
 Studies Program
U of Pittsburgh
Pittsburgh, PA 15260

Pax Center
345 E. 9th St.
Erie, PA 16503

Harrisburg CALC
c/o Clement
332 Blacksmith Rd.
Camp Hill, PA 17011

Mennonite
 Central Committee
21 S. 12th St.
Akron, PA 17501

Brandywine
 Alternative Fund
302 S. Jackson St.
Media, PA 19063

Swarthmore College
 Peace Collection
McCabe Library
Swarthmore, PA 19081

Pendle Hill
338 Plush Mill Rd.
Wallingford, PA 19086

*AFSC
1501 Cherry St.
Philadelphia, PA 19102

Friends Peace Committee
1501 Cherry St.
Philadelphia, PA 19102

National Action/Research on
 the Military
 Industrial Complex
1501 Cherry St.
Philadelphia, PA 19102

*CCCO
2016 Walnut St.
Philadelphia, PA 19103

Philadelphia WRL/WTR
2016 Walnut St.
Philadelphia, PA 19103

*Women Strike for Peace
145 S. 13th St., Rm. 407
Philadelphia, PA 19107

*WILPF
1213 Race St.
Philadelphia, PA 19107

*Movement for a New Society
4722 Baltimore Ave.
Philadelphia, PA 19143

RHODE ISLAND

AFSC
134 Mathewson St.
Providence, RI 02903

SOUTH CAROLINA

South Carolina CALC
20 Waccamaw Circle
Greenville, SC 29605

TENNESSEE

Highlander Center
Box 245 A, RFD 3
New Market, TN 37820

Catholic Worker
c/o Gifford
4385 Giver
Memphis, TN 38122

TEXAS

North Texas CALC
3737 Preston Dr.
Fort Worth, TX 76119

AFSC
1510 Buena Vista
San Antonio, TX 78207

AFSC
704 W. 25th St.
Austin, TX 78705

WRL South Central
P.O. Box 7161
Austin, TX 78712

VERMONT

AFSC
RFD 1
Castleton, VT 05735

CALC
The Schoolhouse RFD #2
St. Johnsbury, VT 05819

VIRGINIA

School of Living
P.O. Box 426
Louisa, VA 23093

WASHINGTON

Seattle FOR
947 Broadway East
Seattle, WA 98102

Women Act for Peace (WSP)
407 Smith Tower
Seattle, WA 98104

Seattle CALC
4759 N.E. 15th Ave.
Seattle, WA 98105

World Without War Council
1514 N.E. 45th St.
Seattle, WA 98105

AFSC
814 N.E. 40th St.
Seattle, WA 98105

Seattle WRL
331 17th East
Seattle, WA 98112

Pacem in Terris House (CW)
331 17th Ave. East
Seattle, WA 98112

Kokopeli Korner (MNS)
811 33rd Ave. E.
Seattle, WA 98112

Women for Peace
3635 S. J St.
Tacoma, WA 98408

Spokane FOR
P.O. Box 661
Spokane, WA 99210

WEST VIRGINIA

Catholic Worker Farm
Rt. 1, Box 308
West Hamlin, WV 25571

Morgantown WRL
345 Prospect St., #607
Morgantown, WV 26505

WISCONSIN

Casa Maria (CW)
1131 North 21st St.
Milwaukee, WI 53233

Center for Conflict
 Resolution (MNS)
520 University Ave.
Madison, WI 53703

AFSC
2006 Monroe St.
Madison, WI 53711

FOREIGN

International FOR
35 Rue Van Elewijck
1050 Brussels
Belgium

War Resisters International
35 Rue Van Elewijck
1050 Brussels
Belgium

PERIODICALS

Akwesasne Notes
Mohawk Nation
via Rooseveltown, NY 13683

Amex-Canada
P.O. Box 187, Station D
Toronto 165
Ontario, Canada

Catholic Agitator
605 North Cummings St.
Los Angeles, CA 90033

Catholic Worker
36 E. First St.
New York, NY 10003

El Malcriado
P.O. Box 62
Keene, CA 93531

Fellowship
Box 271
Nyack, NY 10960

Gamaliel
1335 N St., N.W.
Washington D.C. 20005

The Green Revolution
School of Living
Rt. 1, Box 129
Freeland, MD 21053

*Journal of
 Conflict Resolution*
University of Michigan
Ann Arbor, MI 48104

Journal of Peace Research
Gydas vei 8
P.O. Box 5052
Oslo 3, Norway

Liberation
339 Lafayette St.
New York, NY 10012

Manas
Box 32112
El Sereno Station
Los Angeles, CA 90032

Our Generation
3934 rue St. Urbain
Montreal 131
Quebec, Canada

Peace News
8 Elm Avenue
Nottingham, England

Peacemaker
1255 Paddock Hills Ave.
Cincinnati, Ohio 45229

Peacework
48 Inman St.
Cambridge, MA 02139

Resurgence
24 Abercorn Place
St. John's Woods
London N.W. 8, England

War/Peace Report
218 E. 18th St.
New York, NY 10003

War Resistance
35 rue Elewijck
Brussels 1050, Belgium

WIN
503 Atlantic Ave., 5th Floor
Brooklyn, NY 11217

*Working Papers
for a New Society*
123 Mt. Auburn St.
Cambridge, MA 02139

INDEX

Diana Davies

PRODUCTION NOTES

THE POWER OF THE PEOPLE was produced as a cooperative, non-profit effort by The Power of the People Publishing Project, associated with the Institute for the Study of Nonviolence in Palo Alto and Agape Foundation in San Francisco, California. The project raised approximately $38,000 over a two year period to produce and publish this history book independently. Roughly $12,000 was committed by the 35 cooperating organizations (who were repaid in books), $6000 was generated by pre-publication orders, $3500 was contributed by individuals, and $16,300 was loaned. The project spent approximately $1000 on research, $2700 on photographs, $900 on production, $2500 on typesetting, $6000 on salary, $3800 on administration, $2500 on promotion and fund raising, and $18,500 on printing. Income from the sale of this book will go to repay those who loaned money or donated their work to the project, and then will be used to reprint the book and encourage further nonviolent work.

Two thousand hardbound and six thousand softbound copies of this first edition were printed in the Winter of 1976. The paper used is 70 pound Royal Dull, supplied by the Case Paper Company in Los Angeles. The type is 10 point Caledonia Medium, with 12 point leading, set on a Mergenthaler VIP photocompositor by Intermedia and Johnson Printing Plates in San Francisco. The headlines are Times Roman Medium and the half-tone screen is 133 line. The camera and press work were done by Peace Press, Inc., a worker-controlled shop in Los Angeles which grew out of the peace movement in 1967. Correspondence regarding this book can be addressed to The Power of the People, % Peace Press, 3828 Willat Avenue, Culver City, California 90230.